ACKNOWLEDGEMENTS

I would like to thank Prof. Jimmy Weinblatt, the outgoing dean of humanities and social sciences, Ben-Gurion University, Beersheba, for helping fund the preparation of this book for publication. He has been a constant friend and aid these past few years, and merits far more than these words convey.

I would also like to thank the Rockefeller Foundation for hosting Leah and myself at its estate in Bellagio, in incomparably beautiful and carefree surroundings, where the first draft of this book was produced (itís hard to imagine a place more different from Glubb's adopted country).

Last, I would like to thank Jeff Abel for his help in preparing this book for publication, for trying unfailingly (with scant success) to drag me into this digital age, for our friendship over the past thirty odd years, and for writing these words.

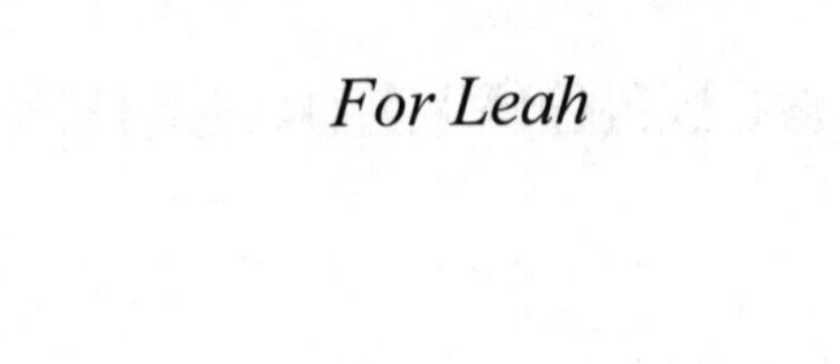

For Leah

CONTENTS

	Abbreviations	vi
	Introduction	1
1	Glubb on Arabs and Jews	9
2	The Arab Revolt 1936-39	33
3	World War II and its Aftermath	56
4	The Road to Jerusalem	91
5	The Invasion	145
6	Border Wars, 1949 - 1956	209
	Conclusion (After 1956)	233
	Bibliography	243
	Notes	247
	Index	289

Abbreviations

AAC	– Anglo-American Commission of Inquiry
ALA	– Arab Liberation Army
BGA	– David Ben-Gurion Archive (Sdeh Boqer, Israel)
CZA	– Central Zionist Archive (Jerusalem)
CAB	– Cabinet (UK)
CO	– Colonial Office (UK)
DP	– Displaced person (post-World War II Europe)
FO	– Foreign Office (UK)
HA	– Haganah Archive (Tel Aviv)
HMG	– His Majesty's Government (British Government)
IDF	– Israel Defence Forces
IDFA	– IDF Archive (Givatayim, Israel)
ISA	– Israel State Archive (Jerusalem)
IWM	– Imperial War Museum (London)
IZL	– *Irgun Zvai Leumi* or National Military Organisation or 'Irgun'
LHI	– *Lohamei Herut Yisrael* or Freedom Fighters of Israel or 'Stern Gang'
MK	– Member of Knesset (Israel)
MP	– Member of Parliament (UK)
NA	– National Archive (Washington)
PRO	– Public Record Office (London)
RAF	– Royal Air Force
RE	– Royal Engineers (British Army)
SAMECA	– St Antony's College Middle East Centre Archive (Oxford)
TJ	– Transjordan
TJFF	– Transjordan Frontier Force
UNA	– United Nations Archive (New York)
UNEF	– United Nations Emergency Force (Egypt)
UNO	– United Nations Organisation
UNRWA	– United Nations Relief and Works Agenncy for Palestinian Refugees in the Near East
UNSCOP	– United Nations Special Committee on Palestine
UNTSO	– United Nations Truce Supervision Organisation
WO	– War Office (UK)

INTRODUCTION

John Bagot Glubb lived most of his long life (1897-1986) in England, where he was born and died. But the 36 years of his main, adult career, as a soldier, were spent in the Middle East, most of them in the Emirate, later Kingdom, of Transjordan, which in 1948 became the Hashemite Kingdom of Jordan. It was there that he made his chief contribution to history.

Glubb was born in Preston, England, in 1897 to a middle class English civil service\military family. His forefathers, from the lesser landed gentry, had included a Member of Parliament (for Okehampton, Devon) in 1313. His father, Frederic Manley Glubb, served in the Royal Engineers (RE), where at the end of World War I he attained the rank of major-general. Glubb, at least initially, followed in his father's footsteps. Educated at Cheltenham College - where he imbibed 'a reverence for the tenets of Christianity',[1] 'a diet of games, classics ... [and] such important Victorian concepts as the stiff upper lip, a sense of fair play, the importance of maintaining appearances, and adherence to an unbending moral code'[2] - and the Royal Military Academy at Woolwich, Glubb, an RE subaltern, was sent to the trenches of Flanders at the end of 1915 where he spent the next three years, twice being wounded (once severely). He was later to treasure the memory of those years of combat in, as he saw it, a just cause, albeit attended by much suffering and loss. He came to regard soldiering as perhaps the noblest profession. 'People who have never been soldiers sometimes imagine the military profession to be brutal ... [and that] the chief preoccupation of soldiers is killing people.' In reality, soldiers spend most of their time at other tasks. Throughout, they are bound together and governed by a worthy ethic of 'brotherhood' and camaraderie.[3] An essentially reserved and solitary man, Glubb in his lifetime enjoyed three bouts of camaraderie - in the trenches with his fellow Englishmen in World War I, with his beduin recruits in the 'Desert Camel Corps' in Iraq in the 1920s, and, lastly, between 1930 and 1956, in the ranks of Jordan's army, the Arab Legion, first as a senior officer and then as its commander.

But while he may have regarded soldiering as a noble calling, Glubb experienced, and well understood, the evils of war. Above all, there was the death of fellow officers and subordinates, the loss of innocent, civilian life and the destruction of property and order. And 'wars never end wars,' he wrote. 'Every war, on the contrary, gives rise to more wars and more violence, hatred and revenge.' Nowhere was this more true than in the Middle East.[4]

Glubb's life in the Middle East began at the end World War I. The bulk of the British Army had been demobilized and Glubb volunteered for service in Mesopotamia (later Iraq), which was occupied by Britain and was about to become a British Mandate. He reached the territory - wracked by tribal and religious conflict - in 1920. At the time, he knew next to nothing of the Middle East, 'its history or culture'; but he craved adventure and interesting work.[5] Initially he served as an engineer. But in 1922 he was appointed an intelligence officer (a 'Special Service Officer'), serving along Iraq's southern frontier among the tribes. There was constant raiding from Saudi Arabia and occasional intervention by the Royal Air Force, with Glubb directing the aircraft to target. In the late 1920s, he organized and commanded the 'Southern Desert Camel Corps'. It patrolled the frontiers of the mandated kingdom and successfully parried Saudi and Syrian marauders and land grabs. Glubb gradually learned the desert Arabs' language and ways and came to love them. They returned that love. 'Glubb ... had a remarkable ability to attract and hold the affection of Arabs,' was how Alec Kirkbride, Britain's longtime representative in Amman, put it. (Kirkbride, an extremely discerning man, implied that this was because Glubb was 'half Irish and half Cornish' rather than a run-of-the-mill Englishman.)[6]

Over the years, Glubb became completely fluent in Arabic; indeed, one Jordanian official in the 1950s described his mastery of the language as 'wonderful and fluent, and few Arabs could match it.'[7]

No doubt, this linguistic achievement helped endear him to the natives. In 1930 Glubb moved to Jordan, itself plagued by beduin marauding and threatened by expansionist Saudi designs. He was appointed second-in-command to Frederick Peake, the founder and commander of the Arab Legion. (Peake and a number of British officials objected - Glubb was a complete outsider, and a non-conventional one at that. But they were overridden.) Glubb, as 'Officer Commanding Desert,' was responsible for keeping order and repelling raiders in the desert areas bordering on Saudi Arabia and Syria. For this task he fashioned a new force, the Legion's 'Desert Patrol.' In March 1939, Glubb succeeded

Peake as commander of the Legion. He was to remain at this post for 17 years.

During World War II, Transjordan was the one Arab state that wholeheartedly cleaved to the Allied cause and stuck by Britain through thick and thin. (Glubb was later to belabour the point in his correspondence with Whitehall, often geared to eliciting additional subsidies and arms.) During the war's first months the Legion, under British auspices, was expanded from a desert gendarmerie into a small, mechanized army and in spring and summer 1941 it participated in the crushing of the pro-Axis government of Rashid `Ali al Ghilani in Baghdad and in the British conquest of Vichy-controlled Syria. It was Glubb's first taste of war in a senior command position and the Legion became the only Arab army to gain combat experience in World War II. After Iraq and Syria, the Legion was used by Britain's Middle East Command to guard and garrison strategic sites and bases around the Middle East. Immediately following the war, and until May 1948, units of the Legion were seconded to the British Army in Palestine and deployed guarding bases and other installations around the country.

In 1948, during the first Arab-Israeli War, Glubb led the Legion, with considerable success, in its occupation of the West Bank and East Jerusalem and in its battles against the Haganah, and later, the Israel Defence Forces (IDF). He remained in command of the Legion during 1949-56, years marked by sporadic Israeli-Arab border warfare and by fear of Israeli conquest of the West Bank. In March 1956, under pressure from Arab nationalists and republicans, King Hussein, Abdullah's grandson and Jordan's ruler since 1953, peremptorily dismissed Glubb and sent him packing back to England. He never again visited Jordan. He spent the following three decades, in retirement, writing volumes of memoirs, political analysis, a biography of Muhammad, and popular histories about recent and not so recent Middle Eastern history. He became a born-again Christian (he served as president of the Deanery Association of the Church of England's Children Society) and published *The Way of Love, Lessons from a Long Life* (Hodder & Stoughton, London, 1974), a mystical, Christian work. He died on 17 March 1986 at his home in Mayfield in Sussex.

Glubb was a major player in the Middle East between 1930 and 1956. As deputy commander of the Transjordan Arab Legion, he helped consolidate the emirate and its borders. Subsequently, as the Legion's commander, he led a detachment of his troops in support of the British Army in its conquest of Iraq and Syria in 1941, when Allied military fortunes around the globe were at a low ebb. And in 1948, he led the Legion in its finest hour to a limited victory in the first Arab-Israeli war. This success, due largely to Glubb's competent preparations and to his more than competent leadership, radically transformed the kingdom's geographic and demographic contours, with far-reaching implications for the region's states and peoples during the following two decades, and, in some important ways, beyond.

During the following eight years, Glubb continued to command the Legion as, in effect, through a system of military governors, the police and the Jordanian intelligence service (all parts of the Legion), it ruled the West Bank and sporadically battled the Israelis along its borders. In Amman, the Legion constituted the Hashemite regime's main prop; in December 1955-January 1956, indeed, it sustained the monarchy in an hour of grave internal crisis. By all accounts, Glubb stood through the crisis like a rock while most of Jordan's politicians lost their heads or nerve.

The 1949-56 period, marked by cycles of Arab infiltration into Israel and Israeli retaliatory raiding into Jordan (and the Gaza Strip), was to set patterns of behaviour, on both sides, that were to characterize Israeli-Arab relations for decades. Glubb's wise handling of the Legion (and cool thinking in the royal palace in Amman) during those years probably helped defer Israel's conquest of the West Bank until 1967.

Besides Glubb's role in the formation of modern Jordan and in the Israeli-Arab conflict, he commands interest as one of the last - and certainly the most influential - of Britain's 'orientalist' corps of officers and officials who stirred the Middle Eastern pot between the First World War and the debacle of Suez in 1956. His story - as well as the policies he helped fashion and the interactions he engaged in - tells us a great deal about a curious sort of 'white man's burden'/Arab-enamoured Englishman as well as something about Britain's ascendant and then declining role in the Middle East.

Throughout his years in Jordan, Glubb fed Whitehall - the War, Colonial, and Foreign offices - directly and indirectly with information and analyses which went into the shaping of British Middle East policy. By and large, his presentation of facts was respected, sometimes even admired, as was the fertility of his mind, which churned out a steady stream of interpretations and solutions to a variety of problems. But he also, at times, tended to exaggeration and alarmism, letting his fears run away with him. As John Beith of the Foreign Office minuted on one of

Glubb's memoranda regarding Egypt in 1956: 'Glubb's intelligence is usually quite good if his treatment of it is at times melodramatic.'[8]

Glubb was regarded by most people who knew him as a somewhat simple though intelligent man, morally upright, reasonable, and honest, usually cool in crisis and sympathetic in adversity. Even one of his chief antagonists, Israel's Moshe Dayan – the IDF chief of general staff from December 1953 to January 1958 - said that he 'seems to be a straightforward man.'[9] General William Riley, the chief of staff of the United Nations Truce Supervision Organisation (UNTSO) in the Middle East in the early 1950s, described him as 'extremely fair-minded.'[10]

But there is also another, minority view of Glubb, as an initially straightforward British officer-type who under the impress of 30 years of diplomacy and irregular warfare in the Middle East had gradually taken on the indirection and mental agility of the desert warrior and casbah intriguer. One British Arab Legion officer put it this way:

> You never knew what was going on with Glubb ... His mind had begun to work like an Arab's. He was all subtleties. He had the kind of mind that could understand the illogic of the Arabs and anticipate it ... He dealt as an Arab with the King's palace, as a beduin with the tribes, as a British officer with London. No one except Glubb knew everything that was going on.[11]

I have focused on Glubb's role in the Zionist-Arab conflict because it was, for a time, important and because examining it affords access to the unusual perspective of someone who was, at one and the same time, both a key and knowledgeable player and an outsider. As an Englishman, Glubb might have been, in some sense, above the Zionist-Arab battle, at least until it involved Jordan itself. And, occasionally, he professed to be so. But he wasn't. From the Zionist side, Glubb was perceived as a pro-Arab mercenary,[12] albeit a somewhat enigmatic one. In crucial months in 1948 he was seen by the Yishuv, the Jewish community in Palestine, as public enemy number one. During the late 1940s and 1950s he was demonized as an anti-Semitic Englishman who had sold his soul to the Arab devil and was the spearpoint of the Arab struggle against the Jewish state – and this at a time when most Europeans, against the backdrop of the recent Nazi destruction of the Jews, sympathized with embattled Israel. Indeed, in May 1948 David Ben-Gurion, Israel's founding prime minister and defence minister, even spoke of arraigning Glubb for war crimes.[13] Somewhat earlier, the extremist LHI (Lohamei Herut Israel – the Freedom Fighters of Israel or 'Stern' terrorist group) had apparently ordered his assassination 'as soon as possible'.[14] Israeli and pro-Israeli histories and memoirists traditionally have portrayed him in a far from favourable light.[15] In embarking on this study, I sought also to examine whether this bad press was fully deserved.

The opening during the past two decades of a great deal of archival material, principally in Britain and Israel, has now made possible a re-evaluation of this image. Moreover, 40-50 years have passed since the events described. No doubt, Glubb's assessment in his autobiography – that 'history gives a truer verdict when the fires of controversy have subsided'[16] – is now at least partially apt.

In the following pages we shall examine Glubb's evolving attitudes towards the Jews and the Arabs, towards the Zionist-Arab conflict and Jewish and Arab policies in the late 1930s, the 1946-48 period, the years leading up to the Sinai\Suez War of 1956, and during the decades of forced retirement thereafter, which he spent writing books on the Middle East - and then describe and analyze his actions in the hope of accurately assessing his contribution to history. The focus inevitably will be on Glubb during that revolutionary upheaval, the 1948 War.

Back in the late 1980s, a spate of books appeared in the West relating to Yishuv\Israeli-Hashemite relations, most notably Avi Shlaim's *Collusion Across the Jordan*, but also Uri Bar-Joseph's *The Best of Enemies* and Ilan Pappe's *Britain and the Arab-Israeli Conflict, 1947-1951.* Taken together, these books persuasively offered a new interpretation – or a 'new historiography' - of Israeli-Jordanian relations which, in turn, shed a new and thought-provoking light on Israeli-Arab relations in general during and on either side of 1948. Both the traditional Zionist and the traditional Arab narratives of that war were in large measure undermined.

Springing to the defence of the official Zionist narrative and forefathers, Itamar Rabinovich of Tel Aviv University, a pillar of Israeli academic conservatism, lambasted these works in his *The Road Not Taken.* He was followed by other Zionist historians (Shabtai Teveth, Anita Shapira, etc.) equally appalled by the Shlaim/Bar-Joseph/Pappe portrayal of Israel and Jordan in 1948 as in cahoots. The conservatives' critique of these 'New Historians' seemed to score some points.

In writing this book, I have undertaken a re-examination of the documentation used, and have made use of a great deal of additional documentation, much of it in the IDF and Haganah archives, which was closed when these works were produced. A certain overlap has been unavoidable – but hopefully it is outweighed by what is new in materials and interpretations. I can only hope that, at the end of the day, this book will add something to our understanding of Glubb and his milieu, and help shed light on the separate, but often contiguous, histories of Israel and Jordan and their unusual relationship.

Chapter 1

GLUBB ON ARABS AND JEWS

Attitude to Arabs

Crucial to understanding Glubb's thinking and actions during his years in the Arab Legion is his attitude toward 'the Arabs.'

'I spent thirty-six years living among the Arabs. During the first nineteen of these years, I lived almost entirely with them, rarely meeting Europeans and sometimes not speaking a word of English for weeks on end ... [In 1925 I decided to] devote my life to the Arabs. My decision was largely emotional. I loved them.' So he wrote in his autobiography, *A Soldier with the Arabs*, published in 1957.[17]

At some point during his years in the Middle East, Glubb began to see his life as a mission:

> I had experienced in myself, as I thought, the feasibility of living simultaneously as an Arab amongst Arabs and as an Englishman amongst Europeans ... It was my idea to help the Arabs by introducing to their country those skills and methods and products in which Europe excelled. I hoped that the Arabs would remain basically Arabs, clinging to and priding themselves on the many fine qualities and traditions inherited by them from their past. But I hoped simultaneously to be able to help them to hold their own in the modern world.

It was no easy task. One problem was that, Jordan apart, 'the Arab countries, and indeed the greater part of Asia, was [sic] becoming increasingly poisoned with hatred and distrust for the West.'[18]

Nor, ultimately, was Jordan - whose people Glubb came to call 'my people' - completely immune. 'The union of Trans-Jordan with Arab Palestine [i.e., the West Bank, in 1948-50] introduced into the country a new population - a population which had suffered an immense injustice as a result of Western policy. Gradually the Trans-Jordanians were partially submerged, and the rock of Jordan, with its wise moderation and its broadminded comprehension of East and West, disintegrated in the flood of hate...' Writing in 1956-57, with the impact of his dismissal by King Hussein still fresh, Glubb glumly concluded: 'I had failed hopelessly in the task to which I had devoted nearly all my life - to promote ever closer cooperation and understanding between East and West.'[19]

But Glubb's emotional ties to 'the Arabs' survived the trauma of dismissal and the decades in 'exile' in England thereafter. Indeed, to judge from the stream of books he churned out in his retirement, his fondness for 'the Arabs' only increased with time and distance. But all along he was a very English, very reserved military man and certainly when commanding the Legion seems to have remained essentially aloof and distant from his Arab subordinates and Jordanian society. One former (British) officer of the Legion noted in the mid-1950s that 'it used to amaze me that he never entered an Arab's house (save in ... parties ... or ... formal visits) and so far as I know, never had a genuine conversation ... with any Arab. It is a strange thing to say that although he lived in the Middle East for 35-odd years, I think it is true that he remained absolutely ignorant and indeed careless of the mood, humour and indeed character of the cultivated Arab.'[20]

IDF Major (later brigadier-general) Dov Steiger (later Sion) in the 1950s tried to place Glubb's sense of 'mission' in an intelligible, wider Anglo-Arab context: 'Glubb is putting into practice the romantic ideals of a group of British statesmen and officers who saw as their life's work the resurrection of the Arab people.' At the core of this attitude was the vision or ideal of 'the Beduin,' the pure, thoroughbred, noble and savage Arab, untrammelled and unpolluted by Western civilisation. 'Glubb,' wrote Sion, 'was captivated by the beduin's virtues and saw him as a creature possessed of natural intelligence, a bold warrior, dedicated, straight and loyal.'[21]

Glubb, of course, was but one in a long string of Englishmen captivated by the nature and lifestyle of the nomads of the Arabian deserts. More than a century before, Sir William Jones, a leading British orientalist, wrote of the Arabs of Hijaz: 'Their eyes are full of vivacity, their speech voluble and articulate, their deportment manly and dignified, their apprehension quick, their minds always present and attentive; with a spirit of independence appearing in the countenance of even the lowest among them.'[22]

Like other British Arabists, Glubb divined in the beduin the supreme virtues of the English gentleman. Back in 1826, an English traveller had written of the Imam of Muscat that he was 'the only Asiatic I ever saw, who gave me the idea of what is conveyed by the English term gentleman.'[23] Or, as one of Glubb's biographers put it, the beduins seemed to embody some of the primary 'virtues of the British gentleman ... The beduin was every Englishman's idea of nature's gentleman.'[24] Beduins, according to Glubb and his intellectual forebears, embodied the characteristics of independence with dependability, hardiness, frankness, proper subordination and loyalty (without servility), good horsemanship and other martial attributes, and a keen intelligence. Indeed, the preeminent analyst of the English romance with the Arabs, Kathryn Tidrick, has persuasively compared the upbringing of those gentleman-travellers, scholars, administrators, and officers - the 'Arabists', who were to represent Britain and its Empire in the Middle East - with that of the beduin:

> The life of an English public school and the life of a Beduin camp have certain things in common: hardship, male comradeship, a delight in sports and outdoor pursuits, and the frequent recital of epic poetry ... Schoolboy loyalty to school and house is mirrored in the Beduin's loyalty to his tribe and clan, and in both societies there is a delicate combination of egalitarianism and respect for authority. Both practice a form of conciliar government, through elders among the Beduin and prefects among the schoolboys ... There was even a common element of nomadism, in the English boy's repeated treks between home and school and the Beduin's regular movements between dry-season wells and wet-season grazing grounds...

For many Englishmen these formative experiences accompanied them (as did the beduins') through adulthood and career. Indeed, for the British administrator, adviser and officer of beduin troops:

> Participation in Beduin life was in some respects like a prolongation of adolescence, a period of life at which many Englishmen of that time and class appear to have been permanently fixated ... They recognized themselves ... in certain of the primitive peoples, usually nomads with strong group feelings and traditions of superiority, with whom the Empire brought them into contact. The Beduin were one of these peoples ...[25]

Given this admiration for and trust of the beduin, it was only natural that Glubb, when raising his Desert Patrol in Transjordan in 1930, recruited only from among the tribesmen and, a decade later, upon assuming control of the Legion and then expanding it, again looked to the tribes for the core of his manpower. Previously, Colonel F.G. Peake, upon founding the Legion in 1920-21 and then gradually expanding it during the following two decades, had relied on recruitment of townspeople and villagers rather than beduin.[26] Indeed, in the second bout of Legion expansion during the 1950s, Glubb did not limit himself to the tribesmen of Jordan but drew also on tribes from various parts of the Arabian peninsula, recruiting from as far afield as 'the Persian Gulf.'[27] It was Glubb who made the Arab Legion synonymous with the beduins, who to this day provide the core of the corps' manpower, especially in its key combat - infantry and armoured - formations.

But Glubb's attitude towards the beduins as towards 'the Arab' in general, was far more complex than is implied by Sion. 'Glubb is by no means blindly pro-Arab. He understands the Arab mentality better than any European I know,' wrote Geoffrey Furlonge, the British Ambassador in Amman, in 1953, 'and naturally he has much sympathy for the people amongst whom he has spent his life. But he recognizes their faults...'[28]

Of the Arabs in general Glubb wrote in 1945:

> They are painfully conscious of their immaturity, their weakness and their backwardness. They show all the instability and the emotionalism of the adolescent ... [characterized by] touchiness and ... [a] readiness to take offence at any sign of condescension by their "elders". Slights give rise to outbursts of temper and violent defiance. Like children they will sometimes be rude, and sometimes [they will be] plunged in despair and self-depreciation ... It is a common error that Arabs are less intelligent than ourselves, and are thus incapable of running an administration, commanding an army or directing a big business. In reality, the Arabs are probably of quicker intelligence than ourselves. Why they cannot run these things so efficiently is owing to their lower sense of duty and public service. They easily slip into nepotism, dishonesty or favouritism. They nearly all realize this in their hearts, but resent our saying so.[29]

Moreover, 'all Arabs today,' he wrote in 1946, 'have an inferiority complex vis-a-vis Europeans ... They are resentful of anything implying that they are today an inferior race ... They fall readily to flattery, but they react with surprising violence against contempt … If the suspicion that they are being insulted can be overcome, they can be delightful comrades and faithful allies.'[30]

Although, as we shall see, Glubb did not regard 'the Arabs' as 'one race', he thought that one could trace

> one or two broad characteristics, which most of them share, and which differentiate them from Europeans. The Arabs in general are hot-headed, hasty and volatile. They are proud and touchy ... But while their hot-headedness makes the Arabs good haters, it makes them also cordial friends. No race can be more pleasant

or charming ... with a ready sense of humour ... To this day I have more friends in Arabia [i.e., the Arab world, in Glubb's parlance] than I have in England,

he wrote in 1957.[31]

Glubb's attitude towards 'the Arabs' was governed - again, as with many of his Arabist predecessors, such as Richard Burton - by an historical-racial world view. His weltanschauung was explicitly and highly racial (though during the 1930s he often inveighed against the Nazi-promoted racist spirit, then abroad in Europe and, in Glubb's view, making inroads in the Middle East as well). While, in Glubb's words, 'the mass psychology of nations is a science as yet imperfectly explored'[32] he was clearly captivated by race theories, including theories of physiognomy, as the following passage illustrates: 'Science corroborates experience and confirms that the Arabs of the Mediterranean countries differ racially from those of the interior. Many people with round heads are found in Syria, Lebanon and among Palestine Arabs. The people of Central Asia are all long-headed.'[33]

Glubb drew a fundamental distinction between the Arabs of the Levant or coast, comprising the townspeople and villagers of western Syria, Lebanon, Palestine and Egypt, the settled Arabs of Mesopotamia, and the essentially nomadic Arabs of the 'interior' desert regions, the beduins. In Glubb's view, most people called 'Arabs' in the 20th Century were not Arabs at all or, at best, highly impure Arabs. Only Arabs of the 'interior,' of the swathe of desert linking eastern Syria, Transjordan, south-western Iraq and Arabia - in short, only beduins - were 'real' Arabs, he believed. In 1951 Glubb set down his views in the matter in an official memorandum:

The characteristics of ... the Central Arabians are the same today as 1,300 years ago. Life is hard in Central Arabia, and the Arabs spend their lives in a bitter struggle for existence against both their enemies and the savage forces of nature. They have no leisure for subtle intellectual discussions, like the peoples of the soft and luxuriant shores of the Mediterranean. The beduin learns to shoot first and ask questions afterwards. They are men used to action rather than words. They are thus excellent military material ... [and] they have not as yet been infected by the European virus of nationalism.

The Muslim conquests of the 7th century imposed the Arabic language upon the countries of the Middle East. To some extent ... it imposed the Muslim religion and Arab culture. Apart from this historical episode, 1,300 years ago, the peoples of the coastal countries of the Mediterranean - Lebanon, Palestine and Egypt - have looked to Europe for their culture rather than to Arabia. Their very

> populations are composed of mixed European races as much as of Arab stock from the hinterland. Today, as in the past, their ideas are almost entirely borrowed second-hand from the west. It is only within the last thirty years that such people have begun to call themselves "Arabs" ... The essential thing to realize is that the Arabs - as the term is used today - are not a race, but a vague cultural zone ... consisting of a great variety of racial stocks. The Lebanese are unlike the Saudi Arabians as the Norwegians are the Greeks ... Arab nationalism is generally speaking confined to the northern Arabic-speaking countries, the populations of which have comparatively little Arab blood in their veins. They might perhaps suitably be called Levantines, except that that term has acquired a certain contemptuous significance ... These people are by no means contemptible. They are intellectually superior to most Europeans, but their extreme intellectual subtlety leads them to unending argument and sophistry. Their cleverness is thus apt to lose itself in intellectual hair-splitting and rarely brings forth practical results in action. Moreover their cleverness leads to political instability ... A certain modicum of stupidity is necessary for political stability and for success in war.[34]

The Arabs of the Levant, then, according to Glubb, were half-breeds polluted by the races that had swept through the region in the course of the centuries.

The Palestinians were part and parcel of the Levant. 'The Arabs of Palestine,' he wrote in 1939, against the backdrop of the end of their rebellion against Britain, 'in reality have probably little Arab blood in their veins ... The townsmen and villagers of Palestine are not of the same race as the [desert] tribes ...'[35] Glubb's views on the Palestinians were not uncommon among Britons serving in the Levant. Stewart Perowne, a teacher at the Arab Training College in Jerusalem and a former secretary to the Anglican bishop in Jerusalem, wrote in 1926:

> The people here are not Arabs ... They are simply Arabic-speaking Levantines, a type which may speak Greek or Turkish or Arabic, but is much more in sympathy with the West than with the East ... In giving them an English education ... one is not really denationalizing them, because for the most part they have not the remotest idea of what their nationality implies...[36]

A decade later, after acquiring immeasurably greater first-hand knowledge in the matter, Glubb expatiated:

> The Palestinians show the main qualities always associated with the Levantine races ... Typical of such qualities are mental acuteness, humour, pleasant manners, an immense absorption in politics, and a tendency to sit all day in coffee

> shops talking fluently, arguing about politics and damning the government. The copious flood of their words and the critical nature of their opinions rarely result in positive action ... [It is said that] wherever you find ten Jews, you will find eleven political opinions ... [This is] equally true of the Palestinians. Thus when dealing with Palestinians it seems necessary to accustom oneself ... to constant reports of hatred entertained by the educated classes for the Government. It is surprising when one meets these conspirators, to find them all bows and smiles...
>
> In addition to these natural qualities, doubtless centuries or millenia old, there are other qualities produced by the past thirty years. The first of these is intellectual snobbery [toward uneducated Arabs, such as beduin] ... [But] these high educational standards have not led to wisdom ... There are three outstanding qualities in the Palestinian town-dwellers and Government officials today: (a) Dislike of foreigners particularly of the West ... (b) ... corruption. Bribery is rife ... (c) ... intrigues against one another.[37]

Later Glubb was to add one further (and somewhat inconsistent) distinction, as between Palestine's rural population and its townspeople. 'The tribesmen and villagers make excellent soldiers - [but] the townsmen are rarely martial,' he wrote. Once again, the reasoning behind this was racial – 'the urban populations are of mixed descent, while the peasants go on, century after century, intermarrying among themselves.'[38]

But generally, Glubb failed to make distinctions between different types of Palestinians. He usually lumped them all together - and painted them with a broad, unsympathetic racial brush. Palestine, a traditional crossroads between Asia, Africa and Europe, Glubb believed, had been 'corrupted' by the criss-crossing passage of foreign influences. And, moreover, over the years, Palestine had succeeded in corrupting its neighbours. 'The mental revolution which takes place in every Arab who lives for even a short period in Palestine is really remarkable. His character seems to be warped, and he becomes mean, hostile and suspicious ... grown accustomed to the idea of disorder and violence.' Again, the backdrop of the Arab Rebellion no doubt influenced Glubb's perceptions at this time.[39] One last, negative collective trait, according to Glubb, marked the Palestinians: ungratefulness. They were ungrateful to Britain for improving their lot and protecting them during the Mandate years and ungrateful to Jordan and the Arab Legion which saved many of them (in the West Bank) from Jewish conquest in 1948, he charged.[40]

Yet, with all this, Glubb was to have an abiding sympathy for the Palestinians in their clash with Zionism and much empathy with their suffering, especially during and following the Naqba - the catastrophe - of 1948. He emerged from the 1948 War filled with admiration for the Palestinians' stoicism. He wrote: 'The depth of the catastrophe is perhaps concealed from the world at large by the immense patience and silent resignation of the victims ... Only those who mix with them intimately know the domestic tragedies which are being daily enacted in the caves in these hills or under the trees of the olive groves of Samaria.'[41] That these sentiments were heartfelt is underlined by the fact that in 1948-49 Glubb adopted two Palestinian (beduin) refugee children - he named them 'Mary' and 'John' - as his own (in addition to his only natural child Godfrey, whom he eventually called 'Faris,' and his adopted daughter, Naomi, a Transjordanian beduin orphan).

'Pure Arab culture', in Glubb's eyes, evolved, and survived, only in the core area of Arabia (the Nejd), in the desert. '"They dwelt in the desert where the air was more pure, the Heaven more open and God more familiar,"' Glubb was to write of his beduin Legionnaires, quoting Origen's description of the early Christian hermits.[42]

For Glubb, the beduins were indivisible from the desert. Glubb was deeply attracted to the desert and often achieved a mystical communion with its vast, wild empty spaces. In his mind the desert was connected with pristine Christian imagery and history, as the retreat and inspiration of a long line of prophets and saints, not to mention Jesus himself. For Glubb, the desert represented the natural, real world; the coast, the artificial and man-made. Glubb once wrote of the Iraqi desert: 'That morning the vast emptiness of the desert seemed to be more than ordinarily full of meaning. It made the silly fussiness of civilisation seem trivial.'[43] And of himself among the beduin in the desert he wrote: 'Only those who have experienced them can understand the joys of evening in the desert, seated in a circle around the campfire in the clean, soft sand, beneath the sparkling Arab stars or in the still white light of the full moon.'[44] In his attachment to the desert, Glubb, once again, was following a long line of British Arabists, who frequently expatiated on the desert's facilitation of communion with nature and the universe and its heightening of the traveller's 'sense of self' and imagination.[45] Nasir al-Din al-Nashashibi says that 'the desert captivated [Glubb's] soul.'[46]

Glubb often wrote about the beduins' physical characteristics, which he saw also as emblematic of that racial purity which they epitomized. These nomads, wrote Glubb, were 'extremely homogeneous' and shared a distinctive nose, which was 'straight, thin and narrow.'[47] Years before, Richard Burton, one of Glubb's orientalist predecessors, had written about the beduins' superior physical attributes, including the 'small but perfectly proportioned penis.'[48]

But alongside this admiration, occasionally bordering on adoration, Glubb remained surprisingly clear-sighted about the beduin - and this too had its roots in his predecessors' observations and stereotypification of the Arabian nomad. Captain George Sadlier, a British traveller through central Arabia in the early 19th century, wrote: 'I have only to repeat that the procrastination, duplicity, falsity, deception, and fraudulence of the Beduin cannot be described by one to an European in language which would present to his mind the real character of these hordes of robbers.'[49] Glubb, of course, was not (like Sadlier) an innocent and much-cheated traveller but, both in Iraq and Jordan, a commander of Beduin troops and (in Jordan) one of the kingdom's potentates, to whom many owed their livelihoods and loyalty. Glubb was generally treated with great deference.

Yet the beduins' faults did not escape his eye. Glubb often talked about their 'emotionalism' and 'childishness':

> There is no point in saying to a beduin NCO [non-commissioned officer] that if he behaves badly, he will lose his chance of a pension later on. No beduin looks so far ahead. They are almost entirely swayed by the emotions of the moment ... As a race, the British as compared to the [beduin] Arabs are like grown up men to school boys. The latter feel more acutely, are more delighted at a success, more depressed at a failure.[50]

As a military man and equestrian, Glubb quite naturally had a great deal of respect for the beduins' camaraderie and martial qualities and inclinations:

> The beduins are a most attractive race of men. They despise work, or agriculture, and consider riding, breeding livestock, or military service as the only possible livelihood for a man of honour. Their only loyalties are personal or tribal. They have no national feeling and pride themselves on selling their swords as mercenaries to the highest bidder. They are open and frank in conversation to a fault, and [are exceedingly] democratic...[51]

In 1942 he wrote in an internal memorandum:

> The outstanding qualities of the beduins are: (1) Vanity or [to?] the point of honour. (2) Fickleness, inconstancy, lack of perseverance ... their generosity is fantastic ... the beduins are very sensitive. They react very readily to those who are

sympathetic to them, and bitterly resent those who are not ... Comradeship is a great tradition among them ... [they are] loyal and remarkably grateful ... In brief, the beduin is often vain, touchy, fickle, childish and importunate. But he is also very alive to honour or shame, quick, intelligent, humorous and capable of great devotion and courage. He is usually loyal to his comrades.[52]

Beduin tribesmen were not always the easiest of companions or subordinates, according to Glubb. Years earlier he had written: 'Uncivilised tribes ... nurse their resentment and when they reach a certain state of desperation, resort to every means of lying, deception and stealth to outwit their rulers.'[53] And in 1936, under the impress of signs of rebelliousness in Transjordan against the British, Glubb wrote:

Beduins are simple souls - plunder, violence, and murder are their element. When ruled with a firm but generous and democratic hand, they are frank, humorous and honest companions and subjects. But they state that, in a pack of wolves, if one be wounded, the others are driven mad by the smell of blood, and turn upon and rend their companion. There is no doubt that the beduins themselves partake of this mentality ... ever ready to rend and devour the weak or faltering... Their delicate nostrils are ever quick to sniff the odour of blood. Rebellion, war, loot, disorder - in a moment dreams of a paradise, half forgotten in six years of slothful peace, awoke in their minds.[54]

Unlike modern-day Europeans, beduins were not wedded to the virtues and value of peace. On the contrary, they tended to see conflict as the natural state of human affairs. 'A prince content to sit down and merely enjoy his natural dominion is regarded by them as hopelessly poor-spirited and effeminate. Moreover, it is not only the prince who conquers his enemies whom they admire. In high politics, successful lying, deceit and subtlety evoke exclamations of admiration.'[55]

Perhaps the Arabs for whom Glubb - again, in line with his Arabist predecessors[56] - had the least respect were the Egyptians. According to Glubb, they (and, by extension, the inhabitants of the Maghreb as a whole), were not really Arabs at all. 'The Egyptians are an entirely different race from the Palestinians,' he once wrote:[57]

The Egyptian seems to be chiefly characterized by pomposity and boastfulness. He has an insatiable lust to be important and applauded. Generally speaking, he is inefficient in action. His big talk rarely results in action. As a soldier, the Egyptian fellah is capable of patient endurance in defence ... The officers rarely, however, have the courage or initiative to act on the offensive. The Egyptians' power

> of speech must not, however, be despised. It is a most formidable weapon. Surrounded by excitable and temperamental races, with whom he shares the Arabic language, the Egyptian is capable of working his neighbours into waves of frenzy during which they may do almost anything ... Radio has enabled Egyptian demagogues to stir up the Arabic-speaking peoples from Morocco to the Persian Gulf ... [Moreover,] Egypt has ... very nearly the only illustrated periodicals in the Middle East, liberally besprinkled with pictures of young females in a manner to appeal to the youthful city dwellers of the East ... The Egyptians have a passion to be rulers ...[58]

Moreover

> as a race, the Egyptians are physically inclined to be lethargical ... After middle age they tend to obesity ... They are extremely expert at intrigue, politics, demagogy ... Physical lethargy combined with intellectual acuteness naturally causes people to sit and argue, and the Egyptians are notorious for their volubility ... In their ruler, volubility may at times degenerate into arrogance.[59]

Both these passages were written under the impress of Nasserist subversion of Jordan. In the last comment Glubb seemed to be specifically referring to Egyptian President Gamal Abdel Nasser.

Attitude to Jews

Over the decades there has been a tendency among Israelis and Jews abroad to identify strong criticism of Israel as tantamount to, or as at least stemming from, anti-Semitism. Zionists routinely branded Glubb an 'anti-Semite', and he was keenly aware of this. 'A number of people, both Jews and Gentiles, are apt to refer to any criticism of Israeli policy as "offensive anti-Semitism," an accusation implying a definite moral lapse. I wish to defend myself against such a charge,' he wrote in his autobiography in 1957.

> "Anti-Semitism", I assume, is an emotion of hatred or dislike towards Jews as a whole, whether considered from the point of view of race or religion. I can state categorically and with all sincerity that I feel no such emotion ... It does not seem to me to be either just or expedient that ... criticisms directed against the Israeli government should brand the speaker with the moral stigma [of] ... anti-Semitism.[60]

'I never felt any hate ... for Jews,' he wrote.[61] Indeed, whenever given an opportunity, he made a point of praising 'the old, generous, cultured liberal Jewry. I have many Jewish friends also.'[62] And: 'Jews, it is said, are good citizens, capable businessmen, civilized, cultured, charming, artistic, wonderful musicians. Much of this is true, at least of west European Jews.'[63]

But the charge of 'anti-Semitism,' as far as can be ascertained, failed to deter Glubb from enunciating his pro-Arab positions or to move him to change them. 'I believe that the creation and maintenance of the State of Israel by armed force was a mistake. That the result has been disastrous for the British and the Arabs alike is only too obvious. It seems to me not improbable that it will ultimately prove to be disastrous for the Jews also,' he wrote in 1957.[64]

But, to judge by his writings, especially after the 1948 war, Glubb's anti-Zionism was tinged by a degree of anti-Semitism. Glubb tended to identify Israel with 'Jewry,' and normally referred to the Israelis as 'the Jews.' Indeed, he often referred to the Arabs' battle against the Yishuv and Jordan's battle against Israel as a battle against 'world Jewry.'[65]

His autobiography is littered with what can only be described as anti-Semitic asides and innuendo. For example, after relating the story of the Jordanian-Israeli battle for Jerusalem in May 1948, he describes a conversation he had with 'a little Greek priest with a thick brown beard, and a gentle sweet smile,' Father Theodosius, who was busy caring for a group of Palestinian refugees. Theodosius showed Glubb 'a picture of the stoning of [St.] Stephen,' and commented: '"Always Jews ... Jews always make trouble." He shook his head sadly and sighed.'[66] Glubb records no effort on his part to correct the priest. Or take Glubb's brief description of Palestine's distant history. He writes that when it was invaded by the Jews in the Second Millennium BC, the country was 'already inhabited by a settled people with a comparatively high culture. The Habiru, or Hebrews, were a backward nomadic tribe by comparison ...'[67] Or, describing the Jews returning to Palestine from their Babylonian exile in the 6th Century BC: 'They fostered ... that aloofness which has served to keep them a peculiar people until the present day.'[68]

Glubb, it appears, reached adulthood without having Jewish friends – while nevertheless imbibing that mild, superficial anti-Semitism that characterized his time, class and upbringing. Occasionally, in his later writings, we hear echoes of it in references to Jews as sharp middlemen and merchants. But Glubb's attitude towards 'the Jews' appears to have hardened and grown more critical with time, especially during and following the years 1948-56, when he personally had had to fight them. It was as if 'the Jews' (in fact, the Israelis) had supplied him with continuous proofs of their negative traits, reinforcing his initial, superficial prejudices. The continuous hostilities between Israel and Jordan – with the IDF usually doing the attacking and Jordan, almost invariably on the defensive, always the weaker and more vulnerable side - during the years 1948-56 aggravated these anti-Semitic tendencies. So did specific Israeli actions and policies during those years, which ran counter to what Glubb accepted as norms of soldierly behaviour.

During the 1930s, World War II, and the immediate post-war years - perhaps under the impress of Nazi anti-Semitism and the Holocaust - Glubb, essentially a fair man, with a soft spot for the underdog, wrote about the Jews (and Zionism) with a measure of ambivalence. 'The life of the Jewish people,' he wrote in 1946,

> is an unending tragedy. Driven ceaselessly from one country to another, they are at first welcomed and then driven out or massacred. Nobody can endure them long because they do not assimilate themselves easily and thus become a state within a state. The tragedy is a vicious circle - other peoples dislike them owing to their character - [and] their unlikeable character has been produced by persecution by other peoples. Persecution and hatred has [sic] bred bitterness in the Jews, and people who hate and sneer are unpopular with their neighbours. The Zionist solution is for them to come out from amongst the Gentiles and live in a country all of their own ... It might be the ideal solution if they could all go to a Pacific island. The fallacy of Zionism is that Palestine is not an island ... There can be only one ending of this struggle [for Palestine] - a pogrom on a scale never yet dreamed of ... If [Jewish settlement] continues against Arab resistance, it can only end, sooner or later, in a terrible disaster for the Jews themselves ... The Crusaders maintained a precarious foothold in the Middle East for 200 years, but in the end not one of them was left. A century or two is nothing in history. Zionism is leading these wretched Jews for one of the worst disasters of their history.[69]

The passage, while conveying an ambivalent sympathy for the Jews' plight, avoids explicit mention of the Holocaust - and implicitly ignores that event, as when Glubb writes of a future 'pogrom on a scale never yet dreamed of.' What pogrom could be greater than the one that had ended barely a year before Glubb wrote these words?

During 1948-56 Israeli troops attacked Arab areas of Palestine, drove out hundreds of thousands of their inhabitants (many ending up as refugees in Jordan), killed hundreds of his beloved Legionnaires, routinely killed Arab infiltrators into Israel (the death toll was in the thousands, most of them destitute refugees or farmers and shepherds), and repeatedly raided Jordanian villages and military bases, killing civilians and soldiers. (See below.) It was perhaps natural that such a daily diet of bloodshed would nurture Glubb's latent anti-Semitism.

Glubb's anti-Semitic proclivities, or at least utterances, grew more pronounced after his removal from public office and his return in 1956 from the Middle East to London. In an indirect way he probably regarded his dismissal by King Hussein as a result, at least in part, of Israel's actions. As he grew older, he became more and more obsessed with racial concepts and categories. In a speech in 1967 he spoke about 'the problem of the Jewish nose'. He maintained that the Hebrew tribes who invaded Canaan (or Palestine) during the Second Millennium BC were 'doubtless' smaller in number than the native inhabitants. In the course of the following centuries 'the distinction between rulers and ruled would be lost by intermarriage ... Thus the Jewish nose turns out not to be Jewish or even Semitic but Hittite and Aryan, the conquered native nose.'[70] He returned to the problem of the Jewish nose in 1971: 'The principal argument [in favour of viewing "the Jews" as an "ethnic group" is the] facial resemblance between them - large nose, sallow complexion, and black hair.' But not all Jews 'have these distinguishing features.' Moreover these features are Middle Eastern rather than Jewish. Russian Jews, for example, 'have considerably less Middle Eastern blood, consisting largely of pagan Slav proselytes or of Khazar Turks. Many eastern European Jews have fair hair and blue eyes.'[71] And again: Modern Jews are not 'descendants of the Judeans ... The Arabs of Palestine are probably more closely related to the Judeans [genetically] than are modern Russian or German Jews.'[72] Of course, an anti-Zionist (as well as an anti-Semitic) point is being made here: The Palestinians have a greater political right to Palestine than the Jews as they, not modern-day Jews, are the true descendants of the land's Jewish inhabitants\owners. (Conversely, Glubb often wrote that the Palestinian Arabs were the genetic descendants of the pre-Israelite inhabitants of Palestine, the Canaanites.)

In 1971 Glubb devoted almost the whole of a fair-sized book, *Peace in the Holy Land*, to Palestine's (and the Jews') history. It was clearly written under the impress of the first years of Israel's often brutal occupation of the Palestinian territories of the West Bank and Gaza Strip. He seems to have been particularly peeved at the idea of Jewish control of Christianity's holy sites, in East Jerusalem and Bethlehem. Glubb's description and analysis is both implicitly and, in parts, explicitly anti-Semitic. He argues that Zionism and the nature of Zionist behaviour towards Palestine's Arabs were not merely facets of Western imperialism's conquest of and dominance over native Third World populations but also a direct and natural outcome of three thousand years of Jewish history. The connections are made on a number of levels. In Glubb's eyes, the Zionist takeover of Palestine during the late Nineteenth and Twentieth centuries replicates the Hebrews' conquest of the land in the 12th-11th centuries BC; and Gentile-Christian persecution of the Jews down the ages bred an aggressive, vengeful Jewish ethos which, once empowered, was as a matter of course unleashed against the Arabs. In fact, argues Glubb, the 'Jewish mentality, Jewish tradition and the Jewish attitude to the rest of the human race has [sic] been passed down without a break from generation to generation.'[73]

Glubb seems to imply that Jewish behaviour and mindset are the fount of such anti-Semitic tracts as *The Protocols of the Elders of Zion* and of ancient Greek descriptions of the Jews as the 'enemies of the human race'. `It is extraordinary,' writes Glubb, `how such phrases recur [throughout history]. Perhaps Jewish solidarity in face of the Gentile world gave rise to the belief in their hatred of the whole of humanity.'[74]

Glubb begins his book with a caveat, asserting that the 'difficulties' of the Middle East are in part traceable to Western 'cynicism and ... unscrupulous politics,' which in turn derive from 'our abandonment of belief in God. For men, if they lose sight of the Spiritual, behave to one another like wild beasts.'[75] *Peace* then sets out to demonstrate why it is 'wrong to depict the primitive Israelite invaders [of Canaan] as peculiarly virtuous'[76] and to assert that God's 'choice' of the Jews - which the author, a believing Christian, does not dispute - by no means rests on their particular virtuousness. He castigates King David's 'expansionist policy'[77] and suggests that

> the principal emphasis in Ezra's reform was the prohibition of marriage between Jews and the rest of humanity. The "holy race" was henceforth to be isolated from mankind. The Israelites had been freely intermarrying with the people of the land [of Canaan] for eight hundred years. [Ezra] seems to have been a "reactionary" ... who wished to recreate the times of Joshua, trying to revive the original conquerors' contempt for the "natives" ... Ezra's reforms were completely opposed [sic] to public opinion today. The idea of a superior race, the blood of which would be contaminated by intermixture with others, is no longer popular. [But] Hitler was not original in his conception of a "master race".

Then, having battered Ezra so mercilessly, Glubb pulls a particularly elusive rabbit out of his hat. He had quite explicitly pointed at the Jews - or Ezra - as the originators of "master race" theory and politics. Glubb now proceeds to point in another direction altogether: 'Aristotle,' he writes, 'is said to have told the young Alexander that the relationship between Greeks and people of other races was like that between human beings and animals. The narrow pride of a single community, believing itself superior to the rest of humanity, has a never-ending appeal to human vanity.' So the Greeks, or the Greeks too, are culprits of "master race" theories. Perhaps Aristotle is introduced in this context as a fig leaf or camouflage or diversion to enable Glubb to parry the charge of anti-Semitism.[78]

Glubb goes on to state that '[the story of] Ezra shows the same confusion between "race" and religion as still befogs Jewry ... Thereby originated that isolationism ... intended to separate those who professed Judaism from the rest of humanity.' But Glubb, an innately fair man, immediately points out, on the basis of such Old Testament books as Jonah and Ruth, that within Judaism there always coexisted a contrasting current of thought as well: '[Some] Jews scattered in the world became advocates of a liberal attitude to all peoples, while others insisted on the narrow isolationism of the "holy nation".'[79]

If there is a direct link between ancient Israel's doctrine of chosenness and master-race thinking, there is also, in Glubb's view, a direct link between Nazism and modern-day Israeli behaviour towards the Arabs. Repeatedly through 1948-56, Glubb was to compare Israeli - usually called 'Jewish' - behaviour to that of Hitler and Stalin. For example, about Israel's demand in spring 1949 in the Israeli-Jordanian armistice negotiations that Jordan cede a strip of West Bank land, Glubb commented: 'The Jewish demand was pure Hitlerite power politics. Transjordan was obliged to sign.'[80] Or: 'The Jews [i.e., Israelis] are playing power politics as crudely as the Russians, [but] on a smaller scale.'[81]

But on a philosophical plane, post-1956 Glubb was to find a deeper layer of causation and confluence - that again harked back to Second Temple Judaism:

> Just as the Nazi persecution produced the present aggressive military state of Israel, so the originally heroic [Jewish] resistance to [the Greek Seleucid King] Antiochus Epiphanes [led by the Maccabbee or Hasmonean family in the 2nd Century BC] transformed Judea into a fanatical and aggressive military principality. John Hyrkanus [grandchild of the original Maccabbee brothers] attacked all his neighbours ... [and] forcibly converted the Idumaeans - a new policy further invalidating any Jewish claim to ethnic unity ... Such was the spirit of the Hasmoneans and we shall encounter it again.[82]

Glubb - somewhat bizarrely, given the context of his ultimately pro-Palestinian argument - is particularly condemnatory regarding the Jewish rebellions against Rome, the 'Great Revolt' of 66-73 AD and the Bar-Kochba Revolt of 132-135. Instead of taking the part of the native, oppressed population, Glubb deems the revolts against the imperial overseer acts of narrow nationalist-religious fanatics. As a life-long agent of the British Empire, Glubb here seems to identify with the empire rather than with its oppressed subjects. According to Glubb, the Great Revolt began when, 'all over the country, the Jews murdered the Gentiles, who retaliated when the occasion offered.'[83] The rebels are dismissed as 'extreme nationalists' and 'gangsters'[84] - one of the leaders of the revolt in the north, Yohanan of Gush-Halav (John of Gischala), is described as 'the local gangster'[85] - and the revolt itself as an act of irrational fanaticism and xenophobia:

> The extremists who rebelled against Rome were not a majority of the Jews in Palestine ... Their motives do not appear to have been religious ... Their motives were perhaps xenophobia, lust of power and greed ... It is probably true that peaceful communities of Jews were protected, not persecuted, by [the Roman leaders] Titus and Vespasian. The treatment accorded [by the Romans] to prisoners was brutal, but in accordance with contemporary custom ... When the Jews took Samaria all the inhabitants had been [sic] massacred ... The educated classes realised that the rebellion must fail. The defenders of Jerusalem were mostly ignorant peasants.[86]

In summary, Glubb writes: 'Under the Romans, Judea broke out once again in bitter, militant isolationism which, as under the Hasmoneans, led to decline of spiritual religion and a rise in race hatreds.'[87] In other words, rebellion against an oppressive, foreign conqueror is dismissed as a form of 'bitter, militant isolationism.'

Glubb subsequently devoted long passages of *Peace* to the unhappy history of Jewish-Christian relations. Here, too, somehow, the much-persecuted Jews are found to be the guilty party; it was they who gave birth to the idea and habit of religious persecution and initiated the sequence of victimisation. 'In the first century and a half after Christ, the Jews seem to have shown this persecuting mentality against the Christians, thereby releasing a chain reaction of persecution down to our own times,' writes Glubb.[88] But the Jews were innovative inasmuch as, while the governments in the ancient world 'were only concerned with the actions of their subjects, not with their thoughts, the Jews seem to have originated religious persecution against people's thoughts ... Thenceforward, not only Jews, but, even more, Christians, were to kill, torture and penalise people for their thought, no matter how innocent their lives.'

Quite naturally, then, 'the Christians had built up bitter resentment against Jews during the first century and a half of persecution,' so that when 'they became strong enough, they were, in most unchristian spirit, eager for their revenge.'[89] Thereafter, Christians persecuted Jews, though not 'continuously.'[90] By the 5th Century, according to Glubb, the Christians caught up with and were 'as violent as the Jews.'[91] But this is not to say that the Jews by this time were blameless; indeed, according to Glubb, they continued to provoke. 'Jews were unwise in their use of mockery. Caricatures of Christ and comic parodies of the crucifixion goaded Christians to fury,' he writes.[92]

According to Glubb, the Christians were not alone among the Gentiles in being goaded by provocations into persecuting Jews. Islamic maltreatment of Jews was also rooted in Jewish actions. In *Peace in the Holy Land*, Glubb wrote the following about the rise of Islam in the 7th Century: 'Muhammad claimed that Islam was the religion of Abraham and Moses, and had hoped that he would be supported by the Jews. Unfortunately, however, the Medina Jews mocked at his revelations and his mission.'[93] Subsequently, he expelled two of Medina's three Jewish tribes. 'The third, however, had communicated with the enemy during the siege of Medina. When the [besieging] Meccans withdrew, seven hundred Jews of this tribe were put to death. The messenger of God presumably regarded the action of these people as organised opposition to the mission with which he believed God had entrusted him.' But, to be sure, individual Jews were allowed to remain in Medina 'unmolested' and Jews and Christians were not compelled to convert to Islam, writes Glubb.[94] Indeed, 'under Islam' the Jews 'received religious freedom ... Jews and Christians were safe, as was their property,' though they were compelled to pay 'a light poll tax but, in return, were exempted from military service,' Glubb tells us - without remarking that this exemption was not of the Jews' asking and had a considerable discriminatory downside.[95] All he says on this point is that, from the Jews' perspective, it was 'probably a profitable bargain' (the phrase itself carries an anti-Semitic overtone).[96]

On Muhammad's and Islam's relations with the Jews Glubb was more forthcoming in his biography of the Prophet, *The Life and Times of Muhammad*, published in 1970. The Jews of Medina, he tells us (on the basis of the Koran and other Muslim texts), frequently challenged Muhammad 'with a view to revealing his ignorance and making him appear ridiculous.' (Glubb compares this to the New Testament description of the rabbis trying `to entangle' Jesus 'in His talk.')[97] Glubb then writes of the Prophet's hope that the Jews would join him in the struggle against the idolaters and comments:

> If the Jews of Medina had been men of wide outlook and generous wisdom, it is possible that they might have discovered a method of peaceful coexistence ... But how could the Jews of Medina be men of broadminded wisdom? ... They themselves were probably early Arab converts to Judaism [again, Glubb is signalling the un-Jewish genetic origin of Jews] ... [Their] rabbis could not resist the temptation to show their superior cleverness by pointing at the factual inaccuracies in the Apostle's [i.e., Muhammad's] versions of the Old Testament stories ... They made the Messenger of God look ridiculous ...[98]

The Jews once again are depicted as too clever by half - and as the cause of their own downfall.

Solely on the basis of the Islamic texts, Glubb suggests 'that the exile or persecution of the Jewish tribes [of the Medina area] was not due to hatred of their religion, but to the fact that they persisted in casting doubts on the mission of the Apostle...'[99] and that 'the Messenger of God at one stage hoped to join forces with the Jews.' But 'the petty vanity of the Judaistic tribes of Medina ... caused the disappointment of his hopes.'[100]

In a giant perversion of the history of Islamic-Jewish relations - in which the Muslims always dominated and the small Jewish minorities were at best second class citizens, and were often oppressed, and at various times and in various places, massacred - Glubb writes: 'It is interesting to note that, once the Jews ceased to be a danger to the survival of Islam, the two faiths once again became allies against Christianity and were to remain so until the rise of Zionism in the twentieth century.'[101] To describe Islam and Judaism, with its small, impoverished and downtrodden communities scattered around the Islamic world, as 'allies' against Christendom or to describe the Islamic attitude towards the Jews at most times as egalitarian, non-discriminatory, or even particularly tolerant, is absurd. But this, in effect, is what Glubb does.

Glubb concludes his book on Muhammad, which was aimed at Anglo-Saxon audiences, with a moving plea for tolerance towards Islam:

> To most Europeans, Islam appears a hard, cruel, savage faith, typified by the hawk-nosed Muslim fanatic, a drawn scimitar in his hand, and the Crescent banner fluttering above his head. This image has perhaps been reinforced in the last twenty years by the bombastic threats of

Levantine politicians, principally Egyptians, about exterminating Israel.[102]

If, during the Middle Ages, Jews lived well in the Islamic world, they did not fare so badly in the Christian world either, according to Glubb. And where, nonetheless, they suffered from the sharp edge of intolerance it was mostly due to their own failings. In the West, between 700 and 1,500 C.E., Glubb writes, the Jews were on the whole tolerated by the Church and protected by secular rulers, but they were 'disliked by the mass of the people.' This was because they served as money-lenders and tax-collectors; because of 'their unsociability, and their refusal to join in public festivals, or even to eat or drink with Christians'; and because of 'their real or imagined contempt for Gentiles.'[103] In the late Middle Ages in northern Europe, 'Jews ... in business with Gentiles ... were sometimes tricky and, feeling self-conscious, often seemed either servile or arrogant.'[104] At the same time, in Medieval Muslim Spain, according to Glubb, 'the Jewish converts tended to support the king against the populace. Again and again in history, we find the Jews, released from repression, rise so rapidly as almost to control their country of residence. Indignant at their power, the people turn against them and a new period of repression ensues.'[105]

In general, Glubb asserts, Jews in Christendom tended to be persecuted 'far less than ... Christian heretics'[106] and less than Christians in the Muslim world. Referring to the Mongol invasions of the Middle East, he writes: 'Certainly the suffering of Christian heretics or Jews in Europe were but a drop in the bucket compared to the agonies of the [Muslim] Middle East from 1220 to 1405.'[107] At the same time, Glubb implies that some massacres of Christians by Christians were in some way instigated by the Jews - as when he writes that Joshua, Gideon and Samuel were Oliver Cromwell's role models, a 'fact which perhaps explains the massacres at Drogheda and Wexford [in Ireland] in 1649.'[108]

All this said, post-1956 Glubb was not completely devoid of any compassion for the Jewish people: 'Even today, it is possible to feel deep sympathy with Jews and their dilemma...,' he wrote in 1971;[109] and 'in many respects we are obliged to sympathize with the Jews of the world in the agonizing dilemma which confronts them, as to whether they should or should not assimilate with the remainder of the human race.'[110] But all in all, Glubb's outlook on the history of the Jews - spelled out in the books written in his years of retirement - is jaundiced, inaccurate, and, at times, blatantly anti-Semitic. It intermixes emphases on Jewish isolationism and sense of superiority with charges of intolerance and over-empowerment.

Beginning in the mid-1930s and even more emphatically in his years of retirement, Glubb was to bewail and assail what he called Jewish 'own[ership], control or influence [over] the greater part of the newspapers, and many of the broadcasting companies in the world.' The Jewish hold on the media, according to Glubb, in large measure explained Israel's dominance of world public opinion; this explained why governments around the world supported the Jewish state. 'It has been found impossible,' he wrote in 1949,

> to get any article published in any American newspaper giving even the mildest suggestion of an Arab viewpoint. This hold over world publicity organizations enables the Jews to play a Jekyll and Hyde policy. In the press of the world, they are the poor, persecuted victims ... In Palestine, the Jews are arrogant military conquerors, driving civilians from their homes, and threatening further military operations against any who refuse to admit their claim to dominate the Middle East.[111]

Glubb at this time had a low opinion of the American Zionist leadership - though perhaps he can be forgiven for this as so did Moshe Shertok (later Sharett), the director of the Jewish Agency Political Department (soon to be Israel's first foreign minister) and Isaiah Berlin, an official at the British Embassy in Washington. In 1943 Berlin wrote to London: 'Shertock [sic] ... says the local Zionists are a shocking collection of incompetents and petty intriguers, which indeed is too true.'[112]

Attitude to Zionism

Glubb viewed Zionism as both a natural outcome of Judaism and Jewish history and as an offspring (or stepchild?) of Western imperialism. In the 18th Century, in the Age of Enlightenment, he argued, some Jews sought to assimilate in Christian societies and 'become ordinary citizens.' But others preferred exclusivity and isolation: 'Zionism [which emerged a century later] was to be one aspect of this fear of absorption [i.e., assimilation].'[113] At the same time, 'Zionism was conceived in the age of imperialism ... [The Jews] made their plans [to take over Palestine] in complete disregard of the "natives" of the Middle East. Zionism and the Union of South Africa alone retain this colonialist mentality today,' he wrote in 1971.[114]

However, Glubb well understood, and to a degree sympathized with (especially before 1948), the wellsprings of Jewish nationalism:

> ... the Jews ... [were] so often the victims of persecution, or at least ostracism and discrimination. They can endure it no longer. They are tired of being everywhere a minority in others' countries. This time they will have a country where they will be their own masters ... For centuries the Jews have been a religion ... The influence of modern nationalism has transformed them into a nation ... We can blame neither Jews nor Arabs for becoming infected with the spirit [of nationalism], for it was western Europe which created modern nationalism ... The Jewish tragedy owed its origin to the Christian nations of Europe and America. At last [in supporting Zionism] the conscience of Christendom was awake,

he wrote in 1948.[115]

And even in his post-1956 years Glubb occasionally wrote about Zionism with a measure of sympathy: 'It is not difficult to understand the Jewish desire for a state where everyone will be a Jew, and the people of which will be free, not only from persecution, but also from insult and social condescension.'[116] But generally, Glubb's tone ranged from negative to extremely negative when discussing Zionism and Zionists. Chaim Weizmann, the foremost Zionist leader after Herzl, the movement's prophet and founder, 'represented the Russian Jews, the sworn foes of assimilation, whose bitter isolationism has been intensified by persecution,' explained Glubb.[117] Moreover - and here one can identify another routine anti-Semitic charge, the charge of dual loyalty or Jewish disloyalty toward their Christian host countries – 'Weizmann's autobiography impresses the Gentile reader with the extreme readiness of the Zionists to change their country. Born in Russia, he lived in Germany, Switzerland and England,' writes Glubb, completely ignoring Weizmann's reasons for moving from country to country and his major scientific contribution to British munitions production in World War I. '... His associates lived similar lives, their loyalty being to Jewry alone,' writes Glubb.[118] Like Weizmann, the majority of the Russian Jews who poured into France, Britain and the United States in the last decades of the 19th Century and the early decades of the 20th Century saw themselves as 'Jews first and only loyal to their countries of residence to a much smaller degree.'[119]

'From the first,' writes Glubb, 'Zionists envisaged the establishment of a Jewish state and the liquidation of the population of Palestine.'[120] To carry out the project, the Zionists always applied a

> little-by-little technique. Weizmann, though clearly envisaging the final objective of the seizure of all of Palestine, always asked for small concessions, moderately worded ... The Zionists, moreover, already followed the policy of harassment, which they have since developed extensively, constantly bringing pressure to bear on those whom they wish to influence. Consequently, waverers agree to their demands, if only for a quiet life, and opponents remain silent to escape constant attack,

he wrote in 1971.[121]

Moreover, Glubb wrote with substantial accuracy, the Zionists always camouflaged with 'doubletalk'[122] their real intentions - statehood and the eviction of the native population.[123] And, during the years of the British Mandate, they proceeded incrementally and by subterfuge, gradually winning one point after another in the international political arena and on the ground in Palestine while enjoying British imperial support and protection. (Throughout his works, Glubb projects an ambivalent attitude towards British imperialism, at once supportive and critical, especially when it was inimical to Arab interests and\or supportive of Zionism.)

And Zionism's victims? The Palestinian Arabs were 'a pleasant and intelligent people' but were unequal to the challenge posed by Zionism, explained Glubb: 'The Zionists...were first class international publicists and politicians, the Palestinians were children. Unfamiliar with the Western world, they made mistakes verging on suicide. One of these was their disastrous habit of boycotting political inquiries.'[124]

Glubb's description of the contrasting natures of Zionist and Palestinian Arab diplomacy is pithy and on target:

> The Jews invariably accepted every promise or concession which they could obtain, even if it were much less than they had hoped for. Having secured any such concession, they then proceeded to demand more, and to enlarge the meaning of the promise which they had received. The Arabs persistently followed the exactly opposite course. They demanded their full programme and rejected categorically any concession which abated by one jot or one tittle from the text of their full demands. The result was catastrophic. The Jews went from strength to strength, securing one partial concession after another ... The Arabs always demanded all or nothing - and obtained nothing.[125]

This brief analysis of Glubb's attitudes toward the Arabs, Jews and Zionism will help us understand his thinking and actions during the 1930s,

1940s and 1950s. His prolonged, successful command of the Arab Legion was made possible by his admiring (though also reserved) view of the beduins; his behaviour toward the Palestinians, both in 1936-39 and during 1948, was at least partly rooted in his (racial) preconceptions. So, too was his inimical attitude toward the Jews, the Zionist settlers and the Zionist enterprise in Palestine, though, between the lines, one also senses both sympathy toward Jewish suffering and a certain admiration for the Zionists' concrete military, political and economic achievements.

Chapter 2

THE ARAB REVOLT 1936-39

In April-May 1936, when the Arab Revolt against the British Mandate government and the Zionist enterprise broke out, Glubb, as second-in-command of the Legion, was responsible for law and order, and the maintenance of Transjordanian sovereignty, in the desert areas of the Emirate. Toward the end of the revolt, in March 1939, Glubb succeeded Peake as commander of the Legion.

The revolt, led, initially covertly and then overtly, by the Grand Mufti of Jerusalem, Muhammad Haj Amin al Husseini, was driven primarily by the massive influx into Palestine of Jewish immigrants from Eastern and Central Europe, fleeing anti-Semitic persecution; in 1935 alone more than 60,000 arrived. The Arabs of Palestine, numbering at the time some one million, feared that if the influx continued, the Jews, who numbered some 350,000, would soon become a majority and Palestine, a Jewish state. Optimally, the rebels hoped to drive out the British and establish an independent Arab-led state; at a minimum, they aimed to force the British to halt or severely reduce the floodtide of Jewish immigration.

Britain, confronted by the triple threat from Nazi Germany in Europe, Fascist Italy in the Mediterranean basin and Africa, and imperial Japan in the Far East and by the fearful prospect that these states might act in concert against her, almost consistently exhibited infirmity of purpose and military weakness in each arena. Without doubt, this spectacle helped to trigger the Arab rebellion in Palestine. Already in September 1935 Glubb had warned - against the backdrop of the Italian assault on Abyssinia - that the Palestinian Arabs might seize 'the opportunity of a European disturbance to hold a general massacre of the Jews.'[126]

In April-May 1936 the Arabs exploited what they saw as their opportunity. While ambivalently sympathetic to the rebels' grievances and aims, Glubb from the first - like his monarch, Abdullah - abhorred their leader, whom he regarded as extremist, terroristic and sly. Haj Amin, Glubb was to write in 1957, after years of himself battling against the Zionists, was

> in reality a fanatical politician. Basically there was considerable justice in the cause he served - resistance to the armed suppression of the people of Palestine, who objected to the mass immigration of Jews against the will of the majority of the inhabitants. But the Mufti's methods were both unwise and immoral - utter intransigence, a complete refusal to compromise and terrorist murders of Palestinians who differed from him.[127]

But the problem wasn't only the character of the rebel leader. While Glubb certainly agreed with Husseini and his Palestinian supporters that the Zionist influx was unjust and must be halted, he was quite naturally antagonistic toward anyone in rebellion against the British Crown and bent on killing Britons, and, besides, was chary about the Palestinians' desire for independence. Sovereignty over Palestine (as over the rest of 'Greater Syria') had long been coveted by his master, Abdullah, a desire quickened by the rebellion and Britain's response to it: The situation seemed, at last, to hold out the promise of a Hashemite takeover of all or parts of Palestine - and Husseini's goal of an independent Arab Palestine ran counter to this ambition.

The rebellion thus sparked within Glubb a set of contradictory emotions and sympathies, which were only resolved when the revolt was finally crushed by the British Army and police in spring-summer 1939. Palestinian hopes for immediate independence were abruptly dashed. But in compensation and to appease the beaten rebels, the British gradually reduced the influx of Jewish immigrants and, in the May 1939 'White Paper,' enunciated a comprehensive reversal of their pro-Zionist (Balfour Declaration) policy of November 1917. Britain announced a severe curtailment of Jewish immigration (15,000 per year for five years, after which further immigration would require the consent of the people, meaning the Arabs, which, it was understood, would not be forthcoming); severe restriction of Jewish land purchases, thus significantly reducing the possibility of establishing new settlements; and a vague promise to grant the country's population - meaning the Arab majority, now assured by the curb on Jewish immigration - independence within ten years.

But in spring 1936, Whitehall's anti-Zionist volte face was still a long way off. And for Transjordan and Glubb the rebellion posed a potential grave challenge. The main danger was of a spillover of anti-British sentiment and, perhaps, violence from Palestine into Transjordan, where there was a small but influential, expatriate Palestinian community.[128] Additionally, it was feared by the authorities that tribal resentments and rivalries as well as a measure of subterranean nationalist feeling among the villagers and beduin might mutate into anti-British and perhaps even anti-Hashemite agitation. Both among the expatriate Palestinians and among some of the Transjordanians there was a natural fellow-feeling for the neighbouring Arab community, under threat from European Zionist encroachment and under the heel of growingly oppressive (due to counter-insurgency operations) British rule.

Glubb worried principally about Britain's position in Transjordan - Britain completely subsidized the Emir's government, which had almost no local sources of revenue, as well as the Arab Legion - and about the physical safety of Britons, like himself, in the Emirate. The Legion, apart from being a small quasi-military formation, also included Jordan's police force and intelligence service.

For people like Glubb, at once a loyal servant of an Arab prince and a loyal subject of the British crown, the rebellion potentially posed a classic dilemma of dual loyalty (perhaps one reason for his lifelong carping about the alleged dual loyalty of British Jewry). Might not the two loyalties, and the interests of the two crowns, collide? ‘To Englishmen who have worked with the Arabs, the situation was tragic in the extreme,’ he wrote in June 1936, six weeks into the rebellion across the river:

> Many of us collaborated with Arabs for [long periods] ... Throughout ... with many ups and downs, we have maintained and enjoyed innumerable friendships ... and in spite of local differences, the great majority of Arabs have maintained their faith that Britain was the greatest, the most generous and the most friendly of the great powers. It is nothing less than tragic to see this faith and friendship turning, before our eyes, into disillusionment and hatred. God alone knows how it will all end.[129]

In May 1936 he had written that the ‘tragedy of Palestine overshadowed all else ... Amman was passionately and vibrantly in sympathy with the Palestine Arabs ... The maintenance [so far] of law and order in Amman,’ he explained, ‘was not due to lack of sympathy for the Palestine Arabs or lack of resentment against the British or the Jews, but rather was an attempt to show that Arabs ... were capable of governing themselves [i.e., controlling their emotions]...’ Outside Amman, the countryside was quiescent because the tribesmen were `not politically minded.’ But the tribal chiefs, he reported, had begun to receive letters ‘from Palestine, urging [them] … to invade Palestine ...’ in support of the rebels. And there were ‘signs’ that ‘[local religious] agitators were seeking to exploit’ the situation.[130] Glubb commented that the introduction of radio had revolutionized ‘the big and the illiterate countries of the world.’ In the Middle East, this had meant that 'Nejd [i.e., central Saudi Arabia] has leaped four centuries as far as news of the world is concerned ... There can be little doubt that, six years ago, a rebellion in Palestine would have been scarcely heard of in the Nejd. Today it is a subject of passionate interest and fiery discussion.'[131] Presumably, this was no less the case in Transjordan itself.

In reporting in early July on the situation among the Transjordan tribes the previous month, Glubb observed that

> the situation in Palestine has entirely dominated the life of Transjordan ... Time had elapsed [since the start of the rebellion] sufficient to allow extremist propaganda to penetrate to the furthest encampment and the poorest beduin family ... This propaganda was of the most inflammatory nature, with a strong religious tinge calculated to excite tribesmen more than nationalistic politics ... The tribesmen began to show signs of a certain truculence, which had been unknown since 1931 ... [and to show a] loss of respect [for] the authorities. All this tended to increase the popularity of King Ibn Saud of Saudi Arabia among the Transjordanian tribesmen, at the expense of the British-aligned Abdullah. The Transjordan tribesmen followed events in Palestine 'with breathless interest. It is the greatest mistake to imagine that beduins are poor ignorant clouts ...

Glubb believed that the pro-Palestinian 'activists' in Transjordan were contemplating two lines of action: (1) Raising levies 'to proceed to Palestine and join in the struggle' (he thought that this was unlikely to 'occur on a large scale'); and (2) a 'local rebellion in Transjordan,' which was the hope of the Palestinian rebel leaders, who believed that this 'would mean a relief of the pressure on themselves by the transfer of half the British forces [eastward] across the Jordan.'

Glubb believed that there was a schism within Abdullah's cabinet but that the tribal leaders largely remained loyal to the government. However, Glubb worried about some of the leaders. The tribes, he argued, had been reduced to poverty by the lack of government grants. 'Haditha al Kurasha, one of the two paramount sheikhs of the Bani Sakhr [a large Transjordan tribe], has been reduced to such poverty that he rarely has enough to eat. Last winter, he and his large family were living largely on cheap barley, of the type used for feeding cattle.' Another sheikh, Mithgal ibn Faiz, had only managed to make ends meet by obtaining a loan from the Jews. 'For the past month, Mithgal ... has made himself the principal instrument of the agitators advocating violence in Transjordan. It is generally believed that his main hope is that the Jews will wash out the debt he owes them, as a bribe to keep him quiet.' Glubb argued that it was a mistake not to pay the tribal chiefs a monthly subsidy.

In Amman itself, the source of potential trouble, according to Glubb, was 'the Nabulsis,' by whom he meant those Palestinians who had settled in the capital since World War I and from among whom hailed many of the Amman government officials, including the Chief (or Prime) Minister, Ibrahim Pasha Hashim. 'With Palestine in its present state, the Nabulsis [i.e., literally, people from the Palestine town of Nablus] are, naturally enough, in great excitement, and have neglected no opportunity to propagand [sic], spread false reports, or taunt the tribal chiefs in the most opprobrious terms for their failure to take up arms.' (Already in late 1935 Glubb had recommended paying subsidies to the sheikhs to forestall rebelliousness.[132])

Glubb believed that this agitation would translate into rebellion only if disgruntled townsmen joined disgruntled tribesmen. But the bulk of the population of Transjordan - about 350,000 strong at the time - lacked any serious anti-Hashemite or anti-British grievance: 'Just as in Palestine every Arab thinks he has a grievance ... in Transjordan, the ordinary Arab has no grievance at all.' Hence, for the time being there would be no rebellion.

But the British must take care not to provide a grievance, Glubb warned. He feared a thoughtless, over-reactive use of British troops or aircraft against protesting Transjordanians. But in the absence of such a spark, he predicted, 'Transjordan will relapse to its former somnolence...'[133]

C.H.F. Cox, the British Resident (i.e., representative) in Amman, thought Glubb somewhat alarmist. In a letter to Sir Arthur Wauchope, the Jerusalem-based High Commissioner for Palestine and Transjordan, he wrote: 'The continued disorders in Palestine have inevitably brought Transjordan nearer the boiling point, but the Amir's [i.e., Abdullah's] authority is still sufficiently great and his determination sufficiently strong to maintain order.' Cox endorsed Glubb's warning to beware of giving the Transjordanians a 'grievance' through a hasty use of British troops. But Glubb, said Cox, was exaggerating with regard to 'the Nabulsis,' 'including the Chief Minister.' The implication was that the Chief Minister (from 1939 on, called Prime Minister), and perhaps other 'Nabulsis,' were not enthusiastic about the Palestine rebellion and\or Haj Amin al Husseini.

But Cox made an important distinction which Glubb had elided. Glubb had divided Transjordanians simply into townsmen and beduin - but he 'has forgotten the villagers, and the leading men among them are a force to be reckoned with, even stronger, in my opinion, than the beduin ...' Cox went on to clear Mithgal ibn Faiz, one of the main chieftains of the Bani Sakhr and Transjordan's leading land owner. He had, indeed, wrote the Resident, borrowed P£1,000

> from the Jews, who have made much use of his name in their propaganda to show the readiness of Transjordan to accept Jewish immigration. [During the 1930s there was much talk among Zionist officials of Jewish purchase of land and settlement in Transjordan]. Mithgal has always said quite frankly that if he [now] sold his land to the Jews, he would destroy them later ...[134]

Partly on the basis of Glubb's reports that summer, Wauchope concluded that 'in order to avoid the spread of disturbances to Transjordan, we must begin to subsidize the Beduin tribes ... I propose that Amir Abdullah should be asked to undertake the distribution of subsidies.' The high commissioner asked London to agree to an initial P£ 5,000 'forthwith.'[135] And two months later, Wauchope reported to the Colonial Secretary, William Ormsby-Gore, that he had sanctioned the following 'disbursements by Major Glubb': 'Minor Bani Sakhr Sheikhs camped near Amman - P£ 200 ...; Turki al Haidar - P£ 25 ...', etc.

Wauchope added that Abdullah himself had already spent

> P£ 3,500 in the following manner:
> Payments to Bedu Sheikhs - 1,590
> Payments to Notables - 660
> Agents in Palestine - 350
> Palestine and Syrian Press - 130
> Religious Personnel in Palestine - 200
> His Highness' [i.e., Abdullah's] own additional expenses [i.e., a special intelligence fund] – 570

According to Wauchope

> both the British Resident and Major Glubb are of the opinion that the subsidizing of tribal sheikhs is proving efficacious, and His Highness the Amir also attaches great importance to this method of keeping the Bedu[in] in hand ... The natural reaction of the Transjordan Arab, whether he is a beduin sheikh or a village notable, when he is called upon to do something for the government ... or merely to refrain from doing something undesirable, is to ask for a quid pro quo ... [such as] payment ... or the grant ... of land ... or the pardon of a relative ...

> I consider that His Highness' remarkable success in preventing the spread of disorder to Transjordan during the past four months is to be attributed in part to the judicious use which has been made in the disbursement of subsidies ... I propose to continue to allot P£ 500 to Major Glubb

and additional sums to Abdullah, concluded Wauchope.[136]

July 1936 saw the waxing of the agitators' efforts to mobilize support in Transjordan for the rebellion - and their failure. Rumours circulated of letters of incitement - both to Transjordan and Hijaz - from Haj Amin, and 'the very name of England' had become 'anathema' in Saudi Arabia, wrote Glubb. 'The hatred which has entered the souls of the people, and the deep impression which they have received of infidel English oppressing Muslims, may well take years to eradicate.' As to Transjordan, Mithgal ibn Faiz had tried to organize a meeting on 2 July of the tribal sheikhs of the emirate 'to consider intervention in Palestine.' The assembly had been sanctioned by the Chief Minister and there were fears that 'a few impassioned speeches' might provoke violence 'which would have dragged the whole country into rebellion.'

Abdullah became 'genuinely alarmed' and threw his whole weight against the meeting. It proved sufficient and, in the end, 'practically no tribal chiefs attended,' only some 'local *fellaheen* [farmers], two agitators from Palestine, a number of politicians from Amman, and the Boy Scouts and the Arab Youth Clubs. (These, black shirts and all, are hotbeds of political agitation),' wrote Glubb. 'Tribally, the affair was a fiasco, and the ultimate result was to strengthen the hand of the Government in the tribal areas.'

By mid-July, the initial excitement in Transjordan had worn off. No doubt, this owed something to the passage of time and to the wearing off of the novelty of the rebellion. Glubb attributed the decline of enthusiasm specifically to the failure of Mithgal's meeting and to 'the small extra sum of special service money' distributed among the sheikhs. Again, Glubb pressed for regular monthly 'salaries' instead of 'one-time lump sums,' whose distribution could be interpreted as an indication of panic and 'weakness.'[137]

Glubb's monthly reports soon began to stray beyond the purview appropriate to a Legion second-in-command responsible for Transjordan's deserts. Indeed, their knowledgeability, scope and depth - often including eccentricities and a tendency to alarmism - seemed to point to higher aspirations and a future political role in the emirate.

Glubb believed that the Palestine rebellion provided an insight into the nature of 20th Century nationalist politics and their relevance to the Middle East. In September 1936 he wrote:

> There can be no doubt that the upheaval in Palestine has profoundly stirred Arab national and Muslim religious sentiment. The combined intervention of the Arab Kings, [of] Iraq, Ibn Saud and [of] the Yemen, and the entry into Palestine of parties of volunteers from Syria and Iraq, have opened up new vistas of [inter-]Arab cooperation in the future ... The Palestine rebellion ... possesses all the elements calculated to stir the passions of every class of Arab - namely the political and nationalist aspect to incite the educated, the religious aspect - Jews and Christians fighting Muslims - to stir the ignorant and fanatical, and alleged military atrocities against Muslim women, to appeal to all ranks and classes ... Even if the rebellion now come[s] to an end, the position of Britain in Arabia [i.e., Glubb often used the term to cover the whole Arab world] will never be the same again.
>
> It is interesting to note that, in connection with the Palestine rebellion, the old arguments are once more being revived to the effect that the Arabs have benefited financially or materially from the presence of the Jews or British, and hence that their rebellion is unjustified, or ungrateful ... These arguments seem to show a fundamental ignorance of human nature, the only powerful incentives of which are not material but spiritual. The masses cannot be swayed by a balance sheet or a treatise on political economy ... The human race, and especially its youth, longs to be heroic ... It is for this reason that Fascism has made such strides with the youth of the world, not least in Arabia ... The young will follow leaders who ask them for sacrifices rather than leaders who give them material benefits...[138]

At the end of October, what turned out to be the first stage of the rebellion in Palestine came to an end, the Arab Kings, at Haj Amin al Husseini's secret behest, having called upon the Palestinians to lay down their arms and give diplomacy a chance. The rebels 'acceded' to the call. The British had promised, should a halt be called to the fighting, to send a royal commission to investigate the 'Palestine problem' and Arab grievances and to propose a solution. In early November, the Peel Commission duly arrived, spending the following eight months travelling around Palestine and interviewing British officials, Palestinian Jews and Arabs and outside Arab leaders, and composing its recommendations, which were published (and formally endorsed by the British Government) in July 1937.

The chief recommendation was to partition Palestine between its Jewish and Arab inhabitants, earmarking 20 per cent of the country for a Jewish State and suggesting that almost all the rest should be fused with

Transjordan to form a large unitary Arab state under Abdullah's rule. About 5 per cent of Palestine, including Jerusalem and Bethlehem and a narrow corridor to the Mediterranean, was, according to Peel, to remain under British control. The commission also recommended that the Arab inhabitants of the area earmarked for Jewish sovereignty should be voluntarily 'transferred' (or forcibly expelled, if necessary) out of the Jewish state area.

The Palestinian Arab leadership, and, in its wake, the Arab world (save for Abdullah) flatly rejected the recommendations and the idea of handing over any part of Palestine to Jewish control, and in September-October 1937 the rebellion was renewed with redoubled vigour. By mid-1938 the British Government shelved the Peel recommendations as unworkable, in effect rejecting the ideas of partition, Jewish statehood, and the transfer of Arabs. The second (and final) stage of the Arab Rebellion was to last until spring-summer 1939, when British troops, marginally assisted by Jewish supernumeraries, at last suppressed it.

During the November 1936-September 1937 intermission in the fighting, Glubb was able to sit back and reflect on the significance of the events. True, the rebellion had not directly affected the political life of the Emirate. But, in reality, 'things have ... never been the same since the Palestine disturbances,' he wrote. 'Previously nobody in Transjordan thought that British authority could be seriously threatened. Now the possibility of its being not only embarrassed, but possibly even defeated, has occurred to every body's [sic] mind.' Meanwhile, reported Glubb, Husseini was busy laying the groundwork for 'unrest in Transjordan should he desire a diversion ... in the event of fresh disturbances in Palestine.' Glubb illustrated his point: Jordanian visitors to Palestine were regularly accosted by rebel agents who tried to recruit them. One sheikh's son from the Kerak area had recently travelled to Jerusalem to receive medical treatment. He had almost immediately been approached and taken before the Husseini-dominated Muslim Supreme Council, where 'he was treated to some wild talk about raising the tribes, and murdering the British officers in Transjordan.' He had been told that Husseini would reward him with P£300 'for services in this direction.' Similarly, an Arab Legion NCO who had travelled in civilian clothes for an eye examination at the Ophthalmic Hospital of St. John in Jerusalem had been harangued about 'the treachery of the Transjordan tribes to the Arab cause and the Muslim religion in not rebelling last summer...' He too had been offered a financial inducement for murdering British officers. 'All the Transjordanians who visit Jerusalem return amazed by the virulence of the abuse of the Amir Abdullah [who is regarded as a British agent],' reported Glubb.[139]

Glubb noted that the winds of subversion and violence had also crossed the river. In April 1937 he reported several shooting incidents in Transjordan and along its borders which he attributed indirectly to the Palestine troubles.[140] Particularly affected, in Glubb's view, were large parts of the Bani Sakhr, which routinely camped around Amman and in the Jordan Valley.[141]

The publication of the Peel Commission recommendations and the subsequent renewal of the rebellion in Palestine, again carrying the threat of disruption of life across the river, gave rise to a further spate of reflections on the Palestine problem, nationalism and the Middle East. Glubb paid particular attention to the commission's transfer recommendation, which called for the removal from the Jewish-designated areas of some 225-300,000 Arab inhabitants so that the new Jewish state should not come into the world with a giant, discontented, and potentially subversive Arab minority in its midst.

In principle, he supported Peel's package of recommendations; after all, they promised to vitally enlarge Abdullah's (that is, his) emirate; and, having (initially) been endorsed by Whitehall, they were, at the same time, the official policy of Her Majesty's Government. They were also favoured by Glubb's superior, Arab Legion commander Colonel Peake: 'We are now in the throes of the controversy over the report of the Royal Commission, and as was foreseen it pleases neither Arab nor Jew,' wrote Peake in July. 'As for me, I think it a very good settlement, as one must look to the future. If we go on as we are, we shall eventually have the whole Arab race hostile.'[142]

Peake was not motivated by philo-Semitism; far from it. As he put it in November:

> I am afraid that the time has passed when it is either profitable or possible to rule these unwilling peoples [i.e., Jews and Arabs], by direct methods. They want to rule themselves and until they do will make direct government by us so difficult that in the end, we must give way. ... Naturally, it would have been much better to have no Jews, but that is now not possible. Rightly or wrongly, there are here [i.e., in Palestine] at least 400,000, whom we cannot leave out, so we must do something about them, that something is "Partition" which I believe the best way out of a bad job.[143]

(But by the end of the following year, with HMG having reversed itself on Partition, Peake followed suit, and with a vengeance (striking probably his true - and appeasing - colours):

> The Churchill-Eden-Amery (a Jew [sic]) pack make me quite furious; they would all willingly plunge England into war for the sake of some obscure Czechs; for years they [i.e. the Czechs] have treated the German minority disgracefully ... I only hope that now Chamberlain will again be big enough to bring peace to Palestine, even though it means reversing our policy of the last few years ... No doubt the Arabs can be cowed into temporary submission ... But when the troops are withdrawn, the rebellion will break out again ... unless we do justice to the Arabs.)[144]

But 'excellent as the [partition] proposals seem to be as offering at least a hope of final peace some day, it is yet remarkable how many pitfalls seem to lie in their way,' wrote a very judicious Glubb. (Looking back in 1971, Glubb on balance was to regard the Peel recommendation in a more favourable light, as 'the most practical solution ever suggested'[145]) His main concern in summer 1937 was with the recommended fusion of the Arab parts of Palestine and Transjordan. The two areas were vastly different, and the mentality of their peoples had grown further apart during the previous 17 years (1920-1937), he argued: 'With the exception of Amman town, Transjordan is still tribal, old-fashioned, Muslim and Arab. In Palestine, the influx of Jews and foreigners, and 17 years of direct British administration, have made the country Levantine or Mediterranean, rather than Arab.' Moreover, should fusion occur, 'the [far better educated] Palestinians are likely to monopolize all the lucrative appointments,' much to the resentment of native Transjordanians.

As well, the transfer proposal raised

> an even more difficult problem ... Peasants are notoriously attached to their native soil, and refuse to leave it, even if better land is available elsewhere. This is a sentiment deep in their character, and not to be argued away by reason. But the difficulty here will not be only in evicting the Arab from Palestine, but in planting them in Transjordan or elsewhere ... The fact that [the] government may spend money to make this land more productive [and allow for the resettlement on it of Palestinian evictees] will not immediately reconcile the Transjordanians to the importation of Palestinian settlements (many of them differing somewhat in culture) into their [midst].

Glubb saw further, tertiary problems: Should Nablus or Amman be the new state's capital? How would Ibn Saud of Saudi Arabia react to the idea of an expanded Hashemite Emirate? And how would Abdullah and Husseini, long-time enemies, be reconciled and co-exist: 'The new constitution appears to reduce the Mufti to insignificance ... But even if the Mufti were eliminated, it is difficult to foresee how His Highness, in an independent Arab state, would consent to be a constitutional monarch with a parliament of Palestinian lawyers?' No doubt such a polity would be wracked by internal turmoil. But, then, 'the Arabs are addicted to turmoil' and are capable of functioning in its midst: 'After all ... they conquered half the world and carried on a succession of civil wars amongst themselves at the same time.' In short, 'to come to Arabia to make war, T.E. Lawrence said, is bringing coals to Newcastle, or as the Arabs have it, hawking dates to the people of Kheibar. But we cannot help feeling that when the politicians from Palestine are turned loose on the tribes of Transjordan, neutrals who value their lives may do well to "stand from under".'[146]

Glubb noted that Ibn Saud was busily denouncing partition and was reportedly in contact with agitators bent on starting or re-starting the 'rebellion ... on the Palestine-Transjordan-Syria frontier'. It was even rumoured that Ibn Saud would issue a call for 'Jihad' against the infidels in Palestine. Glubb commented: 'This is not indeed the first time in history that Palestine has united northern Arabia. At [sic] the period of the Crusades, it took nearly one hundred years to unify the forces of Egypt, Syria and Iraq against the European invaders ... Things move more quickly in these days ... but the Arabs have not yet produced their Saladin.'[147]

In the weeks following the September 1937 resumption of the rebellion, many of its leaders, including Husseini, fled to Beirut and Damascus to avoid the British dragnet. As Glubb saw things, this posed a new and significant threat to Transjordan - one which was to preoccupy him, in one form or another, until the revolt's demise in spring-summer 1939.

In November 1937 Glubb reported that the rebel leaders had concentrated in Damascus and

> from the shelter of this city ... are busy organizing disturbances in Palestine and Transjordan ... In many respects, the easiest way from Damascus to Palestine is east of the Sea of Galilee and through a corner of northern Transjordan. As long as law and order prevails in the country, the free passage of arms and personnel from Syria to Palestine is greatly impeded. To create disturbed conditions in this

country has now therefore become an important plank in the Damascus programme.

Glubb recommended fencing the Transjordanian-Palestinian frontier, in parts with electrification and watchtowers.[148]

The following month, Glubb expatiated on this theme, probably on the basis of fresh intelligence reports. His agents seem to have picked up concrete information: 'The Arab leaders in Damascus decided to make a serious attempt to disturb law and order in northern Transjordan.' Glubb gave several reasons:

> The hope that internal disturbances in Transjordan would occupy the authorities and armed forces, and thereby render them unable to maintain close control of the Syrian frontier ... [and] the increasingly obvious inability of Palestinians [i.e., Palestinian Arabs] alone to secure a victory ... The only hope of victory by violence was thought to be by extending the scope of the disturbances to Transjordan. [And] the personal resentment of a few Transjordanians ... cause[d] them to join the Palestine Arab leaders in Damascus, urging the latter to concentrate on raising revolt in Transjordan.
>
> The plan of campaign elaborated in Damascus consist[s] ... in the enlistment of gangs of men (chiefly from the poorer classes in Damascus), to cross into northern Transjordan where they were to scatter alarm and confusion by cutting telegraph wires, sniping [at] government buildings and highway robbery - methods similar to those employed in Palestine. It was hoped that ... the bands would be gradually ... swelled by volunteers from [among] the Transjordanians themselves.

The authorities in Amman reacted with alacrity:

> on the principle [that if you] "show force ... you may not have to use it." Part of the Arab Legion reserve was called out and a company of the [British-officered Palestinian para-military] Transjordan Frontier Force (TJFF) was sent to Irbid [in northern Transjordan]. These measures and the arrest of a number of Transjordanians in sympathy with the plotters, seem to have caused the latter some consternation. The "rebellion" [was] timed to commence on November 17th, [but] was postponed till December 6th ... [But] as long as the disturbed condition of Palestine continues ... periodic attempts to send terrorist gangs into Transjordan may be expected.[149]

The rebels had apparently considered, or planned, among other things, attempts on the lives of the Legion commanders, Peake and Glubb, and of Abd al Qadir al Jundi, the senior Arab officer in the force.[150]

But nothing came of all this plotting. For months Transjordan remained almost completely unaffected by the rebellion raging on its doorstep. But in July-August 1938, the series of retaliatory bombings in Palestinian Arab public places by the right-wing Jewish group, the IZL (Irgun Zvai Leumi or the National Military Organisation, usually called by the British simply the 'Irgun') 'aroused' the sympathy of the Transjordanians, 'and considerable excitement prevailed in northern Transjordan for some time.' Again, Glubb analysed the sociology of the support in the Emirate for the Palestinian rebels. He thought 'the most nationalistic elements' of the population were 'the government officials' and 'the townspeople of Amman.' The more 'European influence there is in any class or district, the stronger is the national feeling.' But the pro-Palestinian officials, many of whom originated in Palestine, did not translate their sympathies into action because of their official positions. And Amman's townspeople, mainly of Damascene or Palestinian origin, 'were of course largely indifferent to the fate of Transjordan and would be prepared to see the whole country burn, if Nablus thereby would derive any advantage.' But as disturbances would be bad for business and many of the 'Nabulsis' were merchants, they restrained themselves, concluded Glubb.[151]

In September, the brief rebel takeover of the southern Palestine frontier town of Beersheba, with its police station and armoury, and the subsequent withdrawal of the (now isolated and untenable) Mandate police contingents from posts along the 'Arava (in Arabic, Wadi 'Araba) border and at Um Rashrash (present-day Eilat), on the Gulf of 'Aqaba, seriously worried Glubb. He feared that the rebel successes might move the southern Jordanian tribes to dissidence or revolt. He quickly beefed up the Transjordanian outposts along the 'Arava border and himself led a mechanized column down to the seaside village of 'Aqaba (across the way from Um Rashrash) in a show of force. Glubb compared Transjordan to Holland in World War I, 'with a war raging on her frontiers liable at any time to overflow into and overwhelm' it. The situation put a great financial strain on the Emirate and the Legion had to be expanded, he complained.[152]

By November, the British were once again in control of Beersheba (though failed to re-activate its police station). Glubb continued to worry about the attitude of the Bani Sakhr. They were 'not inspired so much by sympathy for their struggling coreligionists as by the impression that all government control was dissolving. The tribesmen assumed an increasingly haughty attitude ... and gave vent to the opinion that the government was finished. The collection of taxes became difficult.' Relations had deteriorated between the tribe and the (Christian) townspeople of Madaba, in southern Transjordan, mildly reflecting what was happening across the border between the *fellahin* and the Jews: 'The Christians are better educated [than the beduin], have ready money, and are shrewd and calculating. The beduin is ignorant, haughty and improvident. Some times he was cheated by the Christian, but more often he sold his land [to Christians] (probably at a very cheap price) out of sheer improvidence, because he was short of cash.' Glubb pacified the Bani Sakhr by surrounding one of their camps and arresting several troublemakers.[153]

Glubb's fears that a Negev (in Arabic, Neqeb) Desert uncontrolled by a permanent police presence might generate lawlessness across the border, in southern Transjordan, merged at the start of 1939 with a new worry - the establishment of Jewish settlements in the Negev, that might provoke beduins on both sides of the border to anger and rebellion. What prompted Glubb's concern was the publication - in the *Journal of the Royal Central Asian Society* (XXV\2, April 1938, pp. 204-18) - of an article entitled 'Southern Palestine and its Possibilities for Settlement' by Major C.S. Jarvis, a former governor of Sinai. (In a previous article published in October 1937, 'The Empty Quarter' (*Journal of the Royal Central Asian Society* XXIV\4, 663-69), Jarvis had advocated Jewish settlement in the area south of Beersheba.) Glubb commented-warned:

> The experience of the past three years has shown that the burning question of Jews and Arabs in Palestine need not necessarily provoke the neighbouring tribal areas to sympathetic rebellion. The support accorded to the "Arabs" of Palestine has been principally based on political nationalism, or race consciousness. This "race consciousness" is often a pure figment of the imagination; the persons "conscious" of their race do not in reality belong to one race at all. This applies with full force to the sympathy of the Arab world for the "Arabs" of Palestine, who in reality probably have very little Arab blood in their veins ... The townsmen and villagers of Palestine are not of the same race as the tribes... or see eye to eye with them.
>
> In the case of the Beersheba district, this fact is proved by [the] non-complicity of the Beersheba tribes in the Palestine rebellion, which has been going on for three and a half years [sic] on their very threshold [even after] the government evacuated their country [i.e., district] in September last. Now statements are periodically made that the Jews should be allowed to occupy the Beersheba area, which formerly supported millions of inhabitants but which now only maintains a "few wretched beduins". But the point to be noted is that the "few wretched beduins" are a different community to the villagers of the north and are not yet completely alienated.

The tribes, if handled properly,

> may yet ... be kept loyal and contented. Moreover, this tribal community is closely connected with the tribes of Sinai and Transjordan. Thus to alienate them would spread the hostility to the tribal communities in neighbouring lands ... The Beersheba district should therefore be treated as a tribal area, and every method should be adopted to keep the tribes happy and contented. On no account should Jews be allowed to settle there, as such a step would merely antagonize the tribal community, as it has antagonized the town and village communities in the north.[154]

Glubb was to return to this theme a few months later, as the outbreak of World War II drew near. The British, he wrote, must make strenuous efforts to keep the region's beduins loyal (perhaps he had in mind the importance of the assistance of the Arabian Peninsula beduins to the British - the 'Arab Revolt' of 1916-18 - during World War I). 'There is here,' he wrote in August 1939,

> the possibility of forming a solid block of tribes covering the Suez Canal, from Ma`an, across the Beersheba area and Sinai, under British influence ... But if Jewish colonies be introduced in the Beersheba area, the keystone of this arch is removed, and not only the Beersheba tribes become hostile, but they will influence those of southern Transjordan and of the Sinai in the same direction.

Retaining the friendship of the beduins, Glubb seemed to be saying, would be more important to the coming British war effort than Jewish sympathy:

> The theory that the presence of Jews [in Palestine] is a strategic asset to the British is now completely exploded. [Glubb was referring here to the pro-Balfour Declaration argument that the existence of a Zionist state in Palestine would help secure the Suez Canal for Britain.] To begin with, if the Jews were not there, the Arabs would be friendly, a much greater strategic advantage. If the Jews arrive, the Arabs become hostile.
>
> It used to be argued that, against this, the Jews would be obliged to be friendly and would thus defend British imperial interests from the hostile Arabs. But experience in northern Palestine has not confined [i.e., confirmed] these hopes. The IPC [i.e., Iraq Petroleum Company] pipeline runs through an area well dotted with Jewish colonies, but this did not prevent the Arabs cutting the pipe in several places every night. The Jews, in practice, are purely occupied with defending themselves, and are (perhaps naturally) not interested in defending British impe-

> rial interests. What is more, no sooner does the policy of HMG cease to meet with the approval of the Jews than [sic] the Jews themselves resort to sabotage!! And the ridiculous position arises that both the Jews and Arabs simultaneously set about sabotaging British imperial interests!![155]

In November, Glubb's fears seemed to be confirmed. News reached him of the landing of a Jewish sailing party at the Gulf of 'Aqaba coastline at Um Rashrash. 'The arrival of Jews and their establishment at 'Aqaba [i.e., at Um Rashrash, 'in the middle of a purely tribal area ... about 140 miles from the nearest Jews in the north'] would be exceedingly unfortunate,' wrote Glubb. 'Infinite complications' would arise over fishing rights in territorial waters and from beduin rights of passage across the gulf shore between Sinai and Transjordan. 'We cannot expect such people to recognize the fantastic geometrical map frontiers in this area,' wrote Glubb. 'The establishment of Jews in 'Aqaba would be a crossing of the Rubicon - the introduction of Arab-Jew hatred into an entirely new area and a new race [i.e., Sinai-southern Transjordan beduin] hitherto untouched.'

Glubb went on to expatiate on this theme, allowing a thimbleful or more of anti-Semitism to show:

> Disturbances would not of course commence immediately. For the history of Jewish immigration into every country in the world is the same. They have been welcomed at first, in England, in Germany, in Poland and in Palestine. They are friendly and polite at first and seem to introduce money and trade. But after a few years, they become highhanded and aggressive, and are found to have laid their hands on all the business and the key positions in the country. The people of the country, who had originally welcomed the arrival of the Jews, will then turn on them, and pogroms, ghettos, bloodshed and brutality result. That this would result in 'Aqaba, as it has resulted in northern Palestine, in Germany and in Poland, there can be no doubt. But in this case, Transjordan, Sinai and Saudi Arabia would assist the Arabs, just as Syria and Iraq have assisted the Palestine rebels in the North. All these future events are almost automatic psychological reactions, which can be foreseen with the accuracy of arithmetic.[156]

Glubb may have had misgivings or fears about the British handling of the rebellion - but he was in no doubt at all about the very negative nature of the eruption (his views, no doubt, coloured by his position and outlook as an agent of the British Empire confronted by the spectacle of a rebellion against British authority with potential to subvert Britain's position, and his own, in Transjordan itself). Nonetheless, nothing could be more effectively designed to incense Glubb - or drive him to absurd argumentation and comparisons - than to describe the Palestine rebellion as 'an outbreak of the destructive spirit of the desert,' as was done by the Zionist leader Chaim Weizmann in late 1938. 'No epigram so brief could convey a more entirely false impression,' he wrote. Rising to the defence of his beloved desert and its inhabitants, he insisted that

> there is nothing whatever of the old spirit of desert tribal war in [the] Palestine rebellion, which, on the contrary, exhibits the most modern features of European post-war mentality - nationalism and terror. It consists, exactly like Fascism and Nazism, in gangs of determined men filled with a fanatical racial creed, and more or less supported by the bulk of the population, who are smarting under a sense of national humiliation.
>
> It is of vital importance to distinguish between these two forms of Arab disturbances, namely an outbreak of desert lawlessness and the new racial fanaticism. Severe military measures are adequate to suppress an outbreak of destructiveness by tribesmen, who become out of hand from a liking for violence. But it is unlikely that military measures can afford any permanent relief in Palestine, where the Arabs are being rapidly forged into a united nation on the latest lines of the European race creeds.
>
> Another interesting comparison between Palestine and Europe may also contain a warning for the future. It is the remarkable similarity between the position of Austria vis-a-vis Germany and Transjordan vis-a-vis Palestine. For Germany, under the prick of national humiliation, developed a fanatical, combatant nationalism, just as Palestine has, while Austria remained old world, religious, influenced by hereditary chiefs. The Nazis left Austria alone in their first year of struggle, but as soon as they were well established, Austria fell into their laps like a ripe plum ...

The starkness and misguidedness of Glubb's comparisons, between Nazism\Fascism and an emergent, anti-colonialist Third World nationalist movement and between Austria and Transjordan (I wonder what either Austrians or Transjordanians would have made of such a comparison at the time?), may have been influenced by the emotional impress of Britain's humiliation and defeat at the Munich Conference of September as much as by the ephemeral successes, in late summer-autumn 1938, of the Palestine Arab rebels.

But Glubb also made a significant - and prophetic - point:

> The increasingly frequent adoption of gang-terrorism as a mode of attaining political ends in the modern world should perhaps cause us to overhaul our methods

> of colonial defence ... The Irish, and now the Palestinian rebellion ... have shown that regular armies are ill adapted to cope with gang warfare, which carries on its activities by the intimidation of private citizens. The only way yet discovered to cope with terrorism is more terrorism [i.e., counter-terrorism] ... Will this soon become an inevitable development in the British Empire also - Navy, Army, Air Force, and - anti-gangster services [i.e., counter-terrorism units] [?].[157]

Glubb took over command of the Arab Legion on 21 March 1939, Col. Peake leaving Transjordan for England five days later. Glubb remained for a while the sole British officer in the Legion (in 1938 there had been six). Glubb had taken over at a critical time, just as the Palestine rebellion - then almost in its death throes - had at last spilled over into Transjordanian territory.

In autumn 1938, there had been a spate of rebel attacks on Transjordanian police posts along the frontier - at Karameh and Shunat Nimrin, in the Jordan Valley, and at Ruman, near Ajlun - but these turned out to be isolated incidents.

Things turned more serious at the end of winter. By late February 1939, the Legion had in hand 'definite information' regarding 'the presence of [Palestinian] armed bands in Transjordan.'[158] The penetration from Syria of the northwestern corner of Jordan by these bands, leavened with foreign (mostly Syrian and Iraqi) volunteers, apparently had a number of purposes. Husseini, with his bands on the run or under siege in Palestine, sorely needed to divert British troops to another theatre of operations: Perhaps if Transjordan seemed under threat, British units would be sent to Amman's aid, relieving the pressure on the rebels in Palestine itself. Perhaps Husseini thought that such incursions might stir disaffected Transjordanians to rebel against Abdullah and the British.[159] Or perhaps he was merely using northwestern Transjordan as a convenient, safe haven and bivouac for tired rebel bands, who could not find rest or safety in Palestine or Syria. Or, lastly, perhaps this area of Transjordan was a convenient, relatively unpatrolled route through which bands re-formed and re-equipped in Syria could be reintroduced into Palestine (the more northerly routes, across the Jordan River north of the Sea of Galilee from the Golan or southwards across the Lebanese-Palestine border, had become less penetrable after the British had sealed the frontiers with barbed-wire fences and a chain of small forts).[160]

On 27 February 1939 a Briton working as a forestry officer was abducted from the village of Dogara, just south of the Yarmuk River, which marked the frontier between Transjordan and Syria, by a band of rebels. A TJFF patrol encountered the group and the forestry officer escaped in the melee. On 9 March a group of 60 rebels, with pack mules carrying 'a considerable quantity of explosives,' crossed the Yarmuk into Transjordan. Two days later the band was spotted by a mounted two-man Legion patrol at the village of Deir as Sana. The patrol escaped under fire and reported back to headquarters; meanwhile, the band began to push on towards the Ajlun Mountain range some five miles away. But before they could reach safety, they were engaged and pinned down by a second, ten-man Legion cavalry patrol. A larger, mixed Legion-TJFF armoured car force then arrived and RAF fighter-bombers strafed the rebels. By nightfall, the band had been overcome. It suffered at least 30-35 casualties, Abu Sha`aban of Lifta, Abu Daoud al Kurdi of Samakh, and Mustafa Nasser of Dogara, being among the dead. The Transjordanians lost two dead (one of them, Lt. Macadam, a British officer) and three wounded.[161]

The Ajlun clash, which according to British intelligence had a 'considerable,' positive effect in Transjordan, especially in the north of the country,[162] was followed by a number of minor rebel attacks on Arab Legion posts in southern Jordan, across the 'Arava frontier (on 12 and 16-17 March), and then by a renewed effort by the rebel leaders in Damascus to stir up the Transjordanian northwest. Glubb reported that rebel bands were 'at large in Transjordan,' with 'their headquarters in the very rough wooded mountains along the northern half of the Jebel Ajlun.'[163] The local villagers 'were deeply apprehensive of the gangs.' Glubb feared that 'if the gangs go long unpunished, the villagers will probably be terrorized into assisting them. And if the gangs appear to be gaining the upper hand, there is a large class of ex-bandits in Transjordan who would be ready to join, not from any political grievance, but out of love for a like [i.e., life] of banditry.'

Transjordan and Britain demanded that the French, who governed Syria, at least restrain the gang-organisers, such as Suleiman Pasha Saudi, and clean up the rebel bases and depots just north of the Yarmuk River, which were the staging posts for the forays into Transjordan. But 'no action has been taken by the French …,' reported Glubb - now the Legion's commander - at the beginning of April.[164]

In early April, two bands of rebels were operating in northern Transjordan - one 40-50 strong led by Abu Mahmoud Hammam of Beit Imrin, and the other, 20-strong, led by Mifleh al Rabadhan ash Sherari and consisting mostly of beduins from the Palestine side of the Jordan Valley. Their numbers seem to have swelled during the following weeks. They holed the IPC pipeline and severed telephone lines. The Legion organized and sent into the Ajlun-Irbid area two mobile mechanized\cavalry columns. On 20-21 April they skirmished with one of the gangs northwest of Ajlun. On 24 April large mechanized and cavalry detachments engaged 100-150 of Hammam's men southwest of Irbid, killing 11 rebels. About 20 wounded were later reported to have reached Damascus. One member of the TJFF was lightly wounded. 'This successful action produced a striking [negative] effect on the gangs. The majority of them split up into small parties and disappeared. Abu Mahmoud Hammam himself recrossed into Syria with twenty-two followers. Mifleh al Rabadhan ash Sherari escaped into Palestine,' reported Glubb. He added that two small bands were still operating in the area, one under Haj Mahmoud ash Shiteiwi, of Samakh, and the other under Saud al Yusef al Khadra, of Tubas. On 26 April the Legion set up a permanent post, with 30 camel-mounted guards, at Ramtha, on the Transjordanian-Syrian frontier. Summarizing the month's activities, Glubb wrote that 'it became evident that Arab [Legion] troops in Transjordan were not only holding their own, but were gaining the upper hand of the rebels, without any need for the importation of British troops.' Moreover, 'public opinion in Syria moved slowly towards the Transjordan side, and more and more people began to say that it was a disgrace for Arabs to be fighting Arabs, while the Jews and English were unmolested.' As to Transjordan, according to Glubb, 'the great majority of public opinion ... supported the government, but in the actual area of the operation, the reputation which the gangs had gained in Palestine was still sufficient to strike terror into the villagers.' Glubb reported that about 20-25 Transjordanians had joined the rebel bands, about half of them from the village of Judeita, 'where a religious community was won over by the announcement of jihad.' Most of these had been caught or killed by the end of April. In mid-April the TJFF and Legion had succeeded in harrying out of the Ajlun Hills and into Syria Aref Abdul Razek, one of the leaders of the rebellion who had come to northwest Transjordan to rest after months of action in Palestine. He was arrested by the French but eventually fled to and settled in Baghdad.[165]

'The gangs [operating in north-western Transjordan in spring 1939] were ... themselves in a delicate position,' according to Glubb. If they refrained from terrorizing the local inhabitants, these would refrain from offering them food or information. But if 'they embarked on a policy of real terrorism, they might well unite the Transjordanians against themselves.' In the end, they chose a middle course, described in a letter from Damascus (from either Izzat Darwaza or Abu Ibrahim the Elder, an important Palestinian rebel band leader) to Hammam intercepted on a messenger at Ramtha: Hammam 'was instructed to act in a friendly and considerate manner to the villagers, but to use extreme severity to [sic] any person who gave information to the government. This policy has been carefully followed by all gangs in Transjordan, and village headmen or watchmen who have given information have been dragged out, flogged, abducted and threatened, with death.' Moreover, a considerable number of government officials, Legion officers and notables had received threatening letters. But the gangs had so far killed no informant. So even though the population had no desire to rebel, the gangs were being kept better informed than the government. Glubb suggested that only a large influx of money - from Ibn Saud or Italy and Germany - could recruit Transjordanians for the rebellion: 'A few thousand pounds go a very long way in Transjordan, and there is a considerable population of retired bandits, who would be quite prepared to resume their old profession, for a financial consideration.'[166]

But Glubb's fears notwithstanding, the Transjordanian success on 24 April 'so discouraged the Arab [rebel] leaders, that they decided to call off the attempt to raise rebellion in Transjordan, at any rate temporarily.' He still feared the occasional terrorist outrage, but for all practical purposes the end of the rebellion in Palestine and the announcement in London of the new White Paper the following month also marked the end of any serious effort to reignite rebellion in Transjordan.[167]

Summarizing the Transjordanian-rebel clashes in northwest Transjordan in March-April 1939, Glubb later wrote: 'The whole of this unhappy affair was a sad misunderstanding. For every man in Transjordan and the Arab Legion sympathized with the cause of the Arabs of Palestine. But their leaders made a profound miscalculation' in trying to foment rebellion in the Emirate.[168]

In order to snuff out the final embers of rebelliousness in Palestine, especially in light of the possibly impending European war, Glubb recommended that Britain announce a pardon for all rebel band members leaving Palestine. In June the French arrested Izzat Darwaza[169] and on 24 July an ambush by Legionnaires managed to capture one of the main Palestinian rebel leaders, Yusuf Abu Durra, while he was moving down the Transjordanian side of the Jordan Valley on his way back to Palestine. He was carrying 'a large number of highly inflammatory proclamations' as well as a prospective rebel 'order of battle,' according to Glubb. Though dressed in civilian clothes, Abu Durra was carrying in his bag 'the uniform of a General, with red cuffs and epaulettes, which he was preparing to don when he crossed the Rubicon of the Jordan.' The arrest caused a sensation in Transjordan, where crowds cheered Abu Durra as he was conveyed through towns on the way to trial in Palestine. There was considerable opposition to his extradition. (He was eventually tried and executed in Palestine in 1940). Ironically, Abu Durra, noted Glubb, had been one of the rebel leaders who had all along opposed raising rebellion in Transjordan.[170]

In July, with the rebellion in Palestine at an end and with the common foe, Germany, about to launch a world war, the French authorities at last acted to destroy the rebels' bases in Syria. French troops swept the Yarmuk Valley in cooperation with the Legion and the TJFF 'for the first time since the commencement of the ... rebellion in 1936.'[171] The Yarmuk River-bed, however, continued for months to play host to ex-rebel bands, financed from Baghdad. In November 1939 the Legion, TJFF and the French launched another, joint sweep on both sides of the river, apparently definitively clearing the area.[172]

In the end, there was very little spillover of the Palestine rebellion into Transjordan. At various junctures, Glubb had feared that there would be - but the traditional loyalties of the tribesmen, reinforced by British subsidies and Arab Legion intimidation, had held rebelliousness in check. And the Transjordanian villagers and townspeople, whatever their sympathies, proved unwilling to translate them into anti-British and\or anti-Hashemite activism. For Glubb, as second-in-command of the Legion and then as its commander, it had been a trying and confusing experience and time, given his sympathy for the rebels' anti-Zionist aims, his distaste for the rebels' leaders and politics, his antipathy for anyone assailing the British Empire, and his fears of a spillover into Transjordan.

Chapter 3

WORLD WAR II and its AFTERMATH

World War II

The outbreak and course of World War II placed Glubb in a difficult position in a number of ways. He was a British commander of an Arab army in an area where the winds of nationalism were increasingly anti-British (and anti-French); and the British were regarded by nationalists as their main oppressor and enemy, and as the main obstacle to Arab self-determination. Few forgot or forgave Britain its bloody suppression of the Palestine revolt of 1936-39 and its periodic suppression of nationalist outbreaks in Egypt and Iraq.

Once Germany, Italy and Japan went to war, putting Britain on the defensive, challenging its power and authority around the globe and highlighting its weaknesses, Arab nationalists became restive and, in some instances, thrusting and rebellious. Perhaps now was the chance to throw off the British imperial yoke once and for all? The Middle East was swept by anti-British (and, in some instances, pro-Axis) propaganda, with the educated classes in most countries setting the nationalist tone. Most appear to have hoped for Britain's defeat. As one Jerusalem educator, Khalil al Sakakini, put it, when informed of the fall of the British bastion of Tobruk, in Libya, in 1942: 'Not only the sons of Palestine were happy when Tobruk fell to the Germans, but the whole Arab world, in Egypt and Palestine and Iraq and Syria and Lebanon. Not because they like the Germans, but because they don't like the British...'[173]

In Palestine, Britain had crushed the nationalist rebels in the nick of time (one can only wonder how much more devastating to British interests would have been the Palestinian revolt had it erupted after September 1939). But in Iraq in April 1941 an anti-British coalition of politicians and army officers, in collaboration with a contingent of exiled Palestinian rebels, led by Haj Amin al Husseini, rose in a pro-Axis revolt. (Following this revolt's demise, Haj Amin fled to Berlin, where he sat out the war years, along with other Palestinian rebel leaders, and was employed by the German Foreign Ministry as a propagandist to the Arab world and as a recruiter of Muslim volunteers for the German army). And in Egypt, a group of officers - that included the young Anwar Sadat - plotted rebellion against Britain as the British Eighth Army advanced across North Africa and thrust into Europe through Sicily. Moreover, for a year, from June 1940 until May-June 1941, Transjordan's northern neighbour, Syria (along with Lebanon), was under the control of the pro-Axis Vichy government, presenting Abdullah, a staunch British ally, with a major potential problem. In 1941 Glubb once again was to find himself at the head of an Arab army fighting other Arabs (in Iraq and Syria, where most of the Vichy troops were Arab). The Legion was the only Arab army to have fought alongside Britain against the Axis.

As if in counterpoint to these generally anti-British winds, the world Zionist movement, and the Yishuv, came out almost to a man in support of the Allied cause - an inevitable stance given Nazi Germany's rabid anti-Semitism. (The only important exception was the minuscule LHI, which continued during 1939-40 to perversely regard the British as the Yishuv's main enemy.) Indeed, 26-28,000 Palestinian Jews volunteered for and served in the British army by 1945 (as compared with only 6,000 Palestinian Arabs - though the Palestinian Arab community was more than twice as large as the Jewish community).[174] To his undoubted chagrin, Glubb found himself on the same side as the Jews.

The news of the German destruction of European Jewry, the Holocaust, which began to filter out to the West in the second half of 1941, only reinforced Zionist support for the Allied war effort. At the same time, this news - and Arab pro-Axis activities - subtly and not so subtly undermined the advocacy of the Arab, and Palestinian, causes among traditionally pro-Arab British officials, including (briefly) Glubb. During the war years, anti-Zionism, for some a mere extension of anti-Semitism, was no longer comfortably or openly enunciated.

During the war's first, ‘phoney’ months, Glubb found himself defending or whitewashing the Arabs (as well as reviewing Transjordanian Air Raid Precautions in anticipation of German or Italian bombardment). With the war only a few days old, Glubb wrote: ‘In spite of the feuds and resentments and recriminations of the last twenty years, there seems to be little doubt that the majority of Arabs today tend to favour the British rather than the German side in the war,’ though he excepted from this line-up the Grand Mufti and the Palestine rebels, Ibn Saud, the king of Saudi Arabia, and elements in Baghdad.[175]

But as the weeks passed, Glubb found this position increasingly untenable. In December 1939 he reported that on 13 November the Amman cinema house had screened a documentary film called ‘The Un-man cinema house had screened a documentary film called 'The Unknown Soldier', which depicted scenes from World War I. 'When the German flag and German troops appeared, a portion of the audience clapped loudly, but the troops of no other nation were applauded,' he wrote. According to Glubb, it later emerged that those who had clapped had been 'seven schoolboys, all Muslims, and members of Transjordan families which had hitherto been known for their sympathy with the Palestine rebels.' Be that as it may, Glubb wrote that

> generally speaking ... *fellahin*, tribesmen and beduins are completely indifferent to the war and to European politics. This does not mean that the war might not move them to sedition, but such a course would be taken by them for local reasons only, not out of preference for, or interest in, any European power ... News of Allied defeats or reductions in local forces, or the forces in Palestine, might encourage outbreaks of disorder. But for the moment, we may rule out the rural population, when discussing sympathy with Germany.

As to the townspeople - consisting, in Glubb's categorisations, of 'officials,' 'well-to-do' or merchant townsmen, and schoolboys and students – 'the latter have been a good deal tampered with, by direct German Nazi propaganda. It is doubtful, however, whether there is much (or even any) genuine pro-German feeling amongst the official or merchant classes.' But some who identified with the Husseini rebels of Palestine, given the Mufti's increasing connection with Germany,

> find themselves ranged ... in sympathy with Germany. This sympathy is due firstly to loyalty to the Mufti's party and secondly to spite against the British over their Palestine policy. All the classes referred to - officials, townsmen and students - are deeply interested in the Palestine question. But while the majority feel considerable resentment [at] ... British policy in Palestine, many are of the opinion that, even so, the British are the best Europeans to have, if they must have any [around].

But the security of Transjordan still lies with the tribes and villages of the country, and 'the Arab Legion [still] maintains a powerful hold on the people ... In tribal districts, the Arab Legion is not only the arm of the law, but the universal guide, philosopher and friend,' he wrote.[176]

Glubb's reports appear to have been designed to calm Whitehall fears of Arab betrayal and place Transjordan in the best possible light. But without doubt Britain's prestige and popularity in the emirate declined with the accumulation of German successes during the following months. By late April 1941, a Zionist intelligence officer reported, against the backdrop of the (temporary) Axis successes in Iraq, that

> the incitement against Britain has greatly increased in Transjordan, as if most of the population belongs to the Fifth Column. The [government] officials spread all kinds of rumours and everywhere people are discussing Germany's greatness and operations ... On 24.4 unknown persons torched the car belonging to the English director of the Accounts Department ... In April telephone and telegraph wires in Transjordan were cut a number of times and in most cases swastikas were painted on the poles.[177]

During the late 1930s, both Italy and Germany had sporadically supported the Palestine Arab rebels, both with propaganda and funds, as part of their global effort to weaken Britain. German anti-British propaganda continued to reach the Middle East during the first months of World War II. Glubb advised the British authorities to mount a counter-campaign, highlighting German race theory, which placed the Arabs far from the top of the human totem pole:

> The writer [i.e., Glubb] has certainly seen somewhere a classified list of the races of the world, issued in Germany comparatively recently, in which the Arabs appeared very low down indeed in the list of race values - in fact right at the bottom somewhere alongside negroes and aborigines. No Arab has ever heard of this race classification. Surely this list could be unearthed [and broadcast] with devastating results. Similarly, more play could be made of German race theory ... regarding the right of the Aryans to dominate the world, and the inferiority of all others, including Semites.[178]

The Arab Legion spent 1939-40 tinkering with Air Raid Precautions and gradually increasing its manpower (by war's end the force numbered 16,000 men). The burgeoning Italian-German presence in North Africa, eventually directed towards Egypt, brought home the possibility that the war might actually reach Transjordan's frontiers. However, the Axis armies never managed to advance east of al Alamein in northwestern Egypt.

But 1941 brought more direct and immediate threats. In June the Germans invaded Russia, the southern arm of their advance pushing towards the Caucuses, threatening a giant envelopment of the Middle East and Suez Canal from the north and west (by Rommel's Afrika Korps). Two months earlier, on 3 April, partly in preparation for Operation Barbarossa, the Germans helped engineer a pro-Axis revolt in

Baghdad, led by elements of the Iraqi Army and supported by the deposed prime minister, Rashid Ali al Ghilani, and by Haj Amin al Husseini and the rest of the exiled Palestinian contingent in the city. It appeared that Iraq might turn into a German base, from which German power would be projected throughout the Middle East. Moreover, since the fall of France in June 1940, Syria and Lebanon were under the control of Vichy-aligned administrators and troops: Once Iraq fell under Axis dominion, these countries too could be expected to host and provide jump-off points for German forces. The whole Middle East seemed to be slipping out of Britain's hands.

Britain acted swiftly. Troops from India were landed at Basra, and began to march up the Tigris Valley toward the Iraqi capital. Simultaneously a small British force assisted by a column (the 'Desert Mechanised Regiment') of the Arab Legion began to make its way through the Transjordanian Desert into western Iraq, via H3, Rutbah, and Habbaniyah, heading for Baghdad. The Legion column, led by Glubb, served as a reconnaissance screen and long-range desert assault unit, capturing the fort at Rutbah and the railway station at Meshahida. The column was reinforced by Indian troops from Basra. Iraqi resistance was light and by 30-31 May, al Ghilani had fled the country, the Iraqi Army (in the form of two officers 'bearing a bath towel on a pole') sued for an armistice, and Iraq was firmly back in British hands.[179] The British force's intelligence officer, Somerset de Chair, later called Glubb's contribution to the recapture of Baghdad 'decisive.'[180]

The British then proceeded to 'sort out' Vichy Syria and Lebanon: Columns from northern Palestine and Iraq converged on Damascus and Beirut, capturing the two capitals in June-July. (It was in the push into Southern Lebanon, spearheaded by Haganah scouts, that Moshe Dayan, later the IDF chief of general staff and antagonist of Glubb, and Defence Minister in the 1967 Six Day War and the 1973 October War, lost his eye to a Vichy sniper, at Iskanderoun.) The Legion, too, participated, Glubb leading his 350-strong mechanized column in the conquest of Palmyra (Tadmor), the vast Roman ruin in the Syrian Desert.[181] Again, Allied casualties were light - but Glubb and his officers now had experience of leading relatively large formations into battle, with all that this entailed in terms of intelligence, logistics, command and control, and combat experience, which was to stand them in good stead in 1948.

The Arabs' pro-Axis activities gave Glubb pause to reflect afresh on the Arab character. 'Are we to conclude from events in Iraq, that the Arabs are fundamentally treacherous and that our policy towards them has been too trusting? Should we in the future treat them with suspicion or endeavour to control them by force alone?' It is difficult, he wrote, 'to correctly appreciate the mentality of another nation.' In the Arab world, Glubb wrote, there is no separation between internal and external politics. The western-backed parties and regimes, he argued, introduced artificially and prematurely, abused their powers, reducing the traditional sway of family, clan and tribe. 'Can we blame them when they hedge or resort to subterfuge and treachery when faced with such threats?' Glubb argued: 'We have no right to accuse the Arabs in general of treachery.' Glubb proposed that British policy should be to give the locals 'generous amounts of freedom' while 'leaving a few first class British officers in key positions.' (In Iraq, by contrast with Transjordan, presumably there hadn't been any.) The Arabs must be 'kept on the rails' - and this involved preventing nepotism, corruption, and terrorism for political ends, he concluded.[182]

Having seen the efficiency and value of Glubb's little gendarmerie, the British set about vastly expanding and militarizing it. In 1939, the Legion had numbered 1,000 men; by 1945 it was the size of a small division, with armoured car squadrons and mortar batteries. After summer 1941, Glubb sought to participate in further British offensives. But the British command preferred to use the Legion as a garrison and guard force, dispersing many of its companies around bases in the region, including in Palestine. Glubb repeatedly pressed for more exacting or rewarding duties.[183] But British headquarters Middle East decided otherwise, perhaps fearing that Legion discipline would crumble when forced to fight fellow Arabs.

Glubb, in Amman for the duration, found himself with a great deal of time on his hands - and proceeded to bombard his superiors with memoranda on the politics of the Middle East, British policy, and the region's post-war future. Some of his attention inevitably focused on Palestine.

In November 1942 Glubb produced a 61-page memorandum entitled 'Note on Post-War Settlements in the Middle East'. He commented that in the wake of World War I there had been strife and bloodshed in every Arab country, much of it due to the uncertainties stemming from conflicting Allied - meaning mainly British and French - policies and promises. It was best, therefore, to decide in advance on the contours of the post-World War II settlement in the Middle East.

Glubb argued for a continued, major British presence in the region. Nationalism was not native to Asia and the term 'independence,' he asserted, was meaningless to most of its peoples. It was the West that had thrust on them such notions. 'In actual fact, a very little consideration would show that the withdrawal of British rule from Asia would be a world catastrophe comparable only to the over-running of the Roman Empire by [the] barbarians, a catastrophe followed by centuries of the Dark Ages.' However, as Britain had promised the Arabs 'an (impracticable) complete independence,' they 'can scarcely be blamed for demanding that the promise be implemented.'

Glubb believed, nevertheless, that Britain should retain 'cantonments' or bases in key sites, such as Tobruk, the Suez Canal, Haifa, Rutbah, and Kuwait, with one division of troops in each, and retain or have mandatory 'responsibility for, all the northern Arab countries [i.e., Palestine-Lebanon-Syria-Iraq-Transjordan], if possible with close American support and cooperation.' France, he thought, must be evicted 'altogether' from the region - its continued presence would only spark Arab antagonism towards the West and rebellions. The British, Glubb felt, perhaps building on his own status in Transjordan, were less obnoxious to Arab eyes.

As to Palestine, to which very little space is devoted in the memorandum, Glubb left his solution somewhat fuzzy, for which he was to be berated by the memorandum's critics. He wrote: 'Even fools may well hesitate to rush into a dissertation on the vexed question of Palestine ... In Palestine we [British] fight the Arabs in the interests of the Jews...' Both Jews and Arabs were busy arming. 'The best hope for peace in Palestine seems to be a generous settlement of the Arab question in other parts of Arabia [i.e., the Arab world], thereby persuading the leaders of the Arabs in other countries to acquiesce in sacrifices in Palestine.' Given the context, the implication seems to be that Glubb favoured partition, involving the eventual establishment of a Jewish state in part of the country. (This implication is strengthened by a passage in his autobiography relating to this period in which he states: 'We in Transjordan produced our own solution. We favoured partition ... [with British garrisons left in Jerusalem and Haifa and the adjoining Arab areas of Palestine being incorporated into Transjordan, Egypt and Lebanon]. Lord Moyne, British Minister of State in the Middle East, to whom I explained the idea, professed himself to be keenly interested. But before he could take up the scheme, he was assassinated in Cairo by Jewish terrorists...').[184] But he did not spell this out. Rather, he seemed to be thinking of partition as a final solution for the not too proximate future. Meanwhile, he wrote:

> a bi-racial [i.e., bi-national, Arab-Jewish] administration [with autonomous Jewish and Arab districts?] in Palestine with Great Britain keeping the peace with a

> large garrison appears inevitable for some time to come. If, however, Palestine were to enter into an Arab federation [of states] and racial animosities were to settle down, the Jews might find a wider scope for their commerce than would be the case if the continuance of the present fanaticism on both sides leaves the Jews confined to a portion of Palestine and encircled by enemies.

In other words, Glubb is arguing for a reunification, in the form of a federation, of the northern-tier Arab states sandwiched between Turkey and Saudi Arabia, while suggesting that the dangled bait of expanded economic ties and benefits might persuade the Jews to forego the establishment of a separate state. He appears to assume that 'the Jews' would sell anything - in this case, their political aspirations - for financial gain.[185]

Glubb sent his memorandum to, among others, Sir Harold MacMichael, the high commissioner for Palestine and Transjordan. MacMichael responded in a closely-argued two-page analysis. He sent copies, along with 13 copies of Glubb's original memorandum, to Colonial Secretary Oliver Stanley, recommending distribution of both among the minister's aides and British Middle East posts.

MacMichael opened by praising Glubb's paper - 'few men have Colonel Glubb's qualifications to paint a picture on so broad a canvas, and the value of the memorandum is proportionate to his knowledge and long experience' - and endorsed a number of its arguments. He, too, opposed the 'tendency to indulge in facile promises of independence' and favoured continued 'regional international control,' but by Britain together with the United States, rather than some looser supervision in a mandates system by a 'decentralised League of Nations,' as Glubb had proposed. MacMichael agreed that, 'if peace is to be kept,' forces must be retained in the region 'indefinitely [and] amply.' The high commissioner also agreed about 'the futility of [the region's] artificial partition at the end of the last war' and posited 'the national and historical indivisibility of the Levantine whole' (implying some form of pan-Arab federation?). MacMichael preferred 'Haifa' as the capital of the prospective federation to Glubb's suggestions of 'Palmyra or Abu Kemal.' He was 'less categorical' than Glubb about the need to completely eject the French from the region though he also thought cooperation with the United States an 'essential requisite' of any post-war arrangement.

MacMichael was critical of Glubb's marginalisation of Palestine: 'The problem of Palestine ... does not seem to me to be given ... the weight which it will certainly carry. Unless it is solved in advance the whole dream-fabric of "federation" is likely to collapse.' MacMichael pointed to the recent 'growth of political maximalism,' which was preventing a compromise:

> The Jews demand Palestine as a Jewish state, and, that achieved, would be ready to talk in terms of a "federation"; the Arabs retort with the obvious counter-reply. The only possible compromise is surely a bi-national Palestine, and, once that is definitely and finally assured and the main cause of friction - uncertainty - thereby removed, negotiations for any form of political unification in the Levant can proceed upon the basis of irrefragable premises.

MacMichael feared

> the likelihood of violent disturbances in Palestine after the war. Once such occur, with Arab and Jew at open loggerheads, I feel that the wave of sympathy among the population of the neighbouring Arab countries may flow so strongly as to sweep away any disposition that may exist in favour of accepting even the moderate and reasonable degree of "sacrifice" involved in bi-nationalism.

Hence, he felt it was necessary to reach a solution to the Palestine problem before any more general plans for unification or 'federation' of the Levant could go forward.[186]

MacMichael's criticisms, and a conversation the two men held subsequently, prompted Glubb to expatiate on his views on the Arab-Zionist conflict and a possible solution. Due to their sometime prophetic qualities and the insight they afford about the character of Glubb's worldview, they are worth quoting from at length.

In his original memorandum, Glubb had suggested that the Arab leaders might be persuaded 'to acquiesce in sacrifices in Palestine.' He now wrote: 'I was somewhat horrified at the idea that my remarks might be interpreted as acquiescence in the proposal for a Jewish state in Palestine. I had intentionally avoided any detailed discussion of the Palestine question in my memorandum' - but now he felt he had to set out his views explicitly, if only to 'avoid misinterpretation.' He seemed to be back-tracking under the pressure of MacMichael's opinions.

Glubb began his explanation with a psychological observation, as was increasingly to be his wont. Perhaps hovering vaguely in the background to his remarks were the recently published revelations about the on-going Holocaust in Europe:

> The psychologists inform us that children who have been brutally brought up by cruel parents, are normally the persons who themselves are cruel to their own

children. This peculiarity is not limited to children. Religious sects which have suffered persecution, are usually the first to persecute other sects, weaker than themselves, when they get the chance. This jungle law by which each community torments those weaker than themselves, is depressing ... One would have hoped that those who had themselves suffered persecution would have vowed never to inflict suffering on others. But unfortunately our observations of human nature do not justify such hopes.

The Jews, who have suffered so much and who make such pathetic appeals to our sympathy when they are the victims of oppression, are entirely without bowels of compassion vis-a-vis the Arabs, when it is within their power to oppress the latter. Somebody has said that the Jews are the cleverest people in the world, but the least wise. Their actions in Palestine have surely confirmed the truth of this opinion ... In Palestine ... greed and fanaticism have characterised their attitude towards the Arabs. [Therefore,] although (or perhaps because) the Jews have long been a persecuted minority themselves, their mentality renders unthinkable any idea of handing another minority over to their tender mercies.

But it must be realized that the proposal to form a Jewish State in Palestine is not the proposal to place a minority under the control of a majority, but the reverse. The Arabs form two-thirds of the population of Palestine!! Nothing could be more undemocratic than to hand over a majority to the rule of a minority and that minority a fanatical people and their professed bitterest enemies ... It is in this connection interesting to note that some Jews demand the right to dominate the Arabs in Palestine on the grounds that they (the Jews) are a superior race compared to the Arabs. This, of course, is the reason why the Germans claim the right to bully the Jews. It is precisely this desire of one "superior race" to dominate the others which we are said to be fighting this war to oppose.

Glubb thought that the Jews, 'by the use of ruthless methods and modern armaments,' might gain control of Palestine, but this would spark 'excitement and hostility' throughout the Arab and Islamic worlds:

At the best it would lead to a boycott of Jewish Palestine goods and an outbreak of persecution of the Jews in other Arab countries. At the worst, it would mean that armed forces from other parts of Arabia would come to the support of the Arabs of Palestine. It would certainly hamper, if not destroy, any plans for Anglo-Arab cooperation after the war.

However,

at the same time [it must] be recognized that the Arabs of Palestine are, on the average, on a lower level of culture than the Jews. Although the Arabs constitute

> a majority, it would not be permissible to hand the Jews over to the tender mercies of the Arabs ... We have ... in Palestine two races ... both greedy and fanatical, and both conspicuously lacking in calm wisdom or broad statesmanship. To hand either race over to the other ... is unthinkable.

So, meanwhile, 'there is ... no possible alternative to the maintenance of a strong central, British administration backed by force,' thought Glubb. (He left open, without stating it, the possibility that, further down the road, eventually, the solution could include partition and the establishment of a Jewish state without a large Arab minority in part of Palestine.) He added, however, that there were still grounds for hope as 'the Jews are a most adaptable race.' With growing commercial ties, the 'spirit of local fanaticism' might 'cool off' and 'the second or third generation of Jews may well become acclimatized in the Middle East and blend in with the local populations.'

Glubb noted that an additional reason for the failure to resolve the Palestine problem was the frequent changes of British policy, so that 'neither side believes that the British Government have the determination to adhere to any decision which they reach.' In general, the government always appears to knuckle under to pressure, thus encouraging 'nationalist extremism.'

Glubb went on to tackle head-on a number of 'Orientalist' Western conceptions (decades before the term had been popularized and given, by Edward Said, its current pejorative meaning). Glubb denounced efforts or hopes to persuade 'India or Arabia' to adopt 'democracy.' 'Human progress is to be reckoned in terms of centuries, not of years.' It was ridiculous to believe that the Arabs could be persuaded to accept 'democracy' in a year or two, because of Western say-so. History - and the East - have their own timetables for development. Glubb - quite unrealistically - proposed that after making a major concession to the Arabs, 25 years be allowed to elapse as a 'probation' period, to see how the change 'takes.' If successful, one could go on to a further concession, again with a 25-year trial period, and so on.

Glubb took issue with MacMichael's assertion that the Arabs 'showed a regrettable lack of wisdom or of statesmanship.' He countered that Ibn Saud, of Saudi Arabia, had shown statesmanship, despite the lack of a formal western education:

> It would almost seem that "education" destroys the natural wisdom of the Arabs. Indeed, the now-despised beduins may well be wiser than many of the so-called educated class ... The results of the present system of education in Arabia may

almost be described as catastrophic. I believe them to be due to the overwhelming dominance of the East by Europe and the United States. Orientals who resent this European dominance think that they can put an end to it, and become equal to Europeans, by having an education on the European model. They therefore endeavour to acquire all the knowledge of law, medicine, engineering, mathematics or whatever it is which is possessed by Europe ... But they miss the point that education is not essentially a question of committing to memory a vast amount of factual knowledge but rather is it the building up of wisdom and "character" ... [These products] of European "education" are as clever as a bag of monkeys, but utterly and ... catastrophically lacking in wisdom. The multiplication of schools which turn out more and more clever, discontented and conceited little monkeys does not appear to be the solution ...

Glubb felt that the Arab 'educated' classes were jealous of Europeans and suffered from a sense of 'inferiority,' which bred in them 'extreme nationalism' and a desire for independence. He added:

Although I have ... repeatedly argued that Eastern nations are not fit to be independent, I do not for a moment believe that Eastern individuals are inferior to ourselves. ... It is largely their institutions which are behind-hand. Centuries of Turkish rule, for example ... left them without educational institutions or economic resources. These things will take several generations to build up. It is quite certain that they will be built up. It is quite probable that a few centuries hence the balance of power will have swung back to Asia, and Europe will be the poor relations ... There is no apparent justification for the offensive airs of superiority which many Europeans assume.

Glubb recommended treating Easterners 'on a perfect social equality' with Britons - and this did not necessitate granting these nations 'political equality,' a 'consummation which may take generations.'[187]

After further reflection, Glubb in mid-1943 produced a second (or third) post-war settlement memorandum – 'A Further Note on Peace Terms in the Middle East'. In it he argued that all the current protagonists – 'Jews, Arabs and French' - remember the way World War I ended in the region, with everyone resorting to violence and 'everybody who used violence ... was successful in retaining permanently what he had seized by force ... Everybody remembers ... and is planning to emulate [these successes at the end of World War II].' The Jews, he said, are preparing 'an armed coup d'etat in Palestine ... Iraq ... will be prepared to intervene against the Jews in Palestine and against the French in Syria and general chaos and bloodshed will cover Northern Arabia [i.e., the northern-tier Arab world].'

To pre-empt such a denouement, Britain must in advance formulate and publicize comprehensive post-war plans for the region, allowing for a three-year intermezzo before final peace terms are reached. There must be United States agreement to the 'main features' of the final settlement.

Britain's main interest in the Middle East 'is the safety of our communications through [this region] to India, Australia and the Far East.' Success in the post-war struggle for the Middle East will go to the side which 'seizes and maintains the initiative.' Ultimately, the decision will be made

> by the use of armed force ... The domination of a disaffected country by armed forces is largely a question of the seizure of key points - cities, railway junctions, buildings on street corners, telephone exchanges ... Unless plans of this nature have been previously considered, the Jews or the Arabs may one day seize these countries themselves ...' In addition to British troops, 'Indians, Africans, Sudanese, Basutos and Arabs [the Arab Legion?] might possibly be employed.

As Glubb saw things, the two main potential problems were the future of Syria and Palestine. If a breakdown occurred in either, 'a general [Middle Eastern] conflagration is probable owing to the ... sympathy felt for these countries in Iraq and Transjordan.'

The problem of Palestine, according to Glubb, was in some ways easier of solution than that of Syria because 'no [other] foreign power has to be consulted as of right, much less has another power to be evicted from the country. There is no competition for the thankless task.' But there were the Arabs and the Jews. Both '(but especially the Jews) are arming with the avowed intention of resorting to violence.' Both sides want all of Palestine:

> The Arabs are twice as numerous as the Jews, but the Jews are far better educated ... The fanatical and disgusting quarrels of two such tiny groups would scarcely have become an imperial problem were it not that both sides have a large gallery of sympathizers outside Palestine ... Unfortunately, the Jews wear the coat of European culture and command sympathy in Great Britain and America...

The situation was deadlocked as 'neither side will hear of a compromise,' and neither can be allowed to rule over the other. Glubb recommended that 'both sides should be told that there is no possibility of the creation of an Arab state or a Jewish state at the end of this war.' The problem was that though the masses in both camps just want 'to live in peace,' 'the fanatics of both sides have become the leaders'. 'The moderates are afraid to come forward' - but they might if 'the mandatory power [took] a firmer hold.' The British must maintain the 'balance ... between the two races [for] a generation or two.'

Glubb believed that there was a natural balance - between the more numerous Arabs and the wealthier and better educated Jews. Domination of one by the other was possible only if the balance could be tilted - so Jewish

> immigration is ... the key to the struggle ... If immigration now ceases, the Arabs feel that they can more or less hold their own. If immigration on a large scale is reopened, the Arabs will interpret it as absolute ruin for themselves. My own opinion is that bloodshed will result.
>
> What the future may hold we cannot foresee. With the destruction of Nazi-ism, Jews may wish to return from Palestine to Europe. At any rate, the end of Jewish persecution in Europe after the war will certainly make the necessity of Jewish migration from Europe less urgent! We must differentiate between the genuine need to save Jews from persecution, and the desire of the local Palestine [Jewish] leaders to pack them into that country in order to achieve political dominance for themselves.

Glubb thought that the immediate post-war years would be a particularly bad time for a resumption of Jewish immigration - because the war's end would result in a local industrial slump; the persecutions in Europe would cease; the countries of 'Northern Arabia' would in any case be 'restless'; and Jewish immigration to Palestine could spark rebellion 'in Iraq and Syria as well as Palestine ... Let us not tempt Providence by ourselves throwing a bombshell into the arena. Let us [for now] leave the White Paper as it stands ... Three years after the armistice will be soon enough voluntarily to court a new small war.'

British policy on Palestine, says Glubb, has been marked by 'vacillation,' and the changes in it have almost invariably been brought about by violence ('The Arabs of Palestine ... only won the White Paper as a result of their rebellion ...'):

> The Jews have perfectly appreciated this fact, and ... many of them are confident that a Jewish armed rebellion ... would immediately cause the abandonment of the White Paper, and an entire reversal of British policy in favour of the Jews. [In fact, the hesitant, on-and-off rebellion of the Jewish armed groups between 1944

> and 1947 led not to the abolition of the White Paper but to Britain's decision to abandon Palestine altogether.] If the Jews start a rebellion, it will be much more efficiently organized than the Arab Revolt ... A high proportion of Jews live in towns, and many of them have seen the Nazi technique [i.e., Glubb seems to be talking about urban terrorism] in Europe ... We do not appear to have taken much trouble to study ... [the art of counter-terrorism], which is ... one extremely distasteful to professional British Army officers ... We should study profoundly the art of city control and street fighting, as practised by such forces as the SS guards [SA?] in the early days of Nazism ... Force is everything in Palestine ... The art of controlling civil disturbances by armed forces, brought to such perfection by the Nazis, is still almost unknown to us. It is an art distasteful to soldiers, but ... unless we can learn and practise this art, we shall be always dragging through rebellions in Palestine.[188]

It would appear from these passages that Glubb, cut off and somewhat isolated in his desert principality, was not really aware of the full lethality of the Holocaust (many, indeed, in Palestine and the West only grasped the full dimensions of the tragedy with the liberation of the extermination camps in 1945) or of the scope of the viciousness and murderousness of the Nazis in keeping down the populations of occupied Europe. Thus, in mid-1943 he was able to speak of a return of refugees from Palestine to Europe after the war and of survivors wishing to resettle and rebuild their lives in the countries of destruction; and thus he was able to speak of adopting 'Nazi methods' to put down rebellion or terrorism in Palestine (or elsewhere in the Middle East). For a man as basically honourable and decent as Glubb, the idea of committing a 'Lidice' after each act of terrorism - as he seems to be advocating here - would have been unthinkable.[189]

Glubb's memorandum of May 1943 sparked enthusiasm among British Middle East hands. The Civil Secretary of the British Administration in Khartoum, Sudan, D. Newbold, responded:

> Re Palestine, I saw and heard enough when I was there in April and May this year to realise the Zionist menace, and I heartily agree with the cessation of Zionist immigration ... The Zionist expansion is astonishing ... The Jewish Agency is an Imperium in Imperio and [David] Ben-Gurion and [Moshe] Shertok [Sharett] are riding for a fall.[190]

It should immediately be noted that Glubb's anti-partition position at this time regarding post-war Palestine substantially diverged from official

British opinion - and, indeed, from an important segment of senior Arab opinion - as the war drew to a close. In late 1943 a special British ministerial committee on Palestine proposed the scrapping of the 1939 White Paper and the establishment of a Jewish state in a partitioned Palestine. In January 1944, under Prime Minister Winston Churchill's guidance, the full Cabinet endorsed the principle while leaving the details (the size and contours of the Jewish state, etc.) to further discussion (which were to remain unconsummated).[191]

Most of Britain's senior Middle East policy-makers and executives endorsed the Cabinet resolution. Lord Moyne, the Minister Resident in the Middle East, at the end of February 1944 held a round of discussions in Jerusalem with MacMichael, Sir Edward Spears, the head of Britain's political mission in Syria and Lebanon, and Alec Kirkbride, the British Resident in Amman. 'It was agreed [among the participants] that partition offers the only hope of a final settlement for Palestine ... There is now widespread discussion both in Arab and Jewish circles of the likelihood of a partition settlement,' according to Moyne. He added that both Jordan's prime minister, Tewfiq Abul Huda, and Egyptian Prime Minister Mustafa Nahas Pasha 'have recognized that a final settlement can only be reached by means of partition' - though these Arab leaders might not be able 'to say this openly.' Moyne (and MacMichael and Kirkbride) clearly conceived that the Arab areas of Palestine not included in the Jewish state would be incorporated in Transjordan.[192]

Abul Huda informed Kirkbride of his position in two conversations, on 2 December 1943 and 16 January 1944. Reporting on the second of these, MacMichael - formally Kirkbride's superior - wrote that Abul Huda had said that 'he did not ... see any alternative to partition, provided always that the division of Palestine was not ... unjust [meaning, that the Jews would get too much of the country].' Abul Huda added that while the Palestinian Arabs would not be enthusiastic, 'they would [ultimately] accept the position.'[193]

By the end of 1944, Arab official opinion in general had fallen into line with Abul Huda's views - at least according to Nuri Said, Iraq's most important politician (he served as prime minister fourteen times during the 1930s, 1940s and 1950s), and Glubb. Nuri Said's own views were clear, according to Kirkbride (who met the Iraqi at the end of November 1944):

> Provided the partition was effected on an equitable basis, it might perhaps be best to lose part of Palestine in order to confine the Zionist danger within permanent boundaries ... Nuri Pasha said that the only fair basis could be the cession to the

> Jews of those areas where they constituted a majority ... [while] the Arab section of Palestine would be embodied in Transjordan.[194]

Moreover, Nuri Said favoured the transfer of the Arab population out of the areas destined for Jewish sovereignty ('...he spoke of the necessity of removing the Arabs from the Jewish state and thought it could be done by exchange').[195]

Toward the end of the war, Glubb wrote one last memorandum on a post-war settlement. In it he toned down a number of his previous suggestions. In 'A Note on the Solution of the Syrian Problem', Glubb reiterated that the White Paper of May 1939, banning Jewish immigration and eventually establishing a 'national [i.e., Arab-dominated] government' in Palestine, must be 'the starting point' of a solution. The Arabs, on this basis, might be induced to accept 'a Jewish National Home' in Palestine - Glubb meant by this an autonomous area, with 'the greatest feasible degree of local self-government' - which would not be tantamount to separate Jewish statehood. The Jews, for their part, would have to accept the impossibility of separate statehood because, 'sooner or later they must realize that no National Home of any sort can survive without Arab acquiescence and ultimately without Arab friendship, and that to win acquiescence and friendship they must make sacrifices.'

Jewish acceptance of such a plan might be facilitated by continued British control of the 'police force for another generation at least' as well as by the 'maintenance of armed British forces' in Haifa or elsewhere in Palestine. These could be trusted to protect the Jews against depredation by Arabs, felt Glubb. However, he was still sure that 'in spite of all that can be done ... the Zionists are going to make a nuisance of themselves to Great Britain and the Arabs for several generations.'

Glubb ended the memorandum by declaring that, in view of the problems presented by France vis-a-vis Syria and Lebanon and Zionism vis-a-vis Palestine, the best that could be hoped for in the area of Greater Syria would be 'a very loose federation,' certainly at the beginning. Perhaps later, 'a closer federation could be formed,' but each of the 'provinces' would still have to enjoy 'a considerable degree of cultural and administrative autonomy.'[196]

In August 1945, three months after the end of the war in Europe, Glubb produced a further, 38-page paper entitled 'The New Relationship, Notes on Certain Aspects of Anglo-Arab Relations in the Near Future', in which he reflected on the universal desire for national independence, or, as he put it, 'the fanatical demand for complete independence.' According to Glubb, there were in Whitehall two responses: Either to agree to quit the Arab countries 'bag and baggage'; or, the 'Victorian' response, to continue to treat all the natives as 'wogs' and to ignore their wishes.

The war had demonstrated that small countries could not resist aggression without great power assistance. On the other hand, the war had equally demonstrated the importance of the Middle East to the well-being of the British Commonwealth. The situation thus made for a compromise in which 'the Arabs' could be admitted 'to the British Empire with something resembling Dominion status. Such a solution would give them a big umbrella in matters of commerce and defence, with local autonomy to live as they like.' The problems in the way of concluding such an arrangement, according to Glubb, were not Arab nationalism, but 'the French' in Syria and Lebanon and 'the Zionists' in Palestine.[197]

1946-47 - Glubb Comes Round to Partition

A Jewish State of Palestine
  If you do it
  You'll rue it
An Arab State of Palestine
  Hardly a proposition
  When you consider the opposition
Federation
  What situation
  Follows separation[?]
  A Divorce[,] of Course
Partition
  To partite and be neighbourly
  Is far less labourly
  Than putting up with banditry
  And blaming the mandatory[198]

In 1937 Glubb had implied that partition was a reasonable, perhaps the only, solution for Palestine, though he heavily qualified this judgement by highlighting a series of major problems that partition would entail. During World War II, as we have seen, he came out more or less consistently and forcefully against partition, at least for the foreseeable future, arguing that it would be unacceptable to the Arabs and hence damaging to British interests. But in the immediate wake of the war, perhaps under the impact of the Holocaust, and certainly mindful of British weakness and the ascendancy in world affairs of the United States, and of Jewish desires and actions in Palestine, Glubb reverted to his support for partition. Partly, no doubt, he was influenced by Abdullah's wishes and the prince's view of Transjordan's interests; perhaps he saw partition as inescapable; and perhaps, however reluctantly, he also came to accept that partition represented a modicum of fairness while all the other alternatives only supplied varying measures of unfairness.

In March 1946 Glubb, apparently unsolicited, submitted a 12-page memorandum entitled 'Is it Feasible?' to the Anglo-American Commission of Inquiry (AAC). The investigative body, consisting of six Britons and six Americans, was appointed at the end of 1945 by the two governments to suggest a solution for the problem posed by the hundreds of thousands of Holocaust survivors wandering around Europe or languishing in Displaced Persons (DPs) camps, in connection with the Palestine problem. Triggering the committee's appointment was pressure by the Zionist movement and some of the DPs to allow them to immigrate to Palestine and pressure by Washington on Britain to allow 100,000 DPs into Palestine immediately.

Glubb wrote that what interested him was not past rights or wrongs, or promises, but 'what was possible.'

> Few people will deny that the Jews have suffered intensely in Europe, and that we should do everything possible to alleviate their present plight and ensure that they will not be persecuted in the future. Other things being equal, if the Jews of Europe want to migrate to Palestine, we should be pleased to facilitate the fulfilment of their wishes. The only obstacle is the opposition of the Arabs.

But could this opposition be overcome?

'The Arabs have not persecuted the Jews in the past 1400 years ... [though] it is true that the Arab Muslims regarded Jews as an inferior class...' But the Palestine problem must be seen within the context of European imperialism and resulting Arab feelings of inferiority and exploitation. 'The Jews who entered Palestine assumed towards the Arabs the haughty manner of the European colonist dealing with a "native" race.'

The Arabs would react to Western-sponsored Jewish immigration with terrorism and rebellion in Palestine and outside it, and on a political level might seek Soviet intercession, Glubb asserted. Glubb compared the introduction of Jews to Palestine with the eastward movement of the Teutonic knights in the Middle Ages and the introduction of Scottish

Presbyterians to Ireland. He also compared the Zionist influx to the Crusader Kingdom of Jerusalem, which collapsed after a century. The Crusaders were 'gradually driven back into the sea.' Glubb saw other parallels: The Crusaders, too, initially, faced a divided Muslim world - but it gradually united and overcame them:

> In precisely the same manner today, Zionism in Palestine is forcing Arab unity and is creating Arab fanaticism ... The Zionists may win this round and the next and the next. They may win for 88 years as did the Crusaders. But there will be 88 years of war, hatred and malice and misery. And in the opinion of the present writer, the Arabs will in the end get the upper hand, even if it be in 200 years, and will push the Jews into the sea again.

Glubb concluded that the decision of the committee should not

> be limited to a solution of the immediate problem of displaced persons. We must also take into consideration the generations and the centuries to come. An error today may create ... one more race problem, which will terminate only, perhaps centuries hence, in the final liquidation of the Jewish bridgehead, after a pogrom of dimensions hitherto unequalled in Jewish history.[199]

The Anglo-American commission's report was published on 20 April 1946. Glubb reacted immediately with 'A Note on the Report of [the] Anglo-American Commission'. The commission had recommended, in line with the United States' position, that 100,000 DPs be immediately allowed entry into Palestine. But, at the same time, it had rejected the idea of partition and recommended a bi-national state under international trusteeship. Glubb reacted with an alarmist, indeed, apocalyptic projection of what might happen should Britain accept the committee's immigration recommendations.

Glubb argued that the commission had been responsible for two glaring omissions: (A) It failed to take account of the possibility that many DPs could be settled in the United States; and (B) it failed to appreciate that a massive influx of Jewish immigrants would be opposed not only by Palestine's Arabs but by the surrounding Arab states.

As to the first point, wrote Glubb, when a sub-committee of the Commission had visited Amman, a number of Arabs had asked one American member why the United States did not accept Jewish immigrants. The American, according to Glubb, replied: '"There are limits to kindness." In an aside to the present writer, the American admitted that the U.S.A. did not want the occupants of the Polish ghettos ... The Arabs,' Glubb continued, 'do not question the tragic plight of the Jews of Europe, or the brutality of Nazi persecution. But they point out that the Jews were massacred by European Christians, and that other European Christians have now decided that the whole burden of this crime against humanity is to be borne by Moslem Asiatics!'

Glubb agreed that the Arab governments 'did not seem to react very generously' when asked to agree to a resumption of Jewish immigration at the rate of 1,500 per month. 'But it must be remembered that internal politics here come into play. The Palestine question has unfortunately become the touchstone of patriotism in every Arab country. No Arab politician dares to agree publicly to any concession ... lest his rivals make political capital of the fact by charging him with lack of patriotism.'

Glubb recommended that henceforward Britain consult the Arab League about such matters before announcing decisions. 'Nothing flatters an inferior like being taken into the confidence of his superior and asked for his advice,' he wrote. Glubb recommended that the United States agree to absorb 30,000 of the DPs, Britain and the Dominions 20,000, and Palestine 24,000. Another 26,000 might be admitted by France and South American and other countries. 'The obvious objection to the proposal is of course that the Jews are alleged not to want to go to Britain, the U.S.A. or other countries, but only to Palestine. If this be indeed true, it is difficult entirely to avoid the suspicion that their wish has been produced by intensive Zionist propaganda...' wrote Glubb.

As in other memoranda, Glubb often puts in the mouths of Arabs his own argumentation. Thus he writes, explaining the origin of the American support for the admission into Palestine of 100,000 DPs: 'The Arabs ... declare ... that the lives of a few tens of thousands of Asiatic natives and the ruin of their homes is not too high a price for the Democratic Party to pay for the New York Jewish vote or to ensure a Second Term for Mr. Truman.'[200]

The Anglo-American committee, according to Glubb, had read previous commission (Peel, etc.) reports on Palestine but had failed to take sufficient account of the maturation of the Arab societies and states in the course of World War II, which rendered their reaction to the Palestine problem more cogent and significant. Hence the committee's throw-away attitude to HMG's ability to implement its recommendations 'takes one's breath away,' he wrote. The Arabs of Palestine 'have handed over the defence of their case to the Arab League' - and Britain had best be apprised of what the League could do in the event that the Committee's recommendations were implemented.

'The regular armies of the Arab states are not formidable opponents,' writes Glubb. But they could be expected to react by launching a 'guerrilla war' – 'the Arab is one of the world's best guerrillas' - in Palestine, with equipment and volunteer contingents streaming in from the neighbouring Arab states. Transjordan would be pressured to contribute volunteers and allow free passage through its territory to Palestine. Britain would need 'three to four divisions' to contain the onslaught. And 'the intense xenophobia' unleashed would result in anti-British disturbances throughout the Arab world, including 'pogroms of [i.e., against] the local Jews.' Britain might even have to 're-conquer' Syria and Iraq. Lastly, one must also consider the possibility of some form of Russian intervention 'on the Arab side,' wrote Glubb.

Glubb recommended that if Britain indeed decided to allow 100,000 immigrants into Palestine, it should first send to the area 12-15 divisions, and crush swiftly and without ado any signs of armed resistance, occupying Damascus, and, if necessary, Baghdad. The Arabs are 'admirers of force,' so this might deter further Arab resistance, and perhaps the Russians as well.

Glubb exhibited a keen awareness of the potential Soviet threat - much as that threat in the immediate post-war years was to weigh heavily on the minds of most British and American leaders and officials. Glubb's predictions were in fact to materialize, but only a decade or two later. 'To profit by playing one power off against another is a principle deeply rooted in the mind of every Arab politician,' Glubb warned. Even though the Arabs naturally 'fear and dislike Russia' (abhorrence of Communist atheism, etc.), a serious Arab-British clash would result if there were an Arab-Russian rapprochement. The Russians would not intervene directly with military forces but would probably 'supply weapons to the Arabs' and military advisory missions. Iraq and Syria might move into 'the Russian orbit' and this might lead to the defection of Turkey and Persia as well.

Presciently, Glubb added:

> Obviously one of the trump cards in the hands of the Arabs is the oil concessions. To what extent ... any Arab country would be willing to denounce [i.e., renounce] their concessions and forcibly close down work at the wells, the writer does not know ... It is possible [moreover] that oil installations and pipe lines might suffer from sabotage or officials of the oil companies be victimized or murdered...

Interestingly, Glubb in this memorandum failed altogether to comment on the AAC's other recommendation, namely the continued international supervision of Palestine and the eventual emergence of a bi-national state. A rejection of partition is implicit throughout the memorandum but the subject is never tackled explicitly or directly.[201]

Glubb's memorandum was to have an embarrassing apotheosis. On 24 May he had been visited at Arab Legion Headquarters by a 'Mr. Hewins,' a correspondent of London's *Daily Mail.* Hewins had spoken of the dangers posed to British interests by the commission's report. 'All this talk,' wrote Glubb subsequently, 'put me off my guard, and resulted in my committing what has now proved to have been a serious indiscretion.' He gave Hewins a copy of his 'Note' on the commission's report - sections of which, attacking the recommendations, Hewins proceeded to publish in his paper, purportedly as an interview with Glubb. Subsequently, there was a question in the House of Commons addressed to Foreign Secretary Ernst Bevin as to steps to be taken to prevent British officers giving 'unauthorised newspaper interviews.' Hector McNeil, Bevin's deputy, answered that Glubb had given no interview and, anyway, he was not a serving British officer.[202]

The anti-partition thrust of Glubb's memorandum reflected the gist of King Abdullah's statement at a meeting, also attended by Glubb, with the new High Commissioner for Palestine and Transjordan, Sir Alan Cunningham, on 1 June 1946. Abdullah was not particularly impressed by the comparison between the Zionists and the Crusaders: 'We do not want to hear about Saladin now. He defeated a few thousand wretched men who came from Europe in sailing ships, half of them being drowned on the journey,' he said - meaning that the Zionists were a far more formidable foe than the Crusaders had ever been. Abdullah believed that the other Arab states, whatever their protestations, would not 'fight for Palestine.' But somehow Palestine had to be protected: It 'must remain an Arab country. His own father King Husayn [the Sharif of Mecca] was buried in Jerusalem [in the Haram ash Sharif, the Temple Mount].' Moreover, if Palestine fell to the Jews, 'the next Arab country to be threatened would be his country, Transjordan, not Syria, or Egypt ... he was in greater danger than any of them.'[203]

Glubb may have hoped that a copy of his memorandum on the AAC would reach Prime Minister Clement Attlee. Be that as it may, he may also have conveyed its gist, highly unusually, in a personal, direct letter to Attlee. In the files of the Jewish Agency from this time there is a Hebrew translation of what purports to be a letter from Glubb to the prime minister, handed to the Zionist leadership by an agent in Jordan in an Arabic translation. The letter states: 'Great is the disappointment of the Arab nation' with the AAC's proposals and with Attlee's initial, favourable comments on them. This, predicted Glubb, would subvert Britain's position in the Middle East. Glubb asked Attlee not to implement the report and 'to solve the Palestine problem in the Arabs' favour' because the country has been theirs for 'a thousand years.' Glubb rejected the argument that should Britain rule in the Arabs' favour, the Jews would cause 'disturbances.' 'Give the Transjordan army a free hand and I can guarantee that it will put an end to what they call the "[Jewish] terrorist organisations" and will bring peace once and for all to the country.'

Glubb went on to plead against partitioning the country 'into two areas, one for the Jews and one for the Arabs.' Such a step would harm both communities and would incite the Arabs to violence. 'One of the things we must fully understand is that the Arabs and their countries are not goods to be purchased with money ... in order to make friends and achieve goals.' Referring to the AAC's '100,000' immigrants proposal, Glubb (with one variation) repeated the formula elaborated in the memorandum: That the United States absorb 30,000, Britain 24,000, and France and southern Africa 26,000; Palestine could absorb no more than 20,000 - and it were better that these be left in Europe, where they could be reabsorbed now that the Nazis had been destroyed.[204]

In June 1946, then, Glubb was still shying away from support for Partition. In a further memorandum from this time, entitled 'A Further Note on the Palestine Question', he argued that demographic realities weighed heavily against the possibility of Zionism's success. In fifty years' time, there would be '70 million' Arabs (without Egypt and the rest of North Africa) as opposed to '2 million' Jews. Thus

> there can be only one ending of this struggle - a pogrom on a scale never yet dreamed of ... The only hope for Jewish settlement in Palestine is that it be carried out with Arab consent. If it continues against Arab resistance, it can only end, sooner or later, in a terrible disaster for the Jews themselves ... The Crusaders maintained a precarious foothold in the Middle East for 200 years, but in the end not one of them was left. A century or two is nothing in history. Zionism is leading these wretched Jews for one of the worst disasters of their history.

Glubb had preceded these conclusions with a sympathetic asseveration (without directly alluding to the Holocaust): 'The life of the Jewish people is an unending tragedy.' But then he explained that this was also the root-cause of their persecution:

> Driven ceaselessly from one country to another, they are at first welcomed and then driven out or massacred. Nobody can endure them long, because they do not

> assimilate themselves easily, and thus become a state within a state. The tragedy is a vicious circle - other peoples dislike them owing to their character - their unlikeable character has been produced by persecution by other peoples ... Persecution and hatred has bred bitterness in the Jews, and people who hate and sneer are unpopular with their neighbours.

The Jews, in fact, suffer 'from the same disease' as the Arabs - an 'inferiority fixation.' 'The Jews are loud in their contempt of [Arab] natives because they have an unpleasant suspicion that the Nordics despise them as natives also...'[205]

But in the course of July, Glubb was to radically change his tune, reverting to his (fleeting) advocacy of partition of 1937. Perhaps he was at last persuaded that no other solution was possible or realistic. He may well have been prompted toward this realization by the IZL bombing of the King David Hotel in Jerusalem, in which some 80 British officers and officials, and Arab and Jewish officials, were killed, on 22 July.

But probably the most important reason for his *volte face* was Abdullah's own abrupt switch in favour of partition over July-August 1946, as expressed in his meetings with British and Jewish Agency officials at the time. (See below.) Whatever the case, Glubb finally penned a memorandum explicitly supporting partition as the only possible solution to the Palestine conundrum, entitled 'A Note on Partition as a Solution of the Palestine Problem'.[206] Curiously, it is probably the most explicitly anti-Semitic memorandum Glubb ever penned - perhaps in psychological compensation for the fact that the memorandum's message was 'pro-Jewish' (supportive of a Jewish state) and represented an admission of defeat for the Arab side.

Glubb defined this memorandum as the third of the series that began with 'Note on the Report of the AAC' and 'A Further Note on the Palestine Problem'. Those had been critical; this one, says Glubb, 'attempts to offer a positive solution.'

Part I is entitled: 'On the Impracticability of All Solutions Except Partition'. In Palestine, argued Glubb, 'it is the safety of the British Empire which is primarily at stake.' A solution 'wholly unfavourable' to the Arabs would bring the Russians into the Middle East:

> Sentimental enthusiasts for the oppressed Jews or the noble Arabs have not got the right picture.

> The sufferings (however much to be lamented) of a few hundred thousand Jews, cannot be weighed in the balance with the future of the British Commonwealth which numbers hundreds of millions.

Should the Russians come in, the result might be 'the premature collapse of the British Empire.'

But despite this ominous preamble, Glubb eventually plumps for partition. He acknowledges that

> any scheme for the partition of Palestine is fraught with difficulties. The reason why it is recommended is because no other scheme offers any possibility of success.
>
> The present writer, for reasons stated more fully in a previous memorandum, believes that Zionism will inevitably end in disaster for the Jews, should the present policy be continued. ... Fifty years hence, the Arab bloc may have a population of 100 millions ... [and] may take its seat with the Great Powers. How is a bitterly hostile and narrow Zionism to maintain its bridgehead on the beaches of Asia in the face of such a growing power?

But in the short term, there was no alternative to partition, however pessimistic the long-term prognosis. The alternative of allowing in more and more Jewish immigrants would ultimately result in a Jewish majority in Palestine, and the 'repression' and 'liquidation' of the Arab minority. The White Paper policy, which had offered 'the best chance the Jews had of survival,' had failed because it was 'long-sighted and none of the protagonists in this struggle are capable of looking ahead.' Continuing the White Paper policy was out of the question.

The alternative of a binational state 'cannot succeed' because of mutual hatred and because neither party was willing to live as a minority in a country governed by a hated, rival majority.

> Every year a narrower and more virulent form of hatred is being injected into the young generation of both races. This applies more to the Jews than the Arabs. Not because the Arabs have any moral scruples at breeding hate, but because they are less efficient at it. Young Jews and Jewesses are educated in Jewish schools [where] ... they employ the Nazi technique for breeding hate in children. The young Jew is as hard, as narrow, as fanatical, and as bitter as the Hitler youth on whom he is modelled...

What Glubb called 'the Jewish mentality' was compounded of two elements – 'the ancient Hebrew tradition' and 'modern East European culture.' Josephus 'shows the Jews [of antiquity] as full of narrow hate and fanaticism as [the Jews of] today.' On to this 'unreasoning Jewish fanaticism' has been 'super-imposed ... a layer of up-to-date Eastern European fanaticism. The characteristics of the Nazi technique have been copied - the theories of race, blood and soil, the terrorism of the gunman, the inculcation of hate into the young, and the youth movements.'

Gentile Britons, used to liberal English Jews, do not realize that a different sort of Jew had emerged in Palestine, argued Glubb. 'Perhaps some of the old Liberal Jews still survive in Great Britain. In Palestine they have been supplanted by the younger generation of totalitarian Nazi Jews' - and these fanatics were daily gaining ground. 'Modern Zionism [was] a compound of ancient Judaism and Nazi-ism,' he argued - and, like the Nazis, they too may 'commit [collective] suicide.' But they might mortally injure the British Empire in the process.

In short, talk of a bi-national state in Palestine 'is twaddle. A bi-national Germano-Jewish state in Prussia would be equally feasible,' concluded Glubb.

Glubb brushed aside economic objections to the partition of so small a country between two states. The Arab part would in any event be united with Transjordan and the Jewish state, if at peace with its neighbours, would be economically viable.

Glubb enumerated the advantages of partition. For one thing, it would result in the curbing of Jewish immigration, as the Jews would not want to over-crowd their state. For another, it would put to rest a conflict that could only otherwise result in the destruction of the Jews. In the absence of an agreed settlement, meaning through partition, 'in the end, the Jews will be exterminated ... perhaps 50, perhaps 100, perhaps 200 years hence, just as they have recently been rooted out of Germany. Partition may thus, in the long run, be the only hope of Jewish survival in Palestine...'

What would be the contours of the partition? 'The Coastal Plain and the Plain of Esdraelon [Jezreel Valley] east to the Sea of Tiberias, will be Jewish; the Nablus area, Hebron, Gaza, and Beersheba will be Arab, and will be united to Transjordan.' But this would still leave a number of problems: (1) the Safad-Acre area; (2) Jaffa; (3) The Holy Places and Haifa.

The largely Arab-inhabited Acre-Safad area (i.e., northern Galilee) could be surrendered to Lebanon; or annexed to Transjordan with a right of transit through Jewish territory, suggested Glubb. And were Transjordan and Syria to become one country 'again' - as Abdullah wanted and as, Glubb argued, was 'more than probable' - then this area would adjoin Syria.

Jaffa, with some 70-80,000 Arabs and surrounded by Jewish settlements, presented a more serious problem. Glubb was uncertain how to resolve it. One possibility was to give Jaffa autonomy inside the Jewish state. Another was continued British rule. A third possibility was to transfer 'the people of Jaffa somewhere else' over a ten-fifteen year period.

Glubb proposed a continued British garrison - with the status of a 'crown colony' - at Rafah on the Gaza-Egypt border, with a '999-year lease.' Haifa, too, should remain in British hands. For Jerusalem Glubb suggested an international or interdenominational administration, with a British high commissioner but 'with no [concealed] imperial objectives.'

Reverting to the Peel Commission recommendations of 1937, Glubb at this point more or less explicitly advocated a massive transfer of Arabs out of the territory of the Jewish state-to-be. Without such a transfer, he implied, partition would solve nothing. 'All that has gone before,' he wrote, 'is ... comparatively easy. The really difficult problem is that of the Arabs left behind in the Jewish state.' The Jews will 'inevitably wish to get rid of their Arab minority as quickly as possible' - to make room for Jewish immigrants. There would also be the problem of the (small number of) Jews left in the territory of the Arab state:

> The best course will probably be to allow a time limit during which persons who find themselves in one or other state against their wishes, will be able to opt for citizenship of the other state. There seems to be little doubt that virtually all of both minorities would opt for the citizenship of the other state. Some might, of course, opt for citizenship ... without desiring to move into and reside in it. The great majority, however, would probably wish to move ... A small proportion of the minorities could move by direct exchange.... But when all such exchanges were over, a large balance of Arabs would be left in the Jewish state. The Jews would want to get rid of them, and would soon find means of making the Arabs wish to move. This, in the writer's opinion, would be the most dangerous aspect of the whole problem.

The Arabs would claim to be maltreated - and appeal to the Arab states 'to save them. A typical "Sudetenland" situation might be created. To avoid this, it would be absolutely essential, before embarking on the scheme, to have plans ready for disposing of the Arab minority.' Glubb estimated that there might be as many as 500,000 Arabs who might have to move. He suggested finding work for the bread-winners among them in public works schemes in the Arab state. 'It is not of course intended to move Arab displaced persons by force, but merely so to arrange that when these persons find themselves left behind in the Jewish state, well paid jobs and good prospects should be simultaneously open for them in the Arab state.'

Glubb envisaged the act of partition as a five-year enterprise, 'with two more years [needed] finally to clear up the details.' By then, the powers - the United States and the Soviet Union - will have been persuaded of its value, and jobs will have been created to absorb the Arabs who had moved. Jewish persecution of the Arabs who might remain behind was a potential powder keg. But the Jews might refrain, out of fear of negative international publicity and reaction. 'By the summer of 1953,' Glubb concluded, 'the Palestine problem should have been finally settled, to the mutual satisfaction of all concerned.'[207]

A month or so later, Glubb followed up this proposal with a further memorandum, entitled 'A Further Note on Partition as a Solution of the Palestine Question', refining some of the original provisions. (One British official, 'J.M.M.', minuted: 'It is in Brigadier Glubb's usual tiresomely long-winded and repetitive style, but it is interesting to see that this officer ... is in favour of partition ...')[208] 'In July 1946,' he wrote, 'I ventured to submit a memorandum in which I advocated partition as the only final solution for the Palestine problem. Nothing which has happened since has caused me to modify this opinion.' In the new memorandum he stressed the integration of the Arab parts of Palestine into Transjordan.

The depiction of the Arabs as fanatics out to murder the Jews for the fun of it is erroneous, he said. 'They are all afraid ... the chief motive of the Arabs is fear ...' But Arab fears of a Jewish state 'seem to be exaggerated,' he reasoned. They fear that the Jews,

> with the vast sums of money at their disposal, would build up an army equipped with the latest aircraft and armoured vehicles, and would then bully, or even declare war on, the neighbouring Arab states. I have pointed out ... that there are not yet a million Jews in Palestine ... and there are about 25 or 30 million Arabs (excluding Egypt). But they reply that with modern chemical warfare, atomic bombs, armour and aircraft, numbers do not count ...
>
> A few more sophisticated people fear that the Jews would fill their part of Palestine to overflowing and then agitate in America for a revision of the frontier. This fear is more reasonable and is more difficult to allay ... It is also feared, and with even more reason, that a Jewish state might ally itself to ... Russia ...

(It is worth noting, perhaps, that, from today's perspective, two out of three of these Arab 'fears,' with certain variations, proved to be realistic.)

Glubb explained his rejection of a straight partition of Palestine into two states, one Jewish and the other Palestinian Arab, by arguing that the Palestinian Arab state would be economically unviable and that it would be controlled by 'extremists,' that is, Husseini and his followers:

> The fact that the Mufti and his supporters have been extremists and supported the rebellion of 1936-1939 would not necessarily render them unfit to lead the new Arab Palestine State. But the experience of the last six months seems to show that the Husseinis, like the Bourbons, have learnt nothing and forgotten nothing in the past 10 years. Scarcely are they back from exile then they begin once more to urge the rejection of every scheme put forward, the boycotting of every conference and the organisation of secret para-military societies to prepare for rebellion. They continue to proclaim that Palestine is a purely Arab country and will always remain so, regardless of the facts of the situation. Moreover, we must not forget that the Mufti spent most of the war in Berlin.

If the Mufti gained control of a Palestine Arab state, 'there can be little doubt that a Nazi despotism would result, anyone not approved of by the Mufti being either eliminated or put in a concentration camp...' Moreover, the Palestine Arabs were inexperienced in self-government 'and their state would probably collapse.'

On the other hand, a fusion of Arab Palestine with Transjordan would create an economically sounder entity, Abdullah had always proven 'unwaveringly pro-British,' and Arab Palestine would remain available to accommodate British bases.

The map which Glubb appended to this memorandum showed a Jewish state smaller than that provided for in the Peel Commission recommendations, consisting of an arc including some of the northern Jordan Valley, the Jezreel Valley, and the Coastal Plain from a point just south of Haifa through Tel Aviv. On the fringes of the Jewish area would be wide 'frontier belts' of as yet undefined sovereignty. The Haifa and Jerusalem areas would remain in British hands, with large British garrisons. The rest of the country was to remain Arab and be incorporated in Transjordan.

Glubb was not unaware of the problems and pitfalls entailed by this scheme. The Jews, filling their state up with immigrants, might well demand more land: 'They could then claim that the situation could only be calmed by the grant of more *lebensraum* to the Jews.' The Jews might seek alliance with the Soviets - but this could be prevented by a pre-emptive Anglo-Jewish treaty. The Syrians would certainly oppose partition.

Glubb thought that surprise and speed of implementation would be crucial to the success of the scheme. The Arab areas should be placed under Transjordanian - meaning Arab Legion - control within 48 hours of the announcement of the scheme; and the Jewish-designated areas handed over to Jewish control with the same speed. 'The vast majority of the [Arab] people of Palestine are sheep, who will follow any determined lead ... With a firm lead of this nature, 80 per cent of the Palestinians could probably swing over to partition.' In the context of this quick, quiet takeover, the British would have to shift units of the Legion into Palestine on the sly, and the Transjordanians would need to organize, before their arrival, 'spontaneous' demonstrations of enthusiasm in the Arab towns. (This last proposal prefigured some of Glubb's efforts in the months before May 1948.)

Implicit in Glubb's scheme is the idea of forcibly transferring the Arab inhabitants of the Jewish-designated areas to Arab-designated areas or out of the country altogether (as is the transfer of the far smaller number of Jews out of the Arab-designated areas to the Jewish area). At one point in the memorandum Glubb writes of Arabs 'who may wish to migrate from the Jewish state...' But at another he writes, more emphatically:

> When the undoubtedly Arab and undoubtedly Jewish areas had been cleared of all members of the other community, work would begin on deciding the actual frontier ... The two races are in places considerably mixed up in the frontier belt, and as the frontier was settled mile by mile, every effort would be made to arrange exchanges of land and population so as to leave as few people as possible to be compensated for cash. This would be the most delicate part of the operation ... [But] it would have to be worked through steadily.

As to the thorny problem of Jerusalem, Glubb proposed a municipality 'administered by a British commissioner and staff, assisted by an elected city council of Jews and Arabs,' with a mixed municipal police force and a brigade of British troops, eventually to be reduced to a battalion. (In his previous, July memorandum, Glubb had proposed that Jerusalem be 'a religious enclave, administered by an international or, rather, inter-religious body...')[209]

Glubb followed up this memorandum with another, in January 1947, entitled 'A Note on the Exact Siting of the Frontier in the Event of the Adoption of Partition', yet again refining his partition scheme. He wrote that partition, with the 'incorporation of the Arab State in Trans-Jordan ... is the only solution which directly effects the Arab Legion and myself.' Hence, he was writing about it. 'The object of this note is to consider the possibility of implementing a frontier more favourable to the Jews than that envisaged in my previous memoranda.'

Glubb reiterated his previous provisions: That Jerusalem remain garrisoned by British troops, with a tri-religious municipality; that Haifa remain a British base; that Jaffa be retained by the Arab state; and that the Acre, Nazareth, and Safad sub-districts form part of the Arab state. Otherwise, the frontier between Jews and Arabs 'very nearly demarcates itself,' according to existing clusters of settlements. 'The remaining outstanding problem would be that of dealing with the considerable areas of Arab land left well within the Jews state. I have already suggested that these Arab owners would have to be bought out and settled elsewhere...' The Jews would thus 'receive an immense increase of land by the migration of the Arabs whose land is now behind the front lines.' But the Jews, and their supporters, may wish to give the Jews even more land. 'To do this it would be necessary to take an area of "virgin" Arab land - not yet penetrated by Jews in any considerable numbers - evict its Arab inhabitants and hand it over to the Jews. It is the feasibility of an operation of this nature which is considered in this paper.'

Whatever solution Britain announces, it is imperative that, this time, it enforce it, and as a final settlement, thought Glubb. 'I believe that ... we could enforce a [partition] frontier based approximately on the existing front line [of Jewish and Arab settlement]. I doubt whether we have the physical power to enforce a frontier which would give the Jews an added area of land, beyond the present [demographic] front line.' What Glubb envisaged was partition between the Jews and Trans-Jordan. But if the plan gave the Jews too large a slice of Palestine, Jordan would be unable to support it against the outrage of the rest of the Arab world:

> Common prudence would seem to dictate that before announcing a scheme to which the cooperation of the Transjordan Government was essential, the agreement of that Government should be obtained. If this were impossible for reasons of secrecy, the scheme must obviously be such that the cooperation of the Transjordan Government was a foregone conclusion ... It is absolutely essential that the partition proposals should be able to command a measure of [outside] Arab support.

> The proposal for partition put forward in previous memoranda did not involve the forcible transfer of any of the population. If the boundary be drawn on the basis of the "existing front line", members of either side who find themselves residing on the wrong side of the boundary will be given the chance to opt for the other state. Should they do so, then the boundary commission will give them land or premises in exchange in the other state, or cash compensation, or will use any other method for facilitating the move for which they have opted. Apart from this, however HMG or British troops will not be concerned with moving anybody - certainly not their forcible eviction from their homes.
>
> If, however, some area now supporting a solely Arab population - and on the Arab side of the front line - is to be allotted to the Jewish state, an entirely different state of affairs will arise. ... The inhabitants will refuse to recognize the validity of the decision, and will refuse to recognize the jurisdiction of the Jewish Government over them. ... They will also of course refuse to abandon their homes and migrate. A complete deadlock will therefore be reached.
>
> It is inconceivable that British troops be used to evict them from their homes. Such things can be done by Germans or Russians but there is no use in our attempting to use frightfulness. British troops are not capable of being frightful enough, and to be a little bit rough is fatal. It merely rouses resentment and fanaticism, without inspiring terror.
>
> To attempt forcibly to transfer large blocks of Arabs by using Jewish troops would lead to civil war, and troops of the Arab states would refuse to do it. The inevitable conclusion therefore seems to be that large blocks of population cannot be moved, and hence that the only frontier which can in practice be implemented is one running approximately along the existing [demographic] front line ... [But isolated communities] will probably opt to move, if not at once, at least in a year or two.

Jaffa, an Arab enclave in a Jewish-majority area, remained a problem. 'To move the inhabitants of Jaffa by force would obviously be impossible [and] ... if ... left behind in the Jewish state ... street fighting would inevitably result,' drawing in external forces. Hence, there was no recourse but to leave it in the Arab state. Glubb recommended establishing a corridor along the Jaffa-Ramle road linking Jaffa to the Arab-populated hill areas of Judea:

> In my previous memoranda, I have never [sic] referred to the possibility of giving a part of the Southern Desert [i.e., the Negev] ... to the Jews. Such a proposal seemed to me altogether too fanciful. But as I see in the press that the Jews are still referring to it, it may be advisable to discuss it. I do not know why the Jews demand this area. Perhaps they have knowledge of some mineral wealth there,

> but this seems unlikely. The statement that this desert is agriculturally valuable (or could be made so) is almost certainly false, and conceals some other motive, probably of a political or strategic nature.

Perhaps a corridor through the Arab areas could be established to the area south of Beersheba. But this would lead to trouble:

> With Jews constantly coming and going across Southern Palestine, they would inevitably try and get in touch with Arabs on the way, lend them money, embark on shady business transactions, and generally throw a spanner in the works ... It is sincerely to be hoped therefore, that HMG will not entertain the idea of an isolated piece of Jewish State in the [Negev] desert.[210]

Glubb's exact definition of the future partition frontiers, and insistence that they must conform to existing front lines of demography and settlement, may have been sparked by a report by his deputy, Col. Norman Lash, who had visited Harold Beeley - director of the Foreign Office's Near East Department - in London. Beeley, according to Glubb, had told Lash that 'it looked as if partition might be the solution but "the frontier would be much more unfavourable to the Arabs than anything I seemed to have dreamed of in my [that is, Glubb's] memoranda".' 'This seems rather alarming,' wrote Glubb.[211] Beeley remained unenthusiastic about partition. In December 1946 Glubb wrote him that the share-out of Palestine between a Jewish state and Transjordan was the 'ideal solution.'[212] Beeley minuted on one of Glubb's partition proposals: 'Although there is much force in these arguments, I do not find them so convincing as the arguments against partition. The difficulties which Brigadier Glubb so rightly fears would have to be faced ... by the British High Commissioner, supported by British forces during the period of transition.'[213] And on 1 February 1947, he wrote Glubb, responding to the January memorandum:

> One idea which has occurred to me ...is that the absorption of the Arab parts of Palestine into the state of Transjordan might represent a danger rather than an advantage for King Abdullah. Is it not likely that the tail would wag the dog and that the Mufti (whether physically in Jerusalem or in Cairo) would prove to be the more powerful of the two?[214]

UN Partition Plan, November 1947

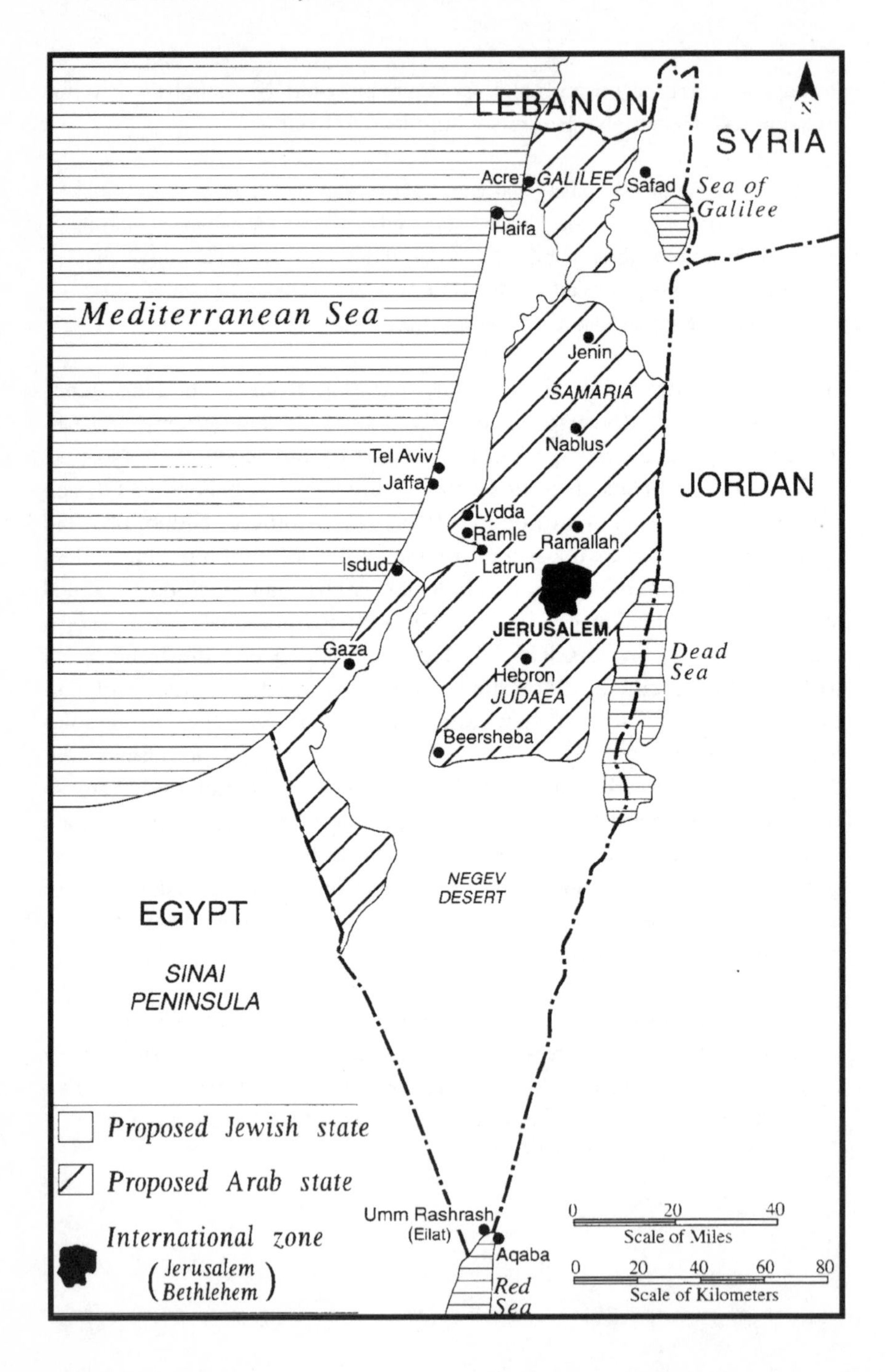

Chapter 4

THE ROAD TO JERUSALEM

1947-1948: Countdown to an Invasion

'The Transjordan Government was suddenly thunder struck by the announcement [in February 1947] of the intended British withdrawal from Palestine,' wrote Glubb in November, just after the United Nations Special Committee on Palestine (UNSCOP), had recommended that Palestine be divided into two independent states, one Jewish, the other Palestinian Arab, and before the United Nations General Assembly had voted to accept the recommendation, on 29 November.[215]

As already suggested, Glubb was aware, probably from its inception in mid-1946, of the Yishuv-Hashemite agreement to divide Palestine between themselves, while denying the Palestinian Arabs sovereignty over any part of the country. Ben-Gurion had outlined his plan for partitioning Palestine between a Jewish state - which he called 'Judea' - and a Transjordanian-Palestinian state - which he called 'Abdulliya' - in a secret memorandum written in mid-July 1946.[216] King Abdullah was already thinking along the same lines. On 29 July 1946 Kirkbride reported that Abdullah - previously a mere 'emir' or prince, he had proclaimed himself 'King' on 25 May – had:

> assumed from the outset that the result of the [planned] discussions [between Jewish and Arab representatives in London] would be partition and that the Arab portion of Palestine would be united with Transjordan ... [But] he anticipates that the other Arab states may press for the creation of an Arab state covering the whole of Palestine because they have committed themselves completely on that point in the past ... He is for partition and he feels that the other Arab leaders may acquiesce in that solution although they may not approve of it openly ... [Kirkbride added that Jordanian Prime Minister Ibrahim Pasha Hashim had told him that] the only just and permanent solution lay in absolute partition with an exchange of populations; to leave Jews in an Arab state or Arabs in a Jewish state would lead inevitably to further trouble between the two peoples. Ibrahim Pasha admitted that he would not be able to express this idea in public for fear of being called a traitor... [He] said that the other Arab representatives at the discussions

> would be divided into people like himself who did not dare to express their true views and extremists who simply demanded the impossible.[217]

On 12 August Abdullah set the Jewish-Hashemite partition ball in motion. He invited Jewish Agency Political Department official Eliahu (Elias) Sasson to his palace at Shuneh, in the Jordan Valley, and presented his plan. The king said that he 'preferred partition [of Palestine with the Jews] and the cooption of the Arab part into Transjordan' to the then British-proposed Morrison-Grady federal solution with separate communal cantons. Abdullah swore Sasson to secrecy and added that 'he wished to expand the borders of Transjordan and to create one large and strong Hashemite kingdom, which would be aligned with Britain and Turkey and would hold the English defence line in the [Middle] East.' He regarded the absorption of 'the Arab part' of Palestine into Transjordan as only a stage in his long-desired cooption of Syria and federation with Iraq. The Jewish part of Palestine would or could then join the federation; Lebanon could either join or not, as it saw fit. He realized that the Arabs of Palestine did not accept his federal plan. Abdullah refrained from talking about the establishment of a Jewish 'state' and spoke merely of a 'Jewish part' of Palestine.

Britain, said Abdullah (responding to a question by Sasson), knew of the plan and (he implied) supported it but thought that it should not be discussed until after the Palestine problem was resolved on the basis of a federal (i.e., Transjordanian-Iraqi-Syrian) solution. The British were wary of re-igniting old Hashemite-Saudi or Hashemite-Egyptian rivalries. Abdullah then backtracked a little and said that if the British insisted on Morrison-Grady, he would agree to it. But he added that if the Jews could persuade Britain and the United States to support partition, he would do likewise.

Abdullah also said that the British had asked that he use the opportunity of the meeting (with Sasson) to try to persuade the Jewish Agency to curb the then raging anti-British terrorism by the Jewish dissident organisations in Palestine; to participate in the proposed trilateral talks in London about the 'Morrison-Grady Plan'; and to refrain from intriguing against Britain in the United States. As for himself, Abdullah asked that Sasson bring him P£10,000 (as a first instalment of a required P£35-40,000) to be used to influence the impending Syrian parliamentary elections in a pro-Hashemite direction and to establish a pro-Hashemite lobby or 'representation' in Palestine.[218]

As arranged, Sasson and Abdullah met again on 19 August. Sasson was to bring the requested P£10,000 and the Jewish Agency's answer to the partition proposal. Sasson arrived bearing only P£5,000, a 'sweetening' (in Sasson's phrase) with which Abdullah was not at all pleased. It was wholly insufficient to meet his immediate needs, he said, and demanded further sums. Abdullah then gave Sasson back P£1,000 of the 'sweetening' asking him to give it to one of his emissaries in Palestine, who was busy mustering support among local notables for the Transjordanian 'partition and federation' plan. But Abdullah declined to go into detail about the prospective partition boundaries, saying only that he would not be 'obstinate.' When Sasson insisted, Abdullah reproved him: 'Do not be egotistical, don't demand only what is good for you. Look at matters within the context of the whole Arab east and its complications, and not only at the Palestine context.' Abdullah agreed to Sasson's suggestion that the matter be covertly discussed by the representatives of the two sides at the forthcoming London talks. Abdullah advised the Jewish Agency to oppose any plan other than 'partition and federation.' This would leave Britain no choice but to accept the plan.[219]

The British Resident in Amman, Kirkbride, informed the High Commissioner in Palestine, who informed the Colonial Secretary, of the contacts between Abdullah and the Jewish Agency, and of Abdullah's stand:

> King Abdullah and Prime Minister of Jordan [Hashim] both consider that partition followed by an exchange of populations [meaning, as all understood, essentially a transfer of Arabs out of the areas of the Jewish state-to-be] is only practical solution to the Palestine problem. They do not feel able to express this view publicly because having regard to the possibility of the Arab area of Palestine being joined to Transjordan they would be regarded as prejudiced. Prime Minister went further and said that if partition was discussed in London any question of the union of the Arab area with Transjordan should be avoided as Saudi Arabia and Syria might turn against the scheme merely in order to prevent Hashemite expansion.[220]

In effect, an in-principle Hashemite-Jewish Agency agreement to partition Palestine between them had been reached. But the regional and international situation were not yet propitious to begin to plan implementation. More than a year was to pass before conditions matured. During 1947 Abdullah blew hot and cold, bending before successive regional and international gusts of wind, sending different signals to different audiences (as was his wont). In July, Abdullah privately told Judge Emil Sandstrom, the chairman of UNSCOP, that partition was the only solution. But in formal session, he testified before UNSCOP that he was opposed to partition - while Kirkbride's deputy, Christopher Pirie-Gordon, assured Bevin that that these were not Abdullah's 'real views' and that he was still interested in taking over 'the Arab areas of Palestine' (that is, he still supported partition).[221] Indeed, Abdullah at this time apparently sent word to Sasson that he was 'ready to sign an agreement on the partition of Palestine - [involving] the establishment in part of the country of a Jewish state and the annexation of the rest by Transjordan.'[222] Yet all the while Abdullah, through Jordan's state-controlled newspapers, and to the acclaim of other Arab leaders, indirectly denounced 'Zionist intrigues' (while privately reassuring Jewish Agency representatives that he would cleave to the agreement of summer 1946).[223]

As 1947 drew to a close and the prospects of a British pullout and Jewish statehood in Palestine became ever more concrete, Glubb - writing in November - became acutely alarmed (in view of the impending UN resolution supporting a Jewish-Palestinian partition) and began almost openly to lobby for a coordinated implementation of the (alternative) Abdullah-Jewish Agency partition plan.

During the previous 16 years, 'Jordan was... one of the happiest little countries in the world ... With the rest of the world in agony, with the neighbouring Arab countries in constant upheaval, in Transjordan nothing could go wrong.'[224] Then the Palestine crisis intruded. As seen from Amman, Britain's February 1947 decision to quit Palestine 'spelt the ruin of Transjordan,' wrote Glubb. 'By settling [the problem of] Palestine, we have reopened the problem of Transjordan.' Until then, two things had 'kept Transjordan alive: An annual Grant in Aid [i.e., subsidy] from Britain;' and the British occupation of Palestine, through whose railway system and ports Transjordan maintained its links with the world (and with its British protector). 'Transjordan is by nature the hinterland of Palestine, and can only live as such ... All her commerce, imports, exports - her very lifeblood - must come in through Haifa or Beirut, over roads and railways controlled by the [prospective] Jewish and Arab states in Palestine, or the Lebanon and Syria [no friends of Transjordan] on [sic] the north.' Moreover, the adoption of the UNSCOP report by the United Nations General Assembly would mean a 'doubling' of Transjordan's enemies. 'She had previously been unfriendly with Syria and Saudi Arabia. Now a Jewish state was to be added on the west, and possibly also an Arab Palestine state, under the Mufti, who would also be hostile to King Abdullah.'

Moreover, Glubb feared Jewish designs on Transjordan itself: 'The leaders of the Jewish Agency do not even today hesitate to state publicly that they consider Transjordan to be part of the Jewish National

Home.'[225] Glubb feared that, to one degree or another, most of Transjordan's neighbours - the Yishuv, Syria, the Saudis and the Palestine Arabs - were intent on partitioning Transjordan between themselves. And the mutual defence pact with Britain might not be sufficient to deter them. One or any combination of these countries, while refraining from declaring war, could launch crippling guerrilla operations or economic sanctions against Amman.

Glubb was certain that in 1948, the Jews would declare their state and 'the disposal of the Arab portions of Palestine may lead to an acute struggle.' The 'Egyptian-Syrian-Saudi League' was 'determined to snatch Arab Palestine.' If the Syrians managed to take the north and the Egyptians the south, Transjordan could scarcely survive. 'The one and only ... solution for Great Britain and Transjordan would be the annexation of the southern Arab part of Palestine to Transjordan ... Britain would thus be able to keep her troops in Palestine,' he wrote.

Glubb proposed that a Transjordanian delegation set out immediately for London to negotiate a continued British subsidy, at present levels. A reduction of the subsidy would mean a crippling of the Arab Legion - and 'Transjordan will [then] cease to exist.' He probably also hoped that during the visit Britain would officially endorse the proposed Transjordanian take-over of the Arab parts of Palestine (including, it would seem, the Negev). But this would have to be done by the Legion - and Britain had announced that it intended to reduce the size of the Legion when it left Palestine.[226]

Since burying the Peel recommendations in 1938, Britain had consistently opposed a partition solution (meaning the establishment of a Jewish state in part of Palestine): Partition was anathema to the Arabs, and British support of partition, it was feared, would alienate the Arab world. But during the second half of 1947, with UNSCOP as background, partition became more and more likely. Without doubt Glubb's (and Abdullah's) lobbying had had a hand, however minor, in beginning to 'turn' Whitehall around.

On 27 August 1947, just before UNSCOP had submitted its report supporting partition, Pirie-Gordon, then acting British minister in Amman, cabled London in support of Transjordanian occupation of the Arab areas of a partitioned Palestine. Like Glubb, he feared that Transjordan was in danger of disappearance - by being gobbled up by one of its larger neighbours:

> A seemingly absolute safeguard against this contingency would be possible if in the event of Partition, the Arab areas of Palestine could in fact be attached to

> Transjordan. The advantages to Transjordan of such an arrangement are obvious, and in as much as it would immensely strengthen the value of [Britain's] Hashemite Alliance and produce a far greater chance of permanency for the Transjordan state without Greater Syria, it would fully meet the requirements of the [British] Chiefs of Staff. The difficulty would of course be overcoming the initial protests of the nationalist politicians in Palestine itself, but I am certain the long-term benefits would more than justify any inconveniences at the start.[227]

By mid-October thinking about a Transjordanian takeover of Arab Palestine had substantially crystallized in the Jordanian capital, but whether it was primarily a matter of Abdullah influencing the local British officials (Kirkbride, Pirie-Gordon, Glubb) or whether they had persuaded Abdullah and his more hesitant aides that the idea was now realistic is impossible to tell. Most likely both sides influenced each other. Be that as it may, in October Kirkbride informed the Foreign Office of a series of talks he had held with Jordan's new Prime Minister (February 1947-December 1947), Samir Rifa`i, who had just returned from an Arab League meeting in Aley, Lebanon. Rifa`i took for granted that Arab armies would at some point have to go in 'to protect the Arab areas of Palestine.' 'It was generally agreed,' said the prime minister, according to Kirkbride, 'that as the armies of Transjordan and Iraq would have to bear the brunt of the fighting, it was only fair that all Palestine should be united to Transjordan if it could be saved.' Kirkbride commented that he did not think the other Arab states, with possibly Lebanon and Iraq excepted:

> would be in favour of the union of Transjordan and Arab Palestine under Abdullah ... My personal conclusion is that King Abdullah would acquiesce to [sic] the formation of a Jewish state in Palestine providing he was certain that the Arab residue came to Transjordan. He does not share the optimism of the others about the ultimate military defeat of the Jews ... [and Rifa`i's] talk of taking over the Jewish area of Palestine with Iraqi assistance must not ... be taken too seriously. In this matter he is not in agreement with his master...[228]

Kirkbride and Glubb did not take pains to hide their views (even though what they were proposing ran counter to UNSCOP's - and subsequently - the United Nations General Assembly proposal to partition Palestine between its Jews and Arabs). Kirkbride that month told two visiting British journalists that Abdullah's ambitions were 'boundless, and quite clearly he would like to rule Nablus and Hebron.' Kirkbride added that 'in his own view it was the logical solution' to the Palestine problem. Of course, all the Arab states were watching each other 'like cats and dogs ... fearful lest one should beat the other to it.'

Glubb also told the journalists:

> a move by Abdullah [into Arab Palestine was] "the obvious thing" ... [but] he was afraid Abdullah might move too quickly ... Both Glubb and Kirkbride discounted any large scale move by [other] Arab armies, and thought the Arabs, after working themselves up, would eventually send [only] arms, money and volunteers to Palestine ... [Kirkbride] did not rule out a move by Abdullah which could be timed to prevent any chaos and minimize strife in Palestine ... Glubb thought it [i.e., Palestine] might have to be allowed to simmer for a while, until Jew and Arab were being worn out, whereupon British intervention via Abdullah would be welcomed. "By that time the Jews might be reasonable and give up Jaffa and the Negev. Western Galilee could go to Lebanon and Syria",

The journalists quoted Glubb as adding: 'The Jews want to pinch the Negev because it's got minerals. So they have put in some settlers. But it's the mineral[s] which they really want, do not forget the oil at Gaza too.' Glubb, they said, opined that 'the Arabs will probably lose the first battles ... but will carry on guerrilla warfare.'

The journalists concluded:

> From the talks with Kirkbride, Glubb and Samir [Rifa'i] Pasha, I [i.e., we] deduce that the Transjordanians have annexation of Arab Palestine in mind, quite definitely ... Abdullah himself is probably thinking of moving in smartly the moment the British withdraw, because he is afraid the Syrians might beat him to it.[229]

It was probably at least partly in response to Kirkbride's cables that Foreign Secretary Bevin began mulling over the idea. On 26 October 1947 he cabled Kirkbride that he was 'considerably preoccupied with the question of the possible participation by the Arab Legion in Palestine after our withdrawal.' The Legion would have to be withdrawn from Palestine with the British evacuation. But 'if at a later stage King Abdullah were to try to send units of the Legion back into Palestine,' Britain would have to pull out the British officers seconded to the Legion and 'consider' stopping the subsidy to Transjordan. Bevin asked for Kirkbride's comments.[230]

Kirkbride replied that 'King Abdullah may act, possibly independently of other Arab States, to forestall the Mufti if we leave a vacuum in Palestine.' Kirkbride argued vigorously against a British cessation of the subsidy to the Legion: 'It would not appear that the subsidy could be withheld because Transjordan sent the Arab Legion back into Palestine after our withdrawal.' He granted that Britain might be forced to withdraw its officers but this, he argued, 'would not immobilise that force as there is an alternative source of supply of Arabs [i.e., Iraqi Army officers] and some British personnel are employed direct by the Transjordan Government.' Kirkbride was set against Iraqis arriving to replace British officers - as the Legion, he feared, would then fall under 'the control of the Iraqi Army and quite outside our influence.' In short, the Minister opposed the withdrawal of the British Legion officers.

Kirkbride was quite firm in his conviction:

> which I have been at pains to conceal from the King and Samir [Rifa`i] ... that strategically and economically Transjordan has the best claim to inherit the residue of Palestine and that the occupation of the Arab areas by Transjordan would lessen the chances of armed conflict between a Jewish state and the other Arab states, in particular Iraq which I hold to be the most dangerous ... King Abdullah would be prepared to acquiesce in the formation of a Jewish state provided Transjordan obtained the rest of Palestine [but] I see no signs of such an attitude of mind on the part of other Arab leaders. A greater Transjordan would not be against our interests, it might be in their favour ... so I see no reason why we should place obstacles in the way of Transjordan. The alternative of a non-viable Palestine Arab state under the Mufti is not attractive.

Kirkbride added that while Abdullah would seek Britain's 'guidance' as to his future course, 'I realise of course that it is probably impossible for HMG to give him any.'[231] In other words, Kirkbride strongly supported a Jordanian occupation of the Arab parts of Palestine with the termination of the Mandate but was reluctant to impart his views to Abdullah or egg him on in this course; at the same time, partly in deference to expected opposition by other Arab countries to such a move, Kirkbride well understood Whitehall's inability to explicitly advise Abdullah to push into Palestine.

Kirkbride's views carried a great deal of weight in Whitehall, given his long service in the Middle East, his close relations with Abdullah, his unassailable knowledgeability about Transjordan (and Palestine), and his intelligence. In a minute to his cable of 29 October, B.A.B. Burrows, Beeley's successor as director of the Near Eastern Department, wrote:

> Would we favour a partition of Palestine [between the Jews and Abdullah?] ... There is a possibility that such an arrangement might come about through agree-

> ment between King Abdullah and the Jews, who we hear from top secret but unconfirmed sources are already in contact. The Chiefs of Staff have said that the incorporation of the Arab areas of Palestine into Transjordan would considerably increase the economic and strategic strength of Transjordan. This would be in our interest.[232]

Burrows was even firmer three weeks later, the day before the UN General Assembly passed the partition resolution:

> There seems to be a general consensus of opinion that both from the point of view of avoiding major bloodshed and from the point of view of our strategical and political interests, it would be extremely advantageous if Abdullah took control of the Arab areas of Palestine (possibly excluding Western Galilee) as we withdraw from them. There is some unconfirmed evidence that Abdullah has already been in touch with Jewish representatives and we have thought that there might be some advantage in previous agreement between him and the Jews. Sir A. Kirkbride argues convincingly against this [i.e., Abdullah making such a prior agreement]. If any such agreement became known, it would inevitably wreck the chances of a peaceful settlement on these lines.[233]

Bevin, in his response, in effect endorsed Kirkbride's views. The 'disadvantages' of the partition of Palestine between the Jews and Abdullah, according to the Foreign Secretary, were that (a) the influx of Jewish immigrants would presumably lead to expansionist urges which would 'sooner or later' cause friction between the Jewish state and 'the neighbouring Arab states,' meaning between Israel and Jordan, over the Jordanian-occupied Arab areas; (b) 'some if not all the Arab states would presumably be violently incensed against King Abdullah. This might however have the countervailing advantage of making him more dependent on us;' (c) 'we should be thought to have engineered the whole scheme and merely to have pretended to evacuate Palestine in order to secure our military requirements there [i.e., in the Jordanian-occupied Arab areas].'

But the 'disadvantage[s],' thought Bevin, were 'balanced' by Kirkbride's arguments and:

> by the probability that in virtue of the Anglo-Transjordan Treaty we should maintain our strategic facilities in a fairly large part of Palestine including presumably an outlet to the Mediterranean; also by the possibility that such a scheme would provide the only way of avoiding major bloodshed in Palestine on our with-

> drawal (on the assumption that King Abdullah would reach prior agreement with the Jews before entering Palestine).
>
> We must however clearly be extremely careful not to be associated with any such scheme at any rate to begin with as this would only increase the opposition of the Arab and Jewish extremists. We might perhaps be able to show guarded approval of the idea of an arrangement between King Abdullah and the Jews in connection with the warnings to be given to him about the Arab Legion on lines described above.

Bevin was referring to the possibility of the Legion becoming 'involved in hostilities in Palestine,' which would lead to world pressure on Britain to halt the subsidy to Transjordan and to remove the seconded British officers.

Bevin recommended that Abdullah be told that:

> if after the end of our civil administration in Palestine the Arab Legion returned there and became involved in hostilities we should be under very strong pressure to cease, while hostilities continued, all payment to Transjordan and to withdraw the British officers ... We should earnestly hope therefore that if he found it necessary to intervene ... he would do so in such a manner as not to become involved in hostilities.

Kirkbride was asked to comment on the content and timing of this proposed 'communication' to Abdullah, and whether Abdullah's 'Greater Syria ambition [which Whitehall was extremely wary about] would be increased or decreased if he obtained extension of his dominions in [i.e., to] Palestine.'[234]

Burrows' and Kirkbride's references to ongoing Hashemite-Yishuv contacts were not unfounded. Indeed, it is difficult to believe that Kirkbride (and Glubb) were not aware of their full purport and extent more or less in real time - though Kirkbride's reluctance to impart the full picture to Whitehall is understandable. All understood, as Burrows had pointed out, that any premature leak about a Hashemite-Yishuv agreement could blow it out of the water. Kirkbride may also have preferred keeping, for a time, certain information to himself. Without doubt, he was aware of the Yishuv-Hashemite contacts and in-principle agreement of July-August 1946. With the UN General Assembly on the verge of endorsing partition, Jordanian-Yishuv contacts matured into a refining, finalizing negotiation about the brass tacks. These culminated in the secret 17 November 1947 meeting between Golda Myerson (Meir), the acting director of the Jewish Agency Political Department, flanked by two aides, Sasson and Ezra Danin, and King Abdullah at Naharayim (Jisr al Majami) on the Jordan River.

Abdullah, reported Sasson, stated that he would 'not allow his forces to collide with us nor cooperate with any other force against us.' If he sent in the Arab Legion, it would 'concentrate [in the] Arab area with a view to prevent bloodshed[,] keep law order[,] forestall [the] Mufti. [He was] prepared [to] cooperate with us [on] this matter.' Abdullah was 'ready [to] sign [a written] agreement with us provided we agree [to] assist [to] attach Arab part [of Palestine] to Transjordan.' Meir replied that 'we prepared [to] give every assistance within frame UN charter.' As usual, according to Sasson, Abdullah asked for additional Jewish Agency funds.[235]

Sasson's above-quoted description of the meeting was a telegraphic abridgement of the proceedings - and essentially omitted the Jewish side of the conversation. Danin in a separate, three-page report was far more expansive. He noted Abdullah's surprise (not to say consternation or disappointment) at meeting a woman at the head of the Agency delegation (in Arabian-beduin custom the idea of a woman as a partner in political dialogue was inconceivable if not downright sacrilegious). After a short exchange about this, Abdullah said that he had told the Arab leaders that he was interested in peace, not war. He told Myerson and her aides that the Yishuv is strong 'and it is necessary to compromise with you. Between the Arabs and yourselves there is no conflict ... Any clash between us is detrimental to both of us. We spoke in the past about partition. I agree to a partition that will not embarrass me in the eyes of the Arab world, when I will have to defend it.' Abdullah meant that the Jewish entity that emerged must not be too large. Abdullah then proposed a 'Jewish republic' in part of Palestine existing 'within a Transjordanian state that will include both sides of the Jordan under my leadership, in which the economy, army and legislatures will be in common.' If the Jews agreed, their area could be enlarged. Meir responded that partition was now under discussion at the UN where 'we hoped it would be decided to set up two states, one Jewish and the other Arab, and that we wished to talk about an agreement on this basis.' Abdullah said that he 'understood' - reluctantly acknowledging that the Jews wanted a full-blown state rather than an autonomous 'republic' under Hashemite rule. Abdullah then cut to the quick and asked what the Yishuv's attitude would be 'to an attempt by him to take over the Arab part of [Palestine]?' The Jewish officials responded that it would be favourable, 'especially if you don't hamper us in establishing our state and don't bring about a clash between our forces and yours and particularly if this [i.e.,

Abdullah's] operation was accompanied by an announcement that the takeover was geared to achieving order and peace until the UN succeeded in establishing a government in that part [i.e., the Arab part of Palestine].' The implication seemed to be that a Palestinian Arab government would be set up after a temporary Transjordanian policing occupation – not exactly what Abdullah had in mind. Abdullah protested that he was interested in the Arab part of Palestine for himself, 'to join it to my state and I do not want to create a new Arab state that will hamper my plans...' Abdullah turned down the Jewish officials' suggestion that perhaps he should contemplate achieving such dominion through a referendum.

When the conversation turned to the idea of introducing an international force into Palestine, Abdullah proposed that it be limited to keeping the peace on the Palestine-Syria and Palestine-Lebanon borders, not on the Palestinian Arab-Jewish and Transjordan frontiers. Abdullah promised that he would not take part in any Arab 'plan' to attack the Jewish state. 'The situation and the circumstances do not justify and do not necessitate war but rather a compromise,' he said.

As to his proposed plans, Abdullah said that Britain's stand was 'not clear to him. No discussions had taken place in this matter, and he was at a loss to interpret their silence.' (True to his word, Kirkbride, up to this point, had not conveyed to the king his or HMG's support for the contemplated Jordanian takeover of Arab Palestine.) According to Danin, Abdullah, in contrast with previous meetings, appeared 'encouraged and forceful' and wanted to sign a written agreement and asked the Jewish official to prepare a draft. But the King added that more practical, detailed discussions would have to wait until after the UN General Assembly voted on the UNSCOP proposals.[236]

During the following months, Zionist officials were repeatedly to refer to the Jewish-Agency-Hashemite 'pact' negotiated and concluded on 17 November. Even as late as 13 May 1948, Yaakov Shimoni, a senior Agency Political Department official, was to refer to the Abdullah-Jewish Agency 'agreement' (*heskem*), albeit questioning whether it was still in effect.[237] And Golda Meir, in her report on her second meeting with Abdullah (that took place on 10 May 1948), said that the first meeting, of 17 November 1947, had been 'conducted on the basis that there existed between us an arrangement and an understanding [*sidur ve'havana*] regarding what he wanted and what we wanted and that our interests did not clash.' She said that she had told Abdullah that the Jews could not promise to help Abdullah's entry into Palestine as the Yishuv was bound by the (prospective) UN decision to establish two states in

Palestine. 'We said that we could not lend an active hand to violating this decision. If [nonetheless] he wanted to go ahead and confront the world and us with a *fait accompli* - the tradition of friendship between us would continue and we doubtless would find a common language about arranging [i.e., safeguarding] our joint interests.' Abdullah, she related, had promised that there would be no clash between his forces and the Yishuv's. Nevertheless, two points had irked her in that first meeting: (A) Abdullah's proposal that the Jews make do with less than full sovereignty, i.e., a 'republic' within an expanded Hashemite kingdom, and (B) that the emergent Jewish entity would be of a size that 'would not embarrass him' (i.e., implying that it should be smaller than what the UN General Assembly was about to allot to the Jews).[238]

But Danin's and Sasson's above-quoted contemporaneous descriptions of what had transpired on 17 November 1947 leave a somewhat more ambiguous impression than that conveyed by Golda Meir six months later. Abdullah, to be sure, had repeatedly and explicitly declared his interest in a Transjordanian takeover of the Arab parts of Palestine and committed himself to non-aggression against the Jewish areas and to non-participation in any aggressively-minded Arab coalition - but he had stopped short of explicitly agreeing to and recognizing a full-fledged Jewish 'state' in those areas. And the Yishuv's representatives had been even less forthcoming or more cagey: They had shied away from explicitly endorsing a Transjordanian military takeover of the Arab parts of Palestine, let alone permanent Transjordanian annexation. Indeed, when mentioning a possible Legion takeover, they had spoken explicitly of it being followed by the establishment of some other - implicitly Palestinian – government. Moreover, at one point the Agency delegates had suggested that perhaps not a military occupation but a plebiscite should be the route Transjordan should pursue in its bid to lay hold of these territories. It would appear that the Agency representatives were bent on leaving the future of the Arab areas - and of understandings about that future - as hazy as possible, perhaps in order to leave open the possibility of eventual Zionist occupation of some or all of them (or – less likely – to leave open the possibility of a last-minute Yishuv-Palestinian deal). War and territorial expansion were definitely in the air - perhaps in Zionist minds as much as in Abdullah's.

Be that as it may, while there were several exchanges of letters, no follow-up meeting took place between Abdullah and Zionist representatives in the weeks and months after the 29 November 1947 UN General Assembly Partition resolution - indeed, until the last-minute Meir-Abdullah meeting on 10 May 1948. Why such a meeting, previewed in the conversation of 17 November 1947, did not take place is not completely clear, though it probably owed much to the breathless pace and violence of the unfolding events in Palestine. In her briefing to the People's Administration on 12 May, Meir had related that during the interim, between 17 November 1947 and 10 May 1948, a go-between had proposed, in Abdullah's name, that the Yishuv give up some of the land allotted to it in the partition resolution - enabling Abdullah to argue in the Arab world that it was he who had extracted this additional territory on behalf of the Arabs. But the Jewish Agency, Meir related, had flatly rejected the idea, saying that 'an [internationally-sanctioned] border is a border' and should be respected by both sides. If, however, it came to war, 'then whoever had the strength would take what he could.'[239]

On 17 November 1947, the day of the first Abdullah-Meir meeting, Kirkbride sent off the following cable to London:

> I submit that prior formal agreement between King Abdullah and the Jews [on a share-out of Palestine] would be dangerous in that secrecy would be impossible. It would act as a focus for the anger of the other Arab states against the King and alienate Palestine Arabs. It might in any case be difficult to secure in the time available. For purposes of publicity (gps. undec.? justification for) Transjordan's intervention in Palestine should be to save the Arabs from possible Jewish aggression and to maintain order. There have been several indications in the Jewish press of late that the acquisition of Arab areas of Palestine by King Abdullah would not be unwelcome to the Jewish Agency. A formal agreement after Transjordan had taken over the Arab areas would be both possible and desirable in due course.[240]

Glubb's position was identical. In a 15-page memorandum penned in December 1947 he advocated 'the annexation of the southern Arab part of Palestine [i.e., presumably meaning at least Judea and the Negev] to Transjordan...' as 'the ideal solution,' in terms of British and Transjordanian interests.[241]

On 29 November 1947 the UN General Assembly, by a vote of 33 to 13, with 10 abstentions, endorsed the core of UNSCOP's partition recommendations and voted for the partition of Palestine into two states, one Jewish, the other Palestinian Arab. Jerusalem and Bethlehem and their immediate environs were to be under international control. The Arab Higher Committee, with the Arab states in its wake, rejected the resolution and announced that the Palestinians, assisted by the Arab states, would resist the emergence of the Jewish state. On 30 November, Arab gunmen ambushed Jewish buses east of Tel Aviv and sniped at Jewish passers-by from positions in Jaffa; anti-Jewish rioting in Jerusalem and a Husseini-ordered three-day general strike ensued. During the following weeks and months, the violence spread throughout the country: Arabs attacked Jewish traffic, settlements and urban neighbourhoods; and the Jewish militias, spearheaded by the mainstream, Jewish Agency-affiliated Haganah, unleashed powerful retaliatory strikes, including devastating bombings in Arab towns. These helped to spread the conflagration to as yet untouched areas. As the British civil administration and military gradually packed their bags and sailed off, the country slipped into full-scale civil war.

In the run-up to the UN vote, as Glubb rightly noted, the Zionists had engaged in 'frenzied lobbying'[242] while the Arabs had lackadaisically looked on, sure of an effortless victory. One reason for the Zionist success was that, for once, Russia and America had 'worked hand in hand.' According to Glubb, 'it is doubtful whether either Russia or America was acting from idealistic motives.' The Russians were interested in anything that might undermine the Western, especially the British, position in the Middle East while the Americans acted from internal political considerations. Simply put, 'the White House had its eye on the Jewish vote in the Presidential election [impending in November 1948].'[243] Glubb added (incorrectly) that 'all' the states of Asia and Africa, except 'the Philippines, South Africa and Liberia,' had voted against partition. And he failed to mention that none of the Western democracies had voted against Israel and that most had voted for (Britain itself had abstained).[244]

While Glubb was critical of the manner of its passage, he was even more critical of the resolution's content. He saw it as blatantly unjust: 'It was unjustly biased in favour of the Jews. It gave sixty per cent of the area of Palestine ... to one-third of the inhabitants'[245] and: 'The greatest injustice in the UNO partition plan had been the award of the Neqeb [Negev]...to the Jews. In this area the population was still preponderantly Arab; the Neqeb had always been Arab in history.' (Curiously, Glubb shared with Ben-Gurion a special attachment to the Negev, albeit for different reasons.)[246] Moreover, the Jews only owned '6' per cent of Palestine's land - and had been allocated its most fertile tracts, in the Coastal Plain and the Jezreel and Jordan valleys.[247] Allocating the Negev to Israel meant blocking 'one of the world's oldest trade routes' and splitting the Arab world in two, Glubb argued.[248]

The passage of the partition resolution made Transjordanian-British agreement on Amman's future course of action urgent and imperative.

Britain's withdrawal from Palestine and the Yishuv's declaration of statehood were now only months away; agreement had to be reached so that the Transjordanian army - led by Glubb - would move with at least tacit British political backing. Glubb had to be assured of British military-financial support and of the integrity of the Legion's British personnel. Indeed, the proposed operation would require additional British funds and equipment. The Legion had to be substantially beefed up in preparation for the occupation of the area today known as the West Bank, which might involve hostilities against the local Arab population, Jewish forces, or even other Arab states' armies. The situation was highly volatile and unclear.

Adding to the lack of clarity was the fluid intra-Arab situation and Abdullah's need to avoid being ostracized by his fellow leaders, wary of Abdullah's expansionist ambitions and suspicious of his relations with Britain and the Zionists. At one point in early December 1947 Abdullah told Kirkbride that he intended to tell the other Arab League members that he planned to take over the Arab areas of Palestine when the British left. Kirkbride 'felt that the proposed step would be premature and harmful.' He advised the King to play along with the other Arab states while 'concealing his own intentions for the time being.' Kirkbride added that Abdullah was 'delighted at the prospect of [such] guidance from London' on this matter.[249]

This lack of clarity - due to the fluid geo-political situation, Abdullah's unclear or shifting thinking and intentions, and his variegated and oscillating statements about his thinking and intentions - was also apparent in Bevin's instructions to Kirkbride in mid-December 1947 regarding the future deployment of the Arab Legion. The Legion's units seconded to the Mandate - on garrison and patrol duties in British bases and along roads in Palestine - would have to return to Transjordan as British rule wound down and British forces were withdrawn. But the British subsidy of the Legion was formally linked to the Legion's services on behalf of the Mandate government. Once its units returned to Jordan and Britain pulled out of Palestine, what would be the fate of the subsidy? Would Whitehall's various departments - Foreign Office, Treasury, Colonial Office, 10 Downing Street - agree to continue to pay, with the Legion no longer directly serving British interests and authorities? And how would it look - to the Zionists, the Americans, the United Nations - if Britain continued to finance the Legion as it acted, in invading Palestine, in contravention and defiance of the UN Partition resolution? Whitehall, wrote Bevin, was looking into the matter. But vis-a-vis the Transjordanians, Kirkbride must tergiversate:

> If King Abdullah asks you what would be our attitude if, after the end of British civil administration in Palestine, the Arab Legion returned there and became involved in hostilities, you should say that while we would expect to be under very strong pressure to cease, while hostilities continued, all payment to Transjordan and to withdraw British officers, we would propose to leave this question over for decision in the light of all the circumstances at the time,

instructed Bevin.[250]

A major British worry was the possible reaction by the other Arab states to a Legion occupation of Arab Palestine. Britain's missions in the Middle East were instructed to sound out their host governments' views. The responses were far from encouraging. Both Iraq and Lebanon's prime minister, Riad a Solh, wanted Transjordan 'to occupy the whole of Palestine including the Jewish areas'; Syria would 'intensely dislike' an occupation 'of any part of Palestine by a purely Transjordan force'; Egypt would regard a Transjordanian push into Arab Palestine as an act of 'Hashemite aggrandizement' but would applaud a Legion takeover of all of Palestine. Saudi Arabia was the most critical: 'Ibn Saud would regard as "treacherous and unjustifiable" any attempt by King Abdullah to seize any part of Palestine...' except by League permission. As to Palestine's Arabs, they would welcome Jordanian intervention - especially if it 'covered the whole country.' In short, the Arab world would ambiguously applaud a Legion occupation of all of Palestine but would regard the takeover only of the Arab areas - effectively, a partition with the Jews - extremely negatively.[251]

Meanwhile, against the backdrop of the spiralling Arab-Jewish violence in Palestine and British inaction and indecision (regarding the proposed Legion push into Palestine), Abdullah became 'increasingly restless.' At a meeting in mid-January 1948 with Kirkbride (attended by the newly appointed Prime Minister and Defence Minister Tewfiq Abul Huda), the King suggested that the Arab Legion units stationed in Palestine could simply stay on when the British withdrew. Alternatively, additional units of the Legion could be sent to Palestine but 'not under the Command of the [Mandate's British] General Officer Commanding.' Kirkbride sharply swatted these ideas, arguing that the Legionnaires had entered the country as part of the mandatory forces; Britain could not leave them behind as its own troops withdrew. 'Prime Minister [Abul Huda] supported me over this point,' Kirkbride comments. Nor could Britain agree to Legionnaires not under its command operating in Palestine - especially in view of the fact that 'in the majority of recent cases [of violence in Palestine] the Arabs were the aggressors.'[252] Abdullah at one point protested that 'he could not possibly agree to the Jewish state having access to the Gulf of Aqaba and so cutting off Transjordan from Egypt.' Kirkbride firmly objected, saying that that was what the United Nations had decided and it was beyond his competence to comment on it.[253]

Abdullah's efforts to try to find out from Kirkbride exactly where Britain stood prompted the Minister to obtain clarifications from Bevin. But Bevin was not yet ready to be drawn. He authorized Kirkbride to deliver an 'oral message' stating that:

> we realise that what King Abdullah really wants to know is whether we think he should intervene in Palestine contrary to the decisions of the Arab League and whether we would protect him at the UN by using the veto if the matter came before the Security Council. We do not feel we can give him any encouragement to act alone [section garbled] ... I am afraid [that is] the best we can do.

Bevin added the following for Kirkbride's information: Britain hoped that (a) the troubles in Palestine would be 'localised' and over as soon as possible; (b) a situation in which Britain would have to cast a veto at the Security Council would not arise; and (c):

> King Abdullah will take no action that might isolate him from the other Arab (states) and thus give rise to the accusation that we are using him to engineer our re-entry into Palestine...
>
> So far as we can see at present it should be possible to satisfy (a) and (b) above, if King Abdullah occupied … Arab areas of Palestine and refrained from sending the Arab Legion into the areas allotted to the Jewish State by the UN. This would however not satisfy (c) above and it is hardly possible at present to think of any course of action which would satisfy all three requirements.[254]

On 17 January 1948 Kirkbride delivered a verbal message from Bevin to Abdullah. Abdullah 'was pleased ... and appeared to concentrate on the fact that he had not been forbidden to move [at the end of the Mandate] into the Arab areas of Palestine...'[255] - though neither had Bevin explicitly endorsed the idea.

It was this lack of clear endorsement of a Transjordanian push into Palestine that underlay Glubb's lobbying, backed by Kirkbride, in December 1947 and early January 1948 for a visit to London by a high-powered Transjordanian delegation. The official, and ostensible, objective of the visit was to negotiate a series of revisions to the Anglo-

Transjordanian treaty of 1946, whose central provisions concerned British military help to the kingdom in case of attack. The Transjordanians sought to amend certain clauses to increase their independence of Britain. But for Glubb, Kirkbride, and Abdullah more important still was the desire to obtain from Bevin and the other British decision-makers clear-cut British support for the intended Legion push into Palestine.

The British at last agreed to the visit and the Transjordanian delegation, headed by Abul Huda ('a quiet, neat, methodical little man, who should have spent his life as an auditor or a chartered accountant ... Few men could have been more unsuited to rule the storms of a world rapidly sliding into chaos' – so Glubb once described him)[256] and including Foreign Minister Fawzi Pasha al Mulki, and Glubb, arrived in London – accompanied by Pirie-Gordon - on 25 January. They began meeting with British officials the following day.

On 30 January 1948 Glubb met with the Director of Military Intelligence, Major-General C.D. Packard, at the War Office. A month later, Packard summarized the conversation:

> ... Glubb made it clear that it was unlikely that King Abdullah would move over the Jewish frontier ... The main objectives of the invading force would be Beersheba, Hebron, Ramallah, Nablus and Jenin, with forward elements in Tulkarm and the area just south of Lydda [i.e., all areas earmarked by the UN resolution for Palestine Arab sovereignty.] King Abdullah had no wish to come into conflict with the Jews ... Jerusalem would of course be inviolate [i.e., the Legion would not occupy it, as it was designated an international zone] ... [As to Abdullah's life-long ambition to rule over 'Greater Syria'], if such an event as the Palestine conquest did in fact take place, King Abdullah's expansionist aspirations would probably be more than satisfied ... His [i.e., Glubb's] personal opinion was that the right tactics for the Arabs were to stand firm on the Jewish frontiers and allow no movement across those frontiers. He feared, however, that the Arabs [i.e., the other Arab states] had not sufficient self-control to carry out this suggestion ... His information led him to believe that the Jewish tactics would be to do nothing unless provoked. Their answer, then, would be on the Nazi lines - for one Jew killed, 10 Arabs would be lined up and shot. Some [Jews] even went further and said that whole villages, men women and children, should be wiped out and their lands ploughed up. This, Brigadier Glubb thought, might be the Jewish undoing, as up to now the Arabs were only "half-annoyed" and if such a situation as he mentioned above did arise, there might be "another Bengal," with a great trek of Jews and Arabs fleeing to their own areas.[257]

But the main meetings took place at the Foreign Office, between Abul Huda and Foreign Office officials. In his memoirs, written some nine years after the event, Glubb remembered the key meeting, between Abul Huda and Foreign Secretary Bevin, with himself attending (officially as 'interpreter'), of 7 February, in a room 'looking out on the Horse Guards' Parade and the black leafless trees in St. James's Park,' thus: Abul Huda opened with a statement declaring that the Palestinian Arabs had not prepared, militarily or politically, for statehood and the likelihood was that:

> the Jews would neglect the UN partition plan and would seize the whole of Palestine up to the River Jordan; or else the Mufti would return and endeavour to make himself ruler of Arab Palestine. Neither of these alternatives would suit either Britain or Transjordan ... During recent weeks, King Abdullah ... had received, and [was] still receiving, many requests and petitions from Palestine Arab notables ... [begging] for the help and protection of the Arab Legion as soon as the British forces withdrew. The Transjordan government accordingly proposed to send the Arab Legion across the Jordan when the British Mandate ended, and to occupy that part of Palestine awarded to the Arabs which was contiguous with the frontier of Transjordan.
>
> Bevin: "It seems the obvious thing to do ... It seems the obvious thing to do ... But do not go and invade the areas allotted to the Jews."
>
> Abul Huda: "We should not have the forces to do so, even if we so desired."
>
> ... Mr. Bevin thanked Tewfiq Pasha for his frank exposition of the position of Transjordan, and expressed his agreement with the plans put forward.[258]

Glubb's remembered version of that meeting is only partly confirmed by the Foreign Office documents written at the time and declassified during the following decades.

The Abul Huda-Bevin meeting had been more than a week in preparation. It had apparently first been requested by Abul Huda through Pirie-Gordon on 27 January. The following day, Pirie-Gordon wrote to Burrows: Abul Huda

> asked me privately last night to request a further meeting with Mr. Bevin ... to explain to him his views on the position in Palestine. The Prime Minister asks that the meeting should if possible be arranged without the knowledge of the Transjordan Foreign Minister or other members of the delegation and that ... it should be attended by Brigadier Glubb...
>
> Tewfiq Pasha explained that he was anxious to put to Mr. Bevin certain opinions on possible developments in Palestine which would not be altogether ac-

ceptable to the Foreign Minister, as representing younger and more Nationalist opinion in the country, and he also naturally did not wish the Foreign Minister to know that the subject of Palestine had been discussed in his absence. Tewfiq Pasha continued further that he quite understood that any action that Transjordan might take in Palestine after the termination of the Mandate was a matter of some delicacy for HMG, in view of their special relationship, and that, while he considered it was only fair that Mr. Bevin should be informed of his own views and intentions, he did not for his part expect Mr. Bevin to give him any definite answer or comment unless he wished to do so.

... I strongly suspect that [Abul Huda] has made the move in response to direct orders from King Abdullah, and that he may well be contemplating the suggestion of some course of action in which an eventual understanding with the Jews is envisaged.

King Abdullah is believed always to have had such a policy at the back of his mind if circumstances should ever make it at all feasible and the previous Prime Minister, Samir Pasha Rifa`i, has also told me on several occasions in private that such a rapprochement with the Jews in the interests of Transjordan was his ultimate aim. The fact that it is so necessary to exclude the Foreign Minister from all knowledge of the meeting suggests that Tewfiq Pasha's proposals may be equally heretical as his predecessor's.[259]

The day before the Bevin-Abul Huda meeting, the Foreign Secretary's aide, Michael Wright, composed a brief for Bevin couched in the following terms:

The Transjordan Prime Minister has expressed a wish to have a private conversation with the Secretary of State on Palestine. He does not wish his own Foreign Minister [Fawzi al Mulki] to be present. He would like Brigadier Glubb to be present as interpreter ... In making this curious request, Tewfik Pasha explained that he wishes to put to the Secretary of State views on possible developments in Palestine which might not be altogether acceptable to the [Jordanian] Foreign Minister...

It seems likely that the Prime Minister may wish to put forward the idea of action by Transjordan in Palestine which would lead to eventual agreement with the Jews. This might take the form of occupation by the Arab Legion after May 15th of some or all of the areas allotted to the Arabs by the UN, but without the occupation of any areas allotted to the Jews. Then after a suitable lapse of time, King Abdullah would come to a de facto agreement with the Jews that they would not encroach on each other's territory...

In the message which the Secretary of State [i.e., Bevin] recently sent King Abdullah ... he warned him of the difficulty which would be caused if King Ab-

> dullah took action which was likely to result in either the UN or the Arab League moving against him. Action on the line suggested above would not upset the UN, but unless handled very carefully indeed, would create very serious trouble with the other Arab states...
>
> Tewfiq Pasha realizes the difficulty of our position and will almost certainly not expect the Secretary of State to make any real reply to the statement which he may make. If it seems impossible to avoid giving a reply, it is difficult to see how the Secretary of State could go beyond the terms of his message to King Abdullah, mentioned above.
>
> It is essential that the Secretary of State should take this opportunity to give a confidential warning that if Transjordan became involved in hostilities against a Jewish state or blatantly contrary to the UN, we should be under strong pressure to suspend the subsidy and to consider the position of British officers seconded to the Arab Legion.[260]

Bevin had previously met Abul Huda and Foreign Minister al Mulki together three times, on 26 January 1948 and on 3 and 6 February 1948 - but the subject of the future of Palestine had not come up.

There are a number of contemporary testimonies to what transpired at the Bevin-Abul Huda-Glubb meeting on 7 February. According to Burrows, summarizing two days later:

> the Secretary of State spoke to Mr. M.R. Wright and myself on February 7th, just after his conversation with the Transjordan Prime Minister about Palestine. He spoke of the possible entry of Transjordan forces into the Arab areas of Palestine, which might in many respects be generally advantageous, but would undoubtedly cause great difficulty with Ibn Saud. He wondered whether we could do anything to promote better relations between Saudi Arabia and Transjordan ... (A) The Prime Minister has told us that it would be generally beneficial if the Arab Legion occupied the Arab areas of Palestine as defined by the United Nations after May 15th. He realized clearly that entry into the Jewish areas would greatly embarrass us, owing to our subsidy [of Transjordan and the Legion].
>
> (B) A development on these lines would seem in many ways the best solution, but we can hardly say so at present, both because, according to the United Nations decision, the Arab state [in Palestine] is supposed to be independent ... and because overt support for these Transjordan plans would antagonize the rest of the Arab states.
>
> (C) This Transjordan plan no doubt would be most acceptable to the US Administration, as providing the best hope of something like the UN Jewish state coming into existence...

> (D) It is tempting to think that Transjordan might transgress the boundaries of the UN Jewish state to the extent of establishing a corridor across the southern [should be northern] Negeb, joining the existing Transjordan territory to the Mediterranean at Gaza. This would have immense strategic advantage for us, both in cutting the Jewish state, and therefore Communist influence, off from the Red Sea and by extending up to the Mediterranean the area in which our military and political influence is predominant and providing [the possibility] of sending necessary military equipment etc. into Transjordan other than by the circuitous route through Aqaba. It would of course be infinitely more difficult to obtain Jewish agreement for a move of this kind than for the occupation of UN Arab areas by the Arab Legion, which the Jews would probably welcome. The Jews would probably be to some extent satisfied [with Transjordanian occupation of the northern Negev] if they received compensation in W. Galilee - but this raises almost insuperable difficulties on the Arab side.[261]

On 8 February Abul Huda cabled the head of Abdullah's court mentioning only that he had had 'a personal meeting with Mr. Bevin in my capacity as Minister of Defence and pure military questions were discussed. I am very pleased at the results and am proud to say that it is due to His Majesty that these results have been attained.'[262] Presumably Abdullah understood from this that his Prime Minister had received the go-ahead from Bevin for the occupation of the West Bank. Clearly at this time both Abdullah and the British contemplated only a Transjordanian (or perhaps Iraqi-assisted Transjordanian) entry into and occupation of Arab Palestine, not a pan-Arab invasion, in which the Transjordanian (or Transjordanian-Iraqi) component would be only a part.

Bevin regarded his meeting with Abul Huda as so important that he sent off two lengthy cables to Kirkbride, describing what had transpired, on 9 and 10 February. On 9 February Bevin said that Abul Huda had asked for the meeting, without his foreign minister being present, in order to pass on 'the point of view of King Abdullah without expecting us necessarily to make any comment or reply.' The return of the Arab Legion after 15 May to 'the Arab areas of Palestine to maintain law and order' would be 'to the public benefit,' said Abul Huda, according to Bevin. Abul Huda appreciated that it would cause Britain 'embarrassment' if the Legion 'attacked any part of the civil population.' But if the United Nations saw that the Legion only reduced bloodshed, 'they would be grateful rather than critical.' Indeed, the Legion's presence in Palestine would facilitate the enforcement of the United Nations partition decision. Abul Huda hoped that 'some solution was ultimately adopted involving a modification of the present arrangements in favour of the Arabs' - i.e., he hoped that there would be a reduction in the size of the prospective Jewish state. Indeed, 'it was possible that the Jews would find that they had opened their mouths too wide [i.e., bitten off more, territorially, than they could chew] and that the United Nations would come to a similar conclusion ...' Abul Huda stressed that Transjordan did not wish to create difficulties for HMG and that any action it took would be 'on Transjordan's responsibility.' Transjordan sought to avoid being isolated in the Arab world.

Bevin informed Kirkbride that he had asked Abul Huda

> whether, when he spoke of the Arab Legion entering Palestine, he referred to the Arab areas as laid down in the UN's decision or whether he thought it would also enter the Jewish areas. Tewfiq Pasha replied that the Arab Legion would not enter Jewish areas unless the Jews invaded Arab areas. He saw that the entry of the Arab Legion into Jewish areas would create such strenuous UN opposition as to cause great difficulty for Transjordan.

Bevin cabled Kirkbride that he had said that he would 'study the statements which his Excellency had made. Tewfiq Pasha repeated that he did not want any reply. If as a result of my study we wished to pursue the discussion he would be glad to do so, but otherwise he would not expect us to refer to the matter again.'

From the contemporary documentation - and in contradiction to Glubb's recollection in *A Soldier with the Arabs* – it appears that Bevin had clearly refrained from fully endorsing Abul Huda's proposal. But Abul Huda, from the first, had acted upon the old Roman law maxim that 'silence is consent' and on the understanding that Bevin understood this.[263]

Bevin's cable to Kirkbride of 10 February was more pithy - but also clearer as to Bevin's position on Jordan's plans:

> Main points [of the meeting with Abul Huda] were as follows: Return of Arab Legion after May 15th to Arab areas of Palestine as defined by UN would be generally beneficial and likely to limit bloodshed and chaos. Transjordan Prime Minister realized that if Arab Legion went further than this and attacked civil population or Jewish state, we should be much embarrassed vis-a-vis UN owing to our subsidy. He hoped that UN might ultimately modify their decision in favour of the Arabs [i.e., give the Arabs more of Palestine] in which case the Arab Legion would be able to help enforce it. Even if the present decision was enforced [i.e., left standing] the presence of the Arab Legion would limit the ensuing chaos and not increase it. Tewfiq Pasha recognized that Transjordan must also be very careful not to become too isolated vis-a-vis other Arab states.

Tewfiq Pasha emphasized that he did not expect any reply from me ... Opportunity was taken in subsequent conversation between Tewfiq Pasha and a member of the [Foreign Office] staff to convey to him the warning [not to attack the Jewish areas] ... to make sure that he realized that we should in the event of aggressive action by the Arab Legion be under serious pressure ... [T]he Prime Minister said that he fully appreciated the position ...[264]

Kirkbride's response to these cables was as follows:

> Both the King and Tewfiq Pasha are, I believe, determined to occupy as much of Arab areas as they can as soon as the mandate is terminated. For publicity purposes they say to the Arabs that they are going to try and occupy the whole of Palestine, but this is merely to forestall the accusation that they are implementing partition. Both realise their inability with the means at their disposal to achieve more than the occupation of Arab areas ...[265]

That Bevin and his aides were not off the mark with regard to Saudi opposition to the contemplated Jordanian move was clearly demonstrated the day before the Bevin-Abul Huda talk. Sir R.I. Campbell, the British Minister in Cairo, met with the Saudi Minister to London, who was passing through the Egyptian capital on his way to his post. The Saudi, Sheikh Hafiz Wahba, told Campbell that King Ibn Saud had the previous week several times mentioned to him reports that 'King Abdullah ... was intending on the withdrawal of British forces to try and seize and occupy in his own name Arab parts of Palestine. King Ibn Saud did not know whether or not the British were behind such a plan. He suspected they might be. He was very uneasy indeed about it all ... Ibn Saud would never agree to such an arrangement and would do everything in his power, even in the last resort go to war, to prevent it. If it should appear that Britain was in fact backing the scheme Ibn Saud's confidence in us would suffer a fatal blow.'[266] Bevin, then, had good reason to worry about a possible leak regarding Britain's backing for Abdullah's scheme.

Nor was Ibn Saud alone in regarding Anglo-Hashemite intentions with suspicion. Cunnningham, the High Commissioner in Jerusalem, was officially left in the dark about the evolving Anglo-Jordanian agreement on Legion intervention at the end of the Mandate (despite his nominal responsibility for the affairs of both Palestine and Transjordan). On 27 January he cabled the Colonial Office for instructions: 'You mention the possibility of Trans-Jordan intervention ... The latest official information I have on this is to the effect that the FO saw some advantage in intervention by Abdullah. You will agree, I am sure, that it is most important that I should know how this matter stands, as soon as possible...'[267]

It is unclear whether Cunningham was informed of the details of the Bevin-Abul Huda conversation. But by the end of February Jordanian intentions were clear to the senior personnel in the British administration in Palestine. For example, the widely distributed British Army in Palestine's 'Fortnightly Intelligence Newsletter' thought that the recent defeat at Tirat Zvi of the Arab Liberation Army - a volunteer force sent by the Arab League to help the embattled Palestinian irregulars - might persuade 'these noble strugglers' to depart Palestine. 'This may well suit King Abdullah's book ... [as this will mean] less opposition to his assumption of control in Arab Palestine.'[268] And the High Commissioner himself was similarly minded. In late February he predicted that the Arabs would be unable to prevent the emergence of a Jewish state ('the Jews should be able to hold the Coastal Plain ... so it might all end in a partition more on the lines of what we would consider fair'), with 'the most likely arrangements [being] ... Eastern Galilee to Syria, Samaria and Hebron to Abdullah, and the south to Egypt, and it might well end in annexation on this pattern...'[269]

On 22 March, Bevin apparently belatedly informed the Cabinet of the details of his talk with the Jordanian leader. The Cabinet was apprised that the Jews during the following weeks might seek to establish a 'Jewish State' in the areas allotted to them in the partition plan 'and the King of Transjordan might seek to assume control of other parts of Palestine ... The Cabinet [as pithily conveyed in the minutes] agreed that ... the British civil and military authorities in Palestine should make no effort to oppose this setting up of a Jewish State or a move into Palestine from Transjordan...'[270]

During the following weeks, Bevin remained remarkably loyal to the scenario charted out in the meeting of 7 February. Just days before the British departure from Palestine and the impending Arab invasion, he cabled Kirkbride in the following terms:

> I am extremely interested in [your] suggestion ... [that] the Arab leaders might content themselves with consolidating the Arab areas of Palestine against further Jewish expansion. This would certainly seem to be far the most sensible course they could adopt in the light of the present military balance of power. It would also make their position internationally far better than if they attacked the Jews. Moreover the maintenance of our own close relations with the Arab States would

> be greatly facilitated if they took this course ... It may well be desirable to say something to [the Arab leaders] in the next few days ... on [these] lines ...[271]

Bevin proceeded to inquire of his various Middle East posts whether such advice should be proffered to the Arab leaders in each country by the British representatives (though it appears that the idea was never, at least formally, acted upon).[272]

And in mid-May, after the Arab Legion invasion and the first Legion-Haganah clashes around Jerusalem, Bevin cabled his American counterpart, General George Marshall:

> We understand that the Jews knew the Arab Legion would enter Arab areas of Palestine, and that this was not unwelcome to them. We have always thought that there might be considerable advantage in an arrangement by which the Haganah and the Arab Legion might be given responsibility for maintaining law and order in different areas [of Palestine]. The Arab Legion have not entered any part of the area recommended for the Jewish state ... The Arab Legion attack on parts of Jerusalem was the direct consequence of the breaking of the [local internationally-mediated] cease-fire by the Jews.[273]

Preparing the Invasion

With his political flanks at least partially secured, Glubb now set about preparing militarily for the impending campaign.

One problem was to gauge the attitude of the inhabitants of various parts of the area soon to be known as the 'West Bank' to the planned invasion and to the prospect of subsequent Hashemite rule. Opinions tended to fluctuate in each town and district month by month in line with local military and political developments. Geographical intelligence also had to be gathered about the routes and objectives of the planned Legion advance.

At the end of January 1948, two months into the civil war in Palestine, one of Glubb's British officers met a Palestinian urban notable and reported:

> The Sheikh hopes that King Abdullah will annex Palestine ... He said that he found the people in Amman more warlike than the Palestinians ... He reported that Gaza, Beersheba and Hebron are anxious to join Transjordan ... Jaffa, he thought, had probably now come over to King Abdullah, and Nablus he thought would. He said that two months ago any talk of King Abdullah's entry would

> have met bitter opposition from many quarters, but now would be accepted with secret relief by the majority ... This is not to deny a strong wish to deny the Jews their National Home. It only means that, in the Sheikh's view, there is not an all-out, do or die, feeling in the Arabs of Palestine as their leaders would have us believe, and he feels that if the economic situation continues to deteriorate and no visible ... improvement of the armed potential occurs, then the majority will be relieved if either a settlement is made with the Jews, or some stable Arab government takes over and imposes order even although [sic] it does not carry on the war against the Jews.[274]

Jewish assessments supported this conclusion. In January 1948 the Haganah Intelligence Service believed that 'the [Palestinian] Arabs had great faith in and had high hopes of the Arab Legion soldiers.'[275] Indeed, its assessment was that 'the Arab town mayors' by and large preferred a Legion takeover to rule by the Mufti. And 'the Mufti clearly is aware of this pro-King Abdullah tendency...'[276]

Embodying pro-Hashemite sentiment at this time was Muhammad Ali al-Ja`abri, the mayor of Hebron, whom Haganah intelligence reported was 'organizing an opposition that would support cooperating with King Abdullah.' Indeed, in late January 1948 Ja`abri was reportedly organizing a petition calling for 'prolonged intervention' by Abdullah.[277] In late February, leading Arab notables - Musa al Alami, Darwish al-Mukdadi, and Yusuf Heikal, the mayor of Jaffa - visited Abdullah in Amman and sought his help. Heikal subsequently related that the moment Husseini's Arab Higher Committee declared a Palestinian Arab government, Abdullah would announce that the Ramallah-Nablus-Tulkarm Triangle was a Jordanian 'protectorate' area. Moreover, Abdullah reportedly had the agreement of Fawzi al Qawuqji, the commander of the ALA, whose units were already deployed in the Triangle, to this 'annexation.'[278]

In January 1948 Arab Legion headquarters asked the British Army to supply it with 30 maps of Palestine's cities ('including all the Jewish towns'). Presumably, the maps were provided (though 'it was unclear [to the recipients of the request] what these maps were needed for).'[279]

During the months before the invasion Glubb, accompanied by staff officers, repeatedly visited Palestine. In January he toured 'Jaffa, Lydda, [and] Ramle' and other Arab settlements and, in his words, 'begged them to prepare to defend themselves.' The Legion also gave the inhabitants barbed wire and 'as many weapons as we could [spare].'[280] In March, he visited and held meeting with notables and local militia leaders in Gaza, Majdal (Ashkelon), Hebron, Ramallah and Beersheba.

Glubb drummed up local support for Abdullah and the prospective Hashemite takeover. Several leaders, including Heikal, apparently pleaded with Glubb (and through him, Abdullah) to send the Legion to 'save' their towns as soon as possible.[281] According to Haganah intelligence, on 20 April Glubb visited the village of Masmiya al Kabira and 'promised King Abdullah's help' and asked the inhabitants 'to support the King.' The inhabitants 'agreed.'[282] No doubt Glubb's visits were also, at least in part, preparatory in a down-to-earth military intelligence sense of learning routes of advance and points of possible local resistance to the Legion entry into the country.[283]

Another preparatory measure involved the securing of the Jordan River bridges even before the Mandate had wound down, with an eye to preventing Haganah sabotage of the vital access routes into Palestine. During the first weeks of 1948 an Arab Legion picket crossed the river into Palestine and guarded the western end of the Sheikh Hussein and Damiya bridges – 'of future potential importance to Transjordan' - each night.[284] But this was clearly insufficient. The Allenby Bridge, east of Jericho, was the focus of Glubb's worries. In late March he warned British Army headquarters in Palestine: '... A Jewish armed car could easily break through and reach the bridge, as was done last month by the Jews at Jisr Sheikh Hussein.' Glubb demanded that the Legion be allowed to secure the Allenby Bridge also from the Palestine side of the river. What is more, by early April Glubb was insisting that the Legionnaires manning the 'road block' on the western end of the bridge, inside Palestine, not come under command of the Mandate military authorities - and the Mandate authorities, though troubled, acceded to this arrangement. Glubb never explicitly declared that the bridge had to be secured in order to enable smooth passage for his columns as they crossed into Palestine on 15 May - but that, of course, was what was at issue.[285] On 10 May, five days before the invasion, Haganah intelligence reported that Allenby Bridge was guarded by 200 Legionnaires 'with their heavy equipment.'[286]

In his memoirs Glubb also referred to the clandestine construction or restoration by West Bank labourers, during April and early May, of one or two dirt tracks fit for four-wheeled vehicles leading from the Jordan Valley up to the Samaria hill-country. Strapped for cash, Glubb paid the £4,000 for the road work out of the Legion's canteen fund. These axes were later used by the Legion as it made its way into Palestine in that vital initial thrust up the escarpment toward Ramallah on Day 1 of the invasion.[287]

But Glubb's most important preparation for the invasion, of course, was the re-organization and strengthening of the Legion. This involved two main areas: (A) the amalgamation and conversion of the force's static garrison companies into combat-capable mechanized battalions; and (B) a major increase in mechanization and firepower, involving the addition of artillery pieces and hundreds of trucks and gun-mounting armoured cars to the Legion's order of battle.

Paralleling and closely following the evolving understanding at the end of 1947 about Transjordanian occupation of the Arab parts of Palestine after the British evacuation and the Glubb-War Office and Abul Huda-Bevin meetings of January-February 1948, Glubb and the British Army moved jointly to beef up the Legion.

The Legion's strength (excluding police) had declined from about 8,500 to 7,500 during April-October 1947.[288] In May 1947 Glubb submitted a plan for re-organizing the force necessitating no major increase in manpower but substantially reinforcing its combat capabilities. The plan was that the existing brigade, with three regiments (battalions), was to be expanded into two brigade groups (each with two battalions), with a third brigade group for the future, to be based on mobilized reserves.[289] The main proposed increment related to armoured vehicles and guns. Britain's annual subsidy, according to the plan, was to increase from £2 million to £2.5 million, and another £1.3 million was to be allocated for additional armaments.[290]

For more than half a year Glubb's proposal gathered dust in a War Office drawer. But the United Nations partition resolution and the growing probability of Legion intervention in Palestine now made it a matter of urgency. On 6 January 1948 officials of the Foreign and War offices and the Treasury met to discuss the Legion's expansion. The Foreign Office representatives explained 'the political background':

> The withdrawal of our forces from Palestine weakens our direct influence in the Middle East ... Our aim is to maintain and indeed strengthen our links with the elements in the Middle East which are known to be favourable to us and of these King Abdullah of Transjordan is one. Further it is very much to our interest that conditions of security should be restored in Palestine as soon as possible after our withdrawal and if King Abdullah and the other Arab leaders agree on the use of the Arab Legion in that part of Palestine allotted to the Arab state by the UN, law and order might be restored to that part of Palestine quite rapidly. There is the further consideration that even if King Abdullah was to hold entirely aloof from Palestine, his own internal security problem is likely to be more serious than before...

The sense of the meeting was to increase the size and capabilities of the Legion.[291]

During February-May, a large amount of equipment and munitions were transferred from the British bases in the Canal Zone to the Legion, mainly by road via Rafah. The major items were dozens of Marmon Harrington armoured cars[292], several dozen 6-pounder guns, and twelve or sixteen 25-pounder artillery pieces and forty 2- and sixty 3-inch mortars.[293] In February the Legion was given ammunition for 10 'contact days' (days of battle) and in May was promised another 30 days' worth. But only part of the promised second allocation was in fact transferred to 'Aqaba, 150 tons consisting mostly of small arms ammunition and 2-pounder shells. The main shipment, of 350 tons of 25-pounder shells and 3-inch mortar bombs, was confiscated, in an act of inter-Arab skull-duggery by the Egyptians, off the freighter Ramses at Suez.[294] By the start of the invasion, the Legion had, according to Abdullah Tall, one of Glubb's senior officers, 24 25-pounders (the most potent gun used in the 1948 War), 38 6-pounder guns, and 40 3-inch mortars.[295]

Nor was manpower ignored. By mid-May 1948 the Legion's numbers appear to have risen to around 9,000[296] - though Glubb in his memoirs puts the number at '6,000 in 1948'[297] and '4,500 ...[in] the field' on 15 May.[298] During the run-up to May 1948, the Legion made a serious effort to recruit specialists from the departing British Army, and dozens of ex-British officers and NCOs joined up just before and just after May 15. A Haganah intelligence report from March states that the Legion tried to mobilize British 'armourers, communications experts, electricians, mechanics ...'[299]

During the months before the invasion and the weeks after it began, the Legion was reorganized, essentially according to Glubb's May 1947 plan guidelines. By May 1948, its three combat regiments or battalions and 12 guard companies had been amalgamated and expanded into four standard battalions, with two brigade headquarters (two battalions per brigade) working under a divisional headquarters. By the end of June, the Legion had been further expanded into a three-brigade (six battalion) army. By November, according to Glubb, through a massive recruitment and training drive, throwing 'financial discretion ... to the winds,' the Legion had 'nearly doubled' in size.[300] By January 1949, the Legion numbered 11,143 men, according to Glubb's memoirs.[301]

The presence of British officers in the Arab Legion during the run-up to 15 May and, indeed, after the start of the invasion, posed a major political-diplomatic problem for Whitehall. Their continued employment was considered vital to the Legion's effective functioning. But their presence seemed to implicate Britain in Abdullah's invasion which was, at least on the face of things, a blatant violation of the terms of UN General Assembly Resolution 181. There were 37 British officers in the Legion on 26 May and there were probably also several dozen NCOs.[302] They had various statuses. All were British subjects. But some were serving British Army officers seconded to the Legion, others were Palestine Government civil servants, and still others were ex-soldiers on private contract with Amman. Before and after 15 May, Britain was concerned about their possible participation in the occupation of the West Bank. And it was even more concerned that Britons might be involved in warfare against the Israelis and Israeli territory, which would place Whitehall in a difficult position in Washington (which, while not supplying the Jewish State with arms, was among its chief political supporters).

Before 15 May, Kirkbride argued against the withdrawal of the British officers if the Legion's role remained a non-belligerent occupation of Palestine's Arab areas. He seemed in part to have been motivated by the consideration that the presence of disciplined, British officers would serve to restrain potentially hot-headed Arab Legionnaires from giving free rein to their nationalist proclivities and attacking Jewish troops and areas. Kirkbride appears to have persuaded Bevin of this.[303] But Kirkbride realized that if, nonetheless, the Legion became involved in clashes with the Jews or invaded Jewish areas, the situation would be completely different and it would be desirable to remove the Britons from the battlefield. Otherwise Britain would be open to charges of direct involvement on the Arab side in the war against Israel.[304]

During the weeks before 15 May the service of a number of seconded British Army officers was terminated, and some, at least, were withdrawn from Palestine back to East Jordan on 30-31 May (in line with the UN Security Council resolution of 29 May banning foreign aid, in war material and personnel, to all parties to the conflict);[305] others were asked or instructed to leave Transjordan or not to take part in the invasion; and still others were simply taken off British government military rolls.

At one point, Bevin suggested that some of the Britons, including Glubb, might be in violation of the Foreign Enlistment Act of 1870. 'Glubb took [this] very badly and wrote [Kirkbride] a long temperamental letter closing with the statement that, unless HMG could promise his officers immunity from a criminal charge, he would resign his post immediately.'[306]

Glubb was annoyed by the apparent disparity in Israeli and British implementation of the embargo regarding personnel: Britain had ordered its nationals serving in the Legion to pull out while the IDF was employing hundreds of foreign nationals, such as Col. Mickey Marcus (Stone), in its ranks. This situation certainly made it easier for Glubb to 'cheat' by informing London (perhaps with a wink) that Britons had been withdrawn back to Amman when, in fact, they had not or, at best, had been briefly withdrawn only to be quickly sent back across the river to rejoin their units.[307]

Nonetheless, in some cases (those officers still formally members of the British Army) Glubb appears to have complied fully, with no little annoyance to the Arab Legion. 'The withdrawal of the British officers [in the second half of May] was a shattering blow. They included all operational staff officers, both the brigade commanders, and the commanding officers of three out of the four infantry regiments, and all the trained artillery officers,' Glubb later wrote, probably with a measure of exaggeration.[308] In truth almost all the officers serving in Palestine in the second half of May and June 1948 were either never removed, or only removed for a day or two, enabling Bevin to state (possibly truthfully) in Parliament on 27 May that all had been moved out of Palestine. Years later, Kirkbride and Desmond Goldie, a senior Legion officer, admitted that, in effect, the Legion had ignored the formal Foreign Office orders in this connection.[309] Indeed, as part of the Legion's overall expansion during the first months of the war, its liaison office in Britain clandestinely recruited new British employees, usually ex-British Army technical personnel and officers. Dozens of these recruits appear to have reached Amman, and then the Legion units in the West Bank, in the following weeks.[310] The subject of seconded British Army officers serving with Legion units in the West Bank, periodically raised by pro-Israeli members of Parliament and in the press, was repeatedly to trouble British officialdom during the following months.[311]

Moreover, Glubb's own continued presence and functioning in the Legion - a British subject and commander of Jordan's army, whatever his institutional affiliations - was a perennial source of embarrassment to Whitehall. A representative of the British chief of staff, in fact, at one point defined Glubb - and two of his senior aides, Norman Lash and Ronald Broadhurst - as 'soldiers of fortune of British nationality.'[312] The situation was such that on 20 May 1948, Bevin seems simply (and absurdly) to have denied 'that Glubb Pasha was leading the Arab Legion' in Palestine.[313]

Before 15 May, Glubb was officially both on the Regular Army Reserve of Officers rolls at the War Office and an official of the Palestine civil service, hence, of the Colonial Office. With the termination of the Mandate, the Palestine civil service ceased to exist - and so did Glubb's position in it. As to the War Office lists, at Foreign Office instigation Glubb's name was removed in mid-May. But none of this vitiated the fact that he continued, de facto, to serve His Majesty's Government and what he (and many in Whitehall) perceived as its interests - as well as Abdullah and his interests.[314]

The civil war between Palestine's Arab and Jewish communities broke out in the immediate wake of the passage of UN General Assembly Resolution 181. Roughly speaking, from late November 1947 until the end of March 1948 the Palestinian Arabs - backed by arms shipments from the Arab states and ALA contingents of volunteers from Iraq and Syria, led by Fawzi al Qawuqji - were on the offensive, attacking Jewish traffic, rural settlements, and urban neighbourhoods. The Haganah (and IZL and LHI) responded with retaliatory strikes. The British Army, gradually withdrawing from Palestine, at first tried to maintain law and order and often assisted those attacked (usually the Yishuv), but generally it maintained a posture of neutrality, its aim being to leave Palestine with as few casualties as possible and with Britain's political, strategic and economic interests in the Middle East intact.

The Yishuv, meanwhile, organized itself for statehood and for the war with the Arab states that its leaders thought more and more likely. At the start of April - due to a concatenation of circumstances, including growing Jewish losses of men and equipment in defence of the convoys along the roads; the stepped up withdrawal of the British military from various areas and from Palestine in general; the growth of Haganah power, due to reorganisation of units and the arrival of clandestine arms shipments from Czechoslovakia; and Washington's signals that it might recant on its support for partition and Jewish statehood - the Haganah went over to the offensive, and during the following six weeks gradually crushed the Palestinian militias and conquered Arab towns (Beisan and Acre) and urban neighbourhoods (in Tiberias, Haifa, and Safad) and swathes of Arab villages (along the road to Jerusalem, in the western Jezreel Valley and around Haifa, and Eastern Galilee). Dozens of Arab villages were razed and hundreds of thousands of villagers and townspeople fled or were driven from their homes into (still-) Arab parts of Palestine or out of the country altogether, into exile.[315]

The evolution of Jordanian policy and actions between late November 1947 and mid-May 1948 must be seen against this backdrop. In mid-November 1947 Golda Meir and King Abdullah agreed in principle to a Yishuv-Jordanian partition of Palestine, with the Arab Legion quietly taking over Arab parts of the country and the Jews declaring statehood in the remainder. But during the period February-early May 1948 the tacit Transjordanian-Yishuv understanding took a severe beating and appeared to unravel. Only later, in retrospect, did it become clear that the agreement had, in fact, substantially held and that Abdullah, like a captain of a storm-battered ship, having set his strategic-political course (partition of Palestine between himself and the Yishuv), had during the following months, while buffeted left and right by stormy seas and alternating pressures (Arab, Yishuv, British), somehow managed, in most major particulars, to adhere to the original course and safely reach the far shore.[316]

But this is to anticipate. During February-15 May 1948, under the impact of events in Palestine, everything appeared up in the air, in flux. The daily bitter clash of Jew and Arab in Palestine's towns and villages seemed to test Abdullah's loyalties and promises to the limit. Would he abide by the non-belligerency agreement? Would he limit himself to a quiet occupation of the Arab areas of Palestine and refrain from attacking Jewish areas and troops?

During April-early May, Haganah intelligence received a steady stream of confirmations that Abdullah indeed intended to adhere to the original understanding. On 19 April, according to one source, Abdullah told 'his people' in Palestine 'that he had no intention of entering the Jewish districts.[317] A senior British official said on 22 April, apparently after a visit to Amman, that 'Abdullah himself agrees to the establishment of a Jewish state.'[318] On 5 May, reporting on the ongoing talks in Amman between the Arab leaders, the Haganah Intelligence Service reported that 'the King promised that he would secure the Arab districts against Jewish aggression...' - implying that he would not attack the Jewish areas. Moreover, according to one source, a delegation of Qalqilya notables at this time was disappointed by their meeting with Abdullah in Amman because 'they understood that the King is in no rush to face the Jews on the battlefield.'[319] In certain areas, appeals to Abdullah led to discord between those favouring a Hashemite takeover and Mufti supporters.[320]

But in the weeks and days leading up to the pan-Arab invasion the original Hashemite-Yishuv understanding nonetheless seemed to teeter on the edge of collapse. Even the Jewish Agency Political Department's

Yaakov Shimoni, a strong advocate of the Hashemite connection and believer in Abdullah's professions of good faith, said on 22 April: 'Until two or three days ago, I thought that he [i.e., Abdullah] would conquer the Arab area, avoiding confrontation with our forces, and after having occupied the Arab area he would negotiate with us. After the latest events [i.e., the Haganah conquest of Arab Tiberias and Arab Haifa] it stands to reason that this is no longer his aim.'[321] In consequence, towards the end of April the Haganah Intelligence Service stepped up its monitoring of the movements of those Arab Legion garrison units still in the country.[322]

According to Glubb, two developments transformed or at least beclouded the planned quiet Transjordanian takeover of the Arab-populated area soon to be known as the 'West Bank': One was the early, gradual British withdrawal from most of Palestine, which enabled the Jewish military forces, primarily the Haganah, to secure much of the Jewish-allotted area and to conquer areas - principally along the Tel Aviv-Jerusalem road and in West Jerusalem - earmarked for Arab sovereignty or international control. The second was the gradually-crystallizing Arab League decision to invade Palestine and attack the Jews, in part in order to save the Palestinian Arabs. During the weeks before the invasion, Abdullah came under growing, indeed intense, pressure to join - indeed, to lead - the other Arab states and armies in the attack on the Jews.[323]

In large measure it was the gradual collapse of Palestinian Arab society under the hammer blows of the 'civil war' of November 1947-May 1948 and more particularly the switch to the offensive by the Haganah in April-early May, triggering the start of the Palestinian mass exodus, that strained the Hashemite-Yishuv agreement. The pressure on Abdullah increased with each new Jewish success and each new episode of Palestinian collapse and flight.

Already on 11 January 1948 Sasson wrote to Abdullah regarding the cycle of 'slaughters and massacres' that were plunging Palestine into chaos and which, implicitly, might affect 'the open and honourable agreement' that had been reached two months before. Sasson expressed a worry that intrigues were afoot in the Arab world that 'push you and your government and army into the cauldron, in order to turn you into our enemies...'[324]

In early May Kirkbride summarized what had transpired during the previous month:

> Amman, already overcrowded, received a fresh wave of refugees from Palestine full of the wildest stories ... Extreme public pressure was brought to bear on King Abdullah and the Transjordan Government to intervene in Palestine immediately with the Arab Legion ... It was only with difficulty that the Transjordan authorities were induced to refrain from intervention.[325]

April 1948 had kicked off with bombs planted near Glubb's house (his wife was slightly injured)[326] and the prime minister's residence. But the crucial event, without doubt, was the conquest, by IZL and LHI irregulars (assisted by a small number of Haganah men), of the Arab village of Deir Yassin on the western outskirts of Jerusalem on 9 April, part of the Haganah's 'Operation Nahshon,' geared to clearing the length of the Tel Aviv-Jerusalem road. The conquest was accompanied, and possibly followed, by the killing, mutilation and rape of dozens of unarmed civilians; altogether, about 110 villagers - most of them women, children and elderly persons - died.[327] Subsequently, British, Jewish and Arab reports of the incident, stressing its gruesomeness, contributed to the precipitation of Palestinian flight from neighbouring and distant villages and towns and sparked feelings of anti-Zionist militancy and vengefulness in the masses and in the political elites in the Arab states. In Transjordan, 'the effect ... of the massacre ... was to create a good deal of indignation and an equal amount of alarm...' reported Kirkbride.[328]

Politicians around the Arab world, including Jordanians, came under pressure from their peoples to intervene to 'save the Palestinians.' Abdullah was immediately pressed to 'do something,' using his fabled Legion. Palestinian notables persistently lobbied the Jordanian court. One Palestinian wrote two days after the massacre pleading with the head of the court 'to assist the Arabs of Palestine out of their affliction,' specifically urging the despatch of the Legion to Palestine, to both take over and protect the Arab areas and also to conquer the Jewish areas of the country.[329] Delegations of Palestinian notables made tracks for Amman to lobby the King to intervene. On 18 April a group of notables from Qalqilya, where 'the fear was great' after Deir Yassin, hammered out a petition to the King 'to ask him for help in defending the town' and on 23 April proceeded to Amman to plead in person. The delegation apparently told the King that the Arab League's ministers were doing nothing but shuttle from meeting to meeting while 'Palestine's Arabs were being slaughtered. If the Arab states lacked the power, they should say so to Palestine's Arabs, and these would then agree to the partition solution [i.e., acquiesce in Jewish statehood and end the hostilities].' The King responded that the Arab Legion was 'too small to alone confront the

Jews, but after the 15th of May other Arab states would join the war and together [the Arabs] would beat the Zionists.' But the delegates from Qalqilya returned home unconvinced and 'largely disappointed,' reported Haganah intelligence.[330]

Immediately after the massacre, Bevin queried Kirkbride about Abdullah's intentions: Did he still intend 'to send the Arab Legion into Palestine after May 15th?'[331] Kirkbride responded that Abdullah's intention to take over the 'Arab areas' of Palestine 'after the 15th of May' remained 'unchanged'[332] - but explicated, probably on the basis of a briefing by Glubb, as follows:

> The general idea seems to be to establish units of the Arab Legion at Hebron, Ramallah and Nablus as a first step and then to decide further moves in the light of events. It is realised that Jerusalem presents too big a problem for the Arab Legion to deal with alone and that Western Galilee is too remote with communications through a Jewish area ... The present intention is to avoid a clash with the Jews but whether or not this will be possible remains to be seen.

Kirkbride added that the notables of 'the Gaza, Hebron and Ramallah' areas openly favoured a Transjordanian occupation, and that Beersheba, 'terrorised by the Jews,' would 'welcome any saviour'; Nablus, with Qawuqji's troops 'at its gates, is more cautious'; while Jaffa, Lydda and Ramleh 'are terrorised by the Mufti's followers who have threatened to murder anyone who has dealings with the Arab Legion.'[333] (Glubb himself, in an interview in the Egyptian daily *Al Ahram*, at this time spoke more vaguely of the Legion entering Palestine after 15 May in order to maintain 'security and order,' if 'the United Nations asked it to do so.')[334]

Deir Yassin and the pressures it spawned prompted Abdullah to ask the British to allow a redeployment of some of the Legion units still in Palestine to defend vulnerable villages. But, as Kirkbride pointed out, there were too many villages – Palestine had about 800 - and too few Legionnaires to effectively change the military picture. The British refused to allow the Legionnaires to be diverted from their originally planned tasks, of defending British lines of communication and bases.[335]

Deir Yassin immediately strained Yishuv-Hashemite relations. To blunt its effect, the Jewish Agency rushed off a letter to Abdullah reiterating the Agency's condemnation of the 'Deir Yassin incident' as 'brutal and barbaric ... [and] not in accord with the spirit of the Jewish people and its cultural heritage.'[336] Abdullah responded that 'the Jewish Agency stands at the head of all Jewish affairs in Palestine and outside it ... and

... and gives rise to [such incidents]' - i.e., the Agency was responsible for Deir Yassin - and 'terrible consequences' would ensue if such incidents continued.[337]

Against this backdrop of 'a general collapse of Arab morale in Palestine,' triggered by Deir Yassin and Qawuqji's parallel defeat in the battle for Mishmar Ha`emek (4-15 April), Abdullah was moved to cable the Arab League Political Committee offering to 'rescue Palestine ... with the Arab Legion.[338] 'Azzam Pasha, the League secretary general, promptly responded by sending General Ismail Safwat, the head of the Arab League Military Committee, to Amman 'to discuss with Your Majesty the necessary measures to be taken to liberate the besieged Arabs and to prevent more massacres taking place...' The League enjoined Abdullah 'to allow the Transjordan Arab Legion to do its duty.'[339] All of this, perhaps, was for the record. 'Azzam no doubt entertained no real hopes that the Legion would rush into or around Palestine in defiance of the British Mandate Government, still nominally the rulers of the land. Moreover, 'Azzam wasn't really interested in giving the Legion a free hand vis-a-vis Palestine. He told a British journalist (who promptly told Glubb, who told Kirkbride) that he agreed to Transjordanian intervention in Palestine only if it was designed to 'take over [Palestine] as a whole' - implying that he did not agree to Legion intervention only in defence of Arab areas and communities.[340]

During the following days, Abdullah, under intense and conflicting pressures, seemed to waver between commitment to his earlier understanding with the Yishuv and the demands of his Arab compatriots. In a statement to the press on 17 April, Abdullah's court chief declared that 'Transjordan opposes vigorously partition' (meaning opposes Jewish statehood) and regards 'Palestine and the Hashemite Kingdom [as] but one thing consisting of coast and inner parts...' This implied that Abdullah was intent on taking over all of Palestine and, perhaps, fusing it with Transjordan.[341] Giving added weight to this view of Abdullah's intentions, Cunningham reported that 'a good Arabic [sic] source' maintained that Abdullah had asked the Iraqis to send a division to Transjordan to 'protect the Legion's rear' while the Legion plunged into Palestine with the initial objective of firmly securing 'Haifa, Jaffa and Gaza.' The implication seemed to be that Abdullah ultimately aimed to take over the Jewish areas as well as Arab Palestine.[342]

With the fall of Arab Tiberias on 17-18 April to the Haganah and the exodus of the town's population (in part to Transjordan), the pressure on Abdullah mounted, both from 'inside and outside Palestine,' to intervene immediately and not wait until the end of the Mandate. Kirkbride seemingly had to use all of his powers of persuasion to keep Abdullah in check - though 'the Arabs do not readily listen to reason when they are in the frenzy of indignation and apprehension...'[343] Needless to say, even without Kirkbride's restraining representations, Abdullah understood that there could be no Jordanian intervention before 15 May; it was not a challenge the British could countenance.

The fall of Arab Haifa on 21-22 April only worsened Abdullah's inter-Arab position and noticeably hardened his anti-Zionist rhetoric. In a statement to the press he declared that after Deir Yassin, Tiberias and Haifa, he had no choice but to intervene, if so invited. The Jews could still achieve a peaceful resolution to the conflict if they agreed to accept local autonomy in their areas but under Arab sovereignty, he said.[344]

By early May, the political pressures were supplemented by economic problems engendered by the waves of refugees pouring across the river. Haganah intelligence reported that 'the cost of living [in Transjordan] was rising from day to day. Fuel prices had increased horrifically and had reached P£2.25 for a can of benzene...' The fuel costs had resulted in a partial stoppage of traffic and 'flour mills had been forced to operate only one day a week.' Basic foods had also risen in price.[345]

In response to these pressures, Abdullah organized or at least permitted the dispatch to Palestine in the first days of May of hundreds of Transjordanian 'volunteers,' many of them former TJFF and ex-Legion troopers, to beef up the Palestinian militias.[346] Even earlier, the Legion reportedly began to recruit as auxiliaries, arm, train, clothe and pay villagers where Legion units were stationed. By early April it was reported that 50 such volunteers had been recruited in Hebron, with smaller numbers being inducted in 'Gaza, Beit Jibrin and Halhul.'[347]

But the Legion itself could not march before 15 May. Abdullah gave vent to his frustrations - and, obliquely, revealed his objectives - in a letter to Cunningham, apprising the High Commissioner of 'Arab feeling in and outside Transjordan' following 'Deir Yassin, [Khirbet] Nasir Eddin,[348] Tiberias and Haifa.' Public opinion in Jordan, he said, was 'so excited and disappointed that nothing can check it except the righting of affairs.' By this the King meant a Jordanian takeover of 'Jerusalem, Nazareth and Bethlehem' with the termination of the Mandate and Jewish acceptance of Arab sovereignty in all of Palestine. This stance, said Abdullah, was 'a true expression [of] the feelings of every Transjordanian who possesses magnanimity and manhood.'[349]

During the weeks before the invasion, Kirkbride and Glubb pulled hard on the reins. A senior RAF officer who had lunched with the King reported on 17 April: 'Recent events in Palestine have made him even more anxious to take drastic action with the Arab Legion but so far Kirkbride and Glubb have managed to exert the necessary restraining influence.'[350] After Tiberias and Haifa, Kirkbride reported: 'Position is that tremendous public pressure is being brought to bear on the King and on the [Iraqi] Regent ['Abd al-Ilah] to intervene with troops in Palestine immediately. The fact that Amman is crowded with refugees and that reports are now coming in of a Jewish offensive in Jerusalem does not make matters easier.' But the Arab leaders were far from optimistic about the possible outcome of intervention:

> There is a general slump of Arab morale and an inclination to indulge in recriminations instead of planning to deal with the situation. King Abdullah ... is losing his nerve. The Regent gave me the impression that his main objective was to calm public opinion in Iraq rather than to save Arab Palestine. The Prime Minister of Transjordan and his colleagues are counselling prudence and are resisting in an admirable manner the hysterical demands for armed intervention by which they are inundated. I have added my own advice to theirs,

reported Kirkbride.[351]

Britain's representatives in Amman bombarded the King with threats and cautions that he hold off until 15 May.[352] Abdullah allowed himself to be persuaded. But others in the Arab world were less attentive to British needs and sensibilities. The gathering of Arab leaders in Amman on the morning of 29 April, which included the Iraqi Regent and 'Azzam, joined later in the day by Syria's prime minister and chief of staff, the Lebanese Prime Minister Riad a Solh and his defence minister, and a representative of the Egyptian Army general staff, 'decided in principle in favour of intervention by the regular Arab armies ...'[353] The day before, 'Azzam had privately told British diplomats that public pressure in each of the states was proving irresistible. 'Their leaders, including himself, would probably be assassinated if they did nothing,' he said. ('Azzam presciently noted that the Jews were 'able to import arms at will despite the [international arms] embargo. He was very sceptical of the embargo on Jewish arms and said the embargo worked only against the Arabs who were not even getting the arms promised them under existing contracts.')[354]

Most of the leaders gathered on 29 April pressed for immediate action, in view of the ongoing, successful Jewish offensives and the Palestinian collapse. 'Azzam privately informed Kirkbride that two Egyptian brigades were poised on the border at Rafah 'and asked whether the

British troops at Rafah would intervene if the Egyptians moved into Palestine.' Kirkbride replied that the British 'would be bound to react to any move before the end of the Mandate.'[355]

At their consultation, some of the Arab leaders suggested that the Arab Legion move into Palestine first and alone, as it was the only Arab army 'on the spot' and ready to act. Jordan's prime minister, Abul Huda, parried that Jordan would not act 'independently' (that is, alone) after the Arab states had decided on 'joint intervention.'[356] Anyhow, Abdullah argued, Jordan could not possibly move before 15 May. And given the Legion's acknowledged pre-eminence among the Arab fighting forces, Jordan's stand proved decisive.[357]

Against this backdrop of Jordanian refusal to rush into premature invasion and successive Palestinian defeats, a number of Arab leaders began inching towards the Jordanian position - of acceptance of a Jewish state, albeit one smaller than that outlined in the UN Partition Resolution. 'Azzam, for one, hinted that such a state 'might be accepted' by the Arabs, prompting Kirkbride to remark to Bevin that this was 'a remarkable change from the earlier objective of occupying the whole of Palestine.'[358]

And the Jordanians remained faithful to their commitments of November 1947 (to Golda Meir) and February 1948 (to Bevin). Exactly a week before the pan-Arab invasion, Kirkbride reported:

> The scheme which was put to you [Bevin] by the Prime Minister [Abul Huda] was that there should be no aggression against the Jewish areas ... In spite of statements made for publicity purposes the intentions of both the King and the Prime Minister remain basically as explained to you. It is not possible however in present circumstances for them to indicate to the Arab world that they propose in effect to accept partition.[359]

It is against this background, of Zionist conquest and Palestinian collapse and flight and pan-Arab confusion, that the following incidents also must be viewed.

The Legionnaires in Palestine - quite remarkably, given their natural sympathy for their embattled Arab brethren - by and large down to mid-May stayed out of the Arab-Jewish fighting. Abdullah may have found it politic during January-March 1948 not to block the passage of ALA troops and supplies through Transjordan into Palestine.[360] And some Legion officers stationed in Palestine during the run-up to May 1948 gave local militiamen basic military drill (and occasionally the odd bullet and grenade).[361] But the Legion stayed out of the civil war.

However, almost inevitably, in view of the existing confusion and tensions, and the proximity of the forces in various areas, a series of Jewish-Arab Legion clashes took place. Seven Legion garrison companies had been seconded to the British Army since the end of the Second World War and had served as guards along Palestine's roads and in various Mandate installations. During December 1947-May 1948 there were points of contact and friction with the Haganah which, quite naturally, regarded the Legionnaires - part of the British Army but nonetheless Arabs - with suspicion. Nevertheless the clashes that occurred by and large involved Legionnaires attacking Jews rather than the opposite (the Jews understood that attacking Legionnaires might embroil them in unwanted hostilities with the British). Such clashes were most frequent during December 1947, the first month of hostilities, their number and frequency gradually diminishing as greater discipline was imposed on the Legionnaires by their British officers and the British Army. On 9 of December, a Legion trooper fired from a military truck at passers-by in Harbour Street, Haifa, wounding three Jews; two days later, on 11 December, a sentry at the gate of 42nd General Military Hospital, Haifa, shot dead a Jew, and on 14 December, in the worst incident, dozens of Legionnaires fired from their Beit Naballah camp at a passing Jewish convoy on its way to Ben-Shemen, killing 14 and wounding 19.[362] The Legionnaires later offered the unlikely story that the Jews had thrown grenades at the camp, provoking their fire. No Legionnaires were hit in the incident.[363]

Nor was Ben-Shemen the last such clash. On 23 December 1947 an Arab Legion unit fired at a Jewish convoy passing by the Lions' Gate outside the Old City. On 25 February 1948 Legionnaires inside the Old City fired at a Jewish school, wounding two children. And on 18 April, Legion armoured cars attacked the Jewish settlement of Neve Ya`akov, just north of Jerusalem, after its defenders repeatedly fired on Arab and British traffic on the Ramallah-Jerusalem road. But, in general, during the period November 1947-late April 1948, the Legion remained both well-disciplined and non-partisan, only rarely clashing with Jewish troops or in any active way assisting the Husseini-led Palestinian militiamen. The Legion officers in Palestine, though they may have had little sympathy for the Jews, no doubt understood that their King regarded Husseini and his supporters as Jordan's main enemies.[364]

But this situation changed, at least to a degree, as Jewish statehood and the Legion push into Palestine drew near. The first serious clash occurred during 27-29 April, when the Legion's 4th Battalion, in violation of the November 1947 Abdullah-Meir understanding (and of international law), mounted a mortar and artillery attack from Transjordan on Haganah forces at the Naharayim (Jisr al Majami) police fort and neighbouring Kibbutz Gesher, on the Palestine side of the international frontier.

The attack, according to the Jordanians, was prompted by the killing of one or more Arab Legionnaires at the site by Haganah snipers[365] or, in another version, was a result of a 'local misunderstanding'[366] - and Glubb, they said, had severely reprimanded the responsible Legion battalion commander, Habis Majali.[367] According to the Haganah, the clash was triggered by the Haganah occupation of the Naharayim police fort, which the British army had evacuated earlier on 27 April.[368]

Be that as it may, the Jordanian attack may also have had an immediate strategic purpose (as understood by Majali or, if authorised by the King, by Abdullah himself): To help clear the way for the prospective pan-Arab invasion of Palestine by driving the Haganah away from one of the main intended crossing points along the Jordan. (On 15 May Naharayim-Gesher was to be the site of the Iraqi invasion and an Iraqi brigade was to spend the following five-six days unsuccessfully trying to take the kibbutz and the neighbouring fort.)

Whether or not there was some initial Haganah sniping, the attack proper began when Legion mortars and armoured cars opened up on the fort and the kibbutz on the evening of 27 April, increasing the volume of fire the following day. But the Legionnaires did not cross the river to assault and take the settlement or fort. (Kirkbride hints that he had a hand in restricting the Legion's operations.)[369] Many of the settlement's buildings were reduced to rubble. But the kibbutz members and the local Haganah force held on, taking casualties. On the morning of 29 April, during a cessation of the shelling, a Legion officer appeared on the scene and demanded, in Abdullah's name, that the Haganah evacuate the fort and surrender the settlement and their arms. The defenders refused. Meanwhile, the Jewish Agency protested to Cunningham, who interceded (via Kirkbride) with Abdullah;[370] separately, a Jewish official, Avraham Daskal, who was friendly with the Jordanian monarch, made direct contact with the palace. Abdullah (or Glubb) then put a stop to the shelling.[371]

The Legion's actions caused 'considerable' embarrassment in Whitehall - after all, Britain's ally was shelling a Jewish settlement in British-administered territory which had been earmarked by the UN for Jewish sovereignty - and prompted a reprimand from Bevin to the Jordanian minister in London. At the same time, Kirkbride was instructed to rebuke Abdullah for an 'aggression against Palestine territory.' Bevin pointed out that Britain was now hard pressed to explain why it was justified in intervening against a contemporaneous Jewish (IZL) attack on Jaffa while desisting from intervention against a Jordanian attack on Gesher.[372]

The second incident was far more serious. As part of their evacuation, the British during April and the first half of May gradually sent back to Transjordan most of the Legion companies that had done garrison duty in Palestine. Initially, the British had planned for the withdrawal of all Legion units back to Transjordan 'by the end of April.' But due to last-minute delays, General Gordon McMillan, the GOC British Troops in Palestine, moved the deadline forward to 12 May.[373] But Glubb was interested in keeping some troops in the West Bank even beyond that date to prepare the way and 'greet' the bulk of the Legion when it crossed the river. It is possible, as well, that for technical reasons - as he later claimed - a number of companies were unable to pull out in time and were left 'stranded' in Palestine (subsequently 'greeting' the bulk of the Legion when it crossed the Jordan on 15-16 May). In all, somewhere between two and six Legion companies failed to leave Palestine by 14 May (though Glubb, in his memoirs, speaks only of one company in Hebron).[374] There is ample evidence that companies or independent platoons remained behind in Ramallah and its environs, and at Latrun, spanning the hours between the British departure and the invading Legion's arrival in the Samarian and Judean hill-country.[375]

During the months before 15 May, Arab civilian and British and Legion military traffic was periodically fired upon along the Hebron-Jerusalem road. The fire came from Haganah militiamen stationed in the Etzion Bloc kibbutzim, four settlements - Kfar Etzion, Revadim, Massu'ot Yitzhak and 'Ein Tzurim - planted during the 1930s side by side just west of the road linking Hebron and Bethlehem. The UN partition plan of 1947 had allocated the area to the Palestinian Arab state but the Haganah command had decided not to evacuate the settlements, despite their vulnerability, both as a matter of principle and precisely because they were 'a sharp thorn stuck in the heart of a purely Arab area,' as Legion officer Abdullah Tall put it[376] and a potential obstruction along a main Arab line of communications. While defending the settlements siphoned off 400-500 Haganah men who could have reinforced the troops guarding Jewish Jerusalem, their presence in the bloc, it was felt, would compel the Arabs, in turn, to expend major resources in besieging or overcoming them, resources that otherwise might have been used to fight for Jerusalem.

During April and early May, the British used the Legion garrison companies to secure the main roads along which they intended to withdraw their men and equipment.[377] These included the Jerusalem-Hebron-Beersheba road, guarded by a Legion company based in Hebron. The British and the Legion - for different reasons - were particularly sensitive about the Jerusalem area roads. The withdrawal of British personnel and equipment from the coastal areas was relatively straightforward, through Haifa port or Rafah to the Suez Canal. But the withdrawal from Jerusalem, whether in the direction of Haifa or southward to Rafah, meant travelling through mixed and often embattled areas, with the danger of British evacuation columns being caught in crossfire. For the Legion, the Jerusalem area was sensitive because of Jerusalem's religious-political importance and because of Abdullah's intention to occupy the West Bank on the heels of the British evacuation. At the end of April, the British substantially reinforced the Legion presence south of Jerusalem: On the 24th and 25th, according to Haganah intelligence (probably exaggerating the numbers), 500-700 Legionnaires reached Hebron and Bethlehem.[378]

The commander of the Hebron detachment, Captain 'Abd al Jawad, according to Haganah intelligence assembled his men in the downtown area and told them 'that the Arab Legion must defeat the Jews and this company has been designated to conquer the Etzion Bloc ... He also addressed the Hebron population and incited them to assist the Legion in the attack ...'[379]

The British may have been interested in beefing up security along the road but Glubb, no doubt, was thinking primarily in terms of the imminent invasion. Seen from Amman, political and military developments seemed hazardous and uncertain and the intentions towards the Etzion Bloc were probably unclear also to the Legion officers in the area. One Legion officer later told an Israeli journalist: 'Arab Legion headquarters in the Hebron area ... intended to receive into its hands control in the whole Hebron area immediately after [the British] left ... A certain plan was drawn up at the beginning of May concerning the takeover in the Hebron area up to the southern approaches to Jerusalem.' But the plan, according to the officer, called not for the conquest but for the neutralization and isolation of the Etzion Bloc. It would appear that Legion units in the Hebron area at this time seem to have received 'conflicting orders from Amman.'[380]

In the last days of the Mandate, according to Glubb's memoirs, the British had ordered the Legion to draw a quantity of stores and vehicles from Egypt. 'We accordingly decided to remove the Kfar [sic] Etzion colonies before they could destroy our convoy and cut us off from Hebron,' he wrote.[381] But this does not appear to be an accurate description of how and why the attack on the Etzion Bloc was finally launched.

Despite 'Abdullah Tall's claims to the contrary,[382] it appears likely that Glubb himself ordered the attack. This is supported by the commander of the Legion's 1st Battalion, Arshid Marshud, who in December 1948 recorded that the order had been given by the Legion's 'chief of staff' (Glubb).[383] Moreover, given the tight discipline in the Legion, it is unlikely that the battalion commander responsible for the Jerusalem-Hebron road, Tall, or the commander of the company stationed in Hebron would have acted without Glubb's permission. Certainly, once hostilities had commenced on 12 May, Glubb's consent would have been necessary for their continuation and for the go-ahead for the final conquest of the settlements the following day.[384]

According to Tall, he had been specifically instructed by Glubb, on 6 April, 'to avoid clashes with the Jews or to harass them in any way.'[385] But the defenders of the bloc, on instructions from Haganah headquarters in Jerusalem, had repeatedly fired on Arab - including Arab Legion - traffic along the road. According to Haganah documentation, the Etzion Bloc units had attacked Arab convoys and individual vehicles on 6, 12, and 30 April and on 1 and 3 May, 'in order to reduce the pressure on [Jewish] Jerusalem' and to prevent Arab arms and irregulars from reaching the city. These attacks included ambushes of Legion units on 12 April and 3 May in which a handful of Legionnaires were killed and wounded.[386] The ambushes, according to the IDF analysis, apparently persuaded the British to 'give the Legion a free hand for aggressive action vis-a-vis the Bloc.' [387] According to one source, the ambushes persuaded the Legion to 'change its policy' towards the bloc, and instead of simply isolating it, the decision was taken to destroy it.[388]

The Haganah was given forewarning. On 4 May, the day after its men ambushed a Legion convoy, a joint force of British, Legion and irregular troops, with tanks, armoured cars, and mortars, launched a heavy punitive attack on Kfar Etzion and its outposts. The Haganah contingent temporarily abandoned one or two positions but generally held its own, and the attackers withdrew. The Haganah suffered 12 dead and some 30 wounded, but it reoccupied the positions. A similar number of Legionnaires were killed, and several dozen were wounded.[389]

It is unlikely that the attackers had intended to capture the settlements. But the result was that the 4 May attack was seen by the Hebronites and the local Legion units as a failure and left them thirsting for revenge and victory. A further Haganah attack on Arab traffic may have taken place during the next day or two. According to one Legion source, on the evening of 5 or 6 May, its officers met and planned the final attack, 'to completely destroy the Etzion Bloc militarily.'[390] The Legionnaires began to train local auxiliaries and to prepare for the final battle. Local notables put pressure on the Legion officers to launch the assault before the British departed.[391] Both the locals and the Legionnaires had an interest in securing the road - and, therefore, uprooting the Bloc - before Abdullah's army crossed the Jordan and occupied the area. It was a matter of logistics and security. But Abdullah, no doubt, also wanted to increase his prestige before the invasion in order to bolster local support for the impending Jordanian takeover.[392] For their part, the Hebron notability - led by Mayor Ja`abri - may have been partly motivated by rivalry with the Husseini-affiliated bands in the Jerusalem hills; the Hebronites, who from April pleaded with Abdullah to move into the area and prevent a Husseini takeover, also wanted to demonstrate combativeness and chalk up a victory over the Zionists.[393]

When Tall was given command of the 6th Battalion, he immediately instructed his units to prepare for action. On 9 and 10 May the Haganah outposts noticed Legion officers reconnoitring the perimeter of Kfar Etzion 'and taking measurements.'[394] At dawn on 12 May parts of two Arab Legion infantry companies (the 6th and 12th), with more than a dozen armoured cars mounting two-pounder guns (from the 1st Battalion and 2nd Garrison Company) and a battery of 3-inch mortars, with hundreds of local irregulars in support,[395] attacked Kfar Etzion and its outposts. According to Tall, Glubb was then (mis)informed of a small-scale clash and reluctantly agreed to send Tall in with reinforcements to help the 'outgunned' Legionnaires.[396] The well-organized Legionnaires, using their superior firepower liberally, gradually churned up the Haganah outworks - the Haganah had no answer to the power and range of the armour, the cannon, and the mortars - and before noon on 13 May had broken through Kfar Etzion's defences and penetrated the centre of the settlement, cutting off the perimeter outposts from each other. The defenders acknowledged defeat. Dozens laid down their arms and began to gather in the courtyard. 'Suddenly fire was opened up on the assembled men.' Those who hadn't been hit ran for shelter and the Arabs began to hunt them down 'in line with Arab tradition,' in the words of the IDF historian of the affair:[397]

> The Arabs who had burst into the settlement from all directions, as they cried "Deir Yassin", killed the living and the wounded and immediately turned to looting and vandalism. [A number of villagers died from land mines as they rushed

> into the settlement to loot.] The Legion's armoured cars opened up with machinegun fire, either taking part in the massacre or in order to stop it (as they told the [Jewish] prisoners afterwards).

The irregulars proceeded to destroy the settlement. Three of the defenders who had been in the courtyard managed to escape - one to Massu`ot Yitzhak and the other two into the hands of Legion officers, who took them prisoner. Two Arabs, whether Legionnaires or villagers is unclear, tried to rape one of the kibbutz women but a Legion officer intervened and shot them dead before taking her prisoner. But according to her testimony, the officer, while taking her to safety, 'shot dead with his pistol [a number of] wounded Jews who showed signs of life.' Both the woman and the man who made it to Massu`ot Yitzhak later testified that 'Legion troops actively participated in the massacre.' But the IDF historian also quotes a Legion officer who explained that there was no formal organized surrender; that after some defenders had surrendered others continued to fire at the Arabs; that villagers indeed massacred surrendering Jews; that Legionnaires killed a number of villagers and two Legionnaires were badly wounded defending three Jewish prisoners who were then taken away by villagers and murdered. Regarding the massacre, the historian explained that 'first and foremost [it stemmed] from a savage mentality, and thirst for revenge and for Jewish blood, and was a direct successor of the massacre [by Arabs] in Hebron in 1929 [of the ultra-orthodox Jewish community, in which 64-66 died] ... In Kfar Etzion 127 persons, including 21 women ... were massacred.'[398]

The Legion's version, as conveyed by Kirkbride to the Foreign Office on 14 May, was somewhat different. Kirkbride was hard pressed to explain why Legion units, seconded to the British Army, had participated in an attack upon and destruction of four Jewish settlements hours before the British pullout. He reported that the Bloc's defenders had triggered the assault by attacking Legion traffic on the Hebron road. Subsequently, the Legionnaires, he (falsely) reported, were simply caught up in an attack on the settlements by irregulars and 'the Arab Legion prevented massacre of inhabitants and looting of colonies which would otherwise have been their fate at the hands of the local Arabs.'[399]

The fall of Kfar Etzion severely shook the morale of the defenders of the other three settlements, whose position had been rendered tactically untenable. Following negotiations during the night between the British, the Red Cross, local Arab leaders and the Jewish Agency, the surrender of the remaining settlements was arranged. Early on 14 May, a Red Cross convoy, augmented by Legion officers, entered 'Ein Tzurim and

Revadim and picked up the wounded. The able-bodied men and women were taken away to Jordanian captivity. A few hours later, Massu`ot Yitzhak surrendered and here, too, the able-bodied were taken to Jordan. Altogether, some 350 of the four settlements' members and defenders became PoWs. A Jewish doctor who accompanied the convoy wrote that, from what he saw in Revadim and `Ein Tzurim on 14 May, 'the Legion troops (officers and men) behaved very well.'[400] In his autobiography, Glubb was at pains to argue that if a massacre had taken place in Kfar Etzion, it wasn't perpetrated by Legionnaires.[401] Abdullah Tall was less cagey (though also not particularly truthful): 'The remaining Jewish combatants continued to resist from a fortified position. This forced our soldiers to kill all of them. We only took three prisoners. All the Jewish combatants were killed.'[402]

In tandem with these Legion-Haganah clashes (and perhaps to a degree egged on by them), Jordan made two clandestine efforts - the first by Glubb and the second by Abdullah - to nail down the November 1947 non-belligerency agreement with the Yishuv before the planned push into the West Bank.

On 10 April 1948 Glubb sent Col. Desmond Goldie, officer in command of the Legion's 1st Brigade, to meet with a Yishuv official named (or code-named) 'Barkai' in Afula. Goldie, saying he had come in Glubb's name, asked 'Barkai' to help set up a meeting with a Haganah representative 'regarding the 15-16 of May.' Goldie said that 'the Arab Legion ... would [then] invade the Arab area of Palestine,' his own brigade in the van. The exact demarcation of the area to be occupied was 'still unclear (the [Nablus-Ramallah-Tulkarm] Triangle, Jerusalem, Acre?),' he said, but the purpose of the requested meeting was 'a discussion on mutual non-belligerency, on those dates [i.e., 15-16 May] and after them.' The meeting concluded with Goldie saying he was returning to Amman and would call 'Barkai' a few days later to 'receive an answer.'[403]

The desired Legion-Haganah meeting, initiated by Glubb but quite likely with King Abdullah's prior consent, at last took place on 2 May. Goldie, accompanied by a staff officer, Major Charles Coaker, drove to Naharayim, the site of the Haganah-Legion clashes three days before, where they met the Haganah's Shlomo Shamir, who was about to assume command of the newly created 7th (Armoured) Brigade, and Nahum Spiegel (Golan), the operations officer (and later commander) of the Golani Brigade.

Goldie had been briefed by Brigadier Norman Lash, Glubb's deputy, rather than by Glubb himself - perhaps in an effort by Glubb to distance himself from the overture. Nonetheless, Goldie told Shamir that he had been sent by Glubb to open a 'line of communication' to the Haganah in order to avoid a Legion-Haganah clash when the Legion pushed into Palestine. Goldie repeatedly spoke of the need for follow-up meetings (perhaps at Kalia, on the northern shore of the Dead Sea) and a pre-arranged method for communication.

Goldie, according to Shamir's report on the meeting, opened with the main point: 'We want contact with you in order to avoid a clash with you. Is this possible?' Shamir responded that 'insofar as the Legion won't fight us and insofar as it won't support attacks by other Arab [armies] ... I see no reason for a clash.'

Goldie then asked whether the Yishuv had in fact accepted partition or 'whether you intend to conquer the whole of the country?' Shamir responded that the future Jewish State's borders was a matter for the Yishuv's political leaders to decide. What would be necessary for the state's security would be conquered 'and if need be, also the whole country.'

How Goldie reacted to this is not stated in Shamir's report. He quotes Goldie as then embarking on a discussion of the Jerusalem issue. 'We are worried about the situation in Jerusalem. How can a [Legion-Haganah] clash be avoided there?,' he asked. On this point Shamir was quite forthcoming: 'To the extent that Jewish Jerusalem will be secure, the road to it [from Tel Aviv] open, and the Jewish settlements around it secure and the road to them safe, I believe there will be no reason for a clash.'

Goldie went on to describe Jordan's general dilemma: 'Understand that we don't want to clash with you but we cannot appear as a brake and traitors to the Arab cause. What can be done?' Goldie felt that a way could be found to avoid battle.

Returning to Goldie's original question, Major Coaker asked whether the attack on Jaffa (by the IZL on 25-27 April) - which had been earmarked in the UN partition plan for Arab sovereignty - signalled the Yishuv's intention to conquer the whole country. Shamir responded in the negative, saying that Jaffa had been attacked because it had harassed neighbouring Tel Aviv 'and this could not be countenanced.'

Now it was Shamir's turn to ask: 'Do you intend to enter Palestine?'

Goldie parried: 'As far as I know, no decision has yet been taken. Maybe the Pasha [i.e., Glubb] knows something. We don't.'

Shamir (pressing): 'But you have already planned the entry into Palestine?'

Goldie: 'True. We have planned several alternative courses but so far nothing has been decided ...'

Shamir dropped the subject and Coaker and Goldie then went on to comment on the previous six months of fighting. Goldie: 'We believed that [Palestinian] Arab morale would collapse but we did not imagine that it would happen so quickly ... The Arabs are not good fighters. The only ones I would rely on are the beduins. They are the only ones who will carry out orders and not run away.'[404]

Shertok subsequently defined the purpose of the Goldie mission or overture as 'to coordinate their respective military plans in order "to avoid clashes without appearing to betray the Arab Cause".'[405] Shamir, more narrowly, defined Goldie's mission as stemming from the Jordanians' - or Glubb's - desire to open a channel of communication for the future; to find out the Haganah's plans; and worry over what was in prospect in Jerusalem, about which the Jordanians would have liked to reach prior agreement.[406] From the text of Shamir's report it would appear that, more generally and above all, Glubb was trying to ascertain whether a non-belligerency agreement could be reached with the Haganah before the Legion plunged into the West Bank.[407] The Haganah, for its part, was probably also keen on mutual non-belligerency and wanted to know the Legion's intentions.

The Goldie-Shamir meeting served as a prelude to the second and last secret meeting, eight days later, on 10 May, between King Abdullah and Jewish Agency representative Golda Meir (Myerson) in Amman. Meir, accompanied this time only by Ezra Danin, was driven to the meeting by Abdullah's secretary, Muhammed Zubeiti, who had earlier transmitted Abdullah's proposals to the Jewish Agency: A unified Transjordan-Palestine kingdom, under Abdullah, with the Jews enjoying autonomy in their majority areas, 'such as Tel Aviv,' but with equal ('fifty-fifty') parliamentary representation for both communities (it is unclear from the documents whether Abdullah meant that the Palestinian Arabs and Jews should each be equally represented or whether the 'fifty-fifty' applied to all Arabs and Jews in the unified kingdom).

The following day, 11 May, Meir, back from Amman, found Ben-Gurion at a meeting of the Mapai Party Centre and handed him a note reporting on the meeting:

> We met amicably. He is extremely worried and he looked terrible. He did not deny that we had [in November 1947] talked and reached an understanding on a

> desirable arrangement [dibbur ve'havana `al sidur ratzui], that is, that he would take the Arab part [of Palestine], but now he is only one of five [aligned Arab leaders]. This is the plan he proposed - a unitary country [i.e., state] with autonomy in the Jewish areas, and after a year it would become one country [i.e., a Transjordan-Palestine state] under his rule.[408]

The following day, 12 May, Meir more fully briefed the Yishuv's political leadership, the 'People's Administration' - which two days later became the 'Provisional Government of Israel.' Abdullah, flanked by Zubeiti, was 'friendly,' she said, but appeared 'very depressed, worried, nervous.' She told Abdullah that his proposals were unacceptable. Abdullah replied that he 'wanted peace not destruction.' Meir said that the Jews and Abdullah had a common enemy, the Mufti's Palestinians, and the Jews had beaten them. Meir proposed that the two sides 'return to the plan that had existed all along and about which there was mutual understanding and there was an agreement.'

Abdullah 'did not deny that that was what he wanted, but in the interim things had happened in the country. There was the matter of Deir Yassin. "[And] then I was one and now I am [only] one of five, and I can't [stick to the agreement]. I have no choice and can do no other."'

Meir responded that the Yishuv was now far stronger and, if there was war, 'we would fight with all our strength ... [and] we will fight in every place, to the extent of our power ... If he reneges on the agreement we had had and if he wants war - then we shall meet [again] after the war.' Meir concluded her report to the Yishuv's leaders by saying that Abdullah was going into this affair 'as a man in a vice, who cannot get out of it.' Danin, who also attended the People's Administration meeting, added: '[Abdullah] said: "I am very sorry and I am sorry about the blood [that will be shed] and about the destruction. Let us hope that we will meet [again] and that our ties will not be broken."' The matter of Jerusalem did not come up at all, perhaps because neither Meir nor Abdullah wished to raise the prickly issue, which almost inevitably would have resulted in disagreement; or, perhaps, because, since 8 May, there had been an internationally-brokered but unofficial truce in the city (which was to last until 14 May), so neither side expected hostilities there to resume or to be sucked into them.[409]

In short, the two leaders had parted after 'agreeing to differ,' in Kirkbride's phrase.[410] After the meeting Zubeiti reportedly told the two Israelis, over dinner, that Abdullah really did not want war - and neither did Talal, his eldest son.[411] But the meeting essentially had ended in failure: Abdullah had refused to re-commit himself to the non-belligerency pact concluded the previous November, and Meir had rejected the idea of Jewish autonomy within an expanded Hashemite kingdom. There would be war and, Abdullah seemed to imply, battle between his forces and the Yishuv. But the monarch seemed also to assume that at its end there would be a Jewish state and renewed Hashemite-Jewish negotiations.

Subsequently, at a press conference in Paris in June, Weizmann vaguely referred to the secret Meir-Abdullah meeting. The palace in Amman quickly denied that any such meeting had taken place. But Kirkbride, asked by the Foreign Office, commented:

> I have reason to believe ... that the lady in question did see the King on May 10th at Amman ...[The] proceedings consisted of both parties stating their case and agreeing to differ. The lady said that the Jews would accept nothing less than [the] United Nations partition [plan] and the King said that he could not go further than Jewish autonomy in an Arab state. It seems that the Jewish leaders had based all their plans on the assumption that Transjordan would not intervene in [Palestine] after the end of the Mandate. In fact the Transjordan army was the most effective opposition with which the Jews had to contend, and they are very cross about it.[412]

According to Tall, who wrote that he had heard about what transpired from people who had been at the meeting, Golda demanded that the King 'declare peace with the Jews, [and] not send his army into Palestine' and promised, for her part, that the Jewish Agency 'would agree ... to Hashemite annexation of the Arab part of Palestine.' Abdullah 'promised that the two armies - Jordan's and Iraq's - would not fight the Jews, but would stop at the partition plan frontiers, and would not cross it.'[413] Tall was to write of how King Abdullah, subsequently, used to 'joke about that Jewess's vulgarity, pride and domineering nature.'[414]

Chapter 5

THE INVASION

Decades later, Kirkbride was to write that 'the last few months before the end of the mandate marked a period of unhappiness for me and I experienced a feeling of helpless horror in much the same way as a bystander watching an impending motor accident knows he can do nothing to prevent it.'[415]

The Arab States Invade Palestine, May 1948

The armies of Egypt, Syria, Iraq, and Transjordan (the Lebanese Army never crossed the border) invaded Palestine on 15-16 May without an agreed, coordinated master plan. During February-April 1948 a number of staff officers, including a young Transjordanian captain, Wasfi Tal, and General Ismail Safwat, the Iraqi ex-chief of staff and Arab League Military Committee chairman in Damascus, had, it appears, worked on a rough plan, involving a coordinated Lebanese-Syrian-Iraqi-Transjordanian thrust, along several north-south and east-west axes, towards Afula. The Arab Legion was supposed to advance into Samaria and then, veering northwestwards, into the Jezreel Valley. Simultaneously the Syrian and Iraqi armies were to cross the borders and push southward and westward toward Afula. Once Afula was captured, severing the Jewish Jordan Valley and eastern Jezreel Valley settlements from the main Jewish concentration of population along the coast, a second-stage push on Haifa - the country's main port - was envisaged, while the Arab Legion, simultaneously, was to push towards the coast somewhere north of Tel Aviv. The Lebanese Army was, it appears, supposed to thrust down the coast road from Ras al-Naqura toward Haifa. With the other Arab armies thus engaged in the north, the Egyptian Army was to cross the border at Rafah and advance directly up the coast road towards Tel Aviv. The 'plan' envisaged a dissection and isolation of the Jewish demographic concentrations and conquest of parts of the Jewish-designated state; it is unclear whether it anticipated anything beyond that, such as the destruction of the Jewish state and\or 'throwing the Jews into the sea.'[416]

Arab States Invade Palestine, May 1948

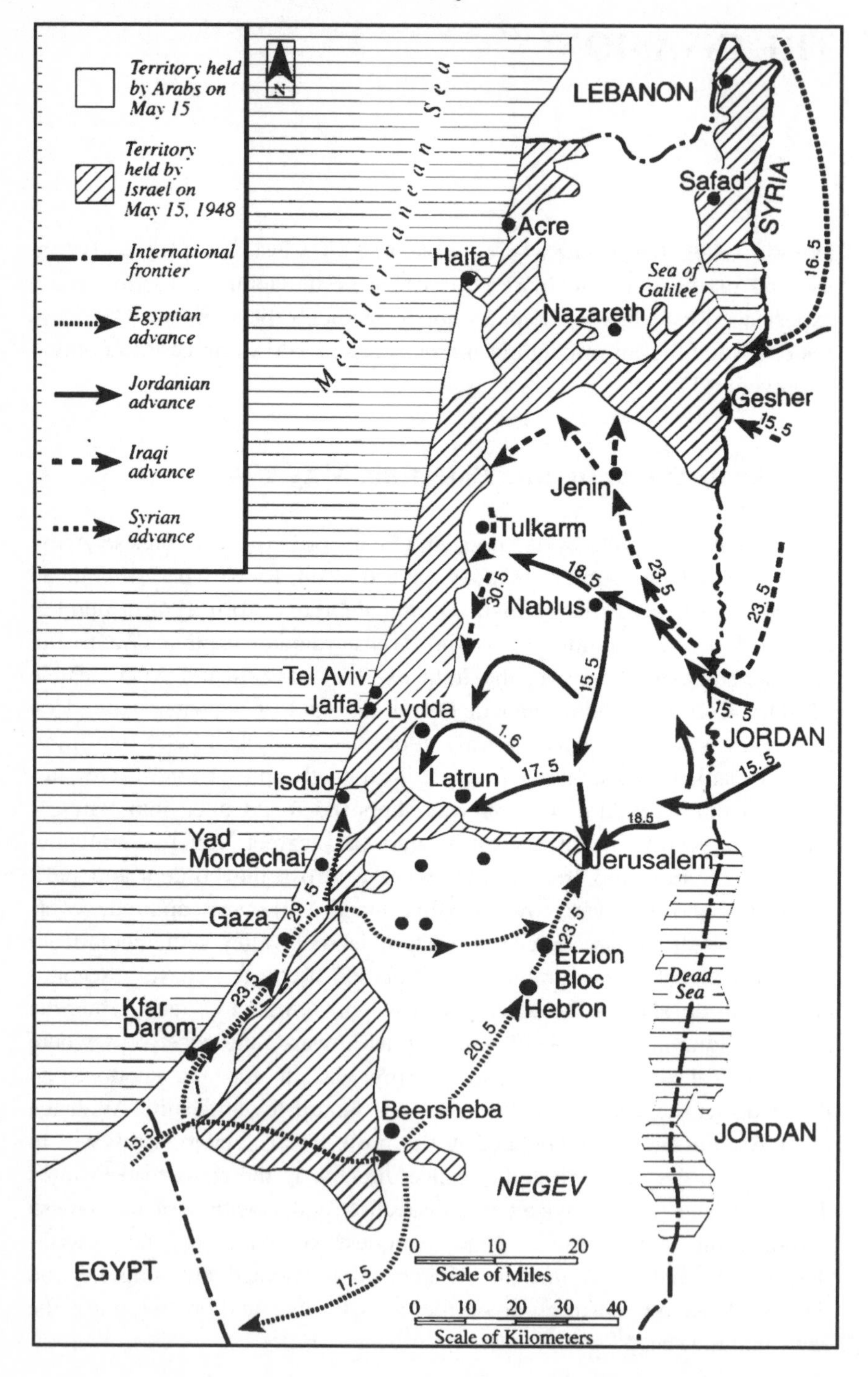

This appears to have been the 'plan' re-worked by General Nur a Din Mahmud, the Iraqi formally appointed at the last minute as the commander-in-chief of the pan-Arab invasion force, and endorsed by he Arab chiefs of staff at their meeting in Damascus on 30 April.[417] But it was never finalized[418] and, in any case, during the last days before the invasion the plan
appears to have been first modified by Mahmud and the various Arab states,[419] and then thoroughly undermined when Abdullah announced at the last minute that he intended simply to take over the Arab-designated area in the centre of the country (more or less an expanded 'West Bank') and when the Lebanese Army made clear its intention not to participate in the invasion.

In the immediate run-up to 15 May, Abdullah in the presence of fellow Arab leaders and British officials blew alternately hot and cold - sometimes appearing to fall in with his fellow leaders' wishes and agreeing to occupy all of Palestine, at other times objecting that he would do no more than take over all or some of the Arab areas. Throughout, the other Arab leaders understood or at least strongly suspected that Abdullah had no intention of taking on the Israelis, if he could help it. According to a Haganah intelligence report from the last week of April, Transjordan told representatives of the other Arab states that it could send no more than '5,000' troops and that its ally Iraq would send only 'two battalions.' As Lebanon and Syria said they would send in only token forces and the Egyptians - at that stage - no troops at all, the Transjordanians argued that 'the offensive was ... doomed to failure, and [the Arabs] must accept partition. Abdullah promised that he could conquer the Arab areas of Palestine and assure their security ...' - meaning that he had no intention of attacking the Jewish state.[420]

Rhetorical oscillations aside, Abdullah in practice cleaved to his original intention - of occupying some of the Arab areas, not attacking the Jewish areas, and avoiding battle with the Haganah. Ultimately, as we shall see, he strayed from the original, British-agreed scheme only in the belated dispatch of the Legion to 'save' the Arab half of Jerusalem from Jewish conquest.[421]

In Amman, the last days before the British pullout and the pan-Arab invasion were, in Kirkbride's words:

> bedlam, the like of which I have never yet experienced. I cannot attempt to recount or record the numerous conversations which I have [had] with Arab leaders going over the same ground again ad again advocating caution, restraint and patience until the end of the Mandate etc., only to have all the work undone by des-

> perate appeals for help from somewhere in Palestine or by the arrival of a new batch of refugees with new rumours. In this atmosphere it is difficult to speculate much about the future.

Nevertheless, he went on to predict that the Arab forces would enter Palestine, but would not be large, and 'the avowed objective of the conquest of Palestine is probably too difficult a task for them.' The Arab leaders might limit themselves to occupying Arab areas and the aim of halting further Jewish expansion - but for one thing: Jerusalem. 'The idea of Jerusalem in Jewish hands drives them beyond reason,' he wrote. 'I am encouraged by Glubb to propagand in favour of the following sequence: (A) A truce for Jerusalem. (B) Occupation of Arab areas by Transjordan alone or by other Arab states too. (C) Talks direct with Jews [some unclear letter groups] in search of a compromise.'[422]

'Azzam Pasha, the Secretary General of the Arab League, spent 10-11 May in Amman, where he apparently proposed to Glubb that he replace Mahmud as pan-Arab commander-in-chief. 'Azzam acknowledged that the Legion was the best of the Arab armies and the only one fully ready to push into Palestine, hence the offer. Glubb politely declined, perhaps sensing that 'Azzam was trying to set him up as a scapegoat for the anticipated failure[423] or to assure Jordanian participation in the fight against Israel - while unable to assure him that any of the Arab armies, apart from Jordan's, would actually obey him. In his memoirs, Glubb wrote, more or less accurately, that, on the eve of the invasion, 'no information was available to Arab Legion headquarters as to what the other Arab armies proposed to do or the strengths which they had available ... Not the least attempt at liaison or cooperation was made ...[And during the fighting], not one word regarding the Egyptian operations was ever available to us, in spite of many requests.'[424]

Indeed, both before and during the fighting there was deep suspicion in each Arab capital and army about the neighbouring leaders' and armies' intentions and objectives. Most believed that Abdullah and Jordan had no real will or intention to fight Israel while Kirkbride, during the invasion's first days, reported (or conjectured) that 'the Egyptian Army seems to have entered into a tacit mutual non-interference pact with the Jewish colonies in the area of Palestine which they occupy ... a case of live and let live ...'[425]

Underlying the lack of cooperation with the other Arab states was Abdullah's and Glubb's assessment that the Jews were too strong and that the pan-Arab attack on Israel would fail. The Jews, as the Transjordanians understood, were better organized, had more men under arms (the Arab armies lacked equipment for some of their troops and others had to be left at home to guard shaky regimes), shorter lines of communication, better financing from abroad, and the support of the two major Powers - in short, they were stronger.[426] Hence, Abdullah preferred and intended to occupy the West Bank without fighting the Jews. Moreover, marching on Jerusalem was never part of his original intention or plan.[427] Or as Glubb later put it: 'The Arab Legion had crossed the Jordan ... with the approval of the British government, to help the Arabs defend the area of Judea and Samaria ... We were strictly forbidden to enter Jerusalem ...'[428] But the previous Jewish occupation of Arab-earmarked territory (Jaffa, etc.), the unfolding threat to (Arab) East Jerusalem, and the growing determination of the other Arab states to invade Palestine themselves, all disrupted the original Transjordanian plan and led to major Arab Legion-Haganah hostilities.

Egypt, Iraq and Jordan invaded Palestine on 15 May; the Syrian Army pushed in, just south of the Sea of Galilee, the following day. The Arab Legion crossed the Jordan on the Allenby Bridge, east of Jericho, at or just before dawn on 15 May. The day before, the Legion's four combat-ready battalions, soon to be joined by two more, had moved out of their bivouac near Zerka, passed through Amman, and then descended westward to the Jordan Valley to the eastern end of the bridge.

Kirkbride - who had not been apprised of the last-minute Syrian and Lebanese changes but knew Abdullah's intentions - on the morning of 14 May summarized what was about to happen thus:

> Present Arab military plans for tonight appear to be that a combined Syrian and Lebanese column will enter Palestine from the Lebanon. Another Syrian column will attack Samakh. Iraqi contingent will attack Jisr Majami and the Arab Legion will adhere to their original scheme and will establish themselves in Hebron, Ramallah and Nablus and then extend the sector over Arab areas.[429]

Until the very last moment Kirkbride was hopeful that a Jordanian-Israeli clash could be averted. Others were less sanguine. Even Bevin was uncertain. On 13 May he wrote to the Secretary of Defence: 'In the event of hostilities breaking out between the Arab Legion and the Jewish State as a result of a Transjordanian attack on the Jewish State within the frontiers laid down by the [General] Assembly, we shall of course have to order all regular British officers to withdraw from and remain outside Palestine ...[430]'

In his memoirs, Glubb described 14 May as his Legion bivouacked on the Jordan, waiting for midnight, and as telephone calls poured into Amman from Arab notables in East Jerusalem calling on Abdullah to save the city. Abdullah and his aides weighed what to do. Glubb argued against committing the army to Jerusalem. 'The Jews were expert in street fighting ... The Arab Legion would lose much of the advantage of its higher standard of tactical training and mobility ... [In Jerusalem] they would be greatly outnumbered by the Jews. With our slender man-power and no reserves, we could not afford a slogging match.'[431] 'If we move into Jerusalem,' Glubb told Abdullah and his aides, 'we shall use up half our army. Then we cannot hold the rest of the country. If the Jews occupy the rest of the country, Jerusalem itself would be out-flanked and fall. So in the end Jerusalem also would fall.' Abdullah 'agreed to wait and hope' but Glubb was 'full of anxious forebodings. I knew the extent of Jewish preparations. I knew that the Arabs had no plan and that there was no cooperation between them. We still had re-ceived no ammunition. The people expected us in two or three days to take Tel Aviv. How was I to act amid so much folly?' Glubb kneeled down and prayed.[432]

Abdullah Tall was later to maintain that, during the countdown to the British departure, he had pressed Glubb to leave behind units of the Le-gion, even in civilian dress, in East Jerusalem to defend the Old City against the Jews. But Glubb had adamantly refused, arguing that Jerusa-lem lay outside the Arab League (meaning, Arab Legion) invasion plans, and the last Legionnaires serving with the British Army in Pales-tine were pulled out of the city on 13 May.[433]

Glubb, then 51, was described as 'short, [with] sandy white hair parted down the middle, bushy little moustache on upper lip, soft gentle voice.'[434] This was the first time that he had led an army in war. In World War I, he had commanded a platoon of engineers. In Mesopota-mia, he had led a company-sized native desert patrol unit. In 1941, he had commanded an under-sized battalion column of Legionnaires on the road to Baghdad and then Palmyra - but essentially these had been scouting expeditions auxiliary to far larger, British-led, combat forma-tions. Now, Glubb was leading an army the size of an undersized British division, whose mission was to occupy a substantial area - about 2,000 square miles - populated by inhabitants of doubtful friendliness and then to hold it against a much larger enemy force, the Haganah\IDF. Jordan could perhaps expect some help from an Iraqi expeditionary contingent (of doubtful quality) and outright antagonism on the part of the other Arab states' armies that might or might not invade Palestine.

Yet, at the end of the day Glubb had managed to hold onto the bulk of the territory, the West Bank, and Abdullah, with substantial but in part unintentional help from the Israelis in clearing the area of foreign volunteers (the ALA), the Egyptian Army, and the Iraqis, was free to annex the territory to his kingdom, which he proceeded to do in 1949-50. Whether this annexation was ultimately beneficial or detrimental to Jordanian, or Hashemite, interests, is another question. But Glubb's success was undoubtedly a major military achievement and the only one of significance among the invading Arab armies. Indeed, one might say that Glubb's Legion was the only army that in the end beat the Israelis, denying them Latrun, the bulk of the West Bank, and East Jerusalem, with the jewel of the Old City at its heart.

In his memoirs, Glubb described the Legion invasion cavalcade on 14 May:

> In ... Amman and in every village along the road, the people were gathered, cheering and clapping wildly as each unit drove past. The flat roofs and the windows were crowded with women and children, whose shrill cries and wavering trebles could be heard above the roar and rattle of the vehicles, and the cheering of the crowds of men beside the road.
>
> The troops themselves were in jubilation. In some trucks, the soldiers were clapping and cheering. In others, they were laughing and waving to the crowds ... Many of the vehicles had been decorated with green branches of pink oleander flowers ... The procession seemed more like a carnival than an army going to war.[435]

On the outskirts of Amman, according to one participant, the units were greeted by the Legion's band, playing themes that 'stimulated the nerves, awakened the hearts and increased the enthusiasm.' The troops then drove down to Shuneh, in the Jordan Valley, where they were addressed by Abdullah (flanked by 'Azzam Pasha), who called on God to see them through.[436]

The Legion crossed the river in the early hours of 15 May, its columns making their way through Jericho and up the escarpments northwestwards, towards Ramallah and Nablus. Kirkbride later described the crucial moment:

> At a few minutes before the hour of midnight on May 14th-15th, 1948, King Abdullah and members of his personal staff stood at the eastern end of the Allenby Bridge across the river Jordan waiting for the mandate to expire officially ... At twelve o'clock precisely the King drew his revolver, fired a symbolical shot into the air and shouted the word "forward". The long column of Jordanian troops which stretched down the road behind the bridge, already had the engines of their cars ticking over and, as they moved off at the word of command, the hum of their motors rose to a roar. They passed through Jericho and went up the ridgeway [to] ... Ramallah ... Other units moved up the Wadi Fara to the heart of the Samaria district [toward Nablus].[437]

The 1st Brigade fanned out around Nablus, the 3rd Brigade from Ramallah westward. In Palestine, the troops were greeted in each town by 'masses of people ... on the sidewalks ... calling for victory with the help of God and the great King [Abdullah].'[438]

Crucial to the Jordanian deployment in the West Bank (and to Israel's continuing possession of West Jerusalem) were Bab al Wad (in Arabic, literally gate to or of the wadi), with its cluster of buildings, including a large Turkish khan, and, a couple of kilometres to the west, the British-built police Tegart fort at Latrun. The two sites were astride the Jerusalem-Tel Aviv road at the eastern edge of the coastal plain as it entered the narrow defile that led eastward and upward to the holy city. Both Bab al Wad and Latrun, it appears, were abandoned by Qawuqji's Arab Liberation Army on 15 May,[439] apparently on Jordanian orders - but a platoon of Arab Legionnaires, from the 11th Garrison Company, supported by several dozen irregulars, stayed on in the fort.[440] On the night of 15 May Glubb, certain that 'the Jews will soon attack Bab al Wad,' ordered 40 Legionnaires from the 4th Battalion, and an indeterminate number of Transjordanian beduin volunteers, to occupy the site.[441] Bab al Wad was duly occupied, either on 16 or early on 17 May. The following day the Legion presence in the nearby Latrun fort and in the surrounding villages was heavily reinforced. It appears that the two sites had not been included in the Legion's original deployment plans - and that Glubb only cottoned on to their importance, especially Latrun's, after his troops had occupied them in force.[442]

It should be noted that when the Legion column crossed the Jordan on 15 May, it made straight for Ramallah and Nablus, refraining from taking the shortest (and paved) route up the Judean escarpment, from Jericho directly to Jerusalem. During the following two-three days, the Legion continued to avoid and bypass Jerusalem (in defiance of all strategic-geographical logic), fanning out to the north and west (and, to a smaller extent, the south) of the city. Abdullah had been reluctant to enter it for the military reasons outlined by Glubb and because he was chary of violating that part of the UN partition resolution that had given the city an international status. Such a move could have caused serious complications with the British and the Americans.

But Abdullah was clearly chafing at the bit; he wanted Jerusalem. Throughout 1946-1947 and the first half of 1948 the city was very much on his mind. He himself was a devout Muslim, for whom Jerusalem was a major holy site. Perhaps, too, the idea of conquering or 'saving' Jerusalem for Islam was linked in his mind to his family's historic role, as the custodians of the two main Muslim holy sites (Mecca and Medina), and to their ouster from the Hijaz by Ibn Saud. If Abdullah couldn't retake the twin holy cities and resume the role of Islam's protector, at least he could lay hold of Islam's third (and Judaism's and Christendom's foremost) holy site. This would give his godforsaken desert principality importance and cachet both in the Arab and Islamic worlds as in the world at large. Moreover, his father Husayn, the ex-sharif of Mecca, was buried in the Old City's Temple Mount compound. Lastly Abdullah no doubt was acutely perturbed by the thought that the Old City would fall into infidel - Jewish or Christian - hands and that, inevitably, he would be blamed by his fellow Muslims and Arabs.

Abdullah's desire to lay hold of East Jerusalem, with the walled Old City at its centre, was not necessarily triggered by the Haganah's unfolding (and very real) threats to the eastern half of the city in late April-early May 1948. Without doubt, the recent Jewish military successes in and around the city increased Transjordanian trepidation and desperation on this score. But evidence of the King's desire to conquer Jerusalem pre-dates by months these Jewish successes and threats. We have already mentioned Abdullah's reference, in his meeting with Cunningham at the end of January 1948, to a possible Transjordanian takeover of East Jerusalem. In mid-February Kirkbride reported that Abdullah 'of late ... has been talking loosely about assuming the duty of protecting the Holy Places in Jerusalem after the termination of the Mandate ...'[443]

Abdullah's mental focus on Jerusalem - it growingly became something of an obsession - seemed to increase as 15 May drew near. He apparently told a United Press International correspondent, off the record, just before 20 April, that 'at the first opportunity he would send Glubb Pasha to conquer Jerusalem...'[444] On 23 April, immediately after the fall of Arab Haifa, he addressed a formal letter to the High Commissioner regarding the situation in 'Jerusalem, Nazareth, and Bethlehem,' cities under Jewish threat and holy to Christians and Muslims. This 'fact ...

makes it necessary that these trusts [i.e., holy sites] be placed in our hands on the termination of the mandate,' he wrote. 'The Jews should not be allowed to do in the Holy Cities and in Jaffa what they did in other places.' Kirkbride commented, in a cable to Bevin, that Abdullah's 'request' was 'unreasonable as he has not the forces to undertake the task' - but added that 'there is little reason current here [i.e., in Amman] at present.'[445]

Abdullah was not alone in fearing for Arab Jerusalem, and was strongly affected by the tide of emotion sweeping through the Arab world. The Arabs, reported Kirkbride on 1 May, seemed to think that Britain 'would let Jerusalem fall into Jewish hands before the end of the Mandate ... No Moslem can contemplate the Holy Places falling into Jewish hands. Even the Prime Minister [Abul Huda] of Transjordan who is by far the steadiest and most sensible Arab here gets excited on the subject.' Kirkbride assured Abdullah and the prime minister that British troops would remain in Jerusalem until 15 May, and that Bethlehem would be 'covered from Jerusalem.' A British garrison would also remain in Nazareth. 'The King's relief was so great that he embraced me.'[446] But despite his reassurances, Kirkbride at the beginning of May continued to fear that Jewish conquest of East Jerusalem was the one thing that could trigger Arab intervention in Palestine before the termination of the Mandate.[447] Jordanian panic - induced by the Haganah assault on Qatamon, a wealthy Arab district in West Jerusalem, that began on 30 April - was such that Abul Huda formally proposed to Britain that it agree to the positioning of Legion units 'to guard the Holy Places as internal security troops' after 15 May or alternatively that Britain propose this to the United Nations.[448] Abdullah followed this up with a letter he handed to Kirkbride for onward transmission to Bevin informing the foreign secretary that he 'was proceeding immediately to Jerusalem at the head of a force in order to protect the Holy Places.' Kirkbride managed to persuade Abdullah to delete this part of the letter but added that he was now 'doubtful whether some such precipitate action can continue to be prevented in the face of the continued Jewish offensive.' The immediate precipitant of what Kirkbride called the King's 'state of mind'[449] was the completion of the Haganah conquest of Qatamon on 2 May. The neighbourhood contained the Iraqi Consulate and a small Arab Legion detachment that guarded it. The Legionnaires withdrew to avoid capture. Abdullah urged Bevin to send in British troops against the Haganah[450] - but the British, only days away from the final pullout, declined.

However, despite the persistent parrying, Abdullah's suggestion that the Legion could in some fashion serve after the pullout as a protector of the Holy Places appears to have struck a responsive chord in Bevin's mind. On 5 May he cabled Kirkbride 'for your own top secret information,' that should a truce be concluded in Jerusalem, 'the idea that the Arab Legion or part of it and the Haganah might [together] be put at the disposal of some neutral commander to preserve order' in the holy city was of 'considerable attraction.' But the time had not yet come to make such a proposal 'in public or to mention it to the Arab Governments.'[451]

The Battle For Jerusalem

The Haganah had, indeed, intended during the Mandate's waning days to take the Old City, and its attacks along the seam between West and East Jerusalem during 13-18 May ('Operation Kilshon') had portended such conquest. On 13 May the Haganah expanded its area of control in the Old City's Jewish Quarter and, with the departure of the British administration and garrison on the morning of the 14th, took over the evacuated British zones ('Bevingrads') in the centre of town (including the central post office and the Russian Church compound). That day, Jewish forces pushed into northern Jerusalem's (Arab-populated) Sheikh Jarah neighbourhood and occupied the Police School and surrounding buildings, and on 18 May conquered the (Arab) Abu Tor neighbourhood to the south.

According to Ben-Gurion, who briefed the Cabinet on 16 May, 'we have conquered almost all of Jerusalem apart from Augusta Victoria and the Old City [he was slightly exaggerating]. The Old City is besieged by the Jews from almost all sides.'[452] Its Arab inhabitants were in 'a terrible panic ... many began fleeing the city,' according to IDF intelligence.[453] The panic was such that a mob collected outside the offices of the local National Committee, demanding permits to enable them to leave. The officials refused, but many got into cars and drove down the road to Jericho anyway. 'Militiamen were sent to stop them by force,' Haganah intelligence recorded.[454]

Paradoxically, the Haganah offensives in Jerusalem in mid-May were at least in part motivated by a genuine fear that the Legion intended to push towards Jerusalem and perhaps even attack West Jerusalem and possibly Israel proper. Its commanders were by no means convinced that Abdullah would cleave to the non-belligerency scenario mapped out in the first Golda Meir-Abdullah meeting. Already on 22 April Yaakov

Shimoni said that while two-three days previously he had believed that Abdullah would 'go ahead and conquer the Arab area [of Palestine] and avoid a clash with us ... after the latest events [i.e., Deir Yassin and the Haganah conquest of Arab Tiberias and Arab Haifa] it is reasonable to assume that this consideration [i.e., policy] no longer exists for him [i.e., guides him].'[455] And less than three weeks later, on 11 May, the Haganah's chief of operations and de facto chief of staff, Yigael Yadin, cabled the Etzioni Brigade, responsible for West Jerusalem: 'From a reliable source it is learned that the Allenby Bridge will be closed tomorrow to civilian traffic and that within two days the Transjordanian army will enter the country [deploying] in various places, and certainly in Jerusalem.'[456] This reflected the appreciation included by the Haganah General Staff in its instruction to all units entitled 'Document No. 32 - 15\1', whose thrust was 'Changes in Plan D – [from] March 1948', dated 11 May 1948. The General Staff now accepted as certain that the regular Arab armies would invade Palestine and try to deliver a 'decisive blow.' The Arab armies might invade simultaneously from 'north, east and south' - or the 'principal regular invader would come from [sic] the Arab Legion - from the east.' The underlying assumption seems to have been that the Legion would not limit itself to occupying Arab areas but would attack the Yishuv.[457]

During 15-18 May, a stream of emotional, even hysterical, appeals from East Jerusalem flooded Amman. For example, according to Haganah intelligence, which monitored the telephone and telegraph lines, in the early hours of 18 May the Arab militia headquarters in Jerusalem rushed off cables to the Arab Legion unit in Hebron and to King Abdullah reading: 'S.O.S. The Jews are near the [Old City] walls, tell the Arab Legion to give help immediately.' To Qawuqji the Arab militia headquarters in Jerusalem cabled: 'The situation is dangerous. A general [Jewish] attack throughout the city. The Jewish guns are on every side. You must send help immediately. The shells are falling inside the [Aksa?] mosque ...'[458] In his memoirs, Glubb recorded the arrival of these cables ('Save us! Help us! They are up to the Jaffa Gate! They have occupied Sheikh Jarah! They are scaling the walls of the Old City! Save us! Help us! ... Our ammunition is finished! We can hold on no longer! Where is the Arab Legion?') and their impact on Jordan's rulers: Abdullah 'looked tired and hollow-cheeked. The Prime Minister was suffering under the strain.'[459]

The impact on the Legion's eventual deployment was almost inevitable. Already on 15 May Kirkbride reported that 'the disturbed situation in Jerusalem' was having 'a disquieting effect on Transjordan plans as it is difficult for the authorities here to resist the appeals for help which continue to arrive from the Arabs still in the city.'[460] And on 16 May Abdullah gave Britain due warning: 'I write to your Excellency [Kirkbride] in the time of the national crisis ... I fully realize my national duties and religious motives towards Palestine as a whole and Jerusalem in particular.' He added that he hoped to avoid, 'as far as is possible, any action' that might embarrass Britain. He seemed to be saying that while he would do his best to avoid complicating Britain's position, he could not allow this consideration to stay his hand with regard to Jerusalem.[461] Moreover, the Legion's initial - essentially logistical - success on 15 May, of fording the river and fanning out unopposed in the West Bank hill country between Ramallah and Nablus, apparently went to heads in Amman. That evening Kirkbride cabled London:

> For no greater justification than existed for the recent collapse of morale, the Arabs here are full of optimism and in no mood to listen to any advice. A reverse in the operations now being undertaken by the regular Arab armies would doubtless dispel this feeling in a matter of hours ... In an informal talk with the Prime Minister ... today, I warned him that if Transjordan went beyond the plan regarding the Arab areas of Palestine, His Majesty's Government would doubtless have to reconsider their position regarding the subsidy and the loan of British officers. He gave me an opening by foretelling a total Jewish defeat in a fortnight. He took [my warning] in good part and said that while he and the King adhered basically to their original intentions, it would be impossible for Transjordan to stop at the frontier of the Jewish state if the other Arab armies were sweeping all before them. In such an event (which I said was unlikely) he would spare us embarrassment by releasing the British officers ... If the subsidy was withheld Transjordan would just have to beg for funds for [sic, from] the other Arab states.[462]

Whether it was this heady whiff of success (the Legion's own and the other Arab armies', real or imagined)[463] or whether Abdullah was intent on hoodwinking his allies is unclear but responding to Haj Amin al Husseini's congratulatory telegram of 16 May, Abdullah wrote: 'We announce to you that the Arab Army [i.e., Legion] has since yesterday captured Lydda airport and in its programme of work will advance together with the Armies of the neighbouring countries until the whole of Palestine has been cleared and handed over to its people like a fragrant ambergris.'[464] On 19 May Abdullah is even said to have told fellow Arab leaders: 'Tomorrow I shall take Jerusalem and one week later - Tel Aviv.'[465] Indeed, as late as 26 May one British official was saying that Abdullah, who then opposed a truce, 'still hoped ... to conquer [West]

Jerusalem and had instructed to concentrate his forces to shell the road [from Tel Aviv to Jerusalem?].'[466]

That Abdullah's thinking for a few days shifted gear or at least teetered on the brink of a major strategic gear-shift was implied in his statements to the press on 13 and 14 May and in his letter to Kirkbride delivered on 17 May (dated '16 May'). In the first report Abdullah was quoted as telling a delegation of Palestinian leaders that, along with the other Arab armies, he intended to conquer 'Palestine.' On 14 May he reportedly said that the termination of the Mandate signalled the invalidation of the Balfour Declaration. 'There was no basis for the Jewish claim to independence. The Arabs were the [true] rulers of the land.'[467] And in the letter to Kirkbride, of 16-17 May, he spoke of his 'national and religious duties in regard to Palestine as a whole and Jerusalem in particular.' The implication, as Kirkbride well understood, was that Abdullah was now contemplating (a) action covering the 'whole' of Palestine and (b) occupying at least East Jerusalem. 'He realises that he has now embarked on an enterprise which may carry him beyond the original scheme for the occupation by Transjordan of some of the Arab areas of Palestine...,' Kirkbride commented. (Kirkbride advised Whitehall to caution Abdullah 'that any departure from the original scheme would of course necessitate a reconsideration of His Majesty's Government's own position.' Whitehall duly instructed Kirkbride to respond to Abdullah's letter in that vein, stressing that 'HMG would particularly deprecate any prolongation of the conflict in the Holy City of Jerusalem.')[468]

But later that day, 17 May, Abdullah seems to have received a cold douche: He visited Jisr Majami and heard how the Syrian invasion was bogged down at Samakh and saw at first hand how the Iraqis at Gesher were 'not much better off.' Indeed, according to Abdullah, the Iraqis were 'declining to commit themselves further unless given support by the Arab Legion. This is not likely to be forthcoming.'[469] Israel was not going to be a pushover, as perhaps it had seemed to some on 15-16 May; perhaps the Legion would do well to stick to its original scheme of occupying only the Arab areas and avoid attacking Israeli territory.

But Jerusalem - not in the UN-earmarked Jewish zone - was another matter. On 16 May Abdullah himself had cabled Glubb:

> The importance of Jerusalem in the eyes of the Arabs and the Muslims and the Arab Christians is well known. Any disaster suffered by the people of the city at the hands of the Jews - whether they were killed or driven from their homes - would have the most far-reaching results for us. The situation does not yet give cause for despair. I accordingly order that everything we [i.e., the Arabs] hold to-

> day must be preserved - the Old City and the road to Jericho. This can be done either by using the reserves which are now in the vicinity of Ramallah or by sending there a force from the general reserves. I ask you to execute this order as quickly as possibly, my dear.[470]

Glubb, reluctant to commit the Legion to battle in Jerusalem, tarried and at dawn the following day, 17 May, he crossed the Jordan to inspect the Legion's dispositions. But no sooner was he across the river than he was assailed by a stream of (even more specific) cables urging him to action. Just before noon, he received an order 'from Amman' saying that 'His Majesty the King orders an advance towards Jerusalem ... He intends by this action to threaten the Jews, in order that they may accept a truce in Jerusalem.' Half an hour later, a second cable, this one from Transjordan's prime minister and defence minister, Abul Huda, explained and expatiated:

> His Majesty ... is extremely anxious and indeed insists that a force from Ramallah with artillery be sent to attack the Jewish neighbourhoods of Jerusalem. The Jews are attacking the gates of the Old City in order to break into it. An attack on the Jews would ease the pressure on the Arabs and would incline the Jews to accept the truce... His Majesty is awaiting swift action. Report quickly that the operation has commenced.[471]

But Glubb continued to stall, apparently spending all of 17 May and much of 18 May 'out of contact' and beyond Amman's reach. He was loath to commit his beloved Legion; he feared a costly and indecisive entanglement in urban street-fighting (in which the Legion's superior firepower and mobility could not be brought to bear); and, perhaps, he feared the political fallout, including anger in Whitehall, which had consistently warned Abdullah against battling the Jews and blatantly violating UN Resolution 181 (which had 'internationalised' the holy city). But the pressure on Glubb, including by his own troops, who were straining at the leash, was intense.

On 19 May Kirkbride described the process:

> Pressure of public opinion in Transjordan and in Palestine together with Jewish offensive in Jerusalem Arab quarters and in Arab areas of Galilee have forced the Arab Legion to move quicker than was at first intended ... Glubb visited the Arab Legion units at Nablus and Ramallah on Monday and Tuesday [17 and 18 May] principally in order to escape insistence of the King and Prime Minister for immediate action. In Palestine he found units in such a state of indignation at not

> having been engaged ... that he felt they might get out of hand if retained in inaction too long.
>
> In both Transjordan and Palestine it is being said that the Arab Legion was merely a tool of the British in order to enforce partition. The Prime Minister went so far yesterday as to ask me whether I was instructing Glubb to avoid action with the Jews or whether Glubb was doing so on his own account. I dealt with this suitably and added that hysterical haste in which the Arab forces were acting might end disastrously unless used their common sense. The Prime Minister climbed down but it was obvious that some definite line would have to be taken immediately.[472]

Kirkbride appears to have reiterated Whitehall's warning against advancing beyond the partition borders and attacking Israel - but with regard to Jerusalem, public pressure was 'too intense' and Abdullah felt unable to resist it.[473]

Bevin was clearly worried by the prospect of the Legion fighting in Jerusalem. Probably he was concerned mainly by the possibility of a Legion assault on West Jerusalem. This, perhaps, is how one should interpret Bevin's cable of the evening of 19 May, in which he instructed Kirkbride to warn the Jordanians against 'a full scale Arab Legion attack on Jerusalem.'[474]

Glubb's response to the pressures from Amman (and East Jerusalem) was gradual, holding off on a massive investment of the Old City for as long as possible. Towards nightfall on 17 May, Glubb moved in two 25-pounders which 'took up a position [possibly at Nabi Samwil] from which they could support an advance if ordered.' Meanwhile, two Legion companies, the 1st and 8th, bivouacked on the Mount of Olives. But the pressure was still on, the Jews themselves fuelling it. The Haganah's repeated efforts on 16-18 May to penetrate the Old City, motivated at least in part by a desire to relieve the Jewish Quarter, apparently were decisive in propelling Abdullah, Glubb and the Legion into Jerusalem proper.[475]

On 18 May, with 'the King haggard with anxiety lest the Jews enter the Old City and the Temple [Mount] area ... [where] his father the late King Husayn of Hijaz, was buried ... The whole responsibility seemed to rest on me [Glubb] alone. I had opposed both the King and the government for forty-eight hours, in the hope of obtaining a truce [in Jerusalem]. If, by any chance, the Old City should suddenly fall, all would be lost.' Glubb ordered one of the companies on the Mount of Olives, the 8th, to descend into the Old City, where, an hour later, 'they were manning the walls' (from which, noted Glubb, always attuned to the echoes of history, 'nearly 1,900 years ago the Jews themselves had cast their darts at the advancing legions of Titus'). 'The die was cast.'[476]

But the lone company could provide the Arabs in the Old City only with temporary relief. And the threat hourly became more immediate; on the night of 18\19 a small Palmah unit managed to break through from Mount Zion via Zion Gate into the Old City, re-establishing the corridor from West Jerusalem to the Jewish Quarter.[477] A much larger force was needed if the Arabs were to secure the Old City, and, perhaps, to take its Jewish Quarter. That night, Glubb ordered in the Legion in force, the attack to begin the following morning, 19 May.

The foregoing raises a question mark regarding the extent of Abdullah's control over his army's dispositions and operations. Or, put another way, how independent was Glubb during the first weeks of the invasion? Some Israeli observers believed that Abdullah's reported irritability during the first week was in part caused by his feeling of impotence or at least, his appearance of impotence, stemming from Glubb's (or the British) control of the Legion. 'He had never before appeared so obviously in the role of a puppet of the British. Glubb Pasha is directing the campaign and Abdullah's orders are thrown into the waste-paper basket' - this, at least, is how Haganah intelligence officer Chaim Herzog reported the situation at the time.[478] But, in fact, Glubb might briefly delay and avoid compliance with the royal commands, but ultimately it was Abdullah who called the shots and determined the Legion's strategic choices. It was he, rather than Glubb, who set the Legion on the road to Jerusalem. (How Glubb would have reacted had Abdullah ordered him to cross the Jewish-Arab UN partition borders and conquer Tel Aviv, is anyone's guess, though one may assume that Glubb and Kirkbride would have succeeded in persuading the monarch to reconsider.)

But it is possible to interpret the interplay between Glubb and Abdullah, and the Legion's ultimate entry into the city, in another way. Without doubt, Glubb, for tactical reasons, was extremely dubious about sending his little army into Jerusalem; he feared that it would be churned up in street fighting. And, unlike Abdullah, he was not as driven by historical-religious motives in desiring the conquest of the city for the Arabs\Islam (though, being extremely history-minded, he would without doubt have looked at his functioning and accomplishments - or failures - through the prism of posterity).

But nonetheless one may question the depth of Glubb's reluctance or hesitancy - as stressed in his memoirs - to do battle in and for the holy city. Probably from the first, he – like his master - was of two minds in the matter. For good strategic reasons Glubb, probably even before the start of the invasion, understood the city's crucial strategic importance; certainly he realized it once he had crossed the Jordan. Put simply, Jerusalem was the West Bank's main communications hub or crossroads: It stood midway on the main axes between Nablus-Ramallah and Bethlehem-Hebron and between Tel Aviv and Jericho. Arab control of the city or at least East Jerusalem would assure contiguity between the northern and southern segments of the West Bank and would bar the easiest access route for Jewish forces to Jericho and the Jordan Valley. Haganah\IDF conquest of East Jerusalem would at a stroke cut off the Arab forces in the Ramallah-Nablus area from those in the Bethlehem-Hebron region and, even more significantly, would open the road down to Jericho and the Jordan Valley. A Haganah push into the Valley, a mere half-hour's drive, would cut off the main axes linking the Legion's bases in Transjordan to its units deployed around the West Bank - effectively either forcing their retreat back across the river or leading to their envelopment and destruction inside Palestine. In short, conquering and holding East Jerusalem was essential to safeguarding and securing the Legion's hold on Samaria and Judea (much as Arab control of Latrun was seen by Glubb as essential to the Legion's continued control of East Jerusalem).

Kirkbride felt, probably on the basis of a briefing by Glubb, that once the Legion had occupied the West Bank's hilly spine, he had faced two choices: To turn

> outwards on [i.e., in] operations which might ultimately lead him [westward] into a Jewish area [i.e., the Coastal Plain] or inwards to relieve Arab areas of Jerusalem. He chose the latter, I think wisely. To have saved the holy places of Jerusalem would give Transjordan greater merit in the Arab world, and [his] troops can be given [the] battle for which they are clamouring without the risk of being involved in what might be described as an act of aggression against the Jewish state.[479]

Whitehall opinion endorsed Glubb's line of reasoning and actions. A minute (perhaps by Beith), from 20 May, stated:

> As the War Office sees it, King Abdullah had two courses open to him. He could either have made a drive to the coast in strength with such other Arab forces as he could collect, cutting off the Jews in Tel Aviv from the Jews in Haifa and in the north, and possibly securing a military victory of the first order. [But] it seems fairly clear that this course would be beyond the powers of the Arab forces at pre-

> sent. The alternative was to concentrate on the capture of Jerusalem, which would give a great fillip to Arab morale and is an operation which lies naturally within the Arab zone. At present the Arab Legion is fighting its way into Jerusalem from the north ... The Jews in the [Jewish Quarter of the] Old City are not likely to be able to hold out much longer ... I think it most important from the Arab point of view that the Arab Legion has not been committed to a major engagement against the Jews' main strength, but has been kept as indicated in [Kirkbride's] telegram to relieve [Arab] Jerusalem.[480]

Thus it was that Glubb, perhaps somewhat reluctantly, ended up battling for East Jerusalem. And a difficult battle it was. Just before dawn on 19 May, a small but heavily armed Legion force - 300 men with armoured cars, four six-pounder anti-tank guns and four 3" mortars, backed by four 25-pounder guns - pushed southwards along the Ramallah-Jerusalem road, re-taking the Sheikh Jarah Quarter at the northern entrance to the city from a small Jewish force that had taken it a few days before. These Legionnaires were reinforced by additional small units that day and the next as they skirmished with Jewish troops at the 'Mandelbaum Gate' and in the Musrara Quarter to the south. But a solid, secure link-up and line of communication from Ramallah, the Legion's headquarters, to the Old City was still in doubt. On 21 May Glubb ordered the Legion's 3rd Regiment (i.e., Battalion), which had been deployed around Nablus since 15 May, into action in Jerusalem. Glubb later described the regiment's soldiers as 'simple and straightforward' beduin, for whom the issue was simple: 'The Holy Places of Jerusalem were being attacked. They would save them' from the Jews.[481] By midnight the regiment had reached Sheikh Jarah[482] and early the next morning, 22 May, it punched its way southwards, finally linking up with the irregulars and Legionnaires manning the Old City walls.[483]

The push on Jerusalem significantly changed the overall strategic picture of the pan-Arab invasion. At Glubb's request, the Iraqi units lackadaisically and unsuccessfully engaged during the first week of the invasion around Naharayim (Jisr Majami), were hastily withdrawn eastward and redeployed (on 22-24 May) in the Tulkarm-Jenin-Nablus triangle of the northern West Bank in place of the Legion units rushed southwards to Jerusalem and westwards to Latrun.[484]

At this point the Arab states - unaware of or indifferent to the Legion's unfolding, desperate battle in Jerusalem - began pressing Jordan to attack Israel rather than merely occupy Arab areas. Abdullah resisted.

The Battle For Jerusalem, May 1948

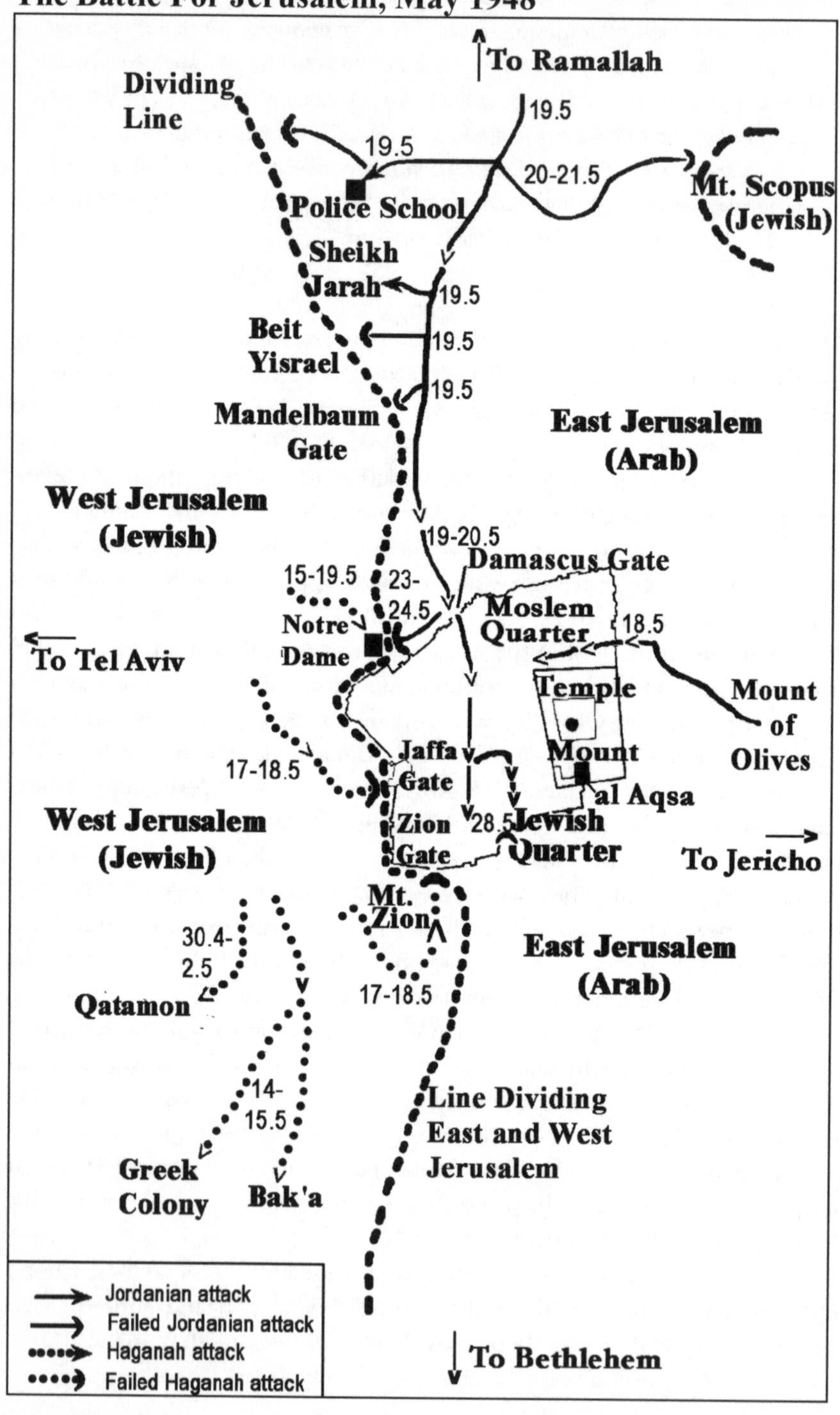

> King Abdullah tells me that it was soon evident that the purpose of the meeting [with the Syrian president on 21 May] at Dera`a was to involve the Arab Legion still further and in particular to get it to move against the Jewish State. [General] Taha al Hashimi [a senior Iraqi officer who sat on the Arab League Military Committee] touched off an explosion of royal Hashemite wrath (which are getting too frequent) by standing up and expressing the opinion that the armies should not be used for political purposes. The King said that after the deplorable shows put up by Syrian and Lebanese forces they were in no position to criticize the Arab Legion and no one with sense would propose attacking the Jewish State with [sic, while] a large Jewish force at Jerusalem [was poised] on the main line of [Legion] communication.[485]

But this still left the north-south axis from Nablus-Ramallah to the Old City, in the section between Shu`afat and the Damascus Gate, insecure: It was enfiladed by Haganah positions at Musrara, and the slope of Musrara was dominated by the massive, fortress-like stone monastery of Notre Dame de France. And the monastery was in Haganah hands. On 23-24 May the 3rd Battalion repeatedly assaulted the structure, a number of times breaking into the building and slogging it out from room to room and storey to storey with grenades and submachine guns. But the nut proved too tough to crack. By the afternoon of 24 May about half of 4th Company's troops were dead or seriously wounded; all of its officers and NCOs save one were out of commission. Glubb called off the attack and, in view of the casualties and a shortage of ammunition, refused to renew it.[486] The building remained in Haganah hands.

Inside the Old City, the Legionnaires were more successful. Between 19 and 28 May they repelled all Jewish efforts to penetrate the walls and gradually, advancing from house to house, constricted the Jewish Quarter, until, on 28 May, its ultra-orthodox inhabitants and 300-odd Haganah defenders raised the white flag. The Haganah men went off to a prisoner-of-war camp in Transjordan and the 1,500 inhabitants were shepherded and transferred, under Red Cross supervision, to Jewish West Jerusalem. ' ... Arab Legion soldiers were seen to be helping along the sick and the old women, and carrying their little bundles of possessions. ... It was our answer to Deir Yassin ...,' wrote Glubb.[487]

Traditional Zionist historiography has maintained that the Legion in the second half of May had tried not merely to reach and secure the Old City but also to conquer West Jerusalem, with its 100,000 Jewish population - and that the thrusts at the 'Mandelbaum Gate' and against Notre Dame, were part of that effort.[488] This was also how Israeli officials saw things at the time. Ben-Gurion, always suspicious of 'perfidious Albion,' its helpers, and intentions, on 19 May told his Cabinet colleagues: 'The Legion has apparently begun its move [i.e., offensive], which has three aims: [Holding] the Old City, [conquering] the whole city and [conquering] its environs.' Indeed, the Arabs' target was not merely West Jerusalem but the whole of Israel: 'According to the information we have from British sources, which more or less can be relied upon, this [pan-Arab] offensive [i.e., the invasion of Palestine] was to have been a lightning operation with the aim of destroying within a few days the [Jewish] state.'[489] Indeed, Ben-Gurion was so angry with the Legion (and Britain) that he gave credence to - and passed on to his Cabinet colleagues - a report that the Legion was about to use poison gas. On 30 May he told his colleagues: 'We have listened to an order to the Legion, an hour ago: To conquer Jerusalem at any price. They especially mentioned Qatamon. An order was given also to use gas. There is no doubt that it will be the British who will give them the gas ...' When several Cabinet colleagues proposed that Israel immediately publicize the information, Ben-Gurion responded: 'It is doubtful that this will stay their hand, because they will stop at nothing ...'[490]

This paranoid view of British intentions, incidentally, was shared at the time by other Israeli leaders - who also (like most Arabs outside Transjordan) regarded the Legion merely as a tool of British designs:

> Am anxious to improve relations with British but see little hope of change [of] heart [on] their part. Bevin's implacability, [UK Ambassador to the United Nations Alexander] Cadogan's casuistry and Glubb's views, Arab Legion shelling [of] Degania A and [Hebrew] University and massing forces for attack elsewhere - point unmistakable inexorable line of crushing Jewish State or reducing it to [minuscule 1938] Woodhead [Commission proposals] size and letting neighbouring beasts devour large part of Palestine,

Foreign Minister Moshe Shertok cabled Zionism's elder statesman, Chaim Weizmann.[491]

But Glubb had no intention of assaulting and taking Jewish Jerusalem and the undermanned Legion made no such effort. After 1948, Glubb always maintained that the fighting for Notre Dame and the Mandelbaum Gate was prompted by Jewish fire and the need to secure the axis to the Old City.[492] Available contemporary documentation supports this. On 21 May, as the attack on Notre Dame was being prepared, Kirkbride apprised London, no doubt on the basis of a briefing by Glubb, that 'in Jerusalem it is not intended to do more than protect the Old City ... but in order to do this an attempt may be made to recapture the Allenby

Square positions [i.e., Notre Dame] which dominate the north west corner of the walls.'[493]

Subsequent internal IDF analysis of what had occurred supports Glubb's version of events - of an unplanned, hand-to-mouth, and, above all (from Glubb's perspective), reluctantly undertaken, defensively-motivated thrust towards East Jerusalem, including the Old City, and protection of the north-south route to the Old City, rather than an assault on Jewish Jerusalem with the aim of conquest. In the most comprehensive and thorough IDF description of the war against the Arab Legion, written in the 1950s, Major Dov Steiger (Sion), Moshe Dayan's future son-in-law who retired in the 1980s as a brigadier general, wrote:

> It is completely clear that at this stage [i.e., the start of the invasion] the Legion had no plan to conquer the whole city [of Jerusalem]. In retrospect, after the event, it appears that there was no serious planning [or] clear intention to carry out such a task. To the extent that there was such a plan, it was not founded on attack and conquest but on siege to force the [Jewish] population to reach some [ceasefire] arrangement. But there is no certainty that Abdullah's aspirations extended that far. It is more likely ... that his aim was to force the Israeli high command to disperse its forces in defence [so that the Legion could continue to hold on to the areas it had occupied in the West Bank and East Jerusalem].[494]

Later in his work, deposited in the IDF Archive and never published, Steiger was to be even more emphatic:

> It is possible to state with complete certainty that Abdullah did not intend to gain control of Jerusalem with Legion forces. The Legion did not plan the conquest of the city as it failed to plan any war on us. The Legion invaded Palestine with one aim only, to conquer the areas in the centre of the country [i.e., the greater West Bank area] that had been earmarked for the Arabs in the partition plan ... His forces were insufficient even for this task, in the eyes of the Legion's commander, let alone for the conquest of a big city like Jerusalem ... Therefore the Legion's commander believed that all efforts must be made to achieve a truce in Jerusalem and to leave it as a demilitarised area outside the battle ... That was the main reason the Legion forces did not enter Jerusalem, and its Arab neighbourhoods, at the end of the Mandate... Contrary to its original intentions, the Legion was sucked into the Jerusalem battles. Glubb hoped until 17 May that the truce committee would succeed in imposing calm in the city and relieve him of [the need for] combat in a built-up area.[495]

Kirkbride nonetheless divined a political silver lining in the unpremeditated battle with the Haganah in Jerusalem. The Arab states, immediately after 15 May, had pressured Abdullah to send the Legion beyond the Arab areas and to fight the Jews as well. The bitter battles which unfolded in Jerusalem and on the road to it to the west enabled Abdullah and Glubb to parry Arab charges that they had avoided war with the Jews and had conspired with the British in an anti-Arab plot. On 22 May, Kirkbride put it this way:

> The original Transjordan plan was upset in that the truce covering Jerusalem ... was broken (by the Jews) immediately the Mandate ended. This meant that the Arab Legion was forced to extend its occupation elsewhere more rapidly than had been intended and to involve itself in the fighting in Jerusalem which the Jews showed every sign of capturing ... Unforeseen commitment of [i.e., to] Jerusalem was however in a sense a benefit for it would have been impossible for the Arab Legion to have arrived at the border of the Jewish State [and] to remain inactive, both on account of the attitude of the men themselves and because of Arab public opinion which would have described the attitude [i.e., inaction] as due to a British plot to effect partition.
>
> Fact that all other Arab states were given roles which caused them to invade the Jewish State immediately hostilities commenced was not entirely accidental, which they have since realized. This realisation and the failure of the Lebanese Syrian Iraqi military efforts make them all the more insistent that the Arab Legion also should advance against the Jewish State.[496]

As the battle for Jerusalem unfolded, Glubb quickly grasped the necessity of occupying and holding Latrun, the vital crossroads mid-way between Tel Aviv and Jerusalem through which Jewish forces and supplies had to pass to reach the capital. Latrun was in the territory earmarked by the UN in 1947 for (Palestinian) Arab sovereignty. In his memoirs, Glubb describes why the Legion occupied Latrun on 17 May. The battle for Jerusalem was on:

> Meanwhile ... the road from Tel Aviv to Jerusalem was open. Weapons, reinforcements and convoys could reach Jewish Jerusalem from the coastal plain ... it did not appear advisable to allow yet more Jewish troops and weapons to reach the city. If they cleared the city, they could drive on down to the Jordan and cut off the whole of Palestine. We accordingly sent our newly raised 4th Regiment [Battalion] to Latrun, to prevent the Jews from using the main road to Jerusalem.[497]

In its post-war analysis of the subsequent battles for Latrun, the IDF History Department (i.e., Steiger) endorsed Glubb's recollected version of events: That the severing of the Tel Aviv-Jerusalem road at Latrun had not been part of the Legion's master plan but that the unfolding battle in Jerusalem had compelled Glubb, as he saw things, to cut the road as a means of (a) preventing the Jews from moving reinforcements and supplies to the city, and (b) diverting Haganah forces away from the city so that the Arabs would be able to hold on in East Jerusalem. In his study of the Legion in 1948, Steiger writes:

> There is no reason to assume that the Legion staff planned these battles [i.e., the battles for Latrun] in advance ... One can assume with confidence that the military plan [to sever the road] ... was born in the Legion in the midst of battle, as a reaction to our objectives ... The [Legion's] original strategic political goal was to capture only the Arab area earmarked for the Arabs in the partition plan ... in the hope that we, too, would make do with controlling the territory earmarked for us. But, when they saw that our military steps were not geared to preserving the area earmarked for the Jews in the [partition] plan but went beyond these parameters, they grasped the need to resort to preventive actions, so that we should not achieve [a dominant] military position ... What emerges is that our operations against the Arab strongholds along the road to Jerusalem prompted the Legion into a deployment different from that originally planned. Our actions against Latrun and [nearby] Deir Aiyub riveted the Legion command's attention to the special value that the road to Jerusalem had for us, [and to the fact that] by simply sitting on the road they could pin down our forces.[498]

The Haganah struck in Latrun on the morning of 25 May with a slapdash collection of poorly equipped battalions. The main target was the Tegart police fort that perched on a hillock overlooking the road and the Ayalon Valley through which it ran. The Legion gunners, on the fort's roof and in the hills to the east, picked off the advancing Israeli infantrymen before they could bring their weapons into range. They never reached the fort. Some, like (the wounded) Ariel Sharon, managed to make it back to Israeli lines; others fell from exhaustion and dehydration (it was over 30 degrees centigrade); still others were hit and died or lay wounded in the fields around the fort. Arab villagers that evening scoured the area for left-behind equipment and, incidentally, finished off the wounded. The Arab Legion reported that the Jews had suffered '600' dead.[499] In truth, 72-74 Israelis died that day. According to Glubb, a further 600 Israelis died in the subsequent two major efforts to take Latrun,[500] on 30\31 May and 8\9 June; in reality these two (also unsuccessful) assaults together cost another 70 Israeli lives.

But these were indeed heavy casualties, given the size of the attacking units and of the Israeli army as a whole, and, without doubt, the battles of Latrun were the most serious defeats suffered by the IDF in 1948. The IDF failed to take Latrun and, indeed, 'the Arab Legion proved itself the master of the battlefield.'[501] Israel was forced to build a makeshift road (dubbed the `Burma Road') around the hillock along which to push supplies to Jerusalem.[502] But the Legion, keeping to its essentially defensive strategy, refrained from seriously disrupting Jewish traffic on this by-pass road or attacking the road itself, so as not to provoke the IDF.[503]

By 29 May, the Legion - in the Jerusalem area and in the first battle of Latrun - had suffered a total of 90 dead and 201 wounded.[504]

As a result of the Yishuv-Palestinian battles before 15 May and of the Haganah\IDF attacks on the Legion subsequently, Abdullah's attitude towards Israel and a possible peace with the Jewish state changed. While Jordanian Minister to London Abdul Majid Haidar was authorised repeatedly to meet with Israel Foreign Ministry official Elias Sasson in Paris in August – to sound him out about Israel's intentions and attitude to Jordanian annexation of the West Bank - Abdullah reportedly remained deeply 'suspicious.' He no longer trusted Israeli assurances that once the other – Iraqi, Syrian and Egyptian - armies withdrew from Palestine, Israel and Jordan could revert to the 'original [Yishuv-Transjordan] partition scheme.' What was to guarantee that after the other Arab armies 'were out of the field ... the Jews would not turn all their forces against the Arab Legion?' he asked. Abdullah instructed Haidar to tell Sasson that the 'expulsion' of the Palestinian Arab population and 'Jewish pretensions' regarding Jerusalem had altered the situation. The return of the refugees and Tel Aviv's acceptance of 'the exclusion of Jerusalem from the Jewish state' were now 'necessary preliminaries to any settlement.'

But according to Kirkbride, Jewish actions and the changed circumstances were not the only bar to Abdullah seriously parleying with the Jews. 'The King realizes his inability [because of inter-Arab considerations] to come to any independent agreement with the Jews but does not wish to' inform Israel of this, reported Kirkbride.[505]

Lydda-Ramle and the End of the War

The Arab invasion of Palestine was to result in repeated United Nations calls for a ceasefire and to the imposition, on 29 May 1948, of a general arms embargo on all the parties involved, including Jordan. By 24 May, Britain was applying strong pressure on Abdullah to support an immediate ceasefire. In a cable to Kirkbride, instructing him on what to say to Abdullah, Bevin noted that 'the Arab Legion had successfully carried out the greater part of its objective of occupying ... Arab areas of Palestine.' In addition, the Legion had become embroiled in 'severe fighting' in Jerusalem and had cut off the road from the coast to West Jerusalem and had secured 'the Moslem Holy places' in the city. 'It therefore appears to us that the purpose according to the Prime Minister's statement [on 7 February] to me has been more or less achieved.' If Abdullah refused to support a ceasefire, Britain would 'find it very hard to avoid reconsidering' its policy regarding the Legion.[506]

Abdullah acceded and Jordan was the first - and at this stage, the only - Arab state to back the United Nations ceasefire call. On 25 May, Abul Huda argued at a meeting of the Arab League Political Committee against the other Arabs' refusal to consider a ceasefire, saying that only the Legion was still actively fighting the Jews and it could not continue to do so alone. The other Arab armies, he charged (correctly), had in effect halted all offensive action ('the Egyptian army refused to move').[507]

But Britain's and Abdullah's efforts notwithstanding, the Arab states tergiversated, coming round only in the second week of June, after their military fortunes and munitions stocks had precipitately declined.[508] By early June, Glubb was predicting that, in the absence of a ceasefire, his army would have to withdraw from Palestine by 14 June at the latest.[509] On 6 June, Kirkbride reported that the Legion had ammunition for 'seven more days fighting only' and that the Iraqis were also 'short of ammunition.'[510]

As to the Security Council prohibitions relating to weaponry, ammunition, spare parts, and foreign fighting personnel, the last British shipment of armaments to Jordan, as described, had taken place on 22-24 May, when two ammunition-laden ships had been dispatched from Suez to 'Aqaba. One had been seized by the Egyptians, who confiscated the cargo of artillery and mortar rounds; almost from the start of the invasion, the Egyptians, too, were feeling the pinch of ammunition shortages. From that point on and until the end of the war, Britain officially desisted from militarily re-supplying Jordan (apart from a stock of barbed wire).[511] Britain also ordered all its nationals serving in the Legion to withdraw east of the Jordan and not to participate in the fighting.[512] Bevin initially demanded that the British personnel be withdrawn by 26 May, when he was due to respond to questions in the House. He explained that the Arab states' rejection of the UN ceasefire resolution compelled him to take this step; he did not want British nationals to defy the UN.[513] As we have seen, many of the Britons duly withdrew across the Jordan, at least for a time - though as Kirkbride admitted in his memoirs, 'I am not sure that they stayed there [i.e., in Transjordan] for long.'[514]

But arms and ammunition supplies were a more serious problem. Britain clearly wished to avoid a rupture with the United States, and vis-à-vis the Jordanians argued, with a degree of reasonableness, that should it defy the Security Council ban, the United States would be forced to do likewise - and supply arms to the Jews, who would emerge the ultimate gainers. No doubt Britain's will to adhere to the embargo was reinforced by the Jordanian-Israeli hostilities around Jerusalem and Latrun. Occupying Arab areas without bloodshed was one thing; fighting a succession of pitched battles against the Haganah\IDF was quite another. Who knew where it might end, perhaps to Britain's embarrassment?

But from Jordan's (and the Legion's) point of view, Britain's behaviour was unfriendly, indeed treacherous, in the extreme. It had been party to the plan for the Legion push into the West Bank, and had known the risks involved. Then, when battle was joined against a growingly superior enemy, Whitehall abruptly cut off supplies. As Kirkbride was to recall, Abdullah complained: 'Allies who let one become involved in a war and then cut off our essential supplies are not very desirable friends.'[515]

Ammunition shortages, bolstered by cut-offs of supplies, were to prove crucial to Arab war-making capabilities immediately after the end of the First Truce, which lasted from 11 June until 8-9 July, when the IDF launched a major offensive ('Operation Dani') against the Legion in the central front.

'From the very beginning of hostilities, I had told both the King and the government that we could not hold Lydda and Ramle,' wrote Glubb.[516] Some ten miles from Tel Aviv, astride the road to Jerusalem, the two Arab towns, each with a population of about 20,000 (additionally swollen during April-June by thousands of refugees from the Jaffa area), were in the plain at the foot of the Judean Hills, northwest of Latrun. Glubb felt that he could hold the hills but nothing below them 'out in the open.' Trying to defend Lydda and Ramle, as well as Latrun and the hill country of Judea and Samaria to the east, Glubb felt, given his minuscule army, would expose Latrun, and the rest of the West Bank, to capture. 'I had explained this situation to the King and Prime Minister before the end of the Mandate and had secured their consent to the principle that Lydda and Ramle would not be defended.'[517]

The inhabitants of the two towns noted that the Legion, in invading and deploying around the West Bank, had initially failed to send units to protect them, and felt exposed and vulnerable. The arrival in early June of a Legion company and several hundred Jordanian volunteers did not substantially alter the strategic picture.[518] Moreover, Jordan initially refrained from appointing a military governor in the two towns (as it had in the other towns it had occupied). The inhabitants rushed off a stream of petitions to Amman. The IDF's Alexandroni Brigade reported: 'A strange thing is the urgent cables from various elements in Ramle, such as the mayor, the military commander of Ramle and sports organisations, to the commander of the Legion, to King Abdullah, to the [Arab] League, [pleading] for immediate help, lest the city be conquered by the Jews and a slaughter like Deir Yassin will take place.'[519]

During the First Truce, the IDF grew enormously, both in manpower and weaponry (mostly from Czechoslovakia). The Arab Legion, like the other Arab armies, largely 'wasted' the month-long ceasefire. Glubb recalled that he had pressed for further recruitment but Abul Huda had said 'no.' 'No more fighting,' he said, 'and no more money for soldiers.'[520] Nonetheless, Glubb went ahead and added and trained new troops.

Abdullah during the truce maintained a militant public facade, declaring that the Arabs would not agree to peace or the existence of a Jewish state but - reverting to his position of early 1946 and May 1948 - would consent to a Jewish minority with the right to 'local administration' within an Arab-governed Palestine.[521] But in private he played a different tune. During the first week of July Abdullah and Abul Huda made great efforts to persuade their allies to agree to extend the truce. Abdullah had made use (and had urged Abul Huda to make use) of Glubb's argument about the Legion's 'serious shortage of ammunition'; Jordan simply could not continue to fight effectively. (It was partly for this reason that Abdullah on 7 July - the day after the Arab League's unanimous decision in Cairo against prolonging the truce - informed Kirkbride that he was ready 'to accept a Jewish state and to come to a separate peace.' Kirkbride commented that Abdullah might not be able 'to survive the popular indignation which would be created in the Arab world by his coming to agreement with the Jews.')[522]

Glubb had apparently lobbied vigorously for an extension of the truce (to which Israel had agreed). He realized that Israel had grown stronger while the Arabs, if anything, had grown weaker. 'I begged Tewfiq Pasha [Abul Huda],' he recalled in his memoirs, '... to insist on the renewal of the truce.' But the Arab League Political Committee decided otherwise. 'I was in a minority of one. All the others wanted to renew the fighting,' Glubb recalled Abul Huda telling him. 'If I had voted alone against it, we should only have been denounced as traitors, and the truce would still not have been renewed.'

'But how can we fight without ammunition?' Glubb had asked.

'Don't shoot unless the Jews shoot first,' Abul Huda had answered.[523]

According to Abul Huda, when he had argued lack of ammunition, the other Arab delegates had countered (a) that their armies still had ammunition and (b) that Britain would 'not let the Arab Legion be defeated' and, when it came to the crunch, would resupply it. Upon his return to Amman, Abul Huda had offered to resign - but the king had rejected the offer, assuring his prime minister of his confidence that he had 'done his best.'[524]

Glubb suspected Abul Huda of playing a double game - in Cairo more or less willingly going along with the warlike majority while, back in Amman, explaining that he had fought tooth and nail for a prolongation of the truce but had been overruled. Glubb noted that Abul Huda (a native of Acre, in Palestine) shared the Palestinian (and Egyptian) trait of impractical extremism and gave an illustration: 'I was one day explaining to him what would happen if the Jews broke through at a certain point, and how we should then have to withdraw from a neighbouring position.

'"You cannot withdraw," he said.

'"But if we do not withdraw, a large part of the army will be cut off and destroyed," I said.

'"Better to have the army destroyed than to give up part of the country to an enemy who has no right to it", retorted the Prime Minister.

'"But if the army is destroyed, the enemy will take the whole country ...", I argued.'

Glubb summarized: 'There may be something admirable in this resolution to demand that which is right, regardless of the cost. But the effect on the fate of the Palestine Arabs was utterly disastrous. Many opportunities for compromise were offered them and might, if accepted, have saved them. But they were utterly intransigent, and, as a result, they were destroyed.'[525]

As a sop to the Jordanians, the Arab states formally agreed to name King Abdullah commander-in-chief of the Arab armies - though in reality the situation remained as before, with the King controlling only the Arab Legion and, indirectly, the Iraqi expeditionary force in Samaria.[526] And so the Arabs reached 8 July, when the Egyptians - a day before the truce officially ended - renewed the war in the south. Bevin pleaded with Abdullah not to allow Jordan to be sucked in and to refrain from 'embarking on [this] unwise course,' threatening that if Jordan initiated a breach of the truce, Whitehall would halt the payment of the subsidy.[527] Even before receipt of Bevin's appeal, Abdullah had ordered the Legion to stay on the defensive and 'to avoid fighting as far as the holding of their present positions permitted'[528] - and on 10 July Glubb toured the Legion units in Palestine in order, according to Kirkbride, 'to make ... arrangements for a phoney war to follow a phoney truce.'[529] According to Ben-Gurion, Abdullah went so far as to officially inform Israel that 'he does not want to fight us and that we should leave him alone. But we could not accept his proposal, as he still held Lydda and Ramle,' Ben-Gurion later informed his cabinet colleagues. Interior Minister Yitzhak Grunbaum subsequently explained the IDF's easy conquest of Lydda and Ramle thus: 'Whoever examined the course of the battles saw that Abdullah did not want to fight.'[530]

In the end, Kirkbride and Glubb endorsed Jordan's decision not to dissent from the Arab League majority opposing the renewal of the truce. Kirkbride argued that Jordan could only have affected 'the issue ... by withdrawing the Arab Legion from Palestine.' But this would have involved 'Transjordan in most serious dangers. It would lead to the collapse of the Arab front in Palestine, to the probable exclusion of Transjordan from the Arab League and to the return of the Mufti to power and favour.' After the start of the Egyptian offensive in the south and on the eve of the renewal of Israeli-Jordanian hostilities, Kirkbride 'tentatively' consulted Glubb and Abul Huda. Glubb, according to Kirkbride, 'considered that there would be serious danger of a mutiny of the Arab Legion ... if they learned that that they were abandoning the other Arab [states'] troops.' Abul Huda argued that 'internal disorders' would break out in Jordan; Jordan simply could not walk out of the Arab League with 'impunity' in the middle of a war.[531]

The IDF went over to the offensive on the Jordanian front on 9 July, embarking on 'Operation Dani,' whose purpose was the conquest of Lydda and Ramle and then Latrun and Ramallah, in order to finally secure the length of the Tel Aviv-Jerusalem road. There was also in IDF command circles a (misplaced) fear that the Legion might use Lydda and Ramle as a springboard for an attack on Tel Aviv; IDF intelligence at this time routinely (and vastly) exaggerated Legion strength in the area.[532] Four IDF brigades were deployed. During the first days of the offensive (9-13 July), the IDF managed to take Ramle and Lydda. But its second stage ground to a halt at the Samarian-Judean foothills, as the Legion held fast and beat back repeated IDF efforts to take Latrun and the first line of hills to the north.

'Operation Dani' and a number of adjunct IDF operations taxed the Legion's resources to the limit. Almost all of its combat strength was deployed in Latrun, along Judea's western foothills, in the hilltops north of the Tel Aviv-Jerusalem road, and in Jerusalem itself; there were no reserves ('a most unfortunate position for a commander,' Glubb dryly noted).[533] In his memoirs, Glubb wrote that to have weakened the Legion garrison in Latrun in favour of Lydda and Ramle 'would have been madness.'[534] Nonetheless, several additional Legion platoons and some volunteers were sent during the First Truce to reinforce the two towns,[535] but otherwise their defence was left in the hands of several hundred local militiamen. These were to be brushed aside by the IDF battalion that occupied the centre of Lydda in late afternoon 11 July. Early on 12 July Ramle's notables surrendered their town without a fight.

The fall of the two towns resulted in a crisis in Legion headquarters and in Amman. Off balance, the Legion momentarily expected the IDF to push eastwards, up the Judean escarpment. Abdullah ordered the troops to stand fast along the line from Latrun-Bab el-Wad northwards. On the night of 11 July Glubb complained that the if he obeyed the order, it might lead to the Legion's destruction. The other alternative was to resign. Kirkbride urged him to hold on 'for a few days.' Glubb clearly felt - thinking like a general, not a politician - that given the Legion's shortages, it 'should begin to fall back while it still had enough ammunition to extricate its units intact.' He seemed to be suggesting a withdrawal back across the Jordan River.[536] The fall of Lydda and Ramle, and the alarming prospect of the destruction of the Legion, badly shook not only Glubb. Prime Minister (and Defence Minister) Abul Huda and Foreign Minister Fawzi al-Mulki both called on Kirkbride on the evening of 12 July 'in ... a state of nerves.'[537]

Compounding the jitters was the arrival of tens of thousands of refugees from Lydda and Ramle in the West Bank and in Transjordan itself following 12 July. At around noon on 12 July, two or three Legion armoured cars, on a reconnaissance mission or perhaps in search of a battalion commander who had gone astray, drove into Lydda sparking, in succession, a firefight with the occupying IDF battalion, an eruption of sniping by local militiamen and, in response, a massacre of some 250 of the townspeople and irregulars by the semi-beleaguered Israeli troops. The IDF command, with Ben-Gurion's authorisation, then ordered the expulsion of the population (and refugees) from the two towns, which was carried out that afternoon and on 13 July. Most of the 50,000-odd evictees made their way eastwards, towards Ramallah, under a blazing summer sun; a handful, and perhaps dozens, died of dehydration and exhaustion. A graphic illustration of the situation, from the Legion's perspective, is provided in a signal from the commander of the 4th Regiment (Battalion) on 14 July: 'Some 30,000 women and children from among the inhabitants of Lydda, Ramle and the area are dispersed among the hills, suffering from hunger and thirst to a degree that many of them have died. All are calling for revenge against the Arab Legion because they think that the Legion is the cause of their misfortune. To calm the situation means must be found to provide them with shelter [and] … food ...'[538] Kirkbride later recalled how some of them poured into Amman: 'I was standing in the main square of the capital as the tide of miserable humanity reached there ... The authorities ... had not made preparations to deal with anything approaching such numbers.'[539]

During the following days the Legion managed to stop the IDF advance - indeed, it gave the Israelis a bloody nose - along the line of the foothills, denying the IDF its follow-up objectives of Latrun and Ramallah. The UN-imposed Second Truce came into effect on 19 July. But the Legion's supply of artillery and mortar shells had been so depleted as to endanger its future deployment in the West Bank – and there were the refugees, needy, noisy and living testimony to the Legion's partial defeat.[540]

The Iraqis and a number of Jordanian Cabinet ministers took the lead in pointing the finger at Glubb, who was suspected of doing Britain's will or, even, of working for the Jews.[541] At a minimum, Glubb was suspected of 'bad faith' and of either 'concealing [the existence of] large quantities' of ammunition in order to persuade the Arab states to accept a truce or of concealing a real shortage of ammunition 'for sinister British reasons.'[542]

Glubb, personally outraged by the massacre at Lydda and the expulsion from the two towns, may have felt somewhat responsible; after all, these communities had been his wards, however thinly protected by the Legion and no matter that he had always said they were indefensible.[543] And 'the refugees in Jordan seemed to make the unfortunate Glubb their particular target for abuse ...,' Kirkbride was later to recall.[544] Unprecedentedly, the West Bank and Transjordan were swept by a wave of street demonstrations directed against the Legion, Glubb, and the British. Two took place in Amman, even before the fighting had died down, on 16 and 18 July. According to one IDF Intelligence report, the demonstrators on 16 July – 'wives and parents of [Legion] soldiers' - intended 'to break into the King's palace ... The disaster in Lydda and Ramle left a terrible impression.'[545] Kirkbride graphically described the second demonstration:

> I was paying a call at the palace one morning, when a couple of thousand Palestinian men swept up the hill towards the main entrance ... screaming abuse and demanding that the lost towns should be reconquered at once ... The King appeared at the top of the main steps of the building; he was a short dignified figure wearing white robes and headdress. He paused for a moment surveying the seething mob before, [then walked] down the steps to push his way through the line of guardsmen into the thick of the demonstrators. He went up to a prominent individual, who was shouting at the top of his voice, and dealt him a violent blow to the side of the head with the flat of his hand. The recipient of the blow stopped yelling ... [and] the King could be heard roaring: "So, you want to fight the Jews, do you? Very well, there is a recruiting office for the army at the back of my house ... go there and enlist. The rest of you, get the hell down the hillside!" Most of the crowd got the hell down the hillside ... A few of the men actually went and enlisted.[546]

According to Pirie-Gordon, 'much of the hostility was against Glubb personally,' and in the demonstration on 16 July the general's car was stoned and two other British officers were 'roughly handled.'[547]

The protests were not restricted to Amman. In Nablus there were 'wild demonstrations' by the townspeople and refugees, vaguely directed against the 'Arab governments and armies,' which were eventually put down by the occupying Iraqi troops.[548] According to Glubb, Legionnaires were stoned in Ramallah's streets and called 'Traitors! Worse than Jews.'[549] Both Glubb and Kirkbride[550] were subsequently to remark on the ungratefulness of the Palestinians: The Legionnaires, said Glubb, 'were at this very moment in battle from Latrun to Deir Tarif against five times their numbers. Already nearly one man in four of those who crossed the Allenby Bridge on May 15th was killed or wounded. I knew that they would go on to the last man - to save that country whose people were now calling them traitors.'[551] There was wild talk among the Palestinians of assassinating the Legion's British officers, and Glubb himself became the butt of rebuke. He was spat on and called a traitor when passing through villages. From then on, he moved about with a team of bodyguards, with a special detail around his house in Amman.[552] Amman was no longer, for him, a hospitable, carefree desert oasis.

And the criticism was not restricted to Palestinian villagers and urban mobs. By 16 July the rumour had reached the Israeli cabinet that 'Abdullah had fired Glubb Pasha.'[553] The truth was somewhat less stark. After writing to Abul Huda urging him (and his fellow Arab leaders) to agree to a ceasefire, lest even worse disasters befall the Arab armies,[554] Glubb was summoned to a meeting of the King and his Council of Ministers on 13 July, where he was roundly upbraided; his previous warnings that he could not defend Lydda and Ramle and would not try were ignored and 'his stories of ammunition shortages were disbelieved.' According to Glubb, Abdullah 'gloweringly' commented: 'If you don't want to serve us loyally, there is no need for you to stay,'[555] or, in another version, 'the King told Glubb in the presence of the entire Cabinet that if he wished to resign there was nothing to stop him.' Glubb asked Pirie-Gordon to ask Bevin whether it were better to have the Legion fight on and 'go under' under his command or whether he should resign (perhaps followed by the rest of the British officers) and to 'leave the Arabs to face the final collapse alone.' Kirkbride thought that of the 'the two evils,' it were better that Glubb soldier on; Pirie-Gordon advised that if the King again suggested resignation, Glubb 'should insist' on a formal letter of dismissal.[556]

But the British were clearly worried by the prospect of Glubb's dismissal. As Pirie-Gordon put it:

> Once the Arab Legion ceases to have a British commander it is goodbye to our influence in Transjordan, and perhaps also in the whole Arab World. The effect of Glubb's dismissal on our prestige in the Middle East would be incalculable: If the puppet state of Transjordan were able to throw off the chains of the imperialist, how much more then should states such as Egypt or Iraq be rid of their ... shackles? It would not, I think, be long before Iraq denounced the Anglo-Iraqi Treaty of 1930. Egypt would ... do the same ...[557]

Whatever his previous position regarding the two towns, Abdullah now found it politic to shoulder Glubb with all the blame, both for their loss and the plight of their inhabitants. The king and his ministers were under pressure from fellow Arab leaders and Palestinians, who believed, or at least charged, that 'Glubb Pasha and the rest of the British commanders of the Arab Legion brought about the fall of these two towns, in order to exert pressure on Arabs and bring about their agreement to [a] ... truce...' The commanders of the Arab armies demanded Glubb's resignation and 'abrogation of [the] Anglo-Transjordan treaty.'[558]

But Glubb refused to carry the can[559] and Abdullah and his ministers were quickly persuaded not to remove the British 'officers from positions of executive authority and [retain] their services in the form of a military mission,' fearing that a much-offended Britain might be prompted to reduce the Legion subsidy (and this, in the middle of the war).[560] (Disregarding Pirie-Gordon's and Kirkbride's advice, Glubb on 17 July offered the King his resignation but Abdullah, 'chagrined at his reopening the subject .. asked him to remain at his post' - though he complained that Glubb depressed him with his flow of forecasts of 'defeat and failure.' The general replied that it was his 'duty' to speak frankly.)[561]

Kirkbride had heard about Lydda and Ramle and Glubb's troubles while in Britain on sick leave. Much annoyed, upon his return to Amman he gave the King an unwonted dressing down: 'One of the first things I did on resuming duty,' reported Kirkbride on 5 August:

> was to reproach the King and the Prime Minister on the subject of the accusations or worse which had been levelled against the British officers of the Arab Legion and against Glubb in particular after the occupation of Ramle and Lydda by the Jewish forces. I said that when things went well the existence of British officers was not mentioned and when a reverse took place all manner of abuse was heaped upon their heads not only by the public but also by certain members of the Council of Ministers.
>
> The King was rather shamefaced and attributed the responsibility to [a] party of Iraqi deputies who had been visiting Amman at the time ... I discussed the matter later with Glubb who did not wish any further action taken for the present...[562]

But the following day, 6 August, Abdullah publicly repented. In a speech before a gathering of notables, with Glubb present, he praised the British officers of the Legion for the 'victory' and asked that his 'satisfaction' be conveyed to every officer and man. Kirkbride: 'King Abdullah now feels he has made amends publicly for any past failure on his part to check attacks on the good faith of the British officers ...'[563]

But Abdullah's gesture of remorse had not substantially altered the situation; Britain had taken a major drubbing in Jordanian public opinion. Or, as Kirkbride put it: 'I am struck [on returning to Amman] principally by the extreme precariousness of our position in Transjordan ...

We have reached a degree of unpopularity which I would have described as impossible six months ago.' The problem was not just the abandonment of Lydda and Ramle and the refugeedom of their populations but the British arms embargo and fear of what the future might hold: 'The main danger now is that of a Jewish attack on the Arab Legion which that force is in no position to resist, being without mortar or artillery ammunition. The anti-British outbreaks which followed the fall of Ramle and Lydda ... [are] an indication of what would happen following a major defeat of [the Legion].'[564] The precariousness of Glubb's - and Britain's - position was highlighted during Glubb's leave of absence in Britain in August-September. At the Arab League meeting in Cairo Arab sources (incorrectly) leaked that Glubb had resigned and would not be returning to his post. An official announcement in Amman seemed to confirm this.[565]

Operation Dani and the 'Ten Days' (as Israeli historians were to call this period of hostilities) ended on 19 July, when the Second Truce went into effect. From Amman's perspective, it came not a moment too soon. The Egyptians, in a 'parade of generosity' (in Pirie-Gordon's phrase), had during the fighting given the Legion some 400 artillery shells - of those they had confiscated from the 'Ramses.'[566] But this was only a drop in the bucket. The Legion was actually saved by the (United Nations) bell. On 18 July Glubb had reported that his supply of mortar and artillery ammunition would 'finally give out some time today or tomorrow at the latest.' Glubb expected that the Legion would then either be 'overrun' or would have to retreat eastward.[567] Moreover, the Legion had suffered serious losses during the 'Ten Days,' according to IDF Intelligence. Of the '2,110' Legionnaires who had participated in the fighting, some '330' had died, '250' had been wounded and '80' had deserted, according to IDF estimates (which may have been high).[568]

At the start of the Second Truce, which was to last until 15 October, when fighting resumed between Israel and Egypt, Abul Huda, no doubt at Glubb's behest, cabled Bevin regarding the Legion's 'desperate' situation. It was suffering from 'exhaustion of equipment and of all ammunition both for artillery and small arms.' In fact, Jordan was 'defenceless'; if the Jews attacked, 'not only would we be unable to maintain ourselves in Palestine for a single day but we would have difficulty even in protecting the road to Amman.' If Britain could not supply Jordan directly, perhaps it could stock ammunition in the RAF station in Amman - and this ammunition could be dispensed to Jordan if a crisis arose, suggested the prime minister.[569]

Abul Huda's appeal was buttressed by a further cable to London from Pirie-Gordon, affirming that Glubb 'confirmed' the prime minister's every word. Given its military state, Jordan had no intention of joining the Arab states should they decide to renew hostilities. But public opinion might not enable Jordan to stand aside. Besides, Pirie-Gordon added, the Legion's situation was now known to the Israelis - and this might prompt 'Jewish dissident groups' to attack the Legion.[570] But neither cable elicited a positive response from Whitehall.

A few weeks later, Glubb decided to try a direct, personal approach. In the second half of August he flew to England for a month's leave.[571] He met Bevin in London on 19 August and handed him a letter from Abdullah, in which the King condemned 'the abominable massacres committed by the Jews' and asked the British to provide Jordan with 'the means' to 'resist ... Soviet expansion' (by which he meant lift the embargo and provide arms with which to resist the IDF). In the letter, the King hinted, or more than hinted, at the Anglo-Jordanian understanding of February 1948 regarding the Legion occupation of Arab parts of Palestine. He wrote: 'I think that we have [i.e., had] at least a partial understanding with you on this subject, according to the information submitted to me by my prime minister, who actually met Your Excellency and discussed this problem.'[572]

Glubb also presented Bevin with two memoranda of his own, 'The Trans-Jordan Situation 12th August 1948' and 'Note by Glubb', dated 19 August 1948 - on the state of Jordan and the Arab Legion - and appealed for ammunition and arms as well as money.[573] (Above all, Glubb sought ammunition for his 25-pounders and 3-inch mortars..)[574]

Glubb presented Bevin with an extremely bleak picture, 'all of it black, suffused with [feelings of] inferiority and failure,' according to Israeli sources. Glubb asserted 'that the Arabs are incapable of any successful military effort. No advantage in numbers or equipment will save them from the breakdown of the moral component in the war effort, from unwillingness to sacrifice themselves, and from a strengthening of the seeds of divisiveness among the various Arab elements ... [Moreover] they are weighed down with a terrible burden, the burden of the refugees.' In short, Glubb felt that a 'pro-Arab policy obliged England to make a giant effort to prevent the Arabs from endangering themselves by renewing hostilities ... Renewal of the war, according to [Glubb's] assessment, means conquest by the Jews of the whole of the country [i.e., Palestine] and the disintegration of the regimes in all the Arab countries.'[575]

Bevin not completely accurately responded that Britain was not responsible for Jordan's difficulties: 'We had never urged the Transjordan Government to take action in Palestine. They had told us beforehand that they intended to do this and we had mentioned the difficulties that might arise for us with the United Nations. We had not been told beforehand that the Arab Legion would go into Jerusalem.' He added that war materiel on a large scale could not be given to the Legion though perhaps could be readied in the Canal Zone for rapid trans-shipment, should Israel break the truce. Glubb 'agreed that it would be unwise to send war materiel at once' but wondered how it could be quickly proven that the Israelis had broken the truce. He pointed out the need for speed in sending assistance as the Legion 'could only hold out for a few days if fighting was resumed.'

Glubb then asked (in Abdullah's name) what Britain 'would do if the Jews, after resuming hostilities, reached the Jordan.' Bevin responded that 'I thought this question ought not to be asked. We had our treaty and we would not go back on it. We would not abandon Transjordan or give up Transjordan territory.' But he cautioned Glubb 'not to rely on this ... assurance to cause an incident.' Glubb was far from reassured: In effect, he had been asking about possible British assistance for Jordanian forces in the West Bank, not about the fate and integrity of the East Bank. But Glubb received one positive reply: Britain would continue subsidizing the Legion, including coverage of the debts incurred in the fighting.[576]

Glubb was marginally more successful with Lord Montgomery, the Chief of the Imperial General Staff. He agreed to support a British warning to Israel that should it attack 'Transjordan,' it would be at war with Britain. Montgomery also favoured the immediate dispatch to British bases in Iraq and Jordan of 'arms and equipment,' so that, when instructed, they could be issued rapidly to the local armies.[577]

Montgomery had, indeed, told Glubb that 'he hoped we would give Transjordan a guarantee that we would go to her help if she was attacked.' But Glubb, while in favour of the assurance, which he had also received from Bevin, was 'strongly against the idea of informing the Jews that it has been given.' He felt that it might 'make it more difficult for the Jews to accept the absorption of Arab Palestine into Transjordan and would also be likely to make the Jews think that they could occupy the whole of Palestine with impunity provided that they do not actually threaten Transjordan territory.'[578]

Despite the foregoing, Glubb apparently did manage to eke out of Bevin a promise of immediate limited supplies of ammunition and spare parts. Shortly after the meeting, Burrows informed Glubb that 'instructions have ... been sent to the British Military Authorities in the Middle East to resume maintenance issues for the Arab Legion on a scale sufficient to meet essential needs for one month ahead,' but without any 'capital equipment or replacement of major items.'[579] The materiel - including thousands of desperately needed 25-pounder high explosive shells and 3-inch mortar bombs - appears to have been shipped to the Legion (and/or to British depots in Jordan) from the Canal Zone via 'Aqaba during the autumn months (in violation of the UN embargo).[580]

Be that as it may, en large, Glubb had proven unable to seriously shake British policy regarding the embargo. The Legion received no additional heavy or light weapons, and no replacements for its destroyed guns, mortars and armoured cars. Nor had it received ammunition in quantities sufficient for more than a week or two of full-scale 'contact.' His Majesty's Government had argued that it had to abide by the Security Council resolution; a violation might sour relations with Washington and trigger an American counter-violation in favour of Israel. Such a spiral would ultimately benefit Israel, went the argument. This left the strategic situation on the Israeli-Jordanian front in the autumn and winter of 1948 essentially unchanged, with the IDF overwhelmingly stronger than the Arab Legion.

Glubb returned to Jordan on 18 September and spent the following months beefing up the Legion with new recruits, including Britons. Glubb also devoted energy to restoring his own position, which had been shaken both by the Lydda-Ramle affair (which somehow completely overshadowed his and the Legion's very real military achievements, of holding East Jerusalem, Latrun and the hill country between) and by revelations about unauthorised over-expenditure on the Arab Legion.

The British government had allocated £2,500,000 for the Arab Legion's upkeep during fiscal year 1948\49. In practise, as a result of the war, Glubb spent some £6 million.[581] How was the excess that had accumulated by autumn 1948 to be covered? Kirkbride reported the following:

> Glubb came to see me yesterday and reported an almost incredible state of affairs financially. Acting on a verbal promise that Arab Legion [i.e., League] funds would be made available ... the latter admits having overspent his current yearly estimates to the tune of about P£400,000 (I fear it may be more) ... The most as-

> tounding feature of the matter is that Glubb did this without any reference to the Jordanian Government ... This Legation was kept equally ignorant...
>
> When Glubb applied to 'Azzam [secretary general of the Arab League] ... a few days ago he received a reply that in view of the failure of the Arab Legion to play its part in recent fighting, no Arab League funds could be spent on the force...
>
> Glubb came to see me ... I was unsympathetic ... he was entirely in the wrong.[582]

Glubb quite reasonably argued that the war had imposed unforeseen expenses and that there had been misunderstandings with the War Office about several items.[583] Eventually, the Jordanian government came up with £300,000, with Whitehall, after much internal bickering, covering the shortfall.[584]

Meanwhile, the Jordanian Council of Ministers moved to impose greater control over Glubb and the Legion. As Kirkbride saw it, it was 'only natural' that the Jordanian Government wished to control its own army's actions. Besides, this cloud definitely had a silver lining. Previously, Glubb had 'exercised something in the nature of a free hand.' Many assumed that he was, in fact, being directed by Whitehall rather than by Abdullah. So Britain was 'blamed for any failure or unpopular action by the Arab Legion.' Now, 'the Transjordan Government cannot evade responsibility ... for the actions of their troops.'[585]

During August and September, while the guns were silent, Glubb was preoccupied by his ammunition shortages, the rivalry with Egypt over control of the southern West Bank, an area comprising the towns of Bethlehem and Hebron and their rural hinterlands, and the burgeoning Palestinian refugee problem.

The ammunition shortages, as we have seen, rendered the Legion incapable of resuming hostilities.[586] The Jordanian government had decided 'not to attack Jewish forces in any circumstances,' reported Kirkbride, and, as we shall see, the Legion was to remain essentially inactive during the following bouts (in October-November and then in December 1948-January 1949) of Egyptian-Israeli hostilities. And the shortages were to have an even more radical effect. As Kirkbride accurately predicted, Transjordan:

> will ... have no option but to negotiate with the Jews. If it were possible to withdraw Arab Legion from Palestine and leave Arab population behind that would be preferable alternative but retreat of Arab Legion would bring with it another

> mass of refugees with which this country could just not cope ... King Abdullah is in touch with Jewish quarters ... Opening talks with Jews would doubtless bring down on Transjordan and probably on ourselves too the wrath of the Arab world ... [But] all this would, in my view, be much lesser evil than probable consequences of trying to hold an untenable position in Palestine ... Glubb agrees with these views.[587]

But Jordan's military inactivity and the resumption of the dialogue with the Jews (which harked back to the pre-war Yishuv-Hashemite entente) was not a product only of ammunition shortages. The unsuccessful pan-Arab assault on Israel had sharpened inter-Arab differences and animosities. As before 15 May so after it, but with added vigour, the Arab leaders were at Abdullah's throat, their traditional enmity compounded by envy of the Legion's good showing against Israel which contrasted with their own generally poor-to-very-poor performances. Indeed, during the Second Truce the situation was such as to move Glubb to report to Whitehall that 'the internecine struggles of the Arabs are more in the minds of the Arab politicians than the struggle against the Jews. 'Azzam Pasha, the Mufti and the Syrian Government would sooner see the Jews get the whole of Palestine than that King Abdullah should benefit.'[588]

A major area of inter-Arab rivalry was the Hebron Hills-Bethlehem area (the southern West Bank), where several companies of Legionnaires had been stationed since mid-May and which had been occupied during the first fortnight of the invasion by the Egyptian Army and its Muslim Brotherhood auxiliaries in brigade strength.

Between the end of May and mid-October the two countries covertly and not-so-covertly vied for dominance in the area (while, at the same time, the Jordanians absorbed or disarmed the Husseini-aligned Palestinian irregular bands).[589] By and large the local population preferred the Jordanians but the Egyptians (rather clumsily) made efforts to win the locals' hearts and minds. Both countries appointed military governors in Bethlehem and Hebron. The Jordanians shipped in supplies and Jordanian stamps; the Egyptians objected, sometimes impounding the supplies and sending them to Gaza. The two sides struggled to win over the local police and municipal officials in Hebron using salaries as bait. On 4 June the Egyptians raised their flag over their headquarters in a disused school building in Hebron. The villagers of Beit Jibrin appealed to Amman to eject the Egyptian garrison from their village. The Egyptians eventually persuaded the pro-Hashemite mayor of Hebron, Muhammad Ali al-Ja`abri, at least momentarily and superficially to support their rule.[590] But Egyptian heavy-handedness soon took its toll. In July the Egyptian authorities began to collect taxes.

Egyptian authorities began to collect taxes. Quite naturally, local opinion shifted against them.[591] In the village of Dhahiriya, south of Hebron, the locals resisted and a number of locals and Egyptians were killed in a firefight. In response, Ja`abri began to incite against Egyptian rule and called for the Legion to re-assert control over Hebron.[592] Villagers at nearby Yata also resisted Egyptian taxation. Again, both sides appear to have resorted to guns and taken casualties.[593] Meanwhile, the Jordanian governor of Hebron, Salah al Majali, waived taxes and stepped up payment of salaries to local officials and policemen.[594]

During the following months the Egyptians, represented on the ground in much greater numbers, retained the upper hand in the Bethlehem-Hebron Hills area while Jordanian supporters, officials, soldiers and policemen campaigned, more or less overtly and with Abdullah's blessing, to undermine their hold. Neither side proved able to force the issue - and, in the end, it was the IDF which decided matters in Operation Yoav, launched on 15 October, by smashing the Egyptian Army in the plains to the west while at the same time not conquering the Hebron-Bethlehem hill-country. Jordanian units quickly filled the vacuum. While small Egyptian units lingered on in Hebron-Bethlehem until February-March 1949, the southern West Bank had effectively fallen into Hashemite hands.

As to the refugees, on 7 September 1948 Glubb produced a five-page memorandum, impressive for its clarity and foresight. He may have been contemptuous of the Palestine Arabs on general, racial grounds, as well as politically and militarily (while at the same time sympathizing with their anti-Zionism), but during 1948 and in later years he was consistently to express empathy with their plight. In his memoirs, he devotes moving passages to graphically describing their trials and tribulations.[595]

In Glubb's estimation, there were (by early September) some 400,000 refugees. The ‘200,000’ or so from areas that were earmarked by the UN for Jewish sovereignty ‘have no chance of returning permanently to their homes,’ he wrote:

> It is possible that the Jews ... may temporarily employ Arab casual labour for a short time, because Arabs work for low wages. But once the Jewish economic situation is re-established, and when more Jewish immigrants arrive, Arab labour will no longer be employed ... The other half of the refugees come from Arab areas which are in Jewish military occupation, and which were Arab in the original UNO partition scheme. In the worst case situation, UNO will fail to evict the

> Jews from these areas also, and we shall have to reckon with 400,000 total irrepatriables. In the best situation, these [200,000] will be able to go back. But when they get home, they will find only the shells of their houses. Everything else will have been totally looted by the Jews. Probably even the door and window frames will have been removed. Certainly these people will have lost all their capital [and moveable property].

But Glubb's implicit, working assumption - and he was right - was that neither category of refugees would be allowed back. Unknown to Glubb, the Israeli Cabinet during June-September 1948 had secretly resolved not to allow the refugees back,[596] a decision that, in the absence of Israeli-Arab peace treaties after the war, in effect sealed the refugees' fate. Glubb, of course, had been completely correct about the more or less universal phenomenon in the Jewish-occupied areas of looting - but seemed to be unaware at this time that many of the empty Arab villages had been already or were being systematically razed, in part to prevent the possibility of a return.

Glubb understood that the war was not yet over and clearly anticipated a substantial increase in the number of refugees during the following months. ‘It may be well to add that there is still a possibility of the truce breaking down ... Should hostilities begin again, a further wave of Arab refugees may be expected to arrive in Transjordan - perhaps 100,000, perhaps 200,000, according to the course of the operations.’ In fact, there were to be an additional 250,000-odd refugees, who were driven out of the south (mainly into the Gaza Strip) by the IDF in Operation Yoav and its aftermath in October-November and out of the Galilee (mainly into Lebanon) in Operation Hiram at the end of October.

Glubb proposed a number of ‘immediate’ and ‘interim’ relief projects, including afforestation, the construction of by-pass roads, fruit canning and agricultural development. Aware that Israel was not going to allow them back, Glubb suggested that the refugees be resettled in Transjordan and the West Bank as well as in Egypt and Iraq. ‘Lebanon would be unlikely to take any. Syria might take a few.’ Glubb bemoaned the fact that Transjordan, ‘both the smallest [sic, Lebanon is much smaller] and the poorest of the Arab countries,’ had to absorb most of the refugees, while the wealthier refugees moved on to Lebanon, Syria and Egypt.[597]

By mid-1949 Glubb's assumption that Israel would never allow a return of the refugees had hardened into a certainty. Interestingly, he added that he, ‘personally ... [was] strongly opposed to Arab refugees going back.’ His argument was that ‘if the Jews do not want them, they will find some means of making life so unpleasant for them that in a month or two they will all come back [to Jordan anyhow].'[598] During the following years Glubb was periodically to propose this or that measure - such as emptying West Bank refugee camps - to alleviate the refugees' plight, which, through infiltration back to Israel, was causing Israeli-Jordanian border tensions and hostilities (see below).[599]

From mid-1948 onwards Jordan was to gradually integrate the West Bank into the Hashemite kingdom, formally annexing the territory in 1950. Thus was Abdullah at least partly to realize his lifelong expansionist ambitions. But the annexation also meant that Jordan, previously an underpopulated, almost homogeneously beduin entity, was now to absorb a local and refugee Palestinian population larger than its original population. This irrevocably 'Palestinized' the Jordanian polity and society. Henceforward, the kingdom would have a population a large part of which resented Hashemite-beduin rule and the monarchy in general. As Kirkbride was later to describe it, 'they came as poor additions to a poor country ... They had no particular reason to be loyal to the ruling dynasty ... and were unforgivingly bitter against the British and the Americans for the ruin which had overtaken all their hopes.'[600]

It was partly for this reason that the Legion, after Egypt's establishment in Gaza in September 1948 of a subservient Palestinian 'government' - the so-called 'All-Palestine Government' - and after deploying in the Hebron hills during the Egyptian retreat in October-November 1948, moved quickly to disarm Palestinian armed bands in the Jerusalem-Ramallah and Hebron areas, principally the 'Holy War Army,' 'Abd al Qadir al Husseini's old armed band that the Mufti had tried to resurrect at the time. The disarming operation was apparently initiated at Glubb's insistence - quite naturally, he didn't want a rival armed group in Legion-controlled territory - and authorized by Jordan's defence minister. The pro-Husseini bands may or may not have planned rebellion against Abdullah, as the Hashemites charged.[601]

Without doubt, Glubb was uneasy about the absorption of hundreds of thousands of Palestinians into the realm. During late 1948-early 1949 he repeatedly expressed fears about the possible benefits the disaffected Palestinian refugee concentrations might bring to the Soviet Union or 'Communism.' In his memorandum from early 1949, 'Suggested Partition Frontiers in Palestine',[602] he wrote: '... the refugee community will provide an exceedingly fertile breeding ground for communistic propaganda, which is already being propagated with great energy and no small success. Internal upheavals, riots and attempts at rebellion may well take place, while pro-Russian or extreme nationalist elements will not lose the opportunity to blame the whole tragedy on British imperialism.'

The fear of Communism at this time ran through the thinking of most British officers and officials, caught up as America's chief ally in the Cold War. Glubb was no doubt aware of the impact of such forebodings on Whitehall and probably hoped that they would propel the West into efforts to solve the refugee problem. (Ironically, Glubb was also prone to reflections on the potential recruitment of the new state of Israel into the Soviet camp. In 1950, for example, he wrote: 'It is perhaps well to remember ... that the Israeli left parties command today one third of the seats in their parliament. These parties claim not to be ideologically Communists in the Russian sense, but they do advocate an alliance with Russia ... This is not surprising when we remember that the great majority of Jews in Israel are natives of countries behind the Iron Curtain.')[603]

By early 1949 Glubb was referring to '700,000 Arab refugees,' approximately the figure reached by various United Nations agencies during the following months (while the Arab states officially spoke of 900,000 or one million refugees and Israel, of 520,000). Glubb was puzzled by the fact that there were not more refugees - or, more accurately, puzzled by the fact that Israel had failed to expel many of the Palestinians from the Galilee during or immediately after Operation Hiram at the end of October 1948. He noted that while 'the Jews forcibly drove out' the inhabitants of Lydda and Ramle and villages west of Jerusalem and Hebron and in the Beersheba area, 'for some reason or other' many of the inhabitants in the Galilee were left in place, unmolested.

As to the refugees, about half the total were living in the West Bank and East Jordan, many of them being taken in by 'very poor ... villagers ... and are sharing with them their food.' The burden on Jordan and its population, he complained, was tremendous. To Transjordan's original population of less than half a million had been added some 400,000 refugees. Glubb argued that Jordan could absorb at most some 100,000. The rest would have to 'return to Palestine or ... die off.' And he maintained - writing during the winter of 1949, when international relief efforts were only beginning to move into high gear - that dying off they were, at a rate of four per cent per month, according to what one British Red Cross officer told him. 'Most of [the 300,000 unabsorbables] will die over the period of the next four years,' he wrote. (In fact, he proved very far off the mark. The refugees were to have a far lower mortality rate, had an extremely high birth rate, and soon benefited from international aid that assured their subsistence. Refugee numbers over the years therefore increased, by leaps and bounds, rather than decreased. Today

UNRWA has on its rolls over three and a half million Palestinian 'refugees' - meaning those who are still alive from among the original refugees and their descendants - while the Palestinian Authority officially claims that the real number of 'refugees' is closer to five million.)

By this time Glubb was acutely aware that Israel was radically transforming the landscape in such a way that none or few of the refugees would have anywhere to return to, even if there was international agreement and Israeli consent. 'All over the conquered areas, Arab towns and villages ... are being filled up with Jews. In some places, whole Arab villages are being demolished and removed, and Jewish colonies being built near by. In others, Arab towns are being completely taken over and transformed into Jewish towns ... This process ... is being carried out with feverish haste.' For Glubb, this meant that it was 'essential ... to fix the frontiers quickly,' before the Israeli *fait accompli* was completed. Glubb warned against agreement to 'cash compensation' to the refugees for their lost property. 'This ... would be disastrous. To give £100 each to every destitute Arab family would be no use ... [and would ultimately leave them] destitute.'[604]

The refugee problem was in large measure a function of battlefield developments. Some 400,000 Palestinians had fled or been driven from their homes by the start of the Second Truce; a further 300,000 refugees were added by operations 'Yoav' and 'Hiram.'

On 14 October, the Egyptians, mustering roughly four brigades, were deployed in Palestine in a rough 'H' formation: Its bulk, the westerly south-north arm of the 'H,' consisted of two brigades strung out along the coast from Rafah through Gaza and Majdal up to Isdud (the present-day Israeli port city of Ashdod); the slightly curved north-south easterly arm of the 'H' was formed by the Egyptian brigade entrenched from Bethlehem through Hebron down to Beersheba. The two arms were connected by a crosspiece formed by Egyptian units of brigade strength strung out from west to east in a chain of fortifications between Majdal and the Hebron Hills, mainly on either side of the Majdal-Beit Jibrin road. This crosspiece served both to connect the main Egyptian troop concentrations and their supply route from Egypt up the coast with the forces in the Bethlehem-Hebron hill country and, at the same time, to cut off the Israeli settlements and troops in the northern Negev south of the road from the main Jewish population centres and troop concentrations to the north, stretching from Rehovot through Tel Aviv and Haifa.

Israel's object in Operation Yoav, launched on 15 October, was two-fold: To defeat the Egyptian Army by destroying its units along the Majdal-Beit Jibrin road and cutting off the easterly right arm of the 'H' from the westerly coastal arm; and to reconnect the Negev, with its semi-isolated Jewish settlements and troops, to the main body of the state to the north.

The Israeli political and military leadership judged that the previous months of fighting had left the various Arab coalition members at loggerheads and deeply suspicious of each other's motives and intentions. Moreover, having all to one degree or another suffered serious losses in men and materiel, and burdened by constricting shortages in arms and ammunition, the Syrians, Iraqis and Jordanians, it was felt, had lost the will and, substantially, the power to fight and would let the IDF operate against the Egyptians unmolested. These assumptions proved correct.

The four-brigade Israeli offensive was provocatively triggered by the dispatch by the IDF of an (empty) supplies column into the Egyptian Majdal-Beit Jibrin crosspiece. The Egyptians, as expected (and in violation of the UN truce provisions, which allowed the supply to the Negev enclave of non-military materials), opened fire and the IDF unleashed its long-planned campaign. Within days, after heavy fighting, the Israelis had punched two large wedges through the Majdal-Beit Jibrin defence lines, isolating large Egyptian units in the process (in what came to be known as 'the Faluja Pocket') and linking up with the Negev settlements, and on 21 October conquered Beersheba. The Egyptian units in the hills to the east, along the Bethlehem-Hebron-Dhahiriya line, were left isolated and cut off and most eventually withdrew southwestwards to the Negev and Sinai.

As soon as Operation Yoav began, Glubb divined the opportunity for Transjordan. On 16 October he dashed off a note to Goldie (which, by the way, offers more than a hint of his attitude toward his Egyptian 'allies' and Israeli enemies):

> If the Jews break through to ... Beersheba, the Egyptians in Hebron will be cut off. We don't want the Jews to capture Hebron too. If we step in and occupy Hebron ... we shall appear as saviours, to rescue Hebron from the Jews when the Egyptians have run away. This Jewish offensive may have good and bad sides. It may finally give the gyppies [i.e., Egyptians] a lesson. On the other hand, it will make the Jews even more arrogant, and if they knock out the Egyptians, they may turn on us ... I don't see how we could let the Jews occupy Hebron if we could prevent it. At the same time, if the Jews are going to have a private war with the Egyptians and the [All-Palestine] Gaza Government we do not want to get involved. The gyppies and the Gaza Government are almost as hostile to us

> as the Jews! ... I imagine that U.N.O. [United Nations Organisation] will not want the Jews to occupy Hebron ... Perhaps we could send a regiment to Hebron ...[605]

Within days, Glubb's expectations were realized; the Egyptians were in retreat. On Abdullah's orders (apparently issued already on 19 October), he hastily organized a Legion force from Jerusalem to reinforce Bethlehem and Beit Jala (against which, unsuccessfully, the IDF had simultaneously mounted a minor push (Operation HaHar and Operation Yekev)) and ordered Goldie to occupy Hebron. The battalion-size Legion column reached the southern town on 21 October. That day, Glubb explained the military, political and economic reasons for the move (which was a major gamble, given the possibility that the Israelis, with overwhelming strength, might push eastward from Beersheba-Beit Jibrin and themselves try to conquer Hebron): 'If the enemy were to take Bethlehem and Beit Jala, our troops in the south [i.e., those left in Hebron since 15 May] would be cut off [from the Legion's main body in Jerusalem-Ramallah-Jericho].' Moreover, if these towns fell under Israeli control, Glubb once again would be held to blame – 'it would again be me who had betrayed the Arab cause' and another flood of refugees, '50,000 to 100,000'-strong, could be expected to pour into Transjordan.[606]

Glubb's move was exquisitely timed: A political window of opportunity had been created by the UN order to all parties to cease fire by 22 October; the Jordanians had thus taken over the southern West Bank just under the wire. It was unlikely that the Israelis would risk angering the UN (and Britain and the United States) by a main assault on Hebron and Bethlehem after the start of the ceasefire.

On the other hand, neither could the Jordanians have allowed themselves to move (and violate the ceasefire provisions) after 21 October. Moreover, the morale of the local population had to be taken into account. During the third week of October the Egyptian defeat and withdrawal, and rumours of impending Israeli attack, had generated panic throughout the Hebron Hills area. Any further delay by the Legion would have resulted in a depopulated southern West Bank. As one Legion officer later recalled, the local inhabitants began 'to leave their places for fear. Had it not been for the Legion companies that arrived to protect their honour and the southern [West Bank] areas [they would have emptied and been conquered by the IDF].'[607]

But successes breed their own problems. Now that Jordan had occupied the (northern and) southern West Bank, the question was: Could it hold the territory? Or, put another way, how could Amman stymie an Israeli attempt to drive out the Legion? Glubb himself told Abdullah and the Jordanian Cabinet on 2 November: 'After the [completion of the ongoing] withdrawal of Egyptian forces [from the Hebron area], the Arab Legion would be unable to maintain its positions if attacked by Jewish forces.'[608] Nor would Britain agree to extend the bilateral defence treaty to cover the West Bank.[609]

One option was for the Legion simply to withdraw back to Transjordan - and leave the West Bank to the Israelis and the other Arab armies to face Israel alone. Glubb and Kirkbride seem occasionally have been tempted. But there were good arguments against such a course: Too much Jordanian blood had been shed in gaining the West Bank to abandon it voluntarily; how would the Legion and the Jordanian public react? And how would the Palestinians, delivered over to Israel's mercies, react? And the other Arab states, who once again would scream 'Jordanian treachery'? On the other hand, leaving the Legion in the West Bank after the other Arab armies were defeated or rendered *hors de combat* was dangerous in the extreme: If the IDF attacked and destroyed the Legion, the West Bank would fall and perhaps the Hashemite regime along with it.[610]

Given pan-Arab weakness, active Arab opposition to the Jordanian conquests, Israel's military preponderance and perceived or suspected expansionist ambitions, and prospective international dubiousness as to the Jordanian claim to the West Bank (ultimately, only Britain and Pakistan recognised Jordan's annexation of the territory), the only alternative - that dictated by wisdom - seemed to be an accommodation with Israel backed by an international (in effect, an Anglo-American) endorsement.

Already in September 1948 Glubb had proposed to the Jordanian and British governments a re-partioning of Palestine with Israel in a way that would give Jordan the West Bank and Egypt, the Gaza and Beersheba districts. Perhaps the Arabs (meaning Egypt) could thus be persuaded to leave the West Bank to the Jordanians? Glubb had hoped that Jordan might enjoy a 'port on the Mediterranean' but doubted whether 'we could pull it off,' given Egyptian control of the coastal strip from Gaza to Isdud and Israeli control of the area to the east of this line.[611] Alternately, Glubb had suggested, all of Arab Palestine, including the West Bank and the Gaza and Beersheba districts, be incorporated into Jordan: Certainly the Palestinians preferred Hashemite to Egyptian rule. Moreover, Glubb sensed that the Egyptians would rather withdraw completely from Palestine than suffer another (losing) bout of hostilities with the Israelis, and the Iraqi expeditionary force, now commanded by the Iraqi Army chief of staff, General Salih Pasha as Saib, was determined to withdraw from Palestine, where it had reaped little glory and might yet face annihilation. The Palestinians themselves were war-weary and Glubb saw no difficulty in the Legion occupying the areas (northern Samaria) eventually to be vacated by the Iraqis or the Hebron-Beersheba-Gaza areas should the Egyptians decide to evacuate them. The Palestinians would prefer that their territory be occupied by one Arab state rather than divided up between several sovereigns.[612] Besides, this arrangement would at last give Jordan the desired outlet to the Mediterranean.

Kirkbride, who had forwarded Glubb's memorandum to Burrows, believed that the general had made 'many sound points.' But Glubb, he wrote, 'over-estimates the desire of the Palestinians for union with Transjordan and underestimates the influence of Haj Amin [al-Husseini] and his associates.'[613]

However, before anyone in London could seriously consider Glubb's various 'plans' the IDF had struck (Operation Yoav), radically changing the geo-political situation. Israel took the Beersheba area and the Legion had responded by taking over Bethlehem and Hebron.

Glubb now set about producing a new plan for a final settlement, taking the new realities at least partially into account. The new draft plan, from late November 1948, recalled the partition plans devised by Glubb back in 1946-1947. Bowing to the *fait accompli*, he now relegated Beersheba and the northern Negev to Israeli rule, but earmarked the central and southern Negev (roughly from a point south of Beersheba to the Gulf of `Aqaba), and the Gaza Strip, for Arab (meaning Jordanian) rule. The West Bank was to be retained by Jordan and the Galilee was to be divided between Israel (the southern half) and Lebanon (the northern half). Glubb asked Kirkbride to submit it 'as your idea, which would carry more weight' - or, if Kirkbride was unwilling, as Glubb's idea, but without negative comment. Kirkbride chose a third option: He simply transmitted it without saying whose plan it was ('I submit for your consideration the following suggestion for a compromise ...').[614]

Israeli-Egyptian hostilities sputtered on intermittently; the IDF occupied Isdud and then Majdal (5 November), the Egyptians retreating southwards along the coastal plain, hunkering down in the narrow coastal area known today as the Gaza Strip and along the international (Egypt-Palestine) border down to al-Auja (later Nitzana) to the south. The Jordanians looked on, passively, without interfering. On 9 November the new ceasefire took effect. But the war, all understood, was not yet over; most of the Negev was still in Arab hands, and Israel was not going to acquiesce in this. But where would the next Israeli blow fall?

Glubb and Kirkbride concluded that Abdullah had no choice: If he wished to hold onto the West Bank, he would have to make peace with Israel - even if this led to Jordan's ostracism and expulsion from the Arab League.[615] Within Jordan, there seemed to be support for this position. The Arab defeats had resulted in a desire to secure 'the best terms they can' before their situation worsened, reported Kirkbride. Senior Legion officers did not want the war to continue.[616] On 30 November Israel and Jordan duly signed a truce, officially ending their shooting war; it was to be a milestone on the way to signing a full armistice agreement and negotiating a final peace settlement.

In a last bout of Israeli-Egyptian hostilities, the IDF, during late December 1948-early January 1949 (Operation Horev), drove the Egyptian Army out of the northern Negev and invaded eastern Sinai, bottling up most of it in the Gaza Strip and threatening it with annihilation. No other Arab army, including the Legion, participated or intervened in the fighting. By operation's end, the Egyptians, pressured by Britain and the United States, sued for a ceasefire, which went into effect on 7 January. With their army defeated and a brigade-size force still stranded and besieged around the northern Negev village of Faluja ('the Faluja Pocket'), Cairo entered into UN-mediated negotiations, and on 24 February 1949 signed at Rhodes a general armistice agreement with Israel. The Lebanese followed suit on 30 March and Iraq officially informed Amman that it intended to withdraw its expeditionary force from the northern West Bank back to Iraq.[617] With Syria (which would sign its own armistice agreement with Israel on 20 July) bent on disengaging from Palestine and, in any case, hostile to the Hashemites, Jordan remained alone to confront the Israelis across the conference table.

The Israeli-Jordanian negotiations - in effect a resumption of the political dialogue halted in May 1948 - began already in November 1948, well before the formal armistice talks and even before the signing of the 30 November truce. During the following months the two sides were to hold two parallel sets of talks, secret political ones geared to reaching a final peace settlement and semi-overt ones concerning an armistice. Abdullah was eager for a deal. He explained his overall situation to Glubb: 'I'll tell you a Turkish proverb ... They say: "If you meet a bear when crossing a rotten bridge, call her - dear Auntie!."'[618]

During August-October 1948, the British, while seeking an end to Israeli-Jordanian hostilities, had been unenthusiastic about Jordan reaching a separate, bilateral deal with Israel. Whitehall feared that such a deal would isolate Abdullah in the Arab world and increase his vulnerability as well as reduce the Arabs' general bargaining power vis-a-vis the Israelis. 'It would be dangerous to suggest bilateral negotiations between Transjordan and the Jews to King Abdullah. He is already flirting with ideas of this kind but both I and the Prime Minister with whom I discussed the tendency some time ago feel he is not really in a strong enough position to ride out the storm which such action would cause in the Arab world,' Kirkbride wrote at the end of August.[619] But by November, Jordan's desperate military and political situation had persuaded Kirkbride and Glubb that Jordan had to negotiate if it hoped to hold onto the hard-won hills of the West Bank, including East Jerusalem. In the absence of a British commitment to come to the Legion's aid in defence of the West Bank, Jordan could either withdraw back to the East Bank or negotiate a peace with Israel which would include acceptance of continued Jordanian occupation of the territory. Abdullah, who for years had sought an accommodation with the Jews, was easily persuaded. Such a course would involve political peril – that is, 'the wrath of the Arab world and ... [possibly] the expulsion of Transjordan from the Arab League. [But] all this, in my view, would be much lesser evil than probable consequences of trying to hold an untenable position in Palestine [without agreement with Israel],' concluded Kirkbride.

Kirkbride was also mindful of the internal problems such negotiations would create. 'Present Prime Minister [i.e., Abul Huda] would not, I am sure, be a party to such negotiations but he could probably be induced to resign beforehand for reasons of health ... Palestine refugees here might be induced to demand negotiations [i.e., support such negotiations] ... Only point on which I am not clear is who could be found to form a Ministry which would carry out new policy. Glubb agrees with these views.'[620] By early December, Kirkbride's views had turned around completely. He cabled London: 'I consider we should now cease to check any tendency of Transjordan to come to terms with the Jews if they can.'[621]

During the following months, the Arab states demanded that Israel withdraw to the 1947 UN partition borders. Israel, for its part, insisted that, with regard to Jordan, the frontiers should be based on the existing military front lines (but with some changes in its favour), and with regard to Syria, on the pre-war partition borders, leaving within Israel both those Arab areas conquered in the course of the war as well as territory that was not yet in Israeli hands but had been allotted to the Jewish state in the partition resolution. With regard to Egypt, Israel preferred the new borders to run along the old Egypt-Palestine international frontier (demarcated by Britain and the Ottoman Empire in 1906), which only in part was identical with the proposed UN Partition Resolution borders. A major problem at this time, from Israel's viewpoint, was the southern Negev, allocated to Israel by the UN vote of November 1947 but physically still loosely in Arab hands (in November 1948 Glubb had dispatched a Legion company to thinly patrol the region).[622]

Glubb's views during the negotiations were clear. He argued:

> It is ironical to think that the Jews for 2,000 years have claimed that armed might conveys no right ... Everywhere [they] denounced their persecutors and looked forward to an age when justice will replace armed power. But now, placed for the first time in a position to persecute others, they suddenly announce that military conquest is the true basis for settlement between nations.[623]

(Glubb (accurately) charged that this attitude characterized Israel's approach to the United Nations in general. It systematically flouted the international arms embargo, by bringing in masses of weapons from Czechoslovakia and from private arms markets, and regularly subjected UN observers who monitored the truces and the embargo to 'indignities' and limitations. Since the assassination of UN Mediator, Count Bernadotte, on 17 September 1948, UN personnel in Palestine had felt so cowed and intimidated that they routinely avoided antagonizing Israel, he wrote.)

Glubb recommended that Israel withdraw from (and hand over to Jordan) the areas earmarked for (Palestinian) Arab sovereignty that it had captured west and south of the West Bank - namely, the Lydda-Ramle and Beersheba areas - enabling the resettlement in them of some '150,000' of the refugees. This, incidentally, was a perennial demand at this time of the Jordanian Government in both the secret peace talks and the armistice negotiations.[624] Perhaps Glubb was in part motivated by a personal feeling of responsibility for the fall of Lydda and Ramle. Glubb also demanded international - and Israeli - agreement to Jordan's retention of the southern Negev wedge around the Gulf of Aqaba, to allow Jordan continued 'land communication' with Egypt and the British Suez Canal bases, while allowing the Jews the use of either 'Aqaba or a new port on the Gulf of 'Aqaba. Glubb recommended, in view of its strategic importance, that Britain retain 'for ever' a garrison in 'Aqaba. He also sought Jordanian access to the Mediterranean: He suggested that the

Gaza Strip be transferred to Jordanian control, and a Jordanian-controlled land bridge from Gaza through Beersheba to Hebron be agreed upon.[625] A corridor from the Hebron Hills to the coast was to be a Jordanian demand throughout the secret political negotiations.

As Israel and Jordan negotiated an armistice (and, secretly, possible peace) during February-March 1949, Israel, exercising its overwhelming military superiority, nibbled at Jordanian-held territory on a number of fronts. This nibbling, as Glubb argued, was a violation of the truce's standstill provisions.[626] In the first and largest of these nibbles, in the south, the Golani and Negev brigades, during 5-10 March 1949, raced southwards from Beersheba to occupy the central and southern Negev and reach Um Rashrash (present-day Eilat) on the Gulf of 'Aqaba (Gulf of Eilat). Israel quite reasonably asserted that it had been promised sovereignty over the area in the UN partition resolution; Glubb and the Jordanians, with a measure of accuracy, argued that the advance was a breach of the Israeli-Jordanian ceasefire agreement and was an exploitation of the just-concluded armistice agreement with Egypt (which assured that the Egyptians would not intervene against the Israeli push). Glubb called the march to Um Rashrash 'an outstandingly flagrant piece of treachery during negotiations.'[627] The Israeli argument referring to the partition boundaries, he asserted, was 'invalid' as 'Galilee, for example, was allotted to the Arabs ... and was now occupied by the Jews.' 'The Jews want to have their cake and eat it,' he was quoted as saying (though, of course, he could have said as much about most nations at most times).[628] Glubb said that the barren, uninhabited southern Negev was not really empty but was 'occupied'[629] by an undersized Jordanian company, which held a 'picket line' some 55 miles north of Um Rashrash[630] and that these troops, indeed, had had to withdraw to Transjordan to avoid clashes and being overwhelmed by the Israelis as they advanced southward.[631]

The IDF columns reached the Gulf of 'Aqaba on 10 March; three days later, in a separate operation, Israeli troops occupied 'Ein Gedi, midpoint on the western shore of the Dead Sea. Glubb was depressed and frustrated by the bloodless Israeli operations, which he knew his forces were inadequate to block or counter. Kirkbride wrote of him, on 9 March, that 'he is one of the most temperamental people produced by Great Britain and is either in a trough of despair or a wave of optimism. He is quite capable of dropping everything in a fit of depression and walking out.' (Indeed, at the time Glubb had threatened to resign after the British Government had turned down his request for a budget increase for the Legion.[632])

During the previous and following days, Israeli troops also made small, nibbling advances along the border with the southern West Bank (west of Idna and Khirbet Beit Awwa) and, moving between Arab Legion positions rather than engaging them, snatched additional bits of territory. 'We were faced with a wild grab for territory, even while the [armistice] negotiators were sitting round the table in Rhodes,' Glubb later recalled.[633] All these moves were designed to give Israel an edge as its negotiators neared completion of the armistice agreement, whose core was the demarcation of the future Israeli-Jordanian frontier.

The armistice talks (much like the parallel political negotiations) went forward under the shadow of Israel's military superiority and more and less blatant military threats. According to American journalist Kenneth Bilby, who interviewed Glubb during the IDF push to Um Rashrash, the Legion commander - aware of Iraq's intention to pull its expeditionary force out of Samaria and of the Legion's weakness - was quite naturally keen on a peace agreement based on 'the present battle lines.' Glubb was willing 'to bargain territory already lost [i.e., Arab-earmarked territory already conquered by the IDF] for the security of territory that was imperilled.' Glubb made the proviso that the final, agreed frontiers had to be guaranteed by the United States and Britain - lest Israel, at a later date, go on to demand or conquer the West Bank or parts of it. Glubb, with Bilby in tow - so Bilby records (and there is no reason to doubt the story) - even went to meet Wells Stabler, the American charge d'affaires in Amman, to see if the United States would indeed offer such a guarantee - but Stabler indicated that Washington would not be forthcoming.[634]

During the second half of March Israel stepped up the pressure on Amman by massing troops along the northern West Bank's border. The message was clear: If Jordan refused to relinquish to Israel the hundred-mile long, several miles-deep strip of land on the western edge of the West Bank, Israel would take it by force, and perhaps additional territory as well. The IDF General Staff was understandably perturbed by the narrowness of the Israeli 'waist' - in places about 10 miles wide - from Qalqilya and Tulkarm to the Mediterranean. An enemy thrust across that waist could cut Israel in two in a matter of minutes. The troop concentrations were designed to compel the Jordanians to cede this strip of land. And neither Jordan nor Iraq, eager to bring its troops home, sought, or was up to, a renewal of hostilities; and both understood that Egypt, Syria and Lebanon were out of the game. 'It is impossible to reproduce the tension and anxiety of those days ...,' recalled Glubb.[635] In exchange, Israel offered to 'allow' the Arab Legion to take over Samaria from the departing Iraqis, in effect conceding and recognizing Jordanian sovereignty over the bulk of the West Bank.

It was clear to the Jordanians that a refusal to hand over the land would result in the destruction of the Legion and the loss of the whole West Bank. It was also clear that ceding the strip, which included 16 Arab villages with 20,000 inhabitants and thousands of refugees from elsewhere, would raise a howl of protest in the Arab world and from the Palestinians. From Amman's perspective, the situation looked exceedingly bleak. Abdullah asked Glubb's advice. The general, according to his memoirs, responded that if hostilities were renewed, 'we could not hold the present line after the Iraqis had gone.' Moreover, the Israelis might then seize 'more territory than they were now asking for.'[636] Nonetheless, Glubb made a personal effort, probably at Abdullah's behest, to save the strip. He appealed to the British charge d'affaires, Pirie-Gordon, to press Whitehall to declare that Britain's treaty obligations also covered the West Bank.[637] But Britain declined.

The crisis peaked at the end of the third week of March. The Israelis presented what amounted to an ultimatum at two meetings with the Jordanians on the 23rd. Glubb described the first meeting, in Jerusalem, thus: '... The Jews demanded that we withdraw 15 kilos. along the whole front opposite the coastal plain. This means about half way to Nablus and Ramallah ...This is of course pure Hitler. Every time it is just one more concession. It looks as if they are determined to have the whole of Palestine and get us back over the Jordan.'[638] When the meeting was renewed, in the evening, the Israelis reduced their demands and the Jordanians caved in and signed the draft agreement. One of the signatories was Lt.-Colonel Coaker, Glubb's chief of staff. Abdullah apparently had asked Glubb to attend but Glubb had declined - saying, according to one witness, that 'he did not want to see the Jews' faces' - and sent Coaker in his stead.[639]

Though his representatives had already signed on the dotted line, Abdullah made a last-ditch, personal appeal - as Glubb had suggested to Pirie-Gordon on 23 March[640] - to both the British and the Americans to intervene and rebuff the Israeli demands. The appeals were unproductive. At a meeting of the Council of Ministers on 26 March, the King - apparently going through the motions for the benefit of his ministers - again asked Glubb about the possibility of resistance. Glubb again replied that, given the Legion's low ammunition stocks and small size, the Israelis could not be successfully resisted.[641]

At a further meeting on 30 March in Shuneh (again with Coaker attending), the Israelis refused to change what had been agreed upon, and on 3 April Jordan and Israel signed the General Armistice Agreement. The Iraqis duly withdrew and the Legion took over the Samaria front on 12 April. The following month, the Legion withdrew from the western and northern fringes of the West Bank, handing over 300-400 square kilometres to Israeli rule.[642] Glubb summarized what had transpired as 'pure Hitlerite power politics.'[643]

Due to the inaccessibility of contemporary Arab documentation, it is difficult to assess Glubb's actual input in the armistice negotiations: How important was his advice in the shaping of Jordan's positions and concessions? A definitive answer must await the opening of Jordan's state archives (which, like the rest of the Arab world's, remain closed to researchers). But from the available evidence it is clear that Glubb's importance and say in Amman somewhat diminished following the end of the Israeli-Jordanian hostilities. At the same time, Abdullah and his key ministers continued to consult him on military-strategic matters and Abdullah no doubt continued to sound out his general on British attitudes and the possibility of influencing British policies. Without doubt, Kirkbride, too, during the armistice talks solicited Glubb's advice regarding the Legion and the Israeli military threat. Moreover, there is evidence that Glubb continued to advise the two men about possible territorial trade-offs in the secret (abortive) peace negotiations that followed the conclusion of the armistice talks.[644]

Israel's behaviour during the armistice talks had made Glubb extremely apprehensive about its future intentions. Immediately following the Iraqi withdrawal and the Israeli takeover of the border strip, an anxious Glubb warned British and American representatives in Amman of a prospective Israeli push to conquer the rest of the West Bank[645] - but his jitters, at least in an immediate sense, proved groundless.

As expected, the Arab states denounced Jordan's cession of the strip to Israel. Their leaders were unimpressed by Abdullah's explanations about Israeli duress. And in Nablus there were riots, the crowds denouncing the Arab Legion and Abdullah, who 'sold our country for cash!' Legionnaires - once again - were publicly denounced as 'Liars, Traitors, Jews.'[646] Abdullah's personal popularity plummeted: 'In conversations in the coffee shops and private houses [in the West Bank] one hears only condemnations of King Abdullah, his government and his [Transjordanian] people ... The Arab people in Palestine have begun to hate the King and his policy, and some 80 per cent of the public opposes him,' IDF intelligence reported.[647] Arab Legion intelligence rated Abdullah's unpopularity even higher:

> Nablus, Tulkarm, and Jenin ... It was found that the moral[e] of the population was extremely low, more so perhaps in the Tulkarm area where they had suffered a great blow by the loss of their lands [through the armistice agreement] ... The hatred of King Abdullah is general, and probably to an extent of 95 per cent if not more [sic]. He is blamed for everything from the failure to capture [West] Jerusalem, handing over Lydda and Ramle and the final blow of the handing over of 300,000 dunams of land in Tulkarm and a large piece of Jenin ... Tulkarm is in a very bad state, the streets empty, and a large part of the market closed. There is no work ... It seems that many of the inhabitants are near starvation, as they do not receive refugee rations. It is estimated that there will be about 17,000 of the villagers and Tulkarm [residents] without any means of earning a living if their lands are not returned.[648]

Glubb responded to the anti-Hashemite groundswell with an anonymous poster, distributed in the West Bank, which stated that the Legion 'is still defending the Holy Land, while the other armies have disappeared. When Jerusalem, the Holy City, was in danger, it was the Arab Legion alone which rescued it ... The Arab Legion inflicted more casualties on the Jews than any other Arab army ... The Arab Legion is still defending the Holy Land from Jewish attack ...'[649]

During the following months, Glubb was indirectly involved in the peace talks between Israel and Jordan. He was never a direct player; given his British citizenship and affiliations, Abdullah made sure that he was formally shut out (Arab critics would have denounced any negotiation he was party to as a 'British sell-out'). But he did interfere through advice and missives to Kirkbride and the Foreign Office (and most probably through direct advice to Abdullah and his ministers). In June 1949, for example, he cautioned Kirkbride against accepting an Israeli offer to trade (Israeli-held) Qatamon and Bak`a (formerly Arab neighbourhoods of West Jerusalem) for the (Jordanian-held) Arab neighbourhood of Sheikh Jarah and the 'Police School' between Jewish West Jerusalem and the isolated Israeli-held enclave of Mount Scopus. Glubb warned that if Sheikh Jarah and the Police School were in Israeli hands, the connection between the southern and northern parts of the West Bank would be severed and the way would more or less be open for the IDF to drive through Bethany down to Jericho. 'It all looks to me merely a subtle [Israeli] trap!,' he wrote. 'I see no indication that they mean to modify their hostility towards us.'[650]

In the end, nothing came of the three years of intermittent secret Israeli-Jordanian peace talks, even though the negotiators produced a number of semi-agreed drafts and, even though, in Glubb's words, 'King Abdullah ... was in favour of peace with Israel.'[651] In a perspicacious analysis, Glubb put his finger on the main problems: The King's efforts to reach a peace settlement 'failed, for two reasons. The first was the intense agitation raised by the other members of the Arab League, which frightened the government, though not the King. The second reason was that the Israelis, though apparently desirous of peace, wanted it only on their own terms. They were not prepared to make adequate concessions. King Abdullah realized that, if he were to make peace, he would have to be able to show substantial advantages therefrom. With Israel unprepared to make concessions, there was little inducement to defy the other Arab states.'[652]

A major obstacle undoubtedly was the co-option into the kingdom of the West Bank, with its native Palestinian population and its large refugee community, and the refugee influx into the East Bank itself. Altogether, more than 600,000 Palestinians had been added to Jordan's population - giving it a 'Palestinian' majority and reducing the original Transjordanian beduin population to a minority (of perhaps 40 per cent). Already in late 1948 Kirkbride had noted the Palestinians' lack of enthusiasm for Hashemite rule. There was a 'growing realization [in Amman] that the Arab areas of Palestine will now be an economic liability and not an asset and that their inhabitants will be political nuisances,' he wrote to Bevin.[653]

Jordan's 'Palestinian' majority was quite naturally embittered and hostile toward Israel, as the Transjordanian beduins had never been and had never had immediate reason to be. Many of the Palestinians were also hostile toward Abdullah, who was seen as a primitive desert chieftain, a British imperial lackey, and a secret friend of Zionism. 'The Palestinians resemble the proverbial Irishman - "Whatever the Government is, they're agin it,"' wrote Glubb in mid-1949. Glubb identified three external factors responsible for the anti-Abdullah agitation in the West Bank – 'The Mufti and the old Arab Higher Committee ... Egypt and Syria [and] ... the Communists directed by Russia.' Glubb believed that the Mufti - who 'is served by a hard core of gangsters and terrorists, who have lived by crime since 1936' - enjoyed 'considerable prestige' among 'ignorant villagers' though had little support among the educated classes. Husseini, believed Glubb, was intent on 'organizing gangs' to carry out a rebellion in Palestine 'synchronized with the murder of King Abdullah.'[654]

But by mid-July 1949, Glubb felt that the initial post-armistice hostility in the West Bank had largely worn off. During the King's tour of the

Ramallah and Jerusalem areas on 14-16 July, he wrote, Abdullah had everywhere encountered 'popular enthusiasm,' according to 'observers.' There was a hiatus between the 'politicians ... pressmen and the stream of propaganda [pouring] out of Syria and Egypt' and 'the opinion of the common people of Palestine.' Partly, according to Glubb's analysis, it was to do with 'divinity still doth hedge a king, as it did in the days of Hamlet.'[655]

And as the months passed, Abdullah's popularity seemed to increase. Glubb reported three months later:

> I was pleasantly impressed ... The King's formal entries into the towns were of course organized by police and officials and I had suspected that the frenzied enthusiasm ... was partly inspired ... [But passing unexpectedly through small towns and villages] casual passers-by applauded ... they were nearly all smiling. It was not frenzied enthusiasm, but it was distinctly warm and friendly. Even when we passed a refugee camp ... a number of people ran out and clapped ... There seems little doubt that amongst the mass of the people of Palestine the King enjoys a considerable popularity ... On the other hand, the official and the educated classes in Palestine are in a peculiar mental state ... [While] it is ... remarkable to watch them elbowing and jostling one another in their eagerness to kiss the Royal hand ... they would turn their coats tomorrow and serve the ex-Mufti, or King Farouk, if they could thereby keep their jobs ... Their attitude to the Jordan Government today differs little from their attitude to the Mandatory Government yesterday ...[and there is] a constant stream of reports of disloyalty ...[656]

A year later, Abdullah's standing in West Bank hearts and minds seemed to have further improved. He toured the West Bank in late April 1950, apparently a day or two before the Jordanian Parliament passed the bill 'unifying' the East and West banks (i.e., annexing the West Bank).[657] Glubb was at his side for at least some of the visit. He reported: 'His reception everywhere was the same and deeply impressive. In every village, the crowds pressed round the royal car, clapping, shouting and cheering. Everybody was laughing. Anyone who has spent many years in the East is familiar with "spontaneous joy" arranged by the police. But there was nothing artificial about the enthusiasm of these demonstrations...' Glubb was particularly struck by the welcome given Abdullah in Qalqilya and Tulkarm, formerly, according to Glubb, 'one hundred per cent supporters of the Mufti ... Ninety per cent of the people ... have taken King Abdullah to their hearts,' as 'the leader so long awaited.'[658]

To be sure, the Hashemite takeover and incorporation of the West Bank was from the start greeted by some Palestinians with joy and relief: Palestinian 'Opposition' families saw Abdullah as a counterweight to, and saviour from, the terroristic Haj Amin al Husseini; for others, he represented stability, order and the rule of law after years of upheaval. As well, albeit reluctantly, many understood that Abdullah had saved the West Bank and East Jerusalem from Israeli conquest. With time, most West Bank Palestinians adjusted or resigned themselves to Hashemite rule.

Nonetheless, as Glubb was aware, a 'thundercloud' darkened the skies of Jordan - the destitute refugees, who constituted about one-third of the country's population and could, potentially, 'cause a collapse of the whole Kingdom.' And, meanwhile, the Mufti, exiled in Egypt, was busy organizing 'disorders in Palestine [i.e., the West Bank] by means of political murders and acts of terrorism.'[659] The ex-Mufti's dislike of Abdullah had, following the events of 1948-50, turned into a deep hatred.

A year later, Abdullah, and, with him, the halting Israeli-Jordanian peace process, were to fall victim to Husseini machinations. On 20 July 1951 Palestinian radicals, connected with the ex-Mufti and the now-exiled Abdullah Tall (he had conspired against King Abdullah), assassinated the King at the entrance to al Aksa Mosque in Jerusalem's Old City. A lone gunman had fired a bullet into the King's head before being himself cut down. It is possible that Tall had been paid 'a large sum' by Egypt or some other country to organize the murder.[660] The assassination was prompted by rumours of Abdullah's secret peace talks with Israel but also by the more basic Palestinian resentment against the desert beduin dynasty and army that had occupied (part of) their land and now controlled their personal and political futures.[661] Ultimately, Glubb - as head of police and of the King's security detail - felt in some way responsible. Indeed, he had been wary of the King's intended visit to the mosque and had assigned Col. Habis Majali to accompany him and 'to be on the alert.' But Majali's efforts to surround the King with a phalanx of guards had been rebuffed by Abdullah - and the assassin had effectively exploited the opening. At the funeral, Glubb broke 'down ... and cried like a child.' Glubb later described Abdullah as 'wise and tolerant,' with a 'broad cosmopolitan outlook ... our beloved master.'[662]

Elias Sasson, the long-time Zionist negotiator with Abdullah, by then Israel's representative in Ankara, saw the King's death as 'a great loss for Jordan, the Arab world, the West and also - Israel.' Abdullah, wrote Sasson, had been the only Arab statesman 'to exhibit understanding of our [i.e., the Jewish people's] resurrection, a sincere willingness to reach an arrangement with us and a realistic attitude to most of our demands and arguments ... despite being an Arab nationalist and a zealous Muslim.'[663] Hashemite fears that the murder would unleash major unrest, and perhaps a Palestinian revolt, were calmed by 'the firm attitude adopted everywhere by the police backed by the … Arab Legion. The public were left in no doubt that anyone who spoke out of turn would suffer for it.' [664] Within minutes of the shooting, the Legion had deployed two infantry battalions in Amman; only a handful of shops were looted in Jerusalem. Would-be rioters or rebels were promptly intimidated into inaction.[665]

Glubb kept Whitehall well-informed about the progress of the investigation of the assassination. Initially, Glubb suspected that the investigation was being carried out with insufficient 'energy' because the police feared reprisals by (presumably Palestinian or pro-Palestinian) 'higher personalities' who were coming under suspicion of involvement.[666] Glubb also suspected official Egyptian involvement (Tall lived in Cairo).[667]

The transition in Amman to a new regime was swift but problematic. Abdullah's son, Talal, succeeded the assassinated King (he was crowned on 6 September 1951) - but only for a year, when his mental illness persuaded Jordan's political and military leaders to appoint his son, Abdullah's grandson, Hussein (who had been by Abdullah's side during the assassination), in his stead. A Regency Council ruled until May 1953, when the 18-year-old prince was crowned king.

The period between the assassination and the consolidation of Hussein's rule was highly volatile. The Legion, with Glubb as its head, served as the mainstay of the transitional regime; without it the country might have slid into chaos or republicanism or been annexed by or partitioned between Syria, Iraq, Israel and Saudi Arabia. For a while it seemed to be touch-and-go, and many foreign observers questioned the kingdom's longevity.

Abdullah had appointed Glubb both deputy Legion commander in 1930 and Peake's successor as Legion chief of staff in 1939. The two had become fast friends, though there was always the master-loyal servant relationship in the foreground (or background, depending on the circumstances). For Glubb the assassination was a terrible personal blow. But, far from diminishing Glubb's personal position, the assassination seemed initially at least to have reinforced it. He emerged as a major anchor in a volatile, unsafe world. Israeli observers spent a relatively large amount of energy trying to accurately trace Glubb's influence and importance in the Jordanian hierarchy.

In June 1954 Mordechai Gazit, first secretary in Israel's embassy in London (and during the 1970s director general of the Prime Minister's Office), said that in the immediate wake of the assassination, Glubb tended to keep away from 'interference in Jordanian state matters.' But 'because of [Kirkbride's successor, British Ambassador in Amman Geoffrey] Furlonge's illness, the interference of the queen-mother and her supporters in the Court, and certain underground factors inspired in the Court, he was pushed into exhibiting political activity.' Thereafter, writes Gazit, Glubb used to meet King Hussein 'almost on a daily basis.' Glubb was extremely influential with the new king. Gazit gives as an example the story about the closing by the prime minister (Fawzi al Mulki), at the instigation of the queen-mother, of a sometime dissentient newspaper *As Sarih*; Glubb intervened and the paper was on the streets again after two days.[668]

Glubb was even more clearly influential as Britain's agent in Jordan, with input into British Middle East policy. In August 1954 Israeli officials reported that Glubb participated in consultations about Britain's 'new deployment ... in the Middle East' and that the British Foreign Office took advice from him on matters concerning 'the Israeli-Jordanian border.'[669] Documents collected by Israeli intelligence tended to confirm this assessment. (Glubb's reach was seen to extend even to purely civilian matters, such as the proposed reactivation in mid-1953 of the Naharayim (Jisr al Majami) hydro-electric plant.)[670]

Chapter 6

BORDER WARS, 1949-56

In assessing the future 'size and shape' of the Legion at the end of the 1948 war, Britain's Chiefs of Staff Committee - in large measure influenced by memoranda from and conversations with Glubb - assessed that the main threats to Jordan, apart from an allegedly expansionist Soviet Union, came from Israel and a variety of Arab states, in that order.

As to Israel, the chiefs wrote: 'The extent to which Israel will menace the integrity of Transjordan depends upon unpredictable future trends within Israel' as well as on the 'final territorial settlement in Palestine.' The chiefs believed that 'extreme Zionism' aimed to absorb 'the whole of Palestine and the greater part of Transjordan into the State of Israel' and there was 'more than a possibility that these extreme elements will come to power and will pursue their claims.'

Much as Glubb was wont to argue, with a great measure of justification, the chiefs wrote that 'if the present flood of immigrants continues ... even the moderate elements will be forced by the pressure of events to demand more territory.' The chiefs were compelled to recommend the expansion of the Legion to 17,000, in part with an eye to that army's ability to deter or at least temporarily stave off Israeli aggression.[671] Israeli commentators, political scientists and historians have over the decades ignored, overlooked or downplayed the importance in Israel's successive bouts of territorial expansion - 1948, 1956 (abortive) and 1967 - and in its perennial confiscations of Arab lands, inside pre-1967 Israel as well as in the occupied territories after 1967, of the demographic factor: The elemental need of a very small country with a rapidly expanding population for more territory in order to have where to absorb and settle the successive waves of immigrants. Zionist immigration, as Arab spokesmen understood and argued since around the turn of the century, would naturally result in expansionism.

From the start of the 1950s, Glubb's focus gradually narrowed concerning the Legion's future role. When he urged Britain to support major enlargement of his army, he at first spoke both of the Legion's usefulness to the West in parrying prospective Soviet aggression and of staving off Israeli expansionism. But his memoranda increasingly left the impression that Israel was his main concern: The Soviet threat, he understood, was certainly not immediate and, in any case, there was little the Legion, however much strengthened, could do about it.

He usually dismissed the Israeli and pro-Israeli argument that the Jewish State was a natural bulwark against Soviet expansionism and would side with the West should it come to an East-West showdown. Israeli politicians and society, he argued, did not have deep-seated political-ideological values (apart from Zionism) one way or another: The Israeli leadership was concerned only with the state's survival. In the context of East-West confrontation, they would bend with the wind: 'I do not believe that the Jews are swayed by any sentimental attachments to East or West, to democracy or communism ... Many of them come from totalitarian governments [i.e., countries] in Eastern Europe. Communism has no terrors for the majority of them.' Besides, 'the minorities of the Middle East have a tradition of keeping a foot in every camp.'[672] At any given moment, he predicted, Israel would side with whatever bloc appeared to be winning - and should the Soviets gain the upper hand in the region, Israel would fall into line and set up a 'pro-Russian' government. (Glubb here revealed not only his anti-Israeli bias but also a deep ignorance of Israeli society and politics.)[673]

Concerning Israel, Glubb's thinking during 1949-56 was dominated by one abiding preoccupation: That it was bent on conquering the West Bank and moving its eastern frontier to the River Jordan. Already in July 1949 he noted that 'many people' believed the Jordan River to be Palestine's 'natural' frontier and 'that the present situation cannot endure for long,' and that 'the Jews' intend to make it Israel's eastern border.[674] Glubb himself argued in the memorandum that, historically speaking, 'more often than not,' Palestine's central massif (Judea and Samaria) - currently largely occupied by the Arab Legion - had been separated from the coastal plain (the core area of the post-1948 Jewish state) and was often fused together with the hill-country of Transjordan, which Glubb called 'the biblical Gilead,' in one political-administrative entity (as Transjordan and the West Bank were fused together between 1949 and 1967). Hence, there was no historical inevitability in the Samaria-Judea hill-country, down to the Jordan River, being absorbed by Israel. However, the recent declassification of Israeli state papers from the 1950s, including IDF material, reinforces the cogency of Glubb's abiding fears: Large sections of the Israeli public, including many in its political and military elite, such as Ben-Gurion, Yisrael Galili, a former head of the Haganah from the Ahdut Ha`Avoda Party, Menachem Begin, the leader of the Herut (Revisionist) Party, and Moshe Dayan, IDF chief of general staff from the end of 1953 until 1958, were keen on expansion, optimally down to the Jordan River.[675]

Nor was such thinking limited to the defence establishment or right-wing opposition factions. Abba Eban, Israel's ambassador to Washington and the United Nations (and, later, the country's foreign minister and deputy prime minister), and a leading liberal and dove, voiced similar aspirations, though he spoke in political rather than military terms:

> There are elements and tendencies in the Triangle [i.e., the northern half of the West Bank] constituting the beginnings of a direction [i.e., move?] towards breaking off from Jordan and turning Palestine westward [i.e., towards alliance or unification with Israel]... The federal system will enable the Triangle to manage its internal affairs ... Under such conditions the present [West Bank-Israel] border will become a purely administrative border ... The concentration of powers in foreign and defence affairs in Israel's capital Jerusalem will constitute, in practise, a type of annexation of the Triangle to Israel, and thus will Israel escape the present asphyxiating frontier ... It is appropriate that we devote thought and work in the coming years to [the idea of realizing this ambition], instead of resigning ourselves to the consolidation of the existing borders for ever.[676]

Reuven Shiloah, Foreign Minister Moshe Sharett's adviser (and previously the founder and first director of the Mossad, Israel's foreign intelligence agency), reacted to Eban's proposal by questioning whether it was worthwhile to nurture such separatist thinking among groups of West Bank notables - but believed that Eban's memorandum necessitated a 'reconsideration of the matter.'[677] Indeed, key Israeli leaders between 1949 and 1956 viewed the Kingdom of Jordan itself as an 'artificial' and 'unnatural' country that could not in the long run survive and would eventually be divided up and absorbed by its more powerful neighbours, with the West Bank going to Israel and the East Bank to Iraq.[678]

Glubb was to spend 1949-56 doing his utmost - essentially, by adopting a policy of military restraint in face of successive Israeli provocations - to frustrate what he believed to be Israel's expansionist aims and to mobilize British political clout to help him. In mid-1950, Glubb tried to persuade Whitehall to contribute to the substantial expansion of the Arab Legion. He argued: 'Jordan's most dangerous potential enemy is ... Israel.' He went on to analyze why this was so, and why Israel must inevitably strive to push its frontier to the Jordan, and he predicted that it would eventually try to conquer the West Bank. To begin with, he argued, Zionism was a naturally dynamic movement 'which cannot long remain stationary.' One facet of its dynamism was its constant demographic growth, through the ingathering of 'millions' of Jewish immigrants. 'The corollary ... can only be a demand for more territory a few years hence.' If this is what characterized the mainstream of Zionism, which governed Israel, to its right were 'extremist parties' who 'demand a renewal of hostilities now, and [they] claim that the whole of [the Kingdom of] Jordan - both sides of the River [Jordan] - should be incorporated in Israel.' Glubb conjectured that these 'extremist' parties - by which he meant primarily Herut (the predecessor of today's Likud) - might take hold of the reins of government following 'the next election.' (He was off by a few decades - the Likud won the premiership only in 1977. But by then a Labour-led government, representing traditional, mainstream Zionism, had already conquered the West Bank and begun to settle Jews in it, and had effectively moved the country's border to the Jordan River. The Likud was to spend the post-1977 decades consolidating - mainly through a series of settlement drives - Israel's hold on this territory and on this border.)

According to Glubb, there were 'other' factors that would or might propel Israel toward a renewal of hostilities - and conquest of the West Bank - a few years hence:

> Strategically, the Jews have acquired a large area of territory in the Beersheba-Gulf of 'Aqaba area in the south [the Negev] and in Galilee in the north. But these two areas are only joined by a narrow strip of coastal plain. The Arab Legion are only a few miles from Tel Aviv and Haifa. Strategically this situation is extremely precarious and the Israeli Army staff are most anxious to drive the Arab Legion back from this vital strategic wasp-waist.

Moreover:

> the religious aspect is equally precarious ... The present Israeli [coalition] government only commands a majority with the support of the religious party in parliament [presumably Glubb was referring to the Mizrahi, later, the National Religious Party]. The religious party have [sic] openly stated that Israel "means nothing" without the capture of all Jerusalem, including the Old City, the Temple of Solomon and the Wailing Wall. If the extreme party [presumably Herut] can convince the religious party that they could capture all Jerusalem, their combined strength might defeat the present government.[679]

Occasionally, Glubb added that Israel's urge to war and expansionism was also indirectly driven by the country's desperate economic plight.

The government used the 'Arab threat' to divert the population's attention away from its economic woes. In June 1952 he wrote Geoffrey Furlonge, the British ambassador in Amman: 'The theoretical [?] explanation of all this is that the economic situation in Israel is more critical than ever, and the government wishes to divert the attention of the people by crying that the enemy is at the gates and it is everybody's duty to stand by the govt. in such a crisis.'[680] What provoked Glubb's reflection was a report from a UN observer that the IDF was deliberately 'working up the tension' along the border in order to provoke Jordan into retaliating and thus giving Israel cause for conquering the West Bank. It is worth remarking that Glubb's suspicion regarding the Israeli government's desire to divert public attention away from internal woes was a mirror image of official Israeli explanations, during the 1950s and 1960s, of the reasons for the Arab leaders' belligerence toward Israel.

In the early 1950s, Glubb anticipated that Israel would be demographically, politically and militarily 'ready' to expand again in 1955. For this reason, he argued, Britain should beef up the Arab Legion; it must be sufficiently strong to hold off the IDF until British forces could reach the battlefield and prevent the fall of the West Bank. (The unstated assumption was that the defence of the West Bank was included among Britain's commitments.) A strong Legion would deter Israel from 'imitating Hitler and Stalin' and launching such an act of aggression, argued Glubb. (Furlonge supported Glubb, arguing that weakening the Legion 'would encourage Israeli chauvinism. If Jordan's forces are incapable of defending the country, the Israelis ... may well take an opportunity in the future of provoking an incident, overrunning Jordan [the West Bank?] and present[ing] the world with a *fait accompli.*') Glubb requested that Britain agree to, and subsidize, the expansion of the Legion from 12,000 to 14,000 men, making possible a mobilisation for war by 1955 of 25,000 all told.[681]

Glubb's thinking remained constant during the following years. In April 1955 he wrote:

> We ... know that the Israel Government is anxious about the possible strength of the Arab states ten or fifteen years hence ... The Israel army are [sic] chiefly anxious to seize the whole of Palestine up to the river Jordan, thereby securing for themselves an ideal defensive line for their frontier, running from the Sea of Galilee to the Dead Sea. The army are [sic] anxious to pick a quarrel with Jordan as soon as possible, to enable them [sic] to seize the Jordan River line.[682]

And in October 1955 he wrote: 'The only country at which Israel really throws covetous eyes is Jordan. Not indeed because Jordan is being troublesome, but because she still holds half Jerusalem and the balance of Palestine. Sooner or later, Israel is almost certain to have a try at moving her frontier to the Jordan.'[683]

Glubb feared that Israel would exploit one of the recurrent frontier skirmishes that characterized Israeli-Jordanian relations during those years to launch such an expansionist offensive:

> Sometimes one wonders whether "infiltration" is not a valuable political asset to Israel...
>
> Is she really seizing on this pretext in order to create an atmosphere favourable for further expansion? ... When the auspicious moment arrives, Israel will then be able to march in, on the Hitlerian pretext that the Jordan Government cannot preserve order and the Israeli Army has had to occupy certain areas in order to restore order. It is a technique with which Nazis and Soviets should have made us familiar.[684]

The skirmishing was in great measure a by-product of the incessant infiltration by Arab peasants and refugees across the line into Israel. During 1950-53, there were, it was estimated, 10-20,000 incidents of infiltration annually. Glubb wrote: 'The Jews recently claimed that there were 20,000 infiltrations a year. As this was Jewish propaganda, 10,000 might be a safer guess ... [or] 11,500.'[685]

Glubb often said, quite accurately, that the vast majority of the infiltrators were Palestinian refugees who lived in the West Bank's towns, villages and 'dreary and sordid' refugee camps,[686] But sometimes, when it suited his political purposes, he claimed that most infiltrations were carried out by border villagers whose lands had been shorn from them in the cession of territory authorised in the armistice agreement of 1949.

In one report, Glubb wrote that the infiltrators' motives were movement from one Arab area to another separated by Israel (for example, from Gaza to the West Bank); smuggling, including of drugs, into or through Israel; reaping crops or picking fruit and vegetables ('in many places, the armistice line divides a house from its garden. In ... Qatana [west of Jerusalem] ... if a man leaves his back door to pick an apple in his garden he is an infiltrator'); attending school in an Arab country and coming home, to Israel, on leave; theft; and avenging past wrongs (Glubb mentioned, in this connection, 'Deir Yassin' and the October 1948 massacre at Dawayima).[687] Glubb's apologetic and justificatory explanations provoked the British Ambassador to Tel Aviv, Frank Evans, to comment that some infiltrators, indeed, were motivated by hatred and revenge and acted like guerrillas, and that the Israelis were therefore 'entitled to fight back.' Nor was infiltration through Israel 'a legitimate way' to travel from Jordan to Gaza. But, quite accurately, he added, 'not revenge, but starvation is the chief motive' of infiltration.[688] According to Glubb, the only solution to the infiltration problem was orderly resettlement of the refugees.[689]

Glubb repeatedly dwelt on the connection between the Palestinians' refugeedom and the infiltration problem. He noted that in the beginning (starting already in the summer of 1948, about midway in the first Arab-Israeli war), the infiltrators 'went back innocently and unarmed. None ... in those days crossed ... in order to fight or injure the Jews. The majority went to try to rescue some of their belongings, or to look for missing relatives ... [or to farm].'[690] (Rather curiously, Glubb failed to mention that many of these early infiltrators actually went back to Israel to resettle in their original villages. Perhaps he felt that admitting this would somehow cast Israel in a favourable light.) The 'ruthless' manner in which the IDF dealt with the infiltrators resulted in many eventually crossing armed and coming at night, leading to Israeli casualties: 'The Arabs armed themselves and began to shoot back,' in Glubb's phrase.[691]

Glubb tended in his descriptions and analyses to downplay (a) the terroristic element in the infiltration; and (b) the very adverse effects the infiltrations, be they terroristic, criminal or agricultural, had on Israel. Quite often, he suggested - and perhaps sincerely believed - that Israel itself or Jewish 'terrorists' were behind the killing of Israelis in order to supply Jerusalem with a provocation in order to attack Jordan. In spring 1953, for example, after a series of particularly murderous infiltrator grenade attacks on Jewish settlers east of Tel Aviv, Glubb absurdly cabled: 'Quite possible Jewish extremists might do this on [i.e., in] order get *casus belli* against Jordan. If Israel Government are doing it themselves, it may be intended to raise more dollars in America or to suppress dissatisfaction in Israel by representing the enemy at the gates.'[692] Glubb linked the possibility that Israel, or Israelis, were behind at least some of the terrorist attacks to Israel's desire to goad Jordan into providing it with a reason to 'capture [East] Jerusalem and drive down to Jericho [and the Jordan River] ... Possible Jews now despair of goading Jordan into [anti-Israeli] reprisals. As a result they are now using their own underground to attack settlements of Yemenite Jews and thus provide casus belli against Jordan.'[693] One British diplomat reported that Glubb had said that 'there were, in Israel, many criminal immigrants from European ghettos. The Jewish terrorist crimes were easily recognizable.

They had been doing it for 20 years during the Mandate. The characteristics were use of Sten guns, mines, hand grenades thrown through windows, and explosives detonated against houses. It took practise and discipline, of which few Jordanians were capable, to be good terrorists.' But by 1957, when publishing his autobiography, Glubb had thought better of this allegation. 'Investigation soon revealed,' he wrote of the spring 1953 terrorist attacks east of Tel Aviv, 'the identity of the new movement. It originated with a group of refugees in Damascus, all of them former [Arab] terrorists employed by the Mufti in Palestine. [In addition] the Saudi Arabia government was arming and subsidizing these men to infiltrate through Jordan into Israel and kill Jews.'[694]

Glubb felt genuine compassion for the refugees, 'driven from their homes by the Jews.' They were kept alive by UNRWA rations which were

> barely enough for subsistence ... People living without employment, with nothing to do by day or night, and receiving only 13\6d [thirteen and a half shillings or two-thirds of a pound sterling] worth of food per month, are liable to wander about and get into trouble. Indeed the surprising thing is that they do not commit more crimes ... [and] they are filled with hatred for Israel ... The nuisance of infiltration is the price the Jews are paying for the brutality with which they liquidated the Arabs residents in their country.

Glubb sympathized with the non-terroristic infiltrators:

> There seems also to be some deep psychological urge which impels a peasant to cling to and die on his land. A great many of these wretched people are killed now, picking their own oranges and olives just beyond the line. The value of the fruit is often negligible. If the Jewish patrols see him he is shot dead on the spot, without any questions. On some occasions they have taken a pair of oxen and a plough and solemnly begun to plough their land, a few hundred yards west of the line, until the Jews came up and shot them dead.[695]

Elsewhere Glubb wrote:

> There is an Arab saying that the cruellest ruler is the man who was himself a slave ... In his recently published book, the Jewish terrorist Menachem Begin claims that the Jews are striking back after all they have suffered. Unfortunately they are revenging themselves on a race of innocent and bewildered peasants, instead of on the Germans, the Russians and the Poles.[696]

Jordan's - and Glubb's – constant policy, but with fluctuating degrees of emphasis and implementation, was to suppress or at least strongly discourage infiltration. 'I can assure you,' Glubb wrote to General William Riley, the chief of staff of UNTSO, the armistice observer corps, in 1951, 'that we are doing everything in our power to prevent it.' He gave Riley exact figures for persons tried for infiltration by Jordanian courts or officers during 1950 in the (Jordanian) Jerusalem District alone (589) and the number of those imprisoned or fined (246 and 280).[697] Glubb's letter, according to Kirkbride, reinforced by certain measures on the ground, had persuaded Israeli leaders of Jordan's sincere 'desire to improve things.'[698]

Glubb's asseverations of Jordan's desire to curb infiltration were not limited to letters to outside observers. He wrote as much in internal correspondence as well: 'Anyone who visits the prisons or the law-courts in West Jordan [i.e., the West Bank] can see for himself that about half the persons in prison are there on charges of infiltration ... [Indeed,] the Government has exposed itself to unending criticism ... because it uses its emergency powers to imprison persons accused of infiltration even when the evidence is inadequate ...'[699] However, Israeli reprisal raids, in which 'innocent' villagers were killed and which triggered popular anger against Israel, curtailed the Jordanian government's ability to punish infiltrators more severely. Thus it was that in 1952 the government's attempt to pass a law providing for 3 to 15 years jail for infiltration into Israel had been rejected by parliament. 'The Government did not ... argue that a man who picked a basket of oranges in his own garden ... deserved 15 years in prison. The argument was ... that, if he does it, the Jews will come and massacre a lot of women and children in some isolated village.'[700] In his autobiography, Glubb maintained, regarding at least 1953-54, that the Legion had strained 'every nerve to prevent infiltration.'[701]

Glubb denied that infiltration was Jordan's fault:

> It is the state of affairs. This state of affairs [i.e., the existence of a refugee problem, Zionism and Israel] was not made by Jordan, but by the Jews, by the policy of Britain and American and by UNO. In truth, it is difficult to find a single wrong act which Jordan has committed. She has always accepted British advice, she has always obeyed UNO orders, she has attempted to conciliate the Jews - but circumstances have been too much for her ... The Jordan authorities are at a loss what further measures to adopt. It is not possible to prevent individuals crossing so long a border line at night. It is not possible to secure Jewish cooperation. Massacres [in reprisal raids] by the Israeli army only make prevention more

> difficult. UNRWA has not yet carried out one [refugee] settlement scheme ... [Jordan has half a million 'vagrants.' Many cross the border into Israel each night.] One third of them are caught by the Jordan police and go to prison. A considerable proportion are killed by the Jews. The remainder live to infiltrate again.[702]

Glubb believed that infiltration was a 'police problem,' and should be handled by Israeli and Jordanian police, in cooperation - rather than by Israeli soldiers. Indeed, the Israelis believed that infiltration was a 'Jordanian problem' and should be prevented by the Jordanians alone. When the Israelis did agree - as occasionally they did - to cooperation along the frontier, the rate of infiltration dropped, he wrote. Glubb suspected that the divergent voices he was hearing from the Israeli side were evidence of a rift in the Israeli leadership 'between the [moderate] Jewish Foreign Office and the Israeli Army. When they agree to cooperate, it means that the Foreign Office have won a chukka. When the agreement is denounced and the shooting [of infiltrators] recommences, the Israeli army has regained the upper hand.'[703] Glubb had presciently, and quite early in the day, noted the well-camouflaged, secret rift in the Israeli government that was to become sharper and more significant in the course of the mid-1950s between the 'Moderates,' led by Foreign Minister Sharett, and the 'Activists' or 'Militants,' led by Prime Minister Ben-Gurion and Dayan of the defence establishment.

Glubb and the Israeli Responses to Infiltration

Glubb was mortified and outraged by some of the means used by the Israelis during these years to deter and punish infiltration. In part it was a matter of ethics and his outlook on how soldiers were supposed to behave; in part, he was influenced by his political and military views on Jordanian interests and vulnerabilities.

Shooting-to-Kill

'The majority of infiltrators caught by the Jews are shot dead on the spot without any semblance of a trial. The conquistadores of Cortez and Pizarro can scarcely have been more haughty and callous to the natives ... It is surely an irony that, at a time when the greatest nations of the west are abjuring their former contempt of eastern people, the persecuted Jews should start a new Imperialism in Asia,' he wrote in 1953.[704] According to most of the available documentation, including internal

IDF and Israel Police records, Glubb was exaggerating, if not actually misleading. While there was a 'free-fire' policy along the borders, in which IDF troops and police and settlement guards shot at almost anything that moved, no questions asked, at most times along most sectors of the border, once infiltrators were captured, the vast majority were not 'shot on the spot' but were either immediately, or after a period of incarceration, expelled to a neighbouring country. A small number who were captured seriously wounded were finished off on the spot.

Interestingly, while Israeli records indicate that IDF troops and other security forces killed somewhere between 2,700 and 5,000 infiltrators during the years 1949-56, Glubb occasionally argued that Israeli statistics in this respect were vastly inflated ('wild'), and designed to demonstrate to the world the dimensions of Israel's infiltration problem. In truth, he once wrote, 'the number of deaths of infiltrators of which the Jordan police obtain information is about seven per cent of the numbers reported killed by "the Israeli Army spokesman".' Glubb argued that the Jordanian authorities almost invariably knew when infiltrators were killed ('the widows weep ... the matter attracts some attention'). The implication is that the real numbers of encounters, and of infiltrators killed, at least on the Jordanian front, was vastly lower than Israel was routinely announcing.[705]

Occasionally, there were cases of IDF troops capturing and executing infiltrators. Usually, the troops involved were punished, albeit very lightly.

Expulsion

Starting in December 1948, Israeli troops regularly scoured empty, half-empty and inhabited Arab villages inside Israel for 'illegal' residents or infiltrators. An 'infiltrator,' for the authorities, was anyone who was not in possession of a valid Israeli permit or ID card issued to all residents during and immediately after October-November 1948 (and to Negev beduin during the following months and years). Most of the infiltrators were in fact inhabitants of Palestine during the pre-1948 period who had fled the country at some point during the war and were not in their homes during the successive censuses (which were held soon after each area was conquered, starting in October 1948). Such infiltrators were rounded up and then either expelled directly, in batches, across the border or thrown in jail and subsequently expelled. Most were expelled into the West Bank though some were shoved across the Lebanese border or into the Gaza Strip.

But on 31 May 1950 the IDF expelled a batch of some 100 Arabs, most of them captured infiltrators, across the border in the 'Arava, the hot flat plain that served as the eastern boundary of the Negev. A few had been tortured in a detention camp before being trucked to the 'Arava; some had been beaten on the trucks. Without water or food, most wandered around, sun-dazed, until they were picked up by beduin or Arab Legion patrols during the following days. By then, some 20-30 of the party had died of dehydration or exhaustion.[706]

Glubb was outraged; a 'bad case of sadism,' he called it. He prepared a detailed file, which he sent to the Mixed Armistice Commission, newspapers and parliamentarians abroad, and to Kirkbride. In the accompanying letter to Kirkbride he wrote (wildly exaggerating - and thereby undermining his case):

> There seems to be little doubt that Arabs in Israel are subjected to the same torture camps technique as the Jews themselves suffered in Nazi Germany, though on a lesser scale ... I do not know if the Jews want peace - I daresay they do. Meanwhile, however, the policy of terrorism and frightfulness towards the Arabs they get hold of, goes on. They have a considerable minority in Israel, and I imagine that the Jews want them all to emigrate. They therefore try to persuade them with rubber coshes and by tearing off their finger-nails whenever they get the chance. I do not know whether this is the policy of the Israel Cabinet, but it must certainly be known and winked at ... The brutality is too general to be due only to the sadism of ordinary soldiers.[707]

Perhaps, Glubb thought, the Israeli leadership genuinely sought peace but thought that the best way to go about it was to 'cow the Arabs' into submission. If so, they were mistaken: 'Indignation in Jordan is mounting. The resentment ... over this ... incident is intense.' More generally, Glubb pointed out that while the Arab infringements of the armistice were committed by impoverished individuals, 'the cruelties and atrocities' from the Jewish side were committed 'solely by Government forces in uniform.'[708]

Reprisals

'Finding that merely killing Arabs did not prevent the refugees from returning to their homes, the Jews started their policy of reprisals,' Glubb wrote in 1954.[709] Glubb accurately described the nature and development of Israel's retaliatory strikes during 1949-53. In the beginning, 'eight or ten Jewish soldiers came over into the nearest Arab village, shot two or three people and withdrew. To resist this, the National

Guard was created, and ten rifles were issued to each village. Jewish soldiers coming over the line were shot. To deal with this the Jews stepped up their operations to platoon level ...'[710] 'A force of about one platoon is normally employed. This enters an Arab village and either shoots the first half dozen people encountered and then withdraws, or surrounds and blows up a house with its inhabitants inside it.'[711] In 1953, the Israelis stepped up the raids to company-size attacks and by the second half of the year were deploying whole battalions; during 1955-56, the raids were often of brigade strength in order to cope with the 'harder' targets selected, such as military camps and police forts. Glubb described (with partial accuracy) the mechanism of this escalation: 'Where force failed to produce any improvement ... they merely thought that the force used had not been enough, and decided to use more force.'[712]

Throughout this period Glubb, in almost every memorandum, pointed to another, psychological, factor that he believed underlay the Israeli strikes:

> Perhaps the explanation is that the Jews have a psychological impulse to use force. Persons or nations who have suffered persecution or who have long been slaves, long to inflict the same hardships on others. The Jews, so long scorned and oppressed, love to prove to themselves that they are not inferior to other races and that they themselves can kill, and smash and crush to powder ... It is suggested ... that the Jews suffer under a sub-conscious urge to smash and kill defenceless people, as a compensation for all they have suffered ... The Israelis have an irresistible desire to be a "herrenvolk" ... Often they state [off the record] contemptuously that Arabs understand no argument but force. They claim that an occasional "punitive expedition" against the natives is the only way to teach them a lesson and keep them in their places.[713]

To this, Glubb responded: 'There is no race in the world which understands only force ... It is ironical to think that such a statement should be made in Palestine, where the Sermon on the Mount was pronounced.'[714]

Glubb argued, at least down to 1954, that the reprisals were always disproportionate to the crime that triggered them and usually hit the innocent, that is, West Bank border villagers [715] - and not terroristic infiltrators or even economic infiltrators, who were mostly refugees.

One of Glubb's main arguments against Israel's reprisal policy was that it simply didn't work. Already in early 1951 he pointed out that 'they have been using reprisals for two and a half years, and ... complain that incidents today are worse than ever.'[716] The reprisals had failed to stem the tide of infiltration. Indeed, often they were counter-productive, themselves provoking further violence. Glubb gave the example of Hamad Hamid, a Legion private, whose cousin had been killed in the Israeli reprisal raid at Beit Liqya on 1\2 September 1954. Hamid – 'following the same policy of retaliation which the Israelis have practised and condoned' - twice attacked Israeli troops at Bir Ma`in, killing two, before himself being shot dead by an IDF patrol. Glubb concluded that 'if the Israelis persist in this policy ... it is only natural that some individuals whose families have suffered casualties will retaliate.'[717] (But Glubb failed to mention that the reprisals policy, especially after 1953, was relatively successful insofar as it prodded the Jordanians into curbing infiltration. Partly due to the deployment of Legion units along the border, the incidence of infiltration gradually fell off over late 1953-56.)

Repeatedly, Glubb raised the possibility that Israel's reprisal raids were designed not to deter or punish infiltration but to compel Jordan to make peace. But if such were Israeli hopes, they were ill-founded. 'Jordan nearly made peace a year and a half ago. Since then, feeling in favour of peace has been getting weaker and weaker, solely owing to Jewish acts of aggression [i.e., mainly reprisal raids],' Glubb wrote in early 1951.[718]

Glubb also suggested another reason for what he regarded as Israel's aggressive frontier policy: 'Life in Israel is not easy. Food is scarce and the cost of living is high. Not only is there conscription but civilian life is constantly disrupted by practise mobilisations and manoeuvres. In order to compel the public to accept such conditions, the Government (or perhaps only the Army) find it useful to be able constantly to cry that the enemy is at the gates.'[719]

During 1949-53, Israeli retaliatory strikes were directed primarily against West Bank border villages, with the aim (a) of deterring the local population or the inhabitants of neighbouring villages, from indulging in infiltration or from hosting or encouraging infiltrators; and (b) of hurting the Jordanian state so that it would be compelled to take measures against infiltrators. The reprisals gave vent to the natural human urge for revenge. The retaliatory policy was also propelled by internal considerations: The need of the dominant party, Mapai, to demonstrate "firmness" against the Arabs ("softness" would have lost them public support and votes); and the IDF's need to train its troops for combat and maintain internal and the border settlers' morale.

But in October 1953, the IDF launched a massive raid against the West Bank border village of Qibya, following the murder by Arab infiltrators of a mother and her two children in a grenade attack on a house in the nearby Israeli settlement of Yehud. The Israeli troops, following explicit Central Command orders, killed about sixty villagers and blew up 45 houses before withdrawing.[720] The outcry in the West, accompanied by some minor American and British sanctions and a reprimand from the Security Council, as well as some muted internal criticism, led the Government and IDF to change the retaliatory policy: Thereafter, almost all raids were directed against military camps and police forts rather than against civilians.

One of the most significant raids was the attack on an Egyptian Army camp and adjoining facilities in the city of Gaza on 28 February 1955. Some 40 Egyptian soldiers died, the largest single toll of Egyptian life in any Israeli raid since 1948. It shook the military junta in Cairo and helped push Egypt into a confrontational policy towards Israel, which involved massive Egyptian rearmament with Soviet Bloc weapons and the periodic dispatch into Israel of terroristic marauders (*fedayeen*), many of them through Jordan.[721] Israel responded with ever larger retaliatory strikes against the Egyptian Army and Jordan. The Gaza Raid thus set in motion the immediate cycle of violence that resulted in the IDF invasion of the Sinai Peninsula in October-November 1956, which was the Israeli contribution to the Franco-British-Israeli Suez War against Nasser's Egypt.

From some point in 1955 on, Israel decided to provoke a war with Egypt in order to crush the Egyptian Army, acquire strategic territory and depose the minatory Egyptian leader, Nasser, who seemed to be on the verge of achieving Arab unity under his guidance and directed against Israel, implicitly threatening Israel with destruction.[722]

But Glubb, from his perch in Amman, saw the Israeli-Egyptian friction in a somewhat different light. Jordan was doing everything it could 'to avoid giving the Jews a pretext' to invade the West Bank, he argued. But Nasser's sabre-rattling and raiding might, by a circuitous route, at last enable Israel to hit Jordan. Glubb charted out the following scenario: Israel would respond to Egypt's provocations by conquering the Gaza Strip; the Egyptians would respond with an offensive of their own; and the rest of the Arab world, including Jordan, egged on by Egypt, would have no option but to join battle at Nasser's side. Thus Israel would get the opportunity to conquer the West Bank.

Indeed, Glubb believed that Ben-Gurion had returned to the Israeli Cabinet (in February 1955) specifically with the aim of 'starting [a] general war against [the] Arabs' and that he and the IDF General Staff had already 'decided on early preventive war with object of moving boundary Israel to River Jordan.' The truth, unknown to Glubb, was that

Ben-Gurion in early April 1955 had tabled a motion to conquer the Gaza Strip but that the Israeli Cabinet had rejected it. Israel did not really want Gaza, with its 250,000 refugees. But Jordan, after the fall of Gaza, would be 'in a most precarious position.' With Israel 'kill[ing] a lot of Palestinians' in Gaza, Jordan would be under 'intense' pressure to intervene, Glubb wrote. 'This might be exactly what Israel wants. The position would be so confused that Israel would claim Jordan had attacked her and that the British [mutual defence] Treaty was inapplicable, and would then throw her whole weight against Jordan.' (Alternatively, the Jordanians might opt for restraint 'and do nothing rash,' but then 'the Egyptians and their friends the Saudis would raise a tremendous howl against Jordan and Britain, over Arab Legion treachery.') Glubb asked that Britain and America threaten 'to use force' against whoever resorts to military operations and also threaten economic sanctions. Should Israel go ahead and nonetheless attack Gaza, Britain and the United States should send air units to Cyprus and Libya 'and give ultimatum to both sides.'[723] Two Foreign Office officials (E.M. Rose and C.E. Shuckburgh) minuted that Glubb's report was 'alarmist' and 'provincial', but Rose thought that 'his views must ... carry weight.' It is worth noting that Glubb's idea, of a double ultimatum to Israel and Egypt, was in fact used by Britain and France as they launched their attack on Egypt in October-November 1956.

By October 1955, Glubb's thinking about Israeli-Egyptian tensions and Israeli and Egyptian policies had solidified - but with a significant change of tack. Egypt, which since February had been struggling against British (and American) efforts to recruit the Arab countries into the anti-Soviet alliance called 'the Baghdad Pact,' regarded pro-British Jordan as a 'thorn in her flesh ... Egypt would, therefore, dearly like to see the disappearance of Jordan from the map. She might well be willing to let Israel move forward to the Jordan, if the East Bank ... were as a result to be divided up between Syria, Saudi Arabia and Egypt.' Certainly Egypt was bent on overthrowing Jordan's Hashemite regime, wrote Glubb.

In this reading, Egyptian-Israeli tensions were merely a Nasserist ploy to 'further [Egypt's] dominion' over the other Arab states. Radically misreading the Middle East map, Glubb pooh-poohed the notion of an Israeli assault on Egypt as 'fantastically remote. The Sinai desert is a formidable obstacle. The great powers would surely intervene before Israel could conquer Egypt, and the former could scarcely send her army to Egypt leaving all the [other] Arabs threatening the territory of Israel.' Therefore, he concluded, 'there would not appear to be a very great danger of war between Egypt and Israel. Israel does not want Gaza.'

But Egypt was

> rendering an immense service to Israel, by all this shouting, threatening and buying arms ... All this Egyptian hoo-has [sic] will make Israel much stronger. She will probably get more arms, much sympathy and perhaps a treaty with the USA. This will not worry Egypt ... The only country at which Israel really throws covetous eyes is Jordan ... [But] the Arab Legion ... cannot embark on an arms race ... Arms perhaps genuinely acquired by Israel out of fear of Egypt, can equally easily be turned against Jordan, when a suitable moment arrives.[724]

One may assume that Glubb was aware of the fragility of this geopolitical analysis - and thus inserted 'extreme conjecturality' into the title.

Glubb and Western Public Opinion

Glubb was a great believer in the power of the press and, unusually for a general in the Arab world, often gave journalists background briefings and, more rarely, interviews, often characterized by inordinate candour.

As we have seen, he credited Jewish control of the Western media with assuring Israel of Western public and, ultimately, governmental support. More than a dash of anti-Semitism obtrudes in his ruminations on the matter. During 1949-56 he was continuously to lament what he saw as the Jews' 'control' of the western media and the inability of the Arab version of any event to get a hearing. 'The result is that the world at large is completely befogged,' he wrote in 1953 regarding Israel's reprisal raids:

> The Arabs ... do not know how to handle publicity. The Jews have it all their own way the whole time. They are the cleverest people in the world. But sometimes one stops to ask what they think they are doing. Precariously clinging to a bridge head in Asia, they spend their time shooting the inhabitants of that continent, pouring scorn upon them, outwitting them, spurning them, hating them. Where do they think they are getting to? ... They need peace but ... they want peace with domination.[725]

He believed that criticism by the Western media of Israel's behaviour would curtail its aggressiveness. 'It was one of the few things they did not like ... The Israelis are sensitive about atrocities [their forces have committed,] and by giving the world the facts ... the atrocities can be stopped ...,' he wrote in 1951. He credited the dossiers the Legion had compiled and distributed in the West about the 'Arava Expulsion and the torture of suspects with ending these practices. Similarly, Glubb was sure that after the compilation that year of a dossier about the 'mutilation of dead [Arab] bodies,' the Israelis would refrain from such behaviour in the future.[726] (I have been unable to locate this dossier.)

Glubb proved less successful when he went to the Western press in person. He was a rather blunt, military man, and highly opinionated. He spoke his mind, often with hyperbole, injecting his own views and emotions into reports of 'the facts.' His press interviews during these years often resulted in embarrassment to his masters in Whitehall (but also in hoots of appreciation by his Arab colleagues).

In July 1949 a journalist named Lawrence Griswold published an 'interview' with Glubb in the North America Newspaper Alliance chain and *The Palestine Post* (Israel). Glubb was quoted as charging 'the Jews' with acting like 'arrogant European conquerors' and predicted that 'the Jews may be completely swept out of Palestine.'[727] Israel's Foreign Minister, Moshe Shertok (Sharett), complained to the British Government that Glubb's 'frequently reported utterances ... breathed ... war' and asked that Britain 'restrain [his] language.'[728] *The Palestine Post* itself, in the leader of 6 July 1949, charged Glubb with 'offending against the spirit of peace.'

An inquiry was set in motion by the Foreign Office, and Pirie-Gordon, Kirkbride's deputy, informed London: '*Palestine Post* report is a fabrication but it is difficult for Glubb to issue a public denial at the moment as he has received numerous congratulatory messages from the Arabs ... Jews have always had a special dislike for Glubb and consider any stick good enough to beat him with. In actual fact, Glubb is extremely discreet on the rare occasions he sees a journalist ...'[729] Another British diplomat added that *The Palestine Post* 'does not cease to exude anti-British venom.'[730]

In the end, it appeared that Glubb had not given Griswold an interview but had briefly spoken with him months before and the journalist had proceeded to publish some of Glubb's (remembered or imagined) remarks as an 'interview.' In the end, the Minister of State at the Foreign Office, Hector McNeil, ruled that 'Glubb ... should have issued a denial immediately. He should be told so.'[731]

More serious was the fallout from an interview with Glubb published in *The New York Times* on 18 June 1953. There, Glubb compared the Israelis to the Nazis and suggested that a recent spate of attacks in Israel had been carried out by Israeli terrorists as an anti-Jordanian provocation, and that the Israeli authorities were aware of this. He argued that motivating Israeli aggressiveness along the borders was a desire to provoke large-scale fighting in which it could expand its territory; and that continuous low-key hostilities along the borders served the political purposes of Israel's leaders in their struggle against right-wing extremists and helped Israel rake in contributions from American Jews. Lastly, he suggested that underlying Israeli aggressiveness was the desire for 'the psychological release of the urge to bully others after having suffered the same thing for centuries.' He also spoke of 'many criminal immigrants [reaching Israel] from the ghettoes of Europe.'[732] Glubb may have been motivated to give the interview to correspondent Kenneth Love, and to say what he did, by the publication the week before, on 14 June, of an extremely pro-Zionist article, entitled 'Israel's "Little War" of the Borders,' by Dana Adams Schmidt, in the *NYT Magazine*.

On 22 June the Israeli ambassador complained to the Foreign Office, charging that Glubb's charges were 'untrue' and 'one-sided' and 'could only encourage the extremists and trouble-makers in Jordan.' Moreover, the Israeli public regarded Glubb as a British agent - and his statements as expressions of British policy. The ambassador asked the British government 'to dissociate themselves from General Glubb's remarks.' The Foreign Office responded that Jordan was constantly being lambasted by Israeli spokesmen so it was 'unsurprising' that Amman should respond. However, it conceded that Glubb's statement had been 'untimely.'[733]

In private, Tony Moore, the British deputy head of mission in Tel Aviv, asserted that Glubb had gone 'too far' - especially in suggesting that the Israeli government 'were perfectly aware' that the outrages 'of which they accused Jordan had been committed by their own terrorists.' Glubb's imputation had been, according to Moore, that the Israeli government not only exploited such crimes but promoted them. Moore charged that Glubb had not a 'shred of evidence' for this 'startling accusation' – nor did the findings of the UN-chaired Mixed Armistice Commission support it. Moore also took issue with Glubb's bald anti-Semitic references to 'European ghettos' and 'the Nazi-like quality of Israel's policy.' Lastly, he wrote that Glubb's remarks - which served the purposes of right-wing anti-government elements in Israel - had only aggravated the problem posed by the fact that Glubb, a British subject, commanded the Arab Legion, an enemy army, which was subsidized by the British government. Moore recommended that Britain press Amman (and Glubb) to use a different spokesman.[734]

But the tussles around Glubb's press appearances, while often illuminating in various ways, were essentially a sideshow; the clashes along the border were the main issue, and without doubt, the succession of Israeli reprisals against Jordanian territory and citizens served to undermine Britain's standing in Jordan and, by extension, the standing of the British officers in the Arab Legion. Politicians and public opinion in Jordan periodically inveighed against Britain's non-intervention or inaction against Israel and, particularly, against Whitehall's non-activation of the Anglo-Jordanian defence treaty. By mid-1953 Glubb was warning the British authorities that 'a complete revolution' had taken place in Jordan's attitude toward Britain. Whereas, before, Jordanians had been 'extremely proud' to be regarded as 'Britain's devoted ally,' and not like the other Middle Eastern states, now, in 1953, 'all this has gone' and Jordanians regard Britain 'as friendly to Israel as to Jordan.' When clashes occur between the two countries, usually on Israel's initiative, Britain invariably proclaims itself 'neutral' - even though bound by treaty to Jordan and not to Israel - and Jordan is routinely lumped together with the rest of 'the Arabs.' Glubb warned that if Britain continued to hold aloof, it would 'lose the friendship of Jordan and eventually the Arab Legion also.'[735]

But in the end, it was not, at least directly, the Jews, or Zionism, or Israel and its behaviour, that resulted in Glubb's dismissal as commander of the Arab Legion and the reduction of Britain's influence and stature in Jordan and the Middle East in general. Since the start of 1955 Nasser and his Jordanian supporters - a mixture of nationalists, republicans, and pan-Arabists - had tried to subvert and overthrow the Hashemite monarchy in Amman, in part to stymie Jordanian entry into the Baghdad Pact. The pact, engineered by Britain (but with Washington in the wings), was designed to establish a chain of allied Muslim and Arab states to counter Soviet penetration, and possible invasion, of the Middle East. Moreover, Nasser suspected that Britain was promoting the pact in order to enhance (Hashemite) Iraq's position in the Middle East, at Egypt's expense.

Jordan, heavily subsidized by Britain and with an army commanded by British officers, had traditionally been regarded by Arab nationalists (and many Israelis) as a cat's paw of British imperial interests. The ruckus around the Baghdad Pact brought matters to a head. The anti-Pact, anti-Hashemite incitement and agitation, orchestrated by the Egyptian Embassy in Amman and the 'Voice of the Arabs' radio station in Cairo, reached a crescendo in December 1955, after the visit to Jordan of Britain's Chief of the Imperial General Staff, General Sir Gerald

Templer, who had come to 'sell' the pact, which promised substantial British strengthening of the Legion, to the Jordanian government.

Jordan's four Cabinet ministers from the West Bank resigned and on 16 December pro-Nasser riots erupted, rocking Amman and the rest of the kingdom. The police proving inadequate, and the Legion was called out to suppress the rioters, who were burning public buildings and looting shops. 'It was heartbreaking work for the troops ... They were abused, periodically stoned and called Jews and traitors,' Glubb recalled. 'Yet whenever they were obliged to fire, they showed perfect steadiness and discipline.' After a month, order was restored. But the kingdom, and its young King, Hussein, had been severely shaken, and all thought of signing the Baghdad Pact was abandoned.[736]

The suppression of the riots embittered the local Nasserist politicians and agitators, who at times thought that they were on the verge of assuming power, and persuaded Cairo to intensify its propaganda against Glubb and the Legion. During the following weeks, Hussein came under intense pressure, from both friends and enemies of the monarchy, at least to 'Arabize' his army by ridding it of its British senior officers.[737] They seemed to symbolize Jordan's (and Hussein's) subordination to British imperial diktats.

Glubb had always insisted that the Legion was an Arab, and Hashemite-controlled, army, not an appendage of the British Empire. The fact that much of its senior staff was British through 1948-56 was due to the absence of Arab officers qualified to fill the appropriate slots, especially in the more technical, sophisticated arms. But once Arabs were sufficiently trained, they would replace the British officers, Glubb explained. According to Glubb, rank and promotion in the Legion were determined by qualification, 'irrespective of race.'

But from 1949 on, Glubb acknowledged the need to 'Arabize' the Legion's upper echelons. 'I think that I am constantly on the look out to reduce [the number of] British officers,' he wrote Kirkbride in 1950, when there were 48 in the force. Glubb feared that 'too rapid promotion' of young and relatively inexperienced Arab officers would reduce the army's efficiency. Nonetheless, the force was gradually being 'Arabized,' he argued. He pointed to the fact that of the Legion's ten infantry regiments, only four had British commanding officers. 'In two or three years, there may well be no British [regimental] C.O.s [commanding officers],' he wrote. 'It will be seen from this example that we are working on the principle that British officers can be dispensed with as soon as competent Arabs are available ...' But Glubb admitted that the situation was not as good in the artillery, engineers and general staff branches, where Arab officers had only begun to be trained and integrated.

In general, Glubb held up the Legion as a well-functioning model of a multi-racial army (and this 'in an age and in a part of the world seething with fanatical Xenophobia and race hatred ... How it works sometimes seems a miracle, but the fact remains that hitherto it has worked').[738]

If there was pressure from within Jordan to 'Arabize' the Legion, there were also continuous countervailing pressures from the British military establishment. Whitehall repeatedly cautioned Glubb that the maintenance (or increase) of the British subsidy depended on the Legion's (perceived) efficiency and that this efficiency was in some measure dependant on the continued presence of a relatively large, highly-qualified core of British officers. Their replacement by less-qualified Arabs - as a result of 'nationalist' or career-motivated pressure from within - would lower the Legion's effectiveness and, hence, usefulness to Britain in the event of war.[739] Glubb was thus caught, during 1949-56, between the need to maintain an effective (i.e., British-led) army and pressures to staff the army with senior Arab officers.

In the confused and crisis-ridden circumstances of 1948, it was perhaps inevitable that Glubb and his fellow British officers would be viewed by suspicious Jordanians and Arabs outside the kingdom as agents of British imperialism (and, occasionally and absurdly, as closet Zionists), whose ultimate loyalty to Jordan was in grave doubt. But they continued to be cast in this role during 1949-56 as well. After each IDF retaliatory strike Jordanian politicians would ask, and outside Arab leaders would taunt - how come the Legion had not interdicted or repulsed the raiders or mounted a retaliatory strike of its own? Always, the finger of accusation was pointed at Glubb (and, occasionally, at Kirkbride as well): 'If anyone asks why force was not used, the reply is always that I and\or Glubb prevented it ... It is believed that we carry out the instructions of His Majesty's Government who are, and always have been, biased in favour of the Jews ... Glubb and I are seriously worried about the present trend here,' reported Kirkbride in 1950.[740] Similar charges were hurled more generally against the Legion and its officers during the following six years.[741] Indeed, within the Legion itself there were occasional 'murmurings' against Jordan's 'restraint' in face of Israeli aggressiveness. [742] No doubt, there were many Arab officers who coveted promotion – and saw the senior British officers as obstacles in their path.

During late 1955 and early 1956, such considerations meshed with the general anti-Western, anti-imperialist, and anti-royalist winds that rocked the kingdom. These helped to precipitate Glubb's downfall. On 1 March 1956 Hussein acted, abruptly dismissing Glubb and ordering his immediate departure from the country. Along with Glubb, the King fired several senior British Legion officers (one of them was Col. Patrick Coghill, director of the Legion's intelligence arm) and a number of senior Arab officers, perhaps suspected of undue loyalty to Glubb.[743] Prodded by young Legion officers, Hussein was gradually persuaded to be more attentive to nationalist demands; and many argued that the 'Arabization' of the Legion was necessary to secure the monarchy against republican and Nasserist criticism.

Glubb's dismissal was perfunctory, rude and graceless in the extreme. Glubb was informed by the prime minister, Samir Rifa`i, that he had 'two hours' in which to leave the kingdom. Glubb balked and Rifa`i, after some haggling, agreed to give him until seven the following morning. Glubb believed that Hussein had dismissed him because of (a) a misunderstanding about ammunition stocks (the king thought that Glubb had allowed them to fall below a reasonable level), (b) the King's 'desire ... to exercise authority unfettered by a middle-aged and cautious adviser,' (c) the King's belief that defiance of Britain would restore his popularity, and (d) genuine nationalist sentiment. Hussein and Glubb had also disagreed over Arab Legion deployment in the West Bank and Glubb's desire to dismiss a number of unreliable officers.[744] Glubb in his autobiography surmised that Hussein had been considering dismissing him 'for at least a year.'[745]

Last-minute intervention by the British Ambassador in Amman, Charles Duke, and Prime Minister Anthony Eden failed to change the King's mind. Following the announcement of the dismissal, Eden sent Hussein a strongly worded message speaking of a 'severe blow' to 'the confidence' on which the Anglo-Jordanian relationship was based, warning that 'the consequences might be disastrous.' The British hoped that Hussein would reconsider[746] but Glubb himself, statesmanlike in extreme adversity, urged Whitehall to exercise restraint and Kirkbride, summoned to the British Cabinet meeting of 9 March, advised against a complete British 'pullout,' which might precipitate Hussein's fall and endanger British interests in Iraq.[747] After a brief interregnum in which General Radi `Innab stood in, Glubb was succeeded as chief of general staff, on 24 May 1956, by 'Ali Abu Nawar, a radical young staff officer who had been a military attaché to Paris and, subsequently, Hussein's aide de camp. Without doubt, Abu Nawar had been among the main instigators of Glubb's ouster.[748]

Britain continued to subsidize Jordan, but not for long. The end of the special relationship, heralded by Glubb's dismissal, was in sight. As one historian put it, '1 March' was 'the deepest cut in the history of the Hashemite state between 1948 and 1967.' It marked Jordan's 'emancipation from British tutelage'; henceforth, it was no longer a British de pendency.[749] As a result of the largely abortive joint Anglo-French-Israeli attack on Egypt in October-November 1956, Britain's general position in the Middle East abruptly declined. Britain's failure to overthrow Nasser - one of the assault's aims - resulted in a massive reinforcement of Nasser's power and prestige, and by extension, of Nasserism and anti-imperialism throughout the Arab world. On 14 March 1957, Jordan unilaterally terminated the Anglo-Jordanian treaty, ending the £12 million annual subsidy, which largely went to the upkeep and development of the Legion. The following month, a group of young officers, apparently led by Abu Nawar, rose in revolt in an attempt to overthrow the monarchy. Swift and courageous action by Hussein, supported by loyal contingents, won the day and Abu Nawar was dismissed and exiled from Jordan. A year later, in July 1958, after a military coup toppled the Hashemite monarchy in Baghdad, Britain flew two battalions of paratroops into Amman to secure Hussein's throne.

But for all practical purposes, the special Anglo-Jordanian relationship - symbolized by Glubb's command of the Legion - was over. Jordan, albeit still a monarchy, became a 'normal' Arab state, joining the inter-Arab shuffle with now Syria, now Egypt, now Iraq, providing Hussein with political backing. At the same time, Jordan benefited from outside injections of American political and financial support and covert Israeli intelligence and, on occasion, military help. But the days of direct Western influence and partial control over Jordan, the days of Glubb, were over.

CONCLUSION (AFTER 1956)

After (and despite) his humiliating ouster from Jordan, Glubb remained 'a convinced champion of the Arab cause.'[750] Indeed, his philo-Arabism, and concomitant anti-Zionism, seemed to have increased with the passage of time and the increase in distance from the Middle East. During the late 1950s and early 1960s Glubb concentrated on producing an autobiography and then a series of histories, rarely giving interviews or sending articles or letters to the editors of newspapers. (No doubt, he held his peace partly in deference to British government sensibilities and wishes.) But from 1967 on, under the impact of the Six Day War and the latest instalment of the Palestinian Arab tragedy, Glubb became a frequent and full-throated pro-Arab propagandist.

Glubb's first book, *The Story of the Arab Legion*, was written in Amman before the outbreak of the first Arab-Israeli war. It was published in 1948. It contains no anti-Zionist or anti-Semitic argumentation or asides. During the following nine years Glubb was preoccupied with war-making and defence against Israeli attacks. He penned a large number of military and political memorandums but had no time for historical writing. But during the three decades after his expulsion from Jordan in 1956, Glubb filled in his time and supplemented his income from a British government pension (the Jordanians refused to give him one) by writing no less than 21 books and extended essays.

His writings and lecturing – he was a much sought-after speaker on the British Middle East circuit – during the last three decades of his life were invariably anti-Zionist and often contained anti-Semitic argumentation. But he was usually careful to maintain at least a facade of objectivity and fair play. (He said of his pro-Arab tract, 'The Middle East Crisis – A Personal Interpretation',[751] published immediately after the Six Day War: 'It was my intention to be entirely objective.'[752]) Among Zionists and Arabs he gained a reputation as a major anti-Israel spokesman, his knowledgeability about the Middle East seemingly guaranteed by his prolonged involvement in its affairs. At the same time, his diffident, reserved demeanour and plain army officer's English and bearing projected solidity and trustworthiness; his status as a retiree and his age sent a message that he was now above the battle.

In 'The Middle East Crisis', he wrote: 'I am an old man, unlikely much longer to grace this mortal scene. For ten years I have tried to avoid violent controversy, seeking refuge in the calmer atmosphere of historical studies. I do not think that I have any remaining passions, hatreds, jealousies and ambitions ... I do not ... dislike anyone ... Syrians, Lebanese, Egyptians or Israelis ...'[753]

But in truth, Glubb's post-1956 writings are all, to one degree or another, imbued with a clear tilt and intent, and his dislikes, if not actual hatreds, are prominently displayed. Glubb portrayed the June 1967 war – precipitated by Egypt's massive violation of Sinai's de facto demilitarisation, the expulsion of UNEF, the United Nations peace-keeping force in Sinai, and the closure of the Gulf of Eilat (Gulf of 'Aqaba) to Israeli shipping – as a result of Soviet machinations and Israeli exploitation of innocent Arab foolishness.[754] Similarly, the IDF's conquest of the West Bank in the course of the Six Day War is lambasted as an unprovoked napalming of innocuous, poorly armed, well-intentioned Arab Legionnaires – without a mention of the fact that it was the Jordanians who had initiated the hostilities along the West Bank border and that Israel had repeatedly asked Jordan to stop shooting (the Jordanians had ignored and then rejected these requests) before unleashing its own (successful) offensive.[755] And Glubb's tone is even sharper when relating to Israel's post-1967 sins of commission: 'When her enemies did not surrender, she resumed her hard line, driving her victims from their homes, bulldozing down whole villages, bombing the refugee camps and the towns and villages of the neighbouring countries ...'[756] Again, no mention is made of the Arab attacks that led to Israeli reprisals, which included such measures as the destruction of homes of suspected terrorists and the bombing of Palestinian guerrilla bases located in or on the fringes of refugee camps, often involving collateral damage. If Glubb occasionally had harsh things to say about Palestinian behaviour, it was usually following a Palestinian attack on the Hashemite regime and was explained away as stemming from the 'similarity' between the Palestinians and the Israelis. Indeed, he attributed the Palestinian rebellion in September 1970 against King Hussein – whose troops had frequently protected them from the IDF - to their 'Jewish' genes. 'Can it be,' he asked, 'that the so-called Arabs of Palestine today are to a considerable degree the descendants of the [Jewish] defenders of Jerusalem against Titus...?'[757]

Moreover, Glubb's memory, overlaid by successive strata of new events and propaganda, grew less and less reliable; his recollection of 1948, for example, grew progressively more anti-Zionist, and less nuanced. In 1957 he was writing: 'It must not be forgotten that the whole problem of embittered refugees was the result of the ruthless expulsion of all Arabs by the Israelis in 1948.'[758] And a decade and a half later he wrote: It was not true that 'the "Arabs" had invaded Israel' in 1948. Rather, 'a careful examination of the dates ... shows that it was Israel that attacked first.'[759] These statements contain breathtaking distortions of the historical record.

In his not infrequent public speeches, interviews, articles and letters to the editor, Glubb consistently defended the behaviour of Jordan and its ruler (despite his own ungrateful and ungracious treatment at King Hussein's hands). In a letter to the editor in February 1968 – against the backdrop of Palestinian guerrilla and terrorist raids from Jordan into the West Bank and Israel and IDF counter-raiding against targets in Jordan – Glubb denied Jordanian 'aggression' against Israel or even that Jordan-based guerrillas were attacking Israel. The 'saboteurs,' he wrote, came from Syria and merely crossed through Jordan on their way to Israel. Jordan, he wrote 'has strained every nerve to prevent infiltration by Syria' - and yet she was consistently pounded by 'massive Israeli retaliation.'[760]

But the focus of Glubb's propagandistic attentions through the late 1960s and 1970s were the Palestinians and, more specifically, the Palestinian refugees. There can be no doubt that Glubb was shocked by Israel's swift victory in 1967 and genuinely angered by its subsequent behaviour in the occupied West Bank and Gaza Strip (the 'creeping annexation' of these territories through the confiscation of Palestinian lands and the establishment of new settlements, the destruction of Palestinian homes and the deportation of Palestinian leaders and activists, etc.). The misery of Palestinian existence certainly touched him; and in some way he may have felt a responsibility for their lot. Or perhaps the Palestinian refugees were simply the most persuasive and effective propaganda tool available to needle or pound Israel in the Western press. Most likely, all these factors played a part in Glubb's unrelenting espousal of the refugees' cause. 'A million and a half of the indigenous people of Palestine' were driven from their homes, he wrote in January 1969 (in fact, the number was about 700,000) – and this he identified as 'the main problem', the core, of the Middle East conflict. He noted that the Palestinians, by 'worldwide acts of violence' had succeeded in drawing the world's attention to their 'grievance.' Any settlement between Israel and the Arab states that did not solve the refugee problem would not last, he concluded.[761]

When talking of the Palestinians, Glubb almost invariably used emotional language, tended to exaggeration and distorted history. 'The Palestinians are the original inhabitants of [Palestine] for thousands of years [sic],' he wrote in a letter to the editor at the end of 1969. In 1948 'the innocent Palestinians [were] evicted from their homes and country.' (Why 'innocent?' After all, they rejected the UN partition resolution of November 1947 and launched, albeit haphazardly, the hostilities that ended in their exodus – and, after 1948, the vast majority, while leaving or being evicted from their homes, continued to reside in 'their country,' Palestine (i.e., the West Bank and Gaza Strip).) He concluded with a peroration:

> I do not write as a propagandist but as a lover of peace and of the Holy Land. As such, I implore the Israeli government to realize that this problem cannot be solved by brute force alone regardless of justice. I am indifferent to the rantings of Nasser, but the fact remains that the Palestinians have suffered grievous injustice. The cure is to redress their grievances, not to make their lives yet more unbearable.[762]

A similar tone informs a letter he sent off immediately after the IDF's Operation Litani of March 1978, in which it briefly occupied southern Lebanon and killed, captured or drove out hundreds of Palestinian gunmen. The operation, argued Glubb, only with a measure of accuracy, was simply an 'implementation' of Ben-Gurion's 'plan' from the 1950s (which proposed installing a Christian government in Beirut, signing an Israeli-Lebanese peace treaty, and Israeli annexation of the area south of the Litani River). And 'it is noticeable that in the recent operations Israel has not only acted against the Palestinians, but has also driven out the native Lebanese, destroying their towns and villages so that they will have no homes to return to. This was the method they employed [in 1948] to drive out the population of Palestine.'[763]

When speaking of the Palestinian refugees, Glubb usually refrained from spelling out what he meant by 'redress'. Perhaps in the 1950s and 1960s he had thought in terms of repatriation. But by the early 1970s - by which time he appears to have resigned himself to Israel's existence[764] - he no longer held out any hope of a massive refugee return to Israel proper. Rather, he hinted that the solution of the problem, through orderly, subsidized resettlement, must lie in (East) Jordan and the West Bank, after Israeli withdrawal from that territory. In 1972, he wrote:

> ... The sine qua non of peace is to provide for these refugees, through the means of an international consortium of powers. (1) Israel should withdraw to the pre-1967 line .. the lands thus released being actively developed to absorb a large [refugee] population. (2) The lands east of the Jordan should be similarly developed, the powers providing the capital cost ... (3) I believe that the refugees could thus be settled and given new hope in life [thus settling] .. their just grievances.[765]

In his eulogy of Glubb, delivered on 17 April 1986 at Westminster Abbey, King Hussein said: 'He was a down-to-earth soldier, with a heart, a simple style of life and impeccable integrity, who performed quietly and unassumingly the duties entrusted to him by his second country, Jordan, at a crucial moment in its history and development.'[766]

Implicit in these words was a (no doubt politically motivated) double devaluation – Glubb projected as mere dutiful servant and portrayed as British mercenary to his 'second country.' Out of modesty, Glubb might have allowed the first characterisation to pass unchallenged. But he most certainly would have taken issue with the second.

To be sure, of all the Britons who drifted through and about the Middle East during the past two centuries, Glubb was the most influential and historically significant both as adviser and as creator and commander of native forces. His influence on Jordan's development and policies, down to 1956, was immense, and the stamp he left on the region's history is ineradicable. But at the heart of his role and contribution lay an enigma and a problem (as highlighted by the King's reference to Glubb's 'second country'). In the years 1947-56, the historically most significant of his career, who did Glubb believe he was serving, Britain or Jordan? And, if both (as he surely believed), where lay his primary loyalty? Some historians, including those of the declining years of the British empire, would by and large endorse Avi Shlaim's judgement: 'Glubb Pasha was really an imperial proconsul, for all his insistence on having served not Britain but the Hashemite Dynasty ... His primary loyalty was to Britain.'[767] Arab nationalists, Jordanian and otherwise, during his years of service in Amman vilified Glubb as nothing less than a 'British agent'; and most Arab journalists and historians of the modern era have followed suit.[768]

But Glubb himself during his years in the Legion always stressed his complete loyalty to the Hashemites and Jordan – and one is tempted to dismiss as a form of apologetics his avowals after his ouster from Amman that his primary allegiance always lay with Britain. In his autobiography, *A Soldier With the Arabs*, Glubb asserted that 'Jordan … has been my country, almost as much as Britain.'[769] But he also wrote, bringing together his love of Jordan and love of God: 'This little tract of country has done more to bring the human race to God than have all the vast continents by which it is surrounded.'[770] And he wrote: 'I had been for more than thirty years in the service of the Hashemite family … I felt myself an old family retainer. I had seen them all grow up and grow old ... Such long and intimate association could not fail to result in devotion.'[771] Glubb, who often wore the traditional beduin head-dress, regularly began paragraphs in public speeches with the phrase 'We the Arabs' (*nahna al-Arab*).[772] And from across the river, Israel's foreign minister, Moshe Shertok (Sharett), pronounced in mid-July 1948: '[Glubb] is more Arab than British.'[773]

Sharett, it seems to me, got it more right than Glubb's Arab critics and detractors. For in the pivotal historical junctions he behaved like a loyal servant of the Hashemite crown rather than an agent of Whitehall's: In 1946-47 Glubb (like his master, Abdullah) supported the partition of Palestine – many months before Whitehall had come round to recognizing the desirability or inevitability of such an outcome; and in mid-May 1948, Glubb sent his troops to occupy East Jerusalem, a move of immense strategic significance that for months Foreign Secretary Bevin and his officials had been cautioning against; and in March 1956, when British and Jordanian interests frontally collided at the moment of Glubb's dismissal – the general held his peace and refrained from any criticism of the young King Hussein, surely an inimitable exhibition of loyalty by a family retainer.

Certainly, through most of his 36-year career in Iraq and Transjordan-Jordan, Glubb felt that British and Arab interests converged and overlapped – and what he did was done in the service of both London and the Arabs. There was an identity or almost complete identity of interests. But when these interests or policies diverged, as for a moment occurred in spring 1948, Glubb followed and served Abdullah. During the 1940s and early 1950s, down to 1956, Glubb continuously fed Whitehall with intelligence about Jordan and advice regarding requisite British policy; indeed, he often tried to help shape British policy – as when, in 1953, he enjoined the British to try to engineer a UN Security Council appeal to both Israel and Jordan to withdraw their armies from the border areas to avoid a clash.[774] And sometimes he was successful in helping shape that policy, as in the persuasion of Bevin and the Foreign Office in late 1947-early 1948 to back a Legion occupation of the West Bank and an Israeli-Hashemite partition of Palestine. But in the end, Glubb was, above all, the Hashemite's obedient and loyal retainer and the Arabs' most successful general.

Glubb grew up in a professional and country gentry milieu in which a genteel superficial anti-Semitism was the norm. Jews were regarded as aliens, and not completely kosher ones at that; they had about them, at the very least, a hint of business malpractice, sharp dealing, manipulation, profiteering. And personal contact with Jews was virtually unknown. Glubb may have come across one or two in school and in the army in Flanders. But he makes no mention of them in his writings.

It appears that it was in the Middle East that Glubb first came into contact with Jewish communities. We know nothing about his contacts, if any, in the 1920s, with Baghdadi Jewry, but he seems, from his perspective, to have seen more than enough of Palestinian Jews in the 1930s and 1940s. They were simply out to 'steal' the Palestinian Arabs' patrimony, and they were doing so using a staggered combination of trickery (buying land and expelling tenant-farmers, while avowing that they had no intention of taking over Palestine but only co-existing with the Arabs) and outright, brute force (1948). This is how Glubb saw the essentials of the Zionist-Palestinian Arab struggle.

Unlike most Palestinian Arabs of his day (or, indeed, of the present time), Glubb had a keen appreciation and knowledge of Jewish history – and of the Jews' historic (second and first millennium BC) ties to the Land of Israel (Palestine). This might have rendered him more sympathetic to Zionist claims. But it didn't. Instead, he preferred to discover, and stress, what he said were the Arabs' 'roots' (Canaanite, Philistine) pre-dating the Hebrews' arrival in Palestine. And he generally ignored the modern and contemporary propellants of Zionism – Eastern European-Russian anti-Semitism and pogroms, and the Holocaust – which could be seen (and were seen, by the late 1940s, by most of the Western world) as supplying the moral underpinnings for the Zionist claims to legitimacy and statehood in their ancient land. Somewhat curiously, Glubb in his books devoted a great deal of space to describing Christian persecution of European Jews down the centuries – but almost not a word about the Germans' murder of six million Jews. Glubb seems never to have internalised what had happened to European Jewry while he was off in the Middle East playing soldier among the Arabs. Certainly he never internalised the Holocaust in the way that he had the tragedy that befell the Palestinian Arabs in 1948, which he was forever lamenting.

Be that as it may, Glubb's encounters with Israel on the battlefields of 1948 and in skirmishes along the borders in 1949-56 sharpened and aggravated his anti-Semitic proclivities. In his post-1948 memoranda to Kirkbride, Bevin and the Foreign Office, he frequently (and not always without reason) depicted Israel ('the Jews') as double-dealing neighbourhood bullies, avenging themselves on the Arab 'natives' for sins committed over the centuries by European Christians against Jews. At the same time, his books on Muhammad, Islam and the Middle East routinely downplayed, and often distorted, the normally miserable, and often tragic, history of Jewish communities in the Muslim and Arab worlds; Muslim and Arab maltreatment of Jews down the centuries, and the frequent, bloody pogroms that punctuated their existence in Morocco and Spain and Iraq and Iran, were meticulously ignored.

Maureen Heaney Norton[775] argues that Glubb 'advocated partition not as a means to protect Arab interests, but as a way to strengthen the [British] Empire.' I think the truth is more complex. By the late 1930s, Glubb had gradually come to feel that pragmatism, if not justice, required that Palestine be partitioned and that the Jews obtain part of the country as a state. And by 1946-47, Glubb was convinced that Palestine should be partitioned between a Jewish state and Abdullah's kingdom, not between the Jews and the Palestinians. Whether out of loyalty to Abdullah and Transjordan or whether out of a realistic appreciation of real options, Glubb became a forceful advocate of such a partition – and then, in May 1948, went on to successfully lead that agent of partition, the Arab Legion, into the West Bank and East Jerusalem. A blow-by-blow, almost day-by-day description of Glubb's thinking and actions during late 1947-May 1948 strongly reinforces the argument of such military analysts as Dov Steiger (Sion) and historians such as Avi Shlaim (*Collusion Across the Jordan*) and Yoav Gelber (*Palestine 1948*) that Jordan invaded Palestine not in order to attack Israel but in order to 'save' its Arab-populated eastern parts from Jewish conquest and, ultimately, to annex them; territorial expansion at the expense of Palestine's Arabs rather than the Jewish state was Abdullah's target.

Jerusalem, even its Arab part, did not figure at all in Glubb's pre-invasion designs. And certainly attacking Jewish West Jerusalem was no part of Glubb's or Abdullah's original planning; both realised that the Legion was simply not strong enough. But eventually, over 18-28 May, Abdullah and, reluctantly, Glubb sent in the Legion to take over East Jerusalem, including the Old City, again, to protect it from Jewish conquest and because it represented a pivotal position in the Legion's deployment throughout the West Bank. Glubb came to realise, in the course of the invasion, that if East Jerusalem fell to Haganah/IDF assault, the rest of the West Bank would follow. Regarding the occupation of East Jerusalem, Abdullah was certainly motivated also by personal and religious reasons connected with his father's tomb and the city's sanctity in Islam.

Abdullah's spiritual and Glubb's strategic concerns regarding Jerusalem found a parallel in Ben-Gurion's approach: Apart from the centrality of Jerusalem as the historical capital and spiritual centre, Ben-Gurion feared that the fall of West Jerusalem, with its 100,000 Jews (virtually one-sixth of the total Jewish population), would so undermine Jewish morale that the whole war effort might collapse. This explains why (against Haganah/IDF advice) he devoted so much effort to taking Latrun.

The Legion's stubborn defence of the Latrun salient should also be seen in terms of the defence of the Legion's general position in the West Bank and East Jerusalem. Latrun's fall could have endangered either or both. And, in any event, Latrun was in an area earmarked by the 1947 UN partition plan for Arab, not Jewish, sovereignty. The three major battles for Latrun, starting with the first on 24-25 May 1948, all represented Haganah-IDF attacks on Arab-earmarked territory, not a Jordanian assault on the Jewish state. Indeed, at virtually no point did Jordanian forces attack and occupy the Jewish state area (for several months toward the end of the war a Legion company did regularly patrol part of the uninhabited southern Negev, earmarked by the partition plan for Jewish sovereignty). If Israel and Jordan entered the 1948 War with a secret, unwritten understanding of mutual non-belligerence, it was primarily Israel that violated it in May and June and then again in July and October 1948, not Jordan.

All of this inevitably opens up the more general question of the Arab states' aim or aims in the invasion of Palestine in 1948. Did they invade in order to throw the Jews into the sea and destroy the Jewish state? Or were their aims more modest and complex? And can one really speak of 'they'? After all, we now know that, Israeli and Lebanese propaganda notwithstanding, Lebanon's army never actually crossed the Israeli border in May 1948; Lebanon may have supplied the Arab Liberation Army, a volunteer force of irregulars, with some logistical and artillery support, but it refrained from taking part in the 'pan-Arab' invasion, whatever its radio stations proclaimed at the time. As to Egypt, Iraq and Syria, whose forces all bit into Israeli territory in the course of their invasions – a large question mark hangs over their real objectives. Did they really intend to drive to the sea (or to Tel Aviv) and destroy the Jewish state? Did their political and military leaderships believe such an objective to be realistic? Or were they, more modestly, aiming at small land grabs to hurt the Jews, score political points and forestall or counter-balance expected Jordanian territorial gains? Only the opening of the Arab states' archives – all, regrettably, closed to researchers - may provide a definitive answer. For the moment, from the evidence afforded by a close look at Glubb's and Jordan's roles, all we can say, with relative certainty, is that the Jordanian invasion, undertaken with Britain's agreement and a measure of cooperation with the Yishuv, was not geared to the destruction of Israel but to the occupation of parts of Arab Palestine – and that Jordan was the military and political lynchpin of the whole invasion.

No doubt there will be historians – 'Old Historians' – who will continue to dispute this picture. But I think the evidence is clear and the conclusion almost ineluctable. What emerges is perforce a far more nuanced and complex picture of the first Arab-Israeli war, its causes and consequences.

As to the years 1949-56, Glubb's role and its import are far less controversial. Some may argue that he did not act as assiduously as emerges from the Legion and British documentation, to curb Arab infiltration into Israel. But there can be no disputing the crucial role he played in restraining the dogs of war by not responding to Israel's retaliatory strikes so that 1956 saw an Israeli-Egyptian rather than an Israeli-Jordanian confrontation. And by so doing, he no doubt saved the West Bank for Jordan for at least a decade. One may conjecture that the anger Glubb exhibited in his post-1967 books, pamphlets and letters to the editor may well, at least in part, have been due to his sense of frustration at the spectacle of Israel's quick conquest of the West Bank and East Jerusalem in the Six Day War. What he, gritting his teeth and eating humble pie, had succeeded in achieving during 1949-56 had been thrown away in the course of a few hasty hours in June 1967. And 35 years later, Palestinian rebellions notwithstanding, the IDF still sits on the Jordan River.

BIBLIOGRAPHY

Archives

David Ben-Gurion Archive – BGA (Sde Boqer, Israel)
Central Zionist Archive – CZA - (Jerusalem, Israel)
Haganah Archive – HA (Tel Aviv, Israel)
Israel Defence Forces Archive – IDFA (Givatayim, Israel)
Israel State Archive – ISA (Jerusalem, Israel)
Public Record Office – PRO (London, England)
St Antony's College Middle East Centre Archive - SAMECA (Oxford, England)
  Glubb Papers
  Haining Papers
  Cunningham Papers
United Nations Archive – UNA (New York, NY, USA)

Newspapers

The Times (London)
The New York Times
The Palestine Post (Jerusalem)

Books and Articles

Asia, Ilan. *The Focus of the Conflict: The Struggle for the Negev 1947-1956* (Heb.) (Yad Ben-Zvi, Jerusalem, 1994)

Bar-Joseph, Uri. *The Best of Enemies, Israel and Transjordan in the War of 1948* (Frank Cass, London, 1987)

Bar-On, Mordechai. *Challenge and Quarrel* (Heb.) (Ben-Gurion University Press, Beersheba, 1991)

- *The Gates of Gaza* (Heb.) ('Am 'Oved, Tel Aviv, 1992)

Ben-Gurion, David. *The War Diary, the War of Independence, 1948-1949* (Heb.) Orren, Elhanan, and Rivlin, Gershon, (eds.). (Israel Defence Ministry Press, Tel Aviv, 1982)

Benziman, Uzi, and Mansour, Atallah. *Sub-Tenants* (Heb.) (Keter, Jerusalem, 1992)

Bilby, Kenneth. *New Star in the Near East* (Doubleday, New York, 1950)

Dann, Uriel. *King Hussein and the Challenge of Arab Radicalism, Jordan 1955-1967* (Oxford University Press, New York, 1989)

Doran, Michael. *Pan-Arabism before Nasser: Egyptian Power Politics and the Palestine Question* (Oxford University Press, New York, 1999)

Etzioni, Binyamin. *Tree and Sword, the Route of Battle of the Golani Brigade* (Heb.) (Israel Defence Forces Press – Ma'arachot, Tel Aviv, 1951)

Gelber, Yoav. *Jewish-Transjordanian Relations, 1921-1948* (Frank Cass, London, 1997)

- *Palestine 1948: War, Escape, and the Emergence of the Palestinian Refugee Problem* (Sussex Academic Press, Brighton, 2001)

Glubb, John. *The Story of the Arab Legion* (Hodder & Stoughton, London, 1948)

- *A Soldier With the Arabs* (Hodder & Stoughton, London, 1957)
- *Britain and the Arabs, a Study of Fifty Years 1908 to 1958* (Hodder & Stoughton, London, 1959)
- 'The Mixture of Races in the Eastern Arab Countries' (Holywell Press, Oxford, 1967)
- 'The Middle East Crisis, a Personal Interpretation' (Hodder & Stoughton, London, 1967 and revised ed., 1969)
- *The Life and Times of Muhammad* (Hodder & Stoughton, London, 1970)
- *Peace in the Holy Land, an Historical Analysis of the Palestine Problem* (Hodder & Stoughton, London, 1971)

Golani, Motti. *There Will be War Next Summer...The Road to the Sinai War, 1955-1956* (Heb.) (Israel Defence Ministry Press, Tel Aviv, 1997)

Ilan, Amitzur. *The Origin of the Arab-Israeli Arms Race: Arms, Embargo, Military Power and Decision in the 1948 Palestine War* (MacMillan\St Antony's, London, 1996)

Israel, State of, and Israel State Archives. *Documents on the Foreign Policy of Israel,* vols. 1-8 (Jerusalem, Israel State Archives, 1981-1995)

Israel Defence Forces, History Branch. *History of the War of Independence* (Heb.) (Israel Defence Forces Press, Tel Aviv, 1959)

Itzchaki, Arieh, *Latrun, The Battle on the Road to Jerusalem* (Heb.) (Cana, Jerusalem, 1982)

Jarvis, C.S. *Arab Command, the Biography of Lt.-Colonel F.G. Peake Pasha* (Hutchinson, London, 1948)

Kadish, Alon, Sela, Avraham, and Golan, Arnon, *The Occupation of Lydda, July 1948*, (Heb.) (Haganah Archive/Ministry of Defence Press, Tel Aviv, 2000)

Kirkbride, Alec Seith. *From the Wings, Amman Memoirs 1947-1951* (Frank Cass, London, 1976)

- *A Crackle of Thorns, Experiences in the Middle East* (John Murray, London, 1956)

Levin, Harry. *Jerusalem Embattled* (Gollancz, London, 1950)

Lunt, James. *Glubb Pasha, A Biography* (Harvill Press, London, 1984)

Masalha, Nur. *A Land Without a People: Israel, Transfer and the Palestinians, 1949-1996* (Faber and Faber, London, 1997)

Meir, Golda, *My Life, An Autobiography* (Futura Books ed., London, 1976)

Messer, Oded. *The Haganah's Operational Plans, 1937-1948* (Heb.) (Tag Publishing House, Israel, 1996)

Milstein, Uri. *History of the War of Independence*, vol. IV (University Press of America, 1998)

Morris, Benny. *Israel's Border Wars, 1949-1956: Arab Infiltration, Israeli Retaliation, and the Countdown to the Suez War* (Oxford University Press, Oxford, rev. ed. 1997)

- 'Operation Dani and the Palestinian Exodus from Lydda and Ramle in 1948,' (*Middle East Journal* 40/1, winter 1986)

- *The Birth of the Palestinian Refugee Problem, 1947-1949* (Cambridge University Press, Cambridge, England, 1988)

al-Nashashibi, Nasir al-Din. *What Happened in the Middle East* (Manshurat al Maktab al Tidjari, Beirut, 1962)

Nevo, Joseph. *King Abdallah and Palestine, A Territorial Ambition* (Macmillan\St Antony's, London, 1996)

Norton, Maureen Heaney, 'The Last Pasha: Sir John Glubb and the British Empire in the Middle East, 1920-1949,' (Ph.D. thesis, Johns Hopkins University, 1997)

Pappe, Ilan. *Britain and the Arab-Israeli Conflict, 1948-1951* (St Antony's/MacMillan, London, 1988)

Porath, Yehoshua. *In Search of Arab Unity 1930-1945* (Frank Cass, London, 1986)

Rabinovich, Itamar. *The Road Not Taken, Early Arab-Israeli Negotiations* (Oxford University Press, New York, 1991)

Royle, Trevor. *Glubb Pasha* (Abacus, London, 1993)

Sakakini, Khalil al-. *"Such Am I, Oh World", Diaries of Khalil al-Sakakini* (Heb.) (Keter, Jerusalem, 1990)

Rabinovich, Itamar. *The Road Not Taken, Early Arab-Israeli Negotiations* (Oxford University Press, New York, 1991)

Royle, Trevor. *Glubb Pasha* (Abacus, London, 1993)

Sakakini, Khalil al-. *"Such Am I, Oh World", Diaries of Khalil al-Sakakini* (Heb.) (Keter, Jerusalem, 1990)

Segev (Sabagh), Shmuel. (ed.) *Through Enemy Eyes* (Heb.) (Ma'arachot, Tel Aviv, 1954)

\- *Behind the Screen* (Heb.) (Ma'arachot, Tel Aviv, 1951)

Sela, Avraham. 'Transjordan, Israel and the 1948 War; Myth, Historiography and Reality,' (*Middle Eastern Studies*, 28\4, 1992)

Shepherd, Naomi. *Ploughing Sand, British Rule in Palestine 1917-1948* (John Murray, London, 1999)

Shlaim, Avi. *Collusion Across the Jordan: King Abdullah, the Zionist Movement, and the Partition of Palestine* (Columbia University Press, New York, 1988)

Tall, Abdullah. *Memoirs* (Heb.) (Ma'arachot, Tel Aviv, 1960)

Tidrick, Kathryn. *Heart-Beguiling Araby, the English Romance with Arabia* (I.B. Tauris, London, 1989 ed.)

Vatikiotis, P.J. *Politics and the Military in Jordan, A Study of the Arab Legion, 1921-1957* (Frank Cass, London, 1967)

Wilson, Mary. *King Abdullah, Britain and the Making of Jordan* (Cambridge University Press, Cambridge, 1987)

Zweig, Ronald. *Britain and Palestine During the Second World War* (Boydell Press for the Royal Historical Society, Suffolk, England, 1986)

NOTES

[1] Royle, *Glubb*, 210.
[2] Royle, *Glubb*, 3.
[3] Glubb, *Soldier*, 261.
[4] Royle, *Glubb*, 65.
[5] Royle, *Glubb*, 67.
[6] Kirkbride, *Crackle of Thorns*, 62.
[7] Avraham Biran, Jerusalem District Commissioner, to the director general, Israel Foreign Ministry, 14 October 1951, ISA FM 2408\13, reporting on a conversation with 'Azmi Nashashibi, the director general of the Jordanian Foreign Ministry. Nashashibi was commenting on Glubb's testimony, in Arabic, at the trial of King Abdullah's assassins. Nashashibi had added that Glubb had adopted 'three beduin children' and that he intended, after retirement, to buy a house and settle in Jordan. 'It is difficult for Glubb to adjust to life in England,' said Nashashibi. See also Jarvis, *Arab Command,* 126-27.
[8] Beith minute, 1 March 1956, to Glubb, 'Note on Egyptian Activities in Jordan,' 22 February 1956, PRO FO 371-121540 VJ1201\2.
[9] 'Memorandum of Conversation,' 18 Nov. 1953, NA RG59, LM60, Roll 5.
[10] Riley (New York) to UNTSO (Jerusalem), 16 June 1952, UNA DAG-1/2.2.5.2.0-1. And the American Ambassador in Amman, Joseph Green, spoke of 'Glubb Pasha's inflexible integrity' (Green to Department of State, 2 March 1953, NA RG 59, LM 60, Palestine and Israel, Foreign Affairs, Roll 2).
[11] Royle, *Glubb*, 412.
[12] See, for example, the editorial in the Israeli Progressive Party daily, *Zmanim*, of 20 October 1953, 'A Sword to Hire,' which called Glubb 'a conscienceless mercenary educated in the tradition of the Black and Tans, representing the dark side of British colonialism'.
[13] Royle, *Glubb*, 343, quoting from Kirkbride to FO, 13 May 1948.
[14] Minute by Burrows, 18 August 1948, PRO FO 371-68831 E11702; and Royle, *Glubb*, 323- 24.
[15] For example, American journalist Harry Levin, in his diary of the 1948 War, *Jerusalem Embattled*, 169, wrote the following entry for 18 May: '[The Arab Legion] must be at about the same place as Titus' cohorts when he "gazed upon Jerusalem the day before its destruction and wept for the sake of the beautiful city". I doubt if Glubb Pasha is weeping.'
[16] Glubb, *Soldier*, 385.
[17] Glubb, *Soldier*, 5.
[18] Glubb, *Soldier*, 6.
[19] Glubb, *Soldier*, 6.
[20] Royle quoting Major R.J.C. Broadhurst, *Glubb*, 451
[21] Dov Steiger (Sion), 'The Arab Legion', undated but from the late 1950s, IDFA 1046\70\\178.
[22] Quoted in Tidrick, *Araby*, 19.

[23] Quoted in Tidrick, *Araby*, 31.

[24] Royle, *Glubb*, 4, 95.

[25] Tidrick, *Araby*, 210-11.

[26] Jarvis, *Arab Command*, 70. I am thankful to Dr. Clinton Bailey for this reference.

[27] Glubb, 'A Note on the Possibility of Raising an Arab Army,' 14 June 1951, PRO FO 816\175.

[28] Furlonge to A.D.M. Ross, FO, 12 February 1953, PRO FO 371-104778 ER1091\63.

[29] Glubb, 'The New Relationship, Notes on Certain Aspects of Anglo-Arab Relations in the Near Future', undated but probably from August 1945, PRO CO 537-2441. Glubb was to repeat many of these points, publicly, in *The New York Times Magazine*, 18 November 1956, in his article (curiously) entitled 'Glubb Pasha Analyzes the Arab Mind'.

[30] Glubb, 'A Note on the Report of [the] Anglo-American Commission', undated but from April-May 1946, SAMECA, Glubb Papers, Transjordan (5).

[31] Glubb, *Soldier*, 37.

[32] Glubb, 'The Situation in Jordania', 15 October 1949, PRO FO 816\148.

[33] Glubb, *Soldier*, 34. Compare this to the 19th Century British ethnologist James Cowles Prichard's descriptions of Middle Eastern head types, as cited in Tidrick, *Araby*, 79-80.

[34] Glubb, 'A Note on the Possibility of Raising an Arab Army', 14 June 1951, PRO FO 816\175.

[35] Glubb, 'A Monthly Report on the Administration of the Trans-Jordan Desert for the Month of January 1939,' 9 February 1939, SAMECA, Glubb Papers, Monthly Reports 1937-1939.

[36] Quoted in Shepherd, *Ploughing Sand,* 166. Perowne was likely speaking of the upper-middle class urban pupils who reached his school rather than poor urban or rural Palestinians.

[37] Glubb, 'The Situation in Jordania', 15 October 1949, PRO FO 816\148.

[38] Glubb, *Soldier*, 269.

[39] Glubb, 'A Monthly Report on the Administration of the Deserts of Transjordan, March 1937', 4 April 1937, PRO CO-831\41\11.

[40] See, for example, Glubb, *Soldier*, 314.

[41] Glubb, 'The Situation in Palestine 10th July 1949', PRO FO 816\147.

[42] Glubb, *Soldier*, 121.

[43] Royle, *Glubb*, 156.

[44] Royle, *Glubb*, 174.

[45] Tidrick, *Araby*, 34.

[46] Al-Nashashibi, *What Happened in the Middle East*, 157. He relates how Glubb spent his leave in 1924 trekking across the Iraqi-Transjordan desert on camel back.

[47] Glubb, 'The Mixture of Races in the Eastern Arab Countries', a lecture delivered in New College, Oxford, on 25 April 1967 (Holywell Press, Oxford, 1967) p.17.

[48] Tidrick, *Araby*, 76.

[49] Quoted in Tidrick, *Araby*, 38.

[50] Glubb, untitled memorandum, undated (but from the 1940s) addressed to 'All British Officers, Arab Legion', SAMECA, Glubb Papers, Transjordan (5).

[51] Glubb, untitled, undated memorandum, SAMECA, Glubb Papers, Transjordan (2).
[52] Glubb, 'Notes on Desert Units', 15 August 1942, SAMECA, Jordan Collection.
[53] Glubb, untitled, undated (but from December 1930) memorandum regarding tribal fighting in southern Transjordan, SAMECA, Glubb Papers, Transjordan.
[54] Glubb, 'A Monthly Report on the Administration of the Deserts of Transjordan, June 1936', 1 July 1936, PRO CO-831\37\3.
[55] Royle, *Glubb*, 185.
[56] See Tidrick, *Araby*, 80-81, on Burton regarding the Egyptians as 'not Arabs,' and 128, on Wilfred Scawan Blunt: 'The Arabic-speaking Copt of the Nile and the Canaanite of Syria are Arab only in language and are without the political instincts inherent in the pure race ... These may never be worthy of their independence, or capable of a self-government of which they have lost the traditions; but they are not real Arabians'
[57] Glubb, 'The Middle East Crisis: A Personal Interpretation' (rev. ed. 1969) 45.
[58] Glubb, 'An (Extremely Conjectural) Memo on Egyptian Policy', 22 October 1955, PRO FO 371-115907.
[59] Glubb, *Soldier*, 32.
[60] Glubb, *Soldier*, 7; and Glubb, *Peace*, 337.
[61] Glubb, *Soldier*, 262.
[62] Glubb, 'Middle East Crisis,' (1969 ed.) 7. See also Glubb to the editor, *The Times* (London), 13 January 1971, where he asserted that he had 'no prejudice whatever against Jews and in many directions I feel for them both sympathy and admiration.' But he also wrote in that letter that the Jews were in many ways responsible for the Gentiles' antagonism towards them (because, for example, of their 'refusal .. to join in the social activities of non-Jews.').
[63] 'Middle East Crisis,' (1969 ed.). One may assume that he was excluding both Sephardi Jews and Israeli Jews from the category of 'west European Jews'.
[64] Glubb, *Soldier*, 7.
[65] See, for example, Glubb, 'Suggested Partition Frontiers in Palestine,' undated but from early 1949, SAMECA, Glubb Papers, Transjordan (5).
[66] Glubb, *Soldier*, 138.
[67] Glubb, *Soldier*, 27.
[68] Glubb, *Soldier*, 28.
[69] Glubb, 'A Further Note on the Palestine Question, June 1946,' PRO CO 537-1856.
[70] Glubb, 'The Mixture of Races in the Eastern Arab Countries.'
[71] Glubb, *Peace*, 243.
[72] Glubb, *Peace*, 274.
[73] Glubb, *Peace*, 243.
[74] Glubb, *Peace*, 242-3.
[75] Glubb, *Peace*, 'Introduction'.
[76] Glubb, *Peace*, 61.
[77] Glubb, *Peace*, 64.
[78] Glubb, *Peace*, 92.
[79] Glubb, *Peace*, 93.
[80] Text of Glubb speech, 6 May 1949, PRO FO 371-75295\E6180.
[81] 'Note by Glubb Pasha,' 19 August 1948, PRO FO 371-68822.
[82] Glubb, *Peace*, 103, 135.

[83] Glubb, *Peace*, 144.
[84] Glubb, *Peace*, 147, 148.
[85] Glubb, *Peace*, 145.
[86] Glubb, *Peace*, 151-2.
[87] Glubb, *Peace*, 155.
[88] Glubb, *Peace*, 160.
[89] Glubb, *Peace*, 161.
[90] Glubb, *Peace*, 163.
[91] Glubb, *Peace*, 167.
[92] Glubb, *Peace*, 161.
[93] Glubb, *Peace*, 178.
[94] Glubb, *Peace*, 178.
[95] Glubb, *Peace*, 183.
[96] Glubb, *Muhammad*, 387.
[97] Glubb, *Muhammad*, 164.
[98] Glubb, *Muhammad*, 196.
[99] Glubb, *Muhammad*, 221.
[100] Glubb, *Muhammad*, 384.
[101] Glubb, *Muhammad*, 294.
[102] Glubb, *Muhammad*, 389.
[103] Glubb, *Peace*, 197.
[104] Glubb, *Peace*, 203.
[105] Glubb, *Peace*, 211-212.
[106] Glubb, *Peace*, 214-5.
[107] Glubb, *Peace*, 230.
[108] Glubb, *Peace*, 214-5.
[109] Glubb, *Peace*, 274.
[110] Glubb, *Peace*, 285.
[111] Glubb, 'Suggested Partition Frontiers in Palestine,' undated but from early 1949, SAMECA, Glubb Papers, Transjordan (5). As we shall see, this charge is also in great measure unfair: Glubb was widely interviewed in the American press and occasionally published articles in important publications, such as *The New York Times Magazine*.
[112] Berlin to Hayter, R. Campbell, Wright (FO, London), 5 April 1943, PRO FO 371-35033.
[113] Glubb, *Peace*, 244.
[114] Glubb, *Peace*, 261.
[115] Glubb, *Arab Legion*, 228-29.
[116] Glubb, 'Middle East Crisis,' 59-60.
[117] Glubb, *Peace*, 262.
[118] Glubb, *Peace*, 263.
[119] Glubb, *Peace*, 263. It is perhaps worth reflecting about Glubb's own problem of dual loyalty at this time.
[120] Glubb, *Peace*, 285.
[121] Glubb, *Peace*, 273.
[122] Glubb, *Peace*, 274.
[123] Glubb, *Peace*, 281.
[124] Glubb, *Peace*, 282.
[125] Glubb, *Soldier*, 45-46.
[126] Gelber, *Jewish-Transjordanian*, 77, quoting Glubb's 'Note on the Reaction in Transjordan in the Event of a European War', 19 September 1935.

[127] Glubb, *Soldier*, 41.

[128] Jarvis, *Arab Command*, 146, says: '... The Arab-Jewish controversy in Palestine [in 1936-1939] did not affect Peake in any way beyond the fact that he did not wish it to spread to the country for which he was responsible.' Jarvis relates an anecdote about several car-loads of Jews from Palestine who visited as-Salt and were stoned 'by about twenty small boys of the village.' Peake had the boys arrested and 'Arab Legionaries caned them soundly on their posteriors to remind them that the people of Transjordan were not concerned in the controversy, and that the old Arab laws of courtesy and hospitality to all comers were to be observed in the country.'

[129] Glubb, 'A Monthly Report on the Administration of the Transjordan Deserts for the Month of May 1936', 11 June 1936, PRO CO 831\37\3.

[130] Glubb, 'A Monthly Report on the Admin of the TJ Deserts for the Month of May 1936', 11 June 1936, PRO CO 831\37\3.

[131] Glubb, 'A Monthly Report on the Administration of the TJ Deserts for the Month of September 1936', 1 October 1936, 'Comments on importance of introduction of radio into Nejd', PRO CO 831\37\3.

[132] See Gelber, *Jewish-Transjordanian*, 77-78.

[133] Glubb, 'A Monthly Report on the Administration of the Deserts of TJ, June 1936', 1 July 1936, PRO CO 831\37\3.

[134] Cox to High Commissioner (Jerusalem), 6 July 1936, accompanying Glubb, 'A Monthly Report ... June 1936', PRO CO 831\37\3.

[135] Wauchope to Secretary of State for Colonies, 27 June 1936, PRO CO 831\39\14.

[136] Wauchope to Ormsby-Gore, 31 August 1936, PRO CO 831\39\14. See also Gelber, *Jewish-Transjordanian*, 93, which gives details of the Jewish Agency's secret financial dispensations to Abdullah at this time.

[137] Glubb, 'A Monthly Report on the Administration of the Deserts of TJ for the Month of July', 1 August 1936, PRO CO 831\37\3.

[138] Glubb, 'A Monthly Report on the Administration of the Deserts of TJ, August 1936', 5 September 1936, PRO CO 831\37\3.

[139] Glubb, 'A Monthly Report on the Admin of the Deserts of TJ, February 1937', 1 March 1937, PRO CO 831\41\11.

[140] Glubb, 'A Monthly Report on the Admin of the Deserts of TJ, March 1937', 4 April 1937, PRO CO 831\41\11.

[141] Glubb, 'A Monthly Report ... March 1937', 4 April 1937, and Glubb, 'A Monthly Report on the Admin of the TJ Deserts, June 1937', 2 July 1937, both in PRO CO 831\41\11.

[142] Peake to Mrs. Ritchie, 18 July 1937, Imperial War Museum (IWM), Peake Papers, Peake Pasha Correspondence, 78\73\3.

[143] Peake to Mrs. Ritchie, 14 November 1937, IWM, Peake Papers, Peake Pasha Correspondence, 78\73\3.

[144] Peake to Mrs. Ritchie, 25 October 1938, IWM, Peake Papers, Peake Pasha Correspondence, 78\73\3. What Peake meant by this vague formulation he made crystal clear the following month: 'In order that the Jews may filch Palestine from the Arabs, we poor British tax-payers must again produce the money [to pay for the troops in Palestine]. All this trouble over some sentimental nonsense about a promise that the Jews should return to Palestine. I do not think that it was ever intended that thousands of Arabs should be shot down in order to carry out a promise which Jews (notorious liars) say was made to them 5,000 years ago. It is a mistake to mix up politics and senti-

ment. There is a sort of clique of sentimental fools in Parliament and the Cabinet who think that we English have a divine mission to put the Jews back in Palestine. Who gave us the divine mission we are not told, nor is it explained why this divine mission should entail killing thousands of Arabs and rendering countless others homeless and miserable...' (Peake to Mrs. Ritchie, 20 November 1938, IWM, Peake Papers, Peake Pasha Correspondence, 78\73\3).

[145] Glubb, *Peace*, 282.

[146] Glubb, 'A Monthly Report on the Administration of the TJ Deserts, July 1937', 2 August 1937, PRO CO 831\41\11. Glubb devoted a page and a half of this report to reflections on the place of 'propaganda' in modern politics. Hitler knew that 'with propaganda any lie could be put across ... It is curious to think that propaganda was almost an English invention - it is generally admitted that it was by studying the British [World] War [I] propaganda that Hitler and Mussolini evolved their methods ... Experiment has proved that the loud and frequent announcement of a simple and forcible idea produces an amazing and overwhelming impression on mass psychology. Hitler partly built up the Third Reich by a continuous repetition of the statement "the Jews are to blame for everything". In Palestine and Transjordan, a not dissimilar wave of mass emotion is being produced by a similar cry, in which, however, the English are replacing the Jews.' It was 'no use' simply dismissing this as 'rubbish,' argued Glubb. He proposed that the British authorities in the Middle East 'exert' themselves to counter such propaganda with 'true ideas.' See also Wilson, *King Abdullah*, 116-24, for Transjordan and the Peel Commission.

[147] Glubb, 'A Monthly Report on the Admin of the TJ Deserts, August 1937', 4 September 1937, PRO CO 831\41\11.

[148] Glubb, 'A Monthly Report on the Administration of the Trans-Jordan Desert for the Month of October 1937', 3 November 1937, SAMECA, Monthly Reports 1937-1939.

[149] Glubb, 'A Monthly Report on the Administration of the Trans-Jordan Desert for the Month of November 1937', undated but from early December 1937, SAMECA, Monthly Reports 1937-1939.

[150] Gelber, *Jewish-Transjordanian*, 127-28.

[151] Glubb, 'A Monthly Report on the Administration of the Trans-Jordan Desert for the Month of August [1938]', 6 September 1938, SAMECA, Glubb Papers, Monthly Reports 1937-1939.

[152] Glubb, 'A Monthly Report on the Administration of the Trans-Jordan Desert for the Month of September 1938', undated but from October 1938, SAMECA, Glubb Papers, Monthly Reports 1937-1939.

[153] Glubb, 'A Monthly Report of the Administration of the Trans-Jordan Desert for the month of November 1938', 4 December 1938, SAMECA, Glubb Papers, Monthly Reports 1937-1939.

[154] Glubb, 'A Monthly Report on the Administration of the Trans-Jordan Desert for the Month of January 1939', 9 February 1939, SAMECA, Glubb Papers, Monthly Reports 1937-1939.

[155] Glubb, 'A Monthly Report for the Month of July 1939', 9 August 1939, SAMECA, Glubb Papers, Monthly Reports 1937-1939.

[156] Glubb, 'A Monthly Report on Transjordan for the Month of November 1939', undated but from December 1939, SAMECA, Glubb Papers, Monthly Reports 1937-1939.

[157] Glubb, 'A Monthly Report on the Administration of the Desert Area for the Month of October 1938', undated but from November 1938, SAMECA, Glubb Papers, Monthly Reports 1937-1939.

[158] Unsigned, 'Summary of Intelligence - Palestine and Transjordan', 24 March 1939, PRO CO-732\84\15.

[159] Glubb, 'Month of March 1939', 8 April 1939, SAMECA, Glubb Papers, Monthly Reports 1937-1939. Apart from relieving the pressure on the rebels, Husseini - who, in Glubb's words, 'aspires to be the Hitler of Palestine' - certainly wished to topple, or at least embarrass, Abdullah, 'his principal competitor in the Arab world.' According to Glubb's intelligence, there was also a group of disaffected Transjordanians in Damascus - Muhammad Ali Bey al Ajlouni, Dr. Subhi Abu Ghanima, and Suleiman Pasha Saudi - who were party to this effort to 'foment rebellion in Transjordan.'

[160] Glubb, 'Month of March 1939', 8 April 1939, SAMECA, Glubb Papers, Monthly Reports 1937-1939. According to Glubb, some rebel band leaders in Palestine objected to setting aflame northern Jordan, fearing that this would endanger 'their lines of communication between Palestine and Syria' (see Glubb, 'Monthly Report for the Month of April 1939', 7 May 1939, SAMECA, Glubb Papers, Monthly Reports 1937-1939).

[161] 'Despatch of the Operations Carried out by the British Forces in Palestine and Transjordan. Period 1st November, 1938 to 31st March, 1939', Force HQ, Jerusalem, 24 April 1939, SAMECA, Haining Papers, puts rebel casualties in the 11 March engagement at '45 dead (24 bodies recovered)' and British-Transjordanian casualties at one dead and five wounded. The Legion captured 23 rifles and 722 sticks of dynamite. See also, Glubb, *Arab Legion*, 235-37, and Jarvis, *Arab Command*, 148.

[162] Unsigned, 'Summary of Intelligence - Palestine and Transjordan', 24 March 1939, PRO CO 732\84\15.

[163] Glubb, 'Monthly Report for the Month of April 1939', 7 May 1939, SAMECA, Glubb Papers, Monthly Reports 1937-1939.

[164] This description of the Transjordanian-rebel clashes in March 1939 is based largely on Glubb, 'Month of March 1939', 8 April 1939, SAMECA, Glubb Papers, Monthly Reports 1937-1939.

[165] 'Despatch on the Operations Carried out by the British Forces in Palestine and Transjordan. Period 1st April, 1939 to 30th July, 1939', Force HQ, Jerusalem, 30 July 1939, SAMECA, Haining Papers; and Glubb, *Arab Legion*, 240-43.

[166] Glubb, 'Monthly Report for the Month of April 1939', 7 May 1939, SAMECA, Glubb Papers, Monthly Reports 1937-1939.

[167] Glubb, 'A Monthly Report for the Month of May, 1939', undated but from June 1939, SAMECA, Glubb Papers, Monthly Reports 1937-1939.

[168] Glubb, *Arab Legion*, 243.

[169] Glubb, 'A Monthly Report for the Month of June 1939', 4 July 1939, SAMECA, Glubb Papers, Monthly Reports 1937-1939.

[170] Glubb, 'A Monthly Report for the Month of July, 1939', 9 August 1939, SAMECA, Glubb Papers, Monthly Reports 1937-1939.

[171] Glubb, 'A Monthly Report for the Month of July, 1939', 9 August 1939, SAMECA, Glubb Papers, Monthly Reports 1937-1939.

[172] Glubb, 'A Monthly Report on Transjordan for the Month of November 1939', undated but from December 1939, SAMECA, Glubb Papers, Monthly Reports 1937-1939.

[173] Khalil al Sakakini, *"Such Am I, Oh World", Diaries of Khalil al-Sakakini*, 212, entry for 27 July 1942.

[174] Glubb, in *Peace*, 289, deliberately papers over this disparity with: 'Both Jews and Palestinians enlisted in the British Army.'

[175] Glubb, 'A Monthly Report for the Month of August 1939', undated but from September 1939, SAMECA, Glubb Papers, Monthly Reports 1937-1939.

[176] Glubb, 'A Monthly Report on Transjordan for the Month of November 1939', undated but from December 1939, SAMECA, Glubb Papers, Monthly Reports 1937-1939.

[177] 'Information from Transjordan', by 'Lemi,' 13 May 1941, CZA S25-22131.

[178] Glubb, 'A Monthly Report on Transjordan for the Month of February 1940', 8 March 1940, SAMECA, Glubb Papers, Monthly Reports 1940. Incidentally, Hitler, who met Haj Amin al Husseini in Berlin on 30 November 1941, came away impressed by the Mufti and his 'blue eyes.' Hitler decided that the Mufti was not a real Arab but of Aryan stock.

[179] Royle, *Glubb*, 259.

[180] Glubb, *Britain and the Arabs,* 237-48; and Somerset de Chair, letter to *The Times* (London), 24 March 1986.

[181] Glubb, *Britain and the Arabs*, 251-62.

[182] Glubb, 'A Monthly Report on TJ for the Month of December 1941', PRO FO 371-31383.

[183] Glubb to Sir Arthur Rucker, office of the Minister of State, Cairo, 12 November 1942, PRO FO 921\47.

[184] Glubb, *Soldier*, 59. Glubb was again to refer to this episode in 1971 in his book *Peace*, 291, where he wrote that 'a few British officers serving the Jordanian Government,' including himself, had 'drawn up a memorandum,' arguing that 'partition seemed to be the only solution,' and Moyne had agreed. But I have found no trace of this memorandum nor have I found any contemporary evidence, from 1942-45, indicating that Glubb at this time favoured partition. Rather, as his subsequent memoranda seem to imply, Glubb appears to have been more inclined during those years towards the Duke of Devonshire's attitude: '...partition scarcely seems worth discussing. It is possible to make a fair division of a partridge or a duck between two reasonable human beings, but to attempt a similar operation for the benefit of two wild animals, both convinced that they are fully entitled to the whole, merely leads to the precipitation of a triangular contest and to incurring the hostility of both beneficiaries. A long experience of my in-laws and a limited one of the Near East have driven me to the conclusion that human beings, when actuated by religious motives, are certainly no less unreasonable than wildcats.' Devonshire, a senior Foreign Office official, seemed to favour giving all of Palestine to the Jews after assuring Arab rule in Libya and Syria, while enabling disenchanted Arabs to 'migrate' from Palestine to Libya (minute by Duke of Devonshire to Secretary of State for the Colonies, 27 January 1943, PRO CO 733\443\10). Lord Moyne was assassinated by LHI gunmen in Cairo in November 1944.

[185] Glubb, 'Note on Post-War Settlements in the Middle East', 15 November 1942, PRO CO 732\88\9. The at the time much-discussed idea, among British, Arab and Zionist officials, of an Arab 'federation,' that might or might not include Palestine, is reviewed in Porath, *Arab Unity*, 58-148.

[186] MacMichael to Stanley, 12 December 1942, SAMECA, Glubb Papers, Monthly Reports 1942.

[187] Glubb to British Resident, Amman, 31 December 1942, PRO CO 732\88\9.
[188] Glubb, 'A Further Note on Peace Terms in the Middle East', 25 May 1943, SAMECA, Glubb Papers, Transjordan\Iraq (8).
[189] It is perhaps worth noting in this connection that Glubb's prejudices or ignorance, or blindness, about the Holocaust led him in 1949 to glibly compare the Palestinians' catastrophe of 1948 to the murder of the six million Jews of Europe (a comparison, indeed, still drawn by many Palestinian Arabs): '...It must be recollected that the Palestinians have suffered, in 18 months, as much as the Jews suffered in the late war in Europe' (Glubb, 'A Note on the Future of Jerusalem', 18 July 1949, PRO FO 816\147).
[190] Newbold to Glubb, 27 June 1943, SAMECA, Glubb Papers, Monthly Reports 1940.
[191] Zweig, *Britain and Palestine*, 175.
[192] Moyne to Foreign Secretary Anthony Eden, 1 March 1944, PRO FO 921\148.
[193] Note by Oliver Stanley, Secretary of State for Colonies, and appended letter MacMichael to Stanley, 16 January 1944, PRO FO 921\148.
[194] Kirkbride to MacMichael, 28 November 1944, PRO FO 921\149.
[195] Author signature unclear, 'Note on conversation with General Nuri Said, the Iraqi Prime Minister and the Iraqi Minister of Foreign Affairs in Baghdad on 5th and 6th December 1944', PRO FO 921\149.
[196] Glubb, 'A Note on the Solution of the Syrian Problem', undated but probably from 1944 or 1945, SAMECA, Glubb Papers, Transjordan (5).
[197] Glubb, 'The New Relationship, Notes on Certain Aspects of Anglo-Arab Relations in the Near Future', undated but from August 1945, PRO CO 537-2441.
[198] Glubb, undated, but from 1946-7, SAMECA, Glubb Papers, Transjordan (5). Perhaps this ditty was appended to 'A Note on the Report of Anglo-American Commission' (see below), serving as its cover sheet.
[199] Glubb, 'Is it Feasible?' with covering note Glubb to Kirkbride, 31 March 1946, PRO FO 916\83. Glubb submitted 15 copies to the committee and 8 to Kirkbride, for onward transmission to London.
[200] Glubb during these years repeatedly stressed the importance of the Jewish lobby in American decision-making regarding the Middle East - but consistently failed to mention that the Holocaust, and its legacy of horror and guilt, as well as Christian philo-Semitic feelings, played a large part in moulding American policy.
[201] Glubb, 'A Note on the Report of Anglo-American Commission', May 1946, PRO FO 816\83, with covering note Glubb to Kirkbride, 13 May 1946.
[202] Glubb to Kirkbride, 11 July 1946, and texts of parliamentary question and answer, both in PRO FO 816/84.
[203] 'Record of a Meeting with His Majesty King Abdullah on 1.6.1946', unsigned, undated, SAMECA, Alan Cunningham Papers, VI\2.
[204] Glubb to Attlee (?), 12 May 1946, CZA S25-7770. The letter exists only in its Hebrew translation; the original English version (if there really was one) is missing. In light of the May 1946 memorandum and its proposed siphoning off to the United States, Britain and the Commonwealth and so on, of batches of DPs, the translation seems to be of a genuine letter. But the differences in the numbers and the destinations, and various phrases used in other parts of the letter, indicate that either the original letter was mistranslated in parts or that a clever hand had used a real letter to someone other than Attlee or a

memorandum by Glubb and grafted on to it additions of his own. The signature – 'Brigadier John Frederic [sic] Glubb' - is also curious (Frederic was the Christian name of Glubb's father). See Gelber, *Jewish-Transjordanian*, 213 and 216 n. 70, for further information on this document.

[205] Glubb, 'A Further Note on the Palestine Question, June 1946', PRO CO 537\1856. For a later comparison between Zionism and the Crusaders, see, for example, Glubb, *Soldier*, 225: 'The Crusaders conquered a greater area of territory and held it for a hundred years - but there are no Crusaders now. Selfish violence sooner or later brings retribution, though it may be long coming.'

[206] Undated but with a covering note from Glubb to Field Marshal Lord Montgomery, 13 July 1946, PRO WO 216\207. Glubb wrote: 'The present situation is so precarious and the introduction of further contingents of Jews might lead to such disastrous results for GB, that I am daily more convinced that partition is the only solution.'

[207] Glubb, 'A Note on Partition as a Solution of the Palestine Problem', PRO WO 216\207.

[208] 'J.M.M.' - possibly John Martin - minute, 20 January 1947, PRO CO 537\1856.

[209] Glubb, 'A Further Note on Partition as a Solution of the Palestine Question', undated but from second half of 1946, PRO CO 537\1856.

[210] Glubb, undated but with covering note Glubb to Kirkbride, 16 January 1947, 'A Note on the Exact Siting of the Frontier in the Event of the Adoption of Partition', PRO FO 816\86.

[211] Glubb to Kirkbride, 10 January 1947, PRO FO 816\86.

[212] Glubb to Beeley, 14 December 1946, quoted in Norton, 'Pasha', 222.

[213] Beeley minute to Glubb memorandum, 20 December 1946, quoted in James Lunt, *Glubb*, 128.

[214] Quoted in Lunt, *Glubb*, 126.

[215] Glubb, 'A Note on the Visit of a Trans-Jordan Delegation to London,' December [should be November] 1947, SAMECA, Glubb Papers, Transjordan (4).

[216] Gelber, *Jewish-Transjordanian*, 205, quotes at length from Ben-Gurion's memorandum of 19 July 1946, which was entitled 'Political Assumptions'.

[217] Kirkbride to T. Wikeley, Eastern Department, FO, 29 July 1946, PRO FO 816\85.

[218] Untitled report by Sasson, 12 August 1946, CZA S25-9036; and Zeev Sharef (Sharif) (secretary of the Jewish Agency Political Department) to I.J. Linton (political secretary of Jewish Agency office, London), 13 August 1946, CZA S25-9036. The Jewish Agency gave the partition plan the appropriate codename 'Solomon.'

[219] Untitled report by Sasson, 19 August 1946, CZA S25-9036. For these Jewish Agency-Abdullah meetings, see Gelber, *Jewish-Transjordanian*, 207-11.

[220] Kirkbride to FO, 23 August 1946 (No. 1387), and Kirkbride to FO, 23 August 1946 (No. 1364), both in PRO FO 816\85. The relations between Kirkbride and Abdullah were such that the King often confided in Kirkbride on the most sensitive issues. As Kirkbride put it in a letter to Burrows in 1948: 'You will probably realize that, as a result of our long association (twenty-seven years), King Abdullah has got into the habit of informing what he has in mind in both official and private matters with a frankness which is some-

times startling and, naturally, I report anything which is of interest to HMG. The position is useful but it has its difficulties ...' (Kirkbride to Burrows, 16 February 1948, PRO FO 371-68819 E2832\14\80G).

[221] Pirie-Gordon to Bevin, 30 July 1947, quoted in Norton, 'Pasha', 241.

[222] Zvi Maimon to Yaakov Shimoni and Reuven Zaslani, 14 September 1947, CZA S25-9013.

[223] Gelber, *Jewish-Transjordanian*, 223.

[224] Glubb, *Soldier*, 26.

[225] This is incorrect. Whereas the minority, right-wing Revisionist school of Zionism still laid claim to Transjordan as part of the eventual Jewish homeland, mainstream Zionism, as represented by the Jewish Agency Executive and its chairman, David Ben-Gurion, no longer seriously advocated such a programme, even in private, and it was certainly no part of the mainstream Zionist policy or platform.

[226] Glubb, 'A Note on the Visit of a Trans-Jordan Delegation to London', December [sic, should be November] 1947, SAMECA, Glubb Papers, Transjordan (4). Glubb also argued, as he was consistently to do in the 1950s, that the Arab Legion also represented a bulwark against Soviet penetration or takeover of the region.

[227] Pirie-Gordon to P. Garran, FO, 27 August 1947, PRO FO 816\88.

[228] Kirkbride to FO, 16 October 1947, PRO FO 816\89. A few days before, Kirkbride had informed the FO of Abdullah's meeting with 'Azzam Pasha and Samir Rifa`i, in which Abdullah - according to Kirkbride - had 'maintained that it was folly to talk of ejecting the Jews from Palestine. He doubted firstly whether the Arabs were capable of doing so and was sure, secondly, that the civilized world would [not] permit them to do so if they were.' According to Abdullah, the others agreed and concurred that 'the wise thing to do' was to 'come to terms with the Jews' while trying to restrict them to 'as small a part of Palestine as was possible' (Kirkbride to FO, 11 October 1947, PRO FO 816\89).

[229] 'Off-the-Record Talks in Transjordan of Two British Correspondents,' unsigned, Amman, 21 October 1947, CZA S25-9038. The 4-page memorandum appears to have been written by one of the two journalists (perhaps Jon Kimche?) and then given to the Jewish Agency. The journalists also quoted Rifa'i as saying that he did not want 'a Jewish state on his eastern border. "The Jews are a people to be feared", he said, "look what they have done in only 27 years. They began with [an] insignificant community of 60,000 in 1920 and now are 700,000 in Palestine, and have mobilized their money and influence to obtain a State from the UNO. Give them another 25 years and they will be all over the Middle East, in our country and Syria and Lebanon, in Iraq and Egypt. ... They were responsible for starting the two world wars we have known in our generation ... yes, I have read and studied, and I know they were behind Hitler at the beginning of his movement."' The two journalists called Rifa`i's statement 'remarkable.' Rifa`i too supported Transjordanian entry into Palestine, but as part of a Greater Syria design: '"We all believe in the Greater Syria scheme, and eventually Arab Palestine, Syria and T.J. will become one country, they must",' they quoted Rifa`i as saying.

[230] Bevin to Kirkbride, 26 October 1947, PRO FO 816\89.

[231] Kirkbride to Bevin, 29 October 1947, PRO FO 816\89.

[232] Burrows minute, 7 November 1947, PRO FO 371-62194 E10206.

[233] Burrows minute, 28 November 1947, PRO FO 371-62194 E10806. As Norton ('Pasha', 250-51) has pointed out, in late 1947 British officials took care to refer to the prospective Transjordanian takeover of the Arab areas of Palestine as 'Abdullah's plan' or 'Transjordan's plan,' as if to deny any British involvement or authorship. The officials were perennially concerned that others might conclude that Britain had 'engineered the whole scheme...'
[234] Bevin to Kirkbride, 11 November 1947, PRO FO 816\89. A number of words were garbled in the telegram's key sentence introducing the subject. It begins: 'The disadvantage of a partition between a Jewish state and (? group omitted ? - an Arab one) would be ...' But from the continuation it is clear that the reference is to Abdullah\Jordan and not a Palestinian Arab state.
[235] Sasson to Shertok, 20 Nov. 1947, CZA S25-1699.
[236] 'Conversation with Abdullah 17.11.47', Ezra Danin, undated, CZA S25-4004.
[237] 'Meeting of the Arab Section of the Political Department of the Jewish Agency (13 May 1948)', in Gedalia Yogev\Israel State Archives, ed., *Political and Diplomatic Documents, December 1947-May 1948*, 789.
[238] Golda Meir at meeting of 12 May 1948, *The People's Administration, Protocols 18 April-13 May 1948*, 40. Meir's much-later version of the 17 November meeting (Golda Meir, *My Life,* 176) is misleading and brief to the point of obfuscation.
[239] Golda Meir statement on 12 May 1948, *The People's Administration*, 41.
[240] Kirkbride to FO, 17 November 1947, PRO FO 371-62194 E10806\30\80. This cable seems to demonstrate that, whatever the depth of Kirkbride's knowledge about developments in Jordan and however profound his relations with Abdullah, he was not, at this time, being kept completely abreast in real time of the king's diplomatic-political moves vis-à-vis the Yishuv.
[241] Glubb, 'A Note on the Effect of the Palestine Situation on the Future of Trans-Jordan', December 1947, PRO FO 371-68818 E2012\14\80.
[242] Glubb, *Soldier*, 60.
[243] Glubb, *Soldier*, 60-62.
[244] Glubb, *Peace*, 298. Most of the Asian and African members of the UN in 1947 were Muslim.
[245] Glubb, *Soldier*, 162.
[246] Glubb, *Soldier*, 146.
[247] Glubb, *Soldier*, 147.
[248] Glubb, *Peace*, 298.
[249] Kirkbride to Burrows, 8 December 1947, PRO FO 816\111.
[250] FO to Kirkbride, 11 December 1947, PRO FO 371-6295 E11610\3\80.
[251] Harold Beeley memorandum, 6 January 1948, PRO FO 371-68364 E101\G.
[252] Kirkbride to Bevin, 12 January 1948, and Kirkbride to Bevin, 13 January 1948, both in PRO FO 816\115.
[253] Kirkbride to Bevin, 12 January 1948, PRO FO-816\115.
[254] Bevin to Kirkbride, 10 January 1948 (dispatched 12 January), PRO FO 816\112.
[255] Kirkbride to Bevin, 20 January 1948, PRO FO 816\112.
[256] Glubb, *Soldier*, 72-73.
[257] Packard, 'Trans-Jordan - A Possible Forecast of Events in Palestine', 5 March 1948, PRO FO 371-68369.
[258] Glubb, *Soldier*, 62-66. Alec Kirkbride, *From the Wings,* 12, pithily supports this version of what happened, on the basis, he writes, of accounts 'given to

me' by Glubb and Abul Huda. Kirkbride had remained in Amman but had been consulted by Whitehall while the Jordanian-British meetings were taking place. 'I advised the Secretary of State that I was convinced that the Jordanians were honest in their plan to restrict their occupation in Palestine to the Arab zone and to avoid a clash between the Arab Legion and the Jewish forces.' But Kirkbride added: '... but it should have been evident to all of us concerned ... that the chances of a peaceful occupation being affected by the Arab Legion were so small as to be negligible ... I reached the conclusion that war between the Arabs and the Jews was inevitable and that, when it came, it would be impossible for the Jordanians to stand aloof from the conflict. Public sentiment throughout the Arab world would be more powerful than the good intentions and promises expressed to Mrs. Myerson ... Glubb and the Jordanian Ministers were not long in arriving at the same conclusion ...'

[259] Pirie-Gordon to Burrows, 28 January 1948, PRO FO 371-68366 E17301\11\65G.

[260] Wright, 'Brief for Conversation with Transjordan Prime Minister on Palestine', 6 February 1948, PRO FO 371-68367.

[261] Burrows, minute, 9 February 1948, PRO FO 371-68368 E2696. A Transjordanian, or joint Transjordanian-Egyptian takeover of the Negev, creating territorial continuity between Britain's Middle East allies or protectorates in the Mashreq and Maghreb - Jordan and Iraq and Egypt - remained a recurrent theme in British geopolitical thinking before, and indeed after, the signing of the Israel-Jordan General Armistice Agreement in April 1949. For example, Bevin again raised the idea of a 'corridor' linking Gaza and 'Aqaba on 25 May 1948 (Bevin to Kirkbride, PRP FO 816\121). For Britain's continuing interest in the idea, see Asia, *The Focus of the Conflict*. In a further minute, Burrows wrote that Bevin 'did not object to the substance of the above minute being confidentially discussed with the State Department' (Burrows addition on 16 February 1948 to minute of 9 February, PRO FO 371-68368 E2696).

[262] Abul Huda, London, to Rais al Diwan, Amman, 8 February 1948, PRO FO 816\112.

[263] Bevin to Kirkbride, 'Conversation with the Transjordan Prime Minister', 9 February 1948, PRO FO 371-68366. As Nevo, *King Abdallah and Palestine*, 91-2, puts it, Abdullah interpreted Bevin's silent response to Abul Huda's statement of intent as tantamount to a 'green light.'

[264] Foreign Office to Amman, 10 February 1948, PRO FO 371-68818 E1788.

[265] Kirkbride to FO, 13 February 1948, PRO FO 371-68367 E2163\G.

[266] Campbell to FO, 7 February 1948, PRO FO 371-68366 E1832\11\65G.

[267] Cunningham to Colonial Secretary, 27 January 1948, PRO CO 537-3901.

[268] British Military HQ, Palestine, 'Extract from "Fortnightly Intelligence Newsletter"', No. 62, 27 February 1948, IDFA 1046\70\\175.

[269] Cunningham to J.M. Martin, CO, 24 February 1948, CO 537-3896. Cunningham had met King Abdullah at Shuneh at the end of January 1948, at the King's 'urgent request.' The King, reported Cunningham, 'was clearly most distressed at our leaving Palestine and asked me once or twice if we were not going to stay on whatever happened. On the Palestine question he was gloomy. He said that every Arab criminal in the Mid-East was pouring in there [a reference to the ALA troops then infiltrating into Palestine] ... He described the areas in Palestine where he himself had a following as being

Nablus and Hebron and made some non-committal remarks about what action he would take when we went ... When I made some remark as to the essential need to safeguard Jerusalem, he immediately asked whether he should take it over when we left. I replied hastily that I was sure satisfactory arrangements would be made ...' (Cunningham to Martin, CO, 2 February 1948, PRO CO 537-3896. Martin responded on 12 February (letter in same file) - after the Abul Huda-Bevin talk in London - with the following: '...Abdullah ... does not seem to have given away much about his future intentions. His Prime Minister, next whom I sat at Louis Spears' Arab Dining Club the other day, was equally non-committal. Is the impression we have here from the latest news about the Arab "militia" dispersed in Samaria correct, that the way may be open for a fairly peaceful transfer to Abdullah's authority in the region as soon as we pull out, or is control from Syria more likely?' It seems that Martin, of the Colonial Office, was not privy to what had transpired in Bevin's office on 7 February.)

[270] Minutes of Cabinet meeting of 22 March 1948, PRO CAB 128\12.

[271] Bevin to Kirkbride, 5 May 1948, PRO FO 816\119.

[272] See Houstoun-Boswall, Beirut, to Kirkbride, 9 May 1948, PRO FO 816\118.

[273] Bevin to Marshall, 'Note', undated but with covering letter M.R. Wright (FO) to Lewis Douglas (US Embassy, London), 22 May 1948, PRO FO 371-68830 E7224\28\80\G. The recurring Transjordanian depiction of the impending push as designed to uphold 'law and order' in the Arab areas of Palestine was, of course, hogwash. From the first, Abdullah's intention - as supported by Whitehall - had been to add the Arab areas of Palestine to Transjordan. But the additional Transjordanian-Glubb explanation, that the invasion-occupation of the West Bank by the Legion was necessary in order to 'save' it from Israeli conquest was probably heartfelt and sincere - and accurate. In the absence of a serious Arab force in place to prevent it, there can be no doubt that the Haganah\IDF would eventually have overrun the West Bank and reached the Jordan River (Glubb, *Soldier*, 96: 'If the Israeli forces had moved forward on May 15th and the Arab Legion had not crossed into Palestine, the Jews in a very short time would have conquered all Palestine up to the Jordan.')

[274] Unsigned, untitled report, Amman, 28 January 1948, with covering note British Legation, Amman, to Eastern Department, FO, 30 January 1948, PRO FO 816\116.

[275] Unsigned, 'The Arab Legion', 7 January 1948, IDFA 500\48\\60.

[276] Unsigned, 'The Mufti and His Relations with the Mayors', 11 January 1948, IDFA 500\48\\60.

[277] Unsigned, 'An Opposition Headed by Muhammad Ali al-Ja`abri', 27 January 1948, IDFA 500\48\\60.

[278] 'Hiram' to Arab Department, Haganah Intelligence Service, 26 February 1948, HA 105\23 gimel.

[279] 'Haganah Intelligence Service Information, Daily Summary', Haganah Intelligence Service, 21 January 1948, IDFA 900\52\\58.

[280] Glubb, 'A Plan for the Military Training of the People', 25 June 1949, PRO FO 816\157.

[281] 'Naim' to 'Tene (Ayin),' 5 April 1948, IDFA 922\1975\\1208; and 'Avner' to 'Tene (Ayin),' 1 April 1948, IDFA 8275\49\\126.

[282] Village file on Masmiya al Kabira, HA 105\134.

[283] For mention of some of these visits, see 'Information from Arab Newspapers', 31 March 1948, and 4 April 1948, both by Haganah Intelligence Service and both in IDFA, 4944\49\\504; 'Arab Affairs Information Bulletin', by 'Yavne,' 22 March 1948, IDFA 500\48\\55; Yogev (ed.), *Political and Diplomatic Documents, December 1947-May 1948*, editorial note, 458; and 'British Connections with Transjordan Arab Legion', 27 May 1948, by Michael Comay, ISA FM 2513\2. See also Nevo, *Abdallah*, 125.

[284] Kirkbride to Bevin, 10 February 1948, PRO FO 816\116.

[285] See Glubb to British Army Headquarters, Palestine, 25 March 1948, and Chief Secretariat, Jerusalem, to British Legation, Amman, 5 April 1948, both in PRO FO 816\117.

[286] 'Annexes to Information Circular No. 223, 10\5\48', Operations\'Hashmonai' to 'Michmash,' IDFA 4944\49\\499.

[287] Glubb, *Soldier*, 82-84. It is possible that the reference to the reconstruction of the 'Wadi Kelt track' in the Haganah intelligence report of 12 April ('Annexes to Intelligence Circular No. 167', 13 April 1948, 'Hashmonai' to 'Michmash,' IDFA 2605\49\\2) should be seen in this context.

[288] J.P.Garran, draft reply to parliamentary question, April 1947, PRO FO 371-62192 E3394, and J.P. Garran, 'The Arab Legion', 15 October 1947, PRO FO 62193 E9748.

[289] Glubb, 'A Note on the Reorganization of the Arab Legion', May 1947, PRO FO 371-62193 E6296; and Glubb, 'Arab Legion Reorganisation Proposal 1947', undated but from November-December 1947, PRO FO 371-62194 E11487.

[290] War Office, 'Cabinet Chiefs of Staff Committee Note by the War Office', 15 January 1948, FO 371-68827 E848G.

[291] Minute by L.F.L. Pyman, FO, 7 January 1948, PRO FO 371-68827 E449. The War Office's view, even before the Abul Huda-Bevin meeting, was quite forthright: 'As a result of our evacuation of Palestine it seems very probable that King Abdullah's influence will be extended over considerable areas of Arab Palestine ... King Abdullah may very well be called upon ... to restore law and order in large areas of Arab Palestine ...' ('Annex I, Appreciation by the Chiefs of Staff of the Minimum Size Which Could be Contemplated for the Arab Legion in Our Own Interests').

[292] At the start of April 1948, the War Office agreed to provide the Legion with '350' Marmon Harrington armoured cars though it seems a much smaller number actually reached the Legion by the end of May (see Norton, 'Pasha', 273).

[293] Various Middle East Land Forces and British ME Office cables in PRO FO 371-68828 E3005\28\80 and E3172\28\80G; and 'Information Sheet No. 180, 21.4.48', 'Hashmonai to 'Michmash', IDFA 4944\49\\499.

[294] Kirkbride to Bevin, 23 May 1948, PRO FO 816\121; and Ilan, *Origin*, 48-49, 121-22.

[295] Tall, *Memoirs*, 67.

[296] Steiger, 'The Arab Legion', cites an intercepted communication from Glubb to Transjordan's defence minister, in which Glubb speaks of '8,900' soldiers in the Legion before 15 May 1948. Sion says that with police, trainees, auxiliary volunteers, and so on, the Legion numbered '10,000.' In his memoirs, Tall (*Memoirs*, 66) speaks of '9,050,' of whom '1,200' were Jordanian irregulars. A Haganah intelligence report of 28 April 1948, 'The Legion Order of Battle at the End of April (Appears Reliable) from Jerusalem [District] In-

telligence Files', by 'Hashmonai,' IDFA 922\75\\283, says the Arab Legion had a complement of 'about 8,500,' with the TJFF, then in the process of disbandment, numbering another '2,600' (some TJFF personnel were at the time being inducted into the AL).

[297] Glubb, *Soldier*, 90.

[298] Glubb, *Soldier*, 92, 94; and Kirkbride, *Wings*, 28. In a memorandum prepared by the FO Research Department and 'redrafted' by Glubb, the total Arab Legion strength crossing the Jordan via the Allenby Bridge was put at 'about 5,000' ('The Part Played by the Arab Legion in the Arab-Jewish Hostilities in Palestine 1948-49', August 1950, with covering note Glubb to Kirkbride, 21 October 1950, PRO FO 816\170). IDF Central Front's intelligence officer, Dan Ram, some time in the second half of 1948 estimated that there were in Palestine some 4000-4500 Legionnaires during the early battles of the war (meaning in the second half of May) (Dan Ram, C Front/Intelligence, 'The Transjordan Army – The Legion', undated, IDFA 863/50//363). The British Chiefs of Staff Joint Planning Staff on 1 April 1948, in 'Trusteeship Proposal for Palestine - Security Problems Involved, Report by the Joint Planning Staff, Appendix', PRO CO 537-3897, wrote that the legion 'comprises three mechanized regiments and fifteen garrison companies totalling 7,400 men, well organised and equipped.' It is worth noting that in September 1948 General Yigael Yadin, the IDF's head of operations, reported to the Israeli cabinet that the Legion 'now' had '4,500' troops in the country 'in active units' - surely an underestimate (see Yadin's report to the cabinet, 8 September 1948, protocols of Israel's cabinet meetings, ISA).

Glubb's numbers tend to be on the low side, with the aim of aggrandizing the Legion's success. Glubb says that the Haganah (later IDF) force that faced his Legionnaires was '65,000' strong. In truth, the Haganah on 15 May numbered 30-35,000. Only part of this force faced the Legion, and some of the troops were initially without arms and many were rear echelon, base camp troops, not combat soldiers (as, essentially, all the Legionnaires who crossed the Jordan in May 1948 were).

In 1948 a British Army regiment normally consisted of two battalions; the Legion's 'regiments', of one battalion each.

[299] 'Haganah Intelligence Service Information, Daily Summary', Haganah Intelligence Service, 2 March 1948, IDFA 900\52\\58.

[300] Glubb, *Soldier*, 210-11, says that some of the new troops reached the line after only '15 days' of training.

[301] Glubb, *Soldier*, 227. Norton, 'Pasha', 296-97, says that the Legion numbered '14,000' soldiers by November 1948.

[302] Norton, 'Pasha' 334-35, suggests that there may have been as many as '190 non-commissioned officers,' but this would seem to be an exaggeration.

[303] Norton, 'Pasha', 333.

[304] Kirkbride to Bevin, 8 May 1948, PRO FO 816\118; and Norton, 'Pasha', 333.

[305] Glubb, *Soldier*, 133.

[306] Norton, 'Pasha', 335; Bevin to Kirkbride, 7 May 1948, PRO FO 816\118; and Kirkbride to Burrows, 13 May 1948, PRO FO 371-68854 E7202. Kirkbride managed to calm Glubb: 'I have become a master in soothing temperamental people, I have had no lack of practice during the past weeks, when my days [sic] work started frequently with the pacification of the King, the Prime Minister and Glubb (in that order).'

[307] Glubb, who probably was not aware of the extent to which non-Israelis were beefing up the IDF - especially the Israel Air Force and Navy - made this point somewhat obliquely in Glubb to Kirkbride, 16 June 1948, PRO FO 816\123.

[308] Glubb, *Soldier*, 134.

[309] Norton, 'Pasha', 350-51.

[310] See, for example, 'Meeting of Brigadier Lash with Arab Legion Officers in Jerusalem', 'Yeruham', IDF Intelligence Service, 8 July 1948, ISA 2569\13, which conveys a report by an Arab agent that Glubb's deputy, Lash, had told a gathering of Legion officers that '75 additional Britons' were about to reach the Legion units in Jerusalem.

[311] See, for example, Kirkbride to Bevin, 15 August 1948, PRO FO 816\127; and Kirkbride to Burrows, 17 August 1948, PRO FO 816\127. Glubb, quoted in the last letter, once explained the British officers' presence in the West Bank thus: 'What happened was that once or twice officers who have got bored sitting doing nothing in Zerka [in East Jordan] ... during the truce, have gone over for a night or two to see their friends [in the West Bank]. They have been told not to do it again.'

[312] Nevo, *Abdallah*, 92.

[313] 'Meeting: S. Silverman, M. Rosette - E. Bevin (Scarborough, 20 May 1948)', unsigned, 20 May 1948, in Yehoshua Freundlich (ed.), *Documents on the Foreign Policy of Israel, May-September 1948*, I, p.41.

[314] Royle, *Glubb*, 353-57.

[315] For the Arab exodus from Palestine, see Morris, *Birth.*

[316] Avraham Sela, 'Transjordan, Israel and the 1948 War: Myth, Historiography and Reality', *MES*, 28\4 (1992), 627, disagrees: 'The central thesis of this article is that the conditions and basic assumptions that had constituted the foundations of the unwritten agreement between Abdullah and the Jewish Agency regarding the partition of Palestine as early as the summer of 1946 were altered so substantively during the unofficial war (November 1947-May 1948) as to render that agreement antiquated and impracticable.'

[317] 'Tene Information, Daily Summary', Haganah Intelligence Service, 19 April 1948, IDFA 900\52\\58.

[318] 'Tene Information, Daily Summary', Haganah Intelligence Service, 25 April 1948, IDFA 500\52\\58.

[319] 'Tene Information, Daily Summary', Haganah Intelligence Service, 5 May 1948, IDFA 500\52\\58.

[320] See Alexandroni Brigade intelligence officer to brigades, Alexandroni battalions, etc., 'Information Circular', 26 April 1948, IDFA 922\1975\\1205, describing 'curses and the drawing of pistols' between representatives of the two factions in Qalqilya's National Committee in the second half of April 1948.

[321] 'Protocol of the Meeting of the [Political Department's] Arab Division, on Thursday 22 April 1948', CZA S25-9664. Shimoni was to somewhat modify this view by 13 May, when he said: 'The feeling is that His Majesty has not completely betrayed the agreement and is not completely loyal to it, but is somewhere in the middle. He will not remain faithful to the 29 November borders, but will not attempt to conquer all of our state,' (see 'Meeting of the Arab Division of the Political Department of the Jewish Agency (13 May 1948)', Yogev (ed.), *Political and Diplomatic Documents, December 1947-May 1948*, 789).

[322] Gelber, *Jewish-Transjordanian*, 273.

[323] Glubb, *Soldier*, 66 and 96.

[324] Sasson to Abdullah, 11 January 1948, in CZA S25-9038.

[325] Kirkbride, 'Monthly Situation Report on Transjordan for the Month of April, 1948', 4 May 1948, PRO CO 537-3962.

[326] Kirkbride to FO, 6 April 1948, PRO FO 371-68820 E4362\14\80; and Glubb, *Soldier*, 66-8.

[327] What actually happened in Deir Yassin has, ever since, been a matter of dispute. Immediately after the incident Arab survivors and spokesmen, and British and mainstream Zionist officials accused the IZL and LHI of committing atrocities; IZL leaders, and combatants who participated in the operation, denied this, charging that the mainstream socialist Zionists were out to get them for internal political reasons and the British and Arabs were motivated by general anti-Zionist feelings. Israeli historian Uri Milstein has recently argued that while some Arab civilians were killed in the course of the fighting (as happened in many villages overrun by the Haganah as well), the IZL and LHI troops involved did not carry out a massacre during or after the battle, or commit atrocities such as rape and mutilation. He dismissed the post-battle British and Arab news reports as (understandable) propaganda, and the internal Haganah intelligence reports as mendacious, motivated and produced with a specific anti-Revisionist (anti-IZL and anti-LHI) political purpose (Milstein, *History of the War of Independence*, vol. IV, 343-96).

But the existing contemporary evidence paints a different picture. One Haganah intelligence report stated: 'Some of the women and children taken prisoner by the LHI were moved to Sheikh Bader [a former Arab district in West Jerusalem]. Among the prisoners were a young mother and a baby ... The guards killed the baby in front of its mother and after she feinted also murdered her. 7 old persons and women taken prisoner by the IZL were paraded through the city streets in trucks. Afterwards the Arabs were taken to Deir Yassin's quarry and murdered' ('The Atrocities Committed by the Dissidents in the Deir Yassin Operation', 'Yavneh' (Yitzhak Levy, commander of the Haganah Intelligence Service in Jerusalem) to 'Tene (D)' (Haganah Intelligence Service HQ), 12 April 1948, IDFA 5254\49\\372). Summing up the operation, Levy wrote: '[There was] confusion among them [i.e., the attacking IZL-LHI force] ... The conquest of the village was carried out with great brutality. Whole families, women, old people, children, were killed and piles of corpses accumulated. Some of the prisoners taken to places of detention, including women and children, were brutally murdered by their guards ... The IZL and LHI men looted and stole quantities of money and food.' ('The IZL and LHI Operation in Deir Yassin', 'Yavneh' to 'Tene (D)', 12 April 1948, IDFA 5254\49\\372).

[328] Kirkbride, 'Monthly Situation Report on Transjordan for the Month of April, 1948', 4 May 1948, PRO CO 537-3962.

[329] 'A Painful Palestinian' (later changed by hand to 'A Suffering Palestinian') to the head of Abdullah's court, 11 April 1948, PRO FO 816\117.

[330] 'Information Circular (Tzror Yediot)', Alexandroni Brigade, 26 April 1948, and 'Information Circular', Alexandrioni Brigade, 28 April 1948, both in IDFA 128\51\\71; and '[Alexandroni] Brigade Circular', 8 May 1948, item from 4 May 1948, IDFA 7011\49\\5.

[331] Bevin to Kirkbride, 10 April 1948 ('despatched 12 April'), PRO FO 816\117.

[332] Kirkbride to Bevin (No. 224), 13 April 1948, PRO FO 816\117.

[333] Kirkbride to Bevin (No. 225), 13 April 1948, PRO FO 816\117.
[334] 'Information from the Arab Press', Haganah Intelligence Service, 18 April 1948, IDFA 4944\49\\504.
[335] Gelber, *Jewish-Transjordanian*, 267, quoting Kirkbride to Burrows, 15 April 1948.
[336] Jewish Agency to King Abdullah, 11 April 1948, CZA S25-1704.
[337] Head of the Royal Diwan, Amman, to Jewish Agency, 12 April 1948, CZA S25-9038.
[338] Kirkbride to Bevin, 16 April 1948, PRO FO 816\117.
[339] 'Azzam to Abdullah, 15 April 1948, PRO FO 816\117.
[340] Kirkbride to Bevin, 16 April 1948, PRO FO 816\117.
[341] 'Statement by the Royal Hashemite Diwan Regarding the Position in Palestine', 17 April 1948, PRO FO 816\117.
[342] High Commissioner, Jerusalem, to Kirkbride, 20 April 1948, PRO FO 816\117.
[343] Kirkbride to Bevin (No. 234), 21 April 1948, PRO FO 816\117.
[344] Kirkbride to Bevin, 23 April 1948, PRO FO 816\117. Kirkbride described Abdullah's statement the previous day as 'a judicious mixture of menace and readiness to negotiate.' The Jewish Agency, unintimidated, responded by rejecting the implied threat and calling for a negotiated settlement (see Sasson to chief of the Royal Diwan, 22 April 1948, CZA S25-9038). But Abdullah officially stuck by his statement, offering the Jews no more than autonomy in 'those areas where they form majority' (chief of Royal Diwan to Sasson, 23 April 1948, CZA S25-9038). But in private, in a talk with Kirkbride, Abdullah admitted that he did not 'expect the Jews to accept such terms' and that the purpose of the message had been 'to keep the door open for negotiations when both sides were in a more reasonable frame of mind' (Kirkbride to Bevin (No. 246), 24 April 1948, PRO FO 816\117).
[345] 'General Survey for the Months of March, April 1948, Population, Economy, Transportation, Among the Arabs', 'Tzuri' to Golani Brigade HQ, 3 May 1948, IDFA 1196\52\\1.
[346] See, for example, 'In the Arab Public', Arab Division of the Political Department, Jewish Agency, 5 May 1948, IDFA 1196\52\\1.
[347] 'Annexes to Intelligence Circular No. 140', 'Hashmonai' to 'Tzuri,' 6 April 1948, IDFA2605\49\\2.
[348] A small village just west of Tiberias, conquered by the Haganah on 12 April. The Jewish troops reportedly killed a handful of Arab non-combatants (see Morris, *Birth*, 71).
[349] Kirkbride to Bevin (No. 244), 23 April 1948, conveying text of Abdullah to Cunningham, 23 April 1948, PRO FO 816\117. The text of the Abdullah telegram (misdated 27 April 1948), is also given in Cunningham to Kirkbride, 26 April 1948, PRO FO 816\118 and, interestingly, is conveyed, in full, in the Haganah Intelligence Service's daily information round-up for 10 May 1948. Apparently Haganah agents obtained a copy of either Abdullah's original letter or of one of the subsequent British cables conveying the text (see 'Tene Information, Daily Summary', 10 May 1948, IDFA 900\52\\58).
[350] HQ RAF Med. M.E. to Air Ministry, London, 17 April 1948, PRO CO 537-3897.
[351] Kirkbride to FO, 25 April 1948, CO 537-3901. A British diplomat in Cairo reported meeting 'Azzam at this time. 'Azzam had 'emphasized the difficult position in which all the Arab governments were now finding themselves.

Their leaders, in fact, including himself, would probably be assassinated if they did nothing ... 'Azzam seemed somewhat depressed' (BMEO (Cairo) to Kirkbride, 29 April 1948, PRO FO 816\118). Lebanon's foreign minister was also described, at this time as 'depressed,' for the selfsame reasons. He predicted - fairly accurately, as it turned out - that 'if the Arabs were defeated in Palestine the governments of Egypt, Iraq and Syria would tumble like a house of cards with repercussions which would be felt throughout the Arab world' (Houstoun-Boswall to FO, 2 May 1948, PRO FO 816\119). As it turned out, the Egyptian prime minister, Mahmud Nuqrashi, was assassinated in November 1948, the Syrian regime was overthrown in March 1949, within months of the end of the fighting, Jordan's King Abdullah and Lebanon's Riad as Sulh were both assassinated two years after the war, Egypt's monarchy was overthrown in 1952 and the Iraqi monarchy was overthrown a decade after the 1948 War. Without doubt, many of these developments owed much to the debacle of 1948.

[352] Kirkbride to Bevin (No. 270), 1 May 1948, PRO FO 816\118.

[353] Kirkbride to Bevin (No. 261), 29 April 1948, PRO FO 816\118.

[354] British Middle East Office, Cairo, to British Legation, Amman, 29 April 1948, PRO FO 816\118.

[355] Kirkbride to Bevin, 1 May 1948, 816\118. 'Azzam during the following days was periodically to approach British officials to request permission for Arab armies to march into Palestine before 15 May, suggesting that HMG could 'turn ... a blind eye' (see, for example, HM Minister, Damascus, to Kirkbride, 5 May 1948, PRO FO 816\119).

[356] Kirkbride to FO, (No. 273), 1 May 1948, PRO FO 816\118.

[357] Kirkbride to Bevin (No. 261), 29 April 1948, PRO FO 816\118.

[358] Kirkbride to Bevin, 8 May 1948, PRO FO 816\119.

[359] Kirkbride to Bevin, 8 May 1948, PRO FO 816\118. This was also the impression that Abdullah had left with the British minister in Beirut (see Houstoun-Boswall to Kirkbride, 9 May 1948, PRO FO 816\119). Kirkbride's mention of Abdullah's belligerent 'statements' apparently referred to interviews in *Al Ahram* and elsewhere that appeared on 9 May in which he spoke of 'a 10-day' campaign in which 'the Zionist bastion would fall in the first attack and the Jews would [be forced to] extend their hand in peace' (see 'Tene Information, Daily Summary', Haganah Intelligence Service, 10 May 1948, IDFA 900\52\\58).

[360] Gelber, *Jewish-Transjordanian*, 250-51; and Nevo, *Abdallah*, 98.

[361] *Through Enemy Eyes*, 130-1, 133, and 136; and Nevo, *Abdallah*, 123-24. Nevo says that Legionnaires trained about 600 men from the Lydda area and 500 from the Ramle area. Mahmud al Ghussan (*Through Enemy Eyes*), a Legion officer, claimed that, while he was posted in a guard company in Haifa, he and other Legionnaires had helped organize and train the city's Arab militia. One Legion officer, Muhammad al Hammad al Huneiti, resigned his commission in order to lead Haifa's militia - until he was killed in a Haganah ambush on 19 March 1948 - and 'many Legionnaires' fought alongside the militiamen, writes Ghussan, probably with exaggeration.

[362] 'Report on Accompanying a Convoy from Petah Tikva to Ben Shemen', by 'Ben Shahar,' 19 December 1947, IDFA 2687\49\\35; 'Schedule of Incidents in Palestine' and appended 'Report on the Ben Shemen Incident', undated and unsigned but accompanied by letter from S. Brodetsky, Chairman of the British Jewish Board of Deputies, to Emanuel Shinwell, War Office, 29 De-

cember 1947, PRO CO 537-3899. Brodetsky also complained to Creech-Jones more generally of the inappropriateness of Britain's employment of the Legion in Palestine.

[363] High Commissioner to London, 15 December 1947, PRO FO 816\111. Gelber, *Jewish-Transjordanian*, says at one point (p. 242) that the offending troops were in reality members of the TJFF, a force organized and controlled by the Palestine Mandate Government, not Legionnaires, but later (p. 249) says that they were Legionnaires.

[364] Gelber, *Jewish-Transjordanian*, 249.

[365] Kirkbride, 'Monthly Situation Report on Transjordan for the Month of April, 1948', 4 May 1948, PRO CO 537-3962. Kirkbride reported that, following the Jewish occupation of the fort, 'an Arab Legion sentry on the Transjordan end of the bridge was shot dead from the post on the 28th of April. The Arab Legion replied with mortar fire from Transjordan territory until the Jews ceased firing ...' Kirkbride was either mistaken or being deliberately misleading: The Jordanians began shooting already on 27 April. In 'Report of a Meeting with Arab Legion Representatives', by 'S.R.' (Shlomo Rabinovich (Shamir)), 3 May 1948, ISA FM 2513\2, a senior Legion officer, Col. Desmond Goldie, is quoted as explaining that Haganah fire, according to the local 4th Battalion Legion commander, Lt. Colonel Habis Majali, had killed '4' of his men, and he had responded as he had, without authorisation from Amman. Majali had added, according to Goldie, that he believed the Jews had intended to cross the river and attack Transjordan (a highly unlikely story). When Glubb heard about the incident, he immediately sent Brigadier Lash, his deputy, to the site to stop the firing, and he had. But when Lash left the scene, the Legionnaires had resumed firing. Again, Majali had maintained that the Jews had fired at his troops. 'The Pasha was very angry and ordered that the Arab Colonel [Majali] be summoned and threatened him' with dismissal.

Majali's explanation of the start of the incident is supported by a Haganah intelligence document that states that, according to an informer, the Legion onslaught was 'a reprisal' for Haganah fire from Gesher. In the course of the incident, three Legionnaires and four local Arabs were killed and five wounded ('Tzuri to 'Tene (Ayin),' 9 May 1948, IDFA 1196\52\\1).

[366] Zaslani (Shiloah) to Shertok (Sharett), 3 May 1948, Yogev (ed.), *Political and Diplomatic Documents, December 1947-May 1948*, 721-22.

[367] 'Report of a Meeting with Representatives of the Arab Legion', by 'S.R.,' 3 May 1948, ISA FM 2513\2.

[368] Golani Brigade Logbook, entry for 27 April 1948, IDFA 665\51\\1; and Etzioni, *Tree and Sword*, 125. My inclination would be to accept the Jordanian version of a local initiative which did not have Glubb's prior authorisation. Glubb was too political an animal and too obedient to British wishes to initiate such a potentially embarrassing attack on Palestine on the eve of the British withdrawal. But the reported presence of Prince Talal, Abdullah's son, the Legion's divisional commander, Lash, and the 3rd Brigade commander, Lt. Colonel 'Teal' Ashton, as well as a variety of Jordanian notables on the site during the shelling (Tall, *Memoirs*, 31; *Through Enemy Eyes*, 41) might point in another direction; indeed, Haganah intelligence reported that Talal had personally 'fired a bit with a machinegun' ('Tzuri' to 'Tene (Ayin)' (Haganah Intelligence Service, Arab Department), 9 May 1948, IDFA 1196\52\\1). It is possible that once the small arms fire began, it was escalated with Abdullah's

agreement (but without Glubb's consent) as an oblique response or counter-signal to the Deir Yassin Massacre and the Haganah conquests of Arab Tiberias and Arab Haifa a few days before.

[369] Kirkbride to FO, 28 April 1948, PRO CO 537-3904: 'I had considerable trouble in preventing action in Palestine at Jisr Majami following the death of an Arab Legionary.'

[370] Cunningham to Kirkbride, 30 April 1948, PRO FO 816\118.

[371] 'Pieces of Information', 'Tzuri' to Haganah Intelligence Service, Arab Department, 9 May 1948, IDFA 1196\52\\1; Tall, *Memoirs*, 31; and Shlaim, *Collusion*, 178-9. IDF History Branch's history of the 1948 War (*History of the War of Independence*, 138) incorrectly states that the Legion tried to conquer the fort and kibbutz, but were 'beaten back.' Shlaim, too, speaks of 'a coordinated attack with infantry, artillery and armour,' implying that the aim was conquest of the settlement. But the engagement had consisted of a protracted shelling and some Haganah counter-fire; Legion units had not crossed the river or attempted a ground assault.

[372] Bevin to Kirkbride (No. 263), 28 April 1948, PRO FO 816\118; Bevin to Kirkbride, 30 April 1948, PRO CO 537-3904; and Bevin to Kirkbride (No. 273), 30 April 1948, PRO FO 816\118.

[373] McMillan to Glubb, 27 April 1948, IDFA 980\85\\44. Perhaps the decision was not motivated solely by technical considerations. McMillan too may have been persuaded to leave some 'welcoming' Legion units *in situ* in expectation of the impending Legion invasion.

[374] Glubb, *Soldier*, 90.

[375] Tall, *Memoirs*, 43-45, says that 'until 13 May' there were more than ten Legion companies in Palestine (identifying them by number), but he fails to tell us how many left Palestine during 13-14 May and how many stayed behind. Sela, 'Transjordan', 644-5, speaks of three Legion units left behind in Palestine on 13-14 May, in Hebron, Ramallah and Nablus. Nevo, *Abdallah*, 125, speaks of 'six' companies left behind. Haganah intelligence placed 'dozens of Legionnaires' in the village of 'Ein Karim, just west of Jerusalem, on the eve of the British pullout ('Ein Karim, 'Mati,' 16 May 1948, IDF 5545\49\\114) and '214' Legionnaires, commanded by a Circassian officer, Muhammad Ishak, in Nablus ('Alexandroni Brigade Bulletin, No. 8', brigade intelligence officer, 14 May 1948, IDF 2323\49\\6).

[376] Tall, *Memoirs*, 41.

[377] Gelber, *Jewish-Transjordanian*, 273.

[378] 'Hashmonai,' 'The Legion Order of Battle at the End of April (Appears Reliable) from Jerusalem [District] Intelligence Files', 28 April 1948, IDFA 922\75\\283.

[379] 'Annexes to Information Circular No. 205, 29 April 1948', 'Hashmonai' to 'Michmash,' IDFA 4944\49\\499. An earlier intelligence report, from 15 April, stated that the Hebron National Committee had discussed the 'impending attack on Kfar Etzion.' One of the commanders of the Legion detachment in the town participated, 'because the Arab Legion was due to take part in the attack' ('Annexes to Information Circular No. 173, 15 April 1948', 'Hashmonai' to 'Michmash,' IDFA 4944\49\\499).

[380] 'On the Fall of the Etzion Bloc', *Hatzofe*, 8 April 1949, IDFA 922\75\\283.

[381] Glubb, *Soldier*, 78.

[382] Tall, *Memoirs*, 36-7, 39-41. Tall claims in his (self-aggrandizing) memoirs that the British and Glubb were chary of launching a large-scale, politically

messy military operation against the Yishuv on the eve of the British departure. He therefore set about organizing a series of provocations designed to compel the reluctant Glubb to issue the necessary authorisations.

383 IDFA922\1975\\693, Arshid Marshud to Glubb, 9 December 1948. But it is unclear whether Marshud was close enough to the decision-making process regarding the Etzion Bloc to have known for certain who gave the order and why.

384 Sela, 'Transjordan', 643, maintains that the attack was launched on 'Glubb's instruction,' though offers no proof other than Glubb's memoirs. Bar-Joseph, *Enemies*, 63-64, offers a contrary assertion: 'Neither Abdullah nor the Legion commander were involved' in the initiative to conquer the bloc. A final determination on this point must await the opening of Jordanian records.

385 Tall, *Memoirs*, 26.

386 Major Yitzhak Yakobson, 'Gush Etzion in the War of Independence' (a comprehensive, undated report, but from the 1950s), 87 and 90-5, IDFA 922\1975\\283.

387 Yakobson, 'Gush Etzion ...', 95. There may be a hint of British foreknowledge about the Legion assault of 12 May on the Bloc in a Haganah Intelligence report from 10 May: 'In [British] military offices in Haifa it is being mooted that on 12 May large-scale military operations will be carried out, which will not be beneficial to the Jews' (see 'Tene Information, Daily Summary', Haganah Intelligence Service, 10 May 1948, IDFA 900\52\\58).

388 'On the Fall of the Etzion Bloc', *Hatzofe*, 8 April 1949, IDFA 922\75\\283.

389 Yakobson, `Gush Etzion ...', 96-104; and 'On the Fall of the Etzion Bloc,' *Hatzofe*, 8 April 1949, IDFA 922\75\\283.

390 'On the Fall of the Etzion Bloc', *Hatzofe*, 8 April 1949, IDFA 922\75\\283.

391 'On the Fall of the Etzion Bloc', *Hatzofe*, 8 April 1949, IDFA 922\75\\283.

392 Steiger, 'The Arab Legion in 1948', 65, IDFA 1046\70\\178.

393 Yakobson, 'Gush Etzion ...', 87-9.

394 Yakobson, 'Gush Etzion ...' 115; and Tall, *Memoirs*, 39.

395 Steiger, 'The Arab Legion in 1948', 66, IDFA 1046\70\\178.

396 Tall, *Memoirs*, 39.

397 Yakobson, 'Gush Etzion ...', 129; and 'The Last Battle of Kfar Etzion', unsigned memorandum based on testimony from the survivors, undated, IDFA 922\75\\283.

398 Yakobson, `Gush Etzion ...', 129-30. It would seem that Yakobson included in the '127' both those who died in the battles of 12-13 May and those who died in the subsequent massacre. One Haganah intelligence report put Arab fatalities at 42 irregulars and 27 Legionnaires.

399 Kirkbride to FO, 14 May 1948, CO 537-3904.

400 'Hashmonai' to 'David,' 'Eldad,' 'Yonatan,' etc., 'Report by Dr. Werth who Visited on 14\5\48 in the Etzion Bloc with the Red Cross Representatives', 14 May 1948, IDFA 5254\49\\145.

401 Glubb, *Soldier*, 78: 'The Arab Legion treated all Jews as prisoners of war. As soon as the Arab Legion withdrew, the villagers of the Hebron district looted the Jewish colonies, leaving not one stone upon another. These colonies had been so aggressive that they had deliberately compelled Arab retaliation.' Glubb returned to the theme a decade later, flatly denying that there had been any massacre. In a letter published in *The Times* (London) on 2 July 1968, Glubb wrote: 'As soon as Kfar Etzion surrendered all firing ceased. The men were conveyed to prisoner-of-war camps. All Jewish women taken by the

Arab Legion were immediately handed back to the Israeli side through the Red Cross. Not a single Jew was massacred at Kfar Etzion.'

402 Tall, *Memoirs*, 40.

403 'Mitzpa' to Political and Arab Departments, Haganah Intelligence Service, 10 April 1948, HA 105\54 aleph.

404 'Report ...', by 'S.R.', 3 May 1948, ISA FM 2513\2. Before writing the report, Shamir on 2 May briefed Ben-Gurion on the meeting (see Ben-Gurion, *The War of Independence: Ben-Gurion's Diary, 1948-1949*, 383. Ben-Gurion's description tallies with Shamir's more detailed report). Shamir's report is the main source of information about what transpired; there is no reason to doubt its general accuracy. See also Shlaim, *Collusion*, 179-86; Lunt, *Glubb,* 13-18; and Royle, *Glubb*, 350-52. Royle states that Goldie handed Shamir a letter from Glubb. Shamir - and Ben-Gurion - make no mention of a letter, and doubtless would have had there been one. Curiously, Glubb made no mention at all of the affair in his autobiography, perhaps a hint that he had dispatched Goldie on his mission without authorisation from Abdullah.

405 Bevin to Kirkbride (reproducing Creech-Jones cable from New York to London), 9 May 1948, PRO FO 816\119. See also 'Meeting: M. Shertok, E. Epstein - G. Marshall, R. Lovett, D. Rusk (Washington, 8 May 1948)', Shertok's undated report on the meeting, in Yogev (ed.), *Political and Diplomatic Documents, December 1947-May 1948*, 758-9.

406 'Report ...', by 'S.R.', 3 May 1948, ISA FM 2513\2.

407 Israel's Foreign Minister, Moshe Shertok (Sharett), referred to the Goldie-Shamir meeting when he briefed the Cabinet on 16 June. Sharett was arguing against the IDF conquest of the whole of Palestine. He then referred to Goldie's assertion-question: 'We don't want to fight you, but we want to know: What are your intentions? If you want to conquer the whole Land of Israel, we will have to resist. But if only part - we will get along' (Protocol of Meeting of Provisional Government of Israel, 16 June 1948, ISA).

408 David Ben-Gurion, *Diary* I, 409, entry for 11 May 1948.

409 Sela, 'Transjordan', 641-3.

410 Kirkbride to Bevin (No. 486), 14 June 1948, PRO FO 816\123.

411 Israel State Archives, *The People's Administration, Protocols 18 April-13 May 1948*, 40-44; and Shlaim, *Collusion*, 205-10.

412 Kirkbride to FO, 14 June 1948, PRO FO 371-68821 E8053. See also Kirkbride, *Wings*, 22.

413 Tall, *Memoirs*, 50.

414 Tall, *Memoirs*, 50.

415 Kirkbride, *Wings*, 25.

416 Gelber, *Jewish-Transjordanian*, 287 writes: 'Highly bellicose propaganda accompanied the [Arab coalition] invasion that was motivated primarily by domestic considerations and secondly by inter-Arab considerations. Nevertheless, the invasion's purpose was not to push the Jews into the Mediterranean but to save the Palestinians from total destruction ...'

417 An approximate outline of this plan is to be found in 'The Arab Attack Plan After the 15th of May', unsigned, 5 May 1948 ('with certain reservations'), IDFA 5942\49\\53.

418 Glubb, *Soldier*, 93 writes: 'The Israelis subsequently claimed knowledge of an Arab master plan, combining the strategy of all the Arab armies. No such plan existed, nor had any attempt been made to prepare one.'

[419] S. Segev (Sabagh) ed., *Behind the Screen*, 148-49. See also 34, for the Iraqis' post-war appreciation that the Arab armies had fought disparately and with different purposes.

[420] 'The Legion Order of Battle at the End of April (Appears Reliable) from Jerusalem [District] Intelligence Files', 'Hashmonai,' 28 April 1948, IDFA 922\1975\\283.

[421] Gelber, *Jewish-Transjordanian*, 287, writes of Jordanian aims: 'Abdullah, of course, had [an] ulterior motive for his participation - the annexation of Arab Palestine to his kingdom ... Abdullah remained faithful to his previous agreement with the Jewish Agency. His Legion did not cross the borders of the [UN-defined] Jewish state ...'

[422] Kirkbride to FO, 2 May 1948, PRO CO 537-3901. A slightly different version of this cable is quoted in Gelber, *Jewish-Transjordanian*, 274-75. Gelber, dating it 1 May 1948, quotes the last part as saying: 'I am encouraging Glubb to propagate in favour of the following sequence ...' One might say that, taken together, the two versions aptly reflect the symbiosis between Kirkbride and Glubb, each feeding the other ideas, proposals, and advice in such a fashion as almost to make their positions and (political) actions indistinguishable and inseparable during the crucial weeks of the invasion.

[423] Kirkbride, *Wings*, 22-23. At a follow-up meeting with Kirkbride, 'Azzam announced that the Arab armies intended to invade Palestine. Kirkbride asked him for his estimate of the Jewish forces the Arabs would come up against. 'Azzam 'waved his hands and said: "It does not matter how many there are. We will sweep them into the sea!"' (*Wings*, 24).

[424] Glubb, *Soldier*, 94-95.

[425] Kirkbride to Bevin (No. 462), 7 June 1948, PRO FO 816\122. Kirkbride was wrong, but the fact that he wrote this is indicative.

[426] Glubb, *Soldier*, 93-96.

[427] Sela, 'Transjordan', 627.

[428] Shlaim, *Collusion*, 239.

[429] Kirkbride to FO, 10:10 AM, 14 May 1948, PRO CO 537-3904. A variant of this cable - speaking of the Legion's intent to 'extend [its control] cautiously over Arab areas' beyond Hebron and Nablus, sent at 12:10 hours - is in PRO FO 816\120. Lebanon at the last moment decided not to send its forces across the border. Partly in response, Syria changed plans and, instead of invading Palestine via Lebanon, shifted its army south-eastwards and ended up invading Palestine - and attacking Israeli territory - in one thrust just south of the Sea of Galilee, at Samakh and then Degania, on 16 May and 20 May respectively.

[430] Quoted in Shlaim, *Collusion*, 222. Alexandre Parodi, French ambassador to the United Nations and President of the Security Council, predicted on 9 May that there would be 'clashes between the Arab Legion and the Haganah' and believed that 'an agreed partition between Abdullah and the Zionists arrived at in this manner after small-scale fighting was probably the best solution.' Parodi thought that the two sides would probably succeed in avoiding 'major battle' (UK Delegation to UN to FO, 9 May 1948, PRO FO 816\119).

[431] Glubb, *Soldier*, 98.

[432] Glubb, *Soldier*, 101.

[433] Tall, *Memoirs*, 42-3.

[434] 'Off-the-Record Talks in Transjordan of Two British Correspondents', unsigned, Amman, 21 October 1947, CZA S25-9038.

[435] Glubb, *Soldier*, 99.

[436] Arshid Marshud, OC 1st Battalion, to Glubb, 9 December 1948, IDFA 922\1975\\693.

[437] Kirkbride, *Wings*, 28. The exact hour in which the lead Legion units crossed the river is unclear. It appears that Kirkbride was wrong and that this occurred around dawn, 15 May 1948.

[438] Arshid Marshud to Glubb, 9 December 1948, IDFA 922\1975\\693.

[439] S. Segev (Sabagh), ed. and translator, *Through Enemy Eyes (Heb.)*, 148. *Through Enemy Eyes*, published by the IDF Press (Tel Aviv, 1954), is a collection of three abridged and translated books by Arab participants in the 1948 War. The third of these is an abridged, translated version of Mahmud al Ghussan, *Ma`arak Bab al Wad* (the battle of Bab al Wad). Ghussan served in 1948 as a staff officer in the Legion's 4th Battalion and these are his war memoirs.

[440] Segev (ed.), *Through Enemy Eyes*, 151 and 153. Like the Legion company in Hebron, this force had not withdrawn from Palestine and stayed on during and after the final British pullout, awaiting the arrival of the invading Arab armies.

[441] Glubb to Ahmad Sadeq Bek, 22:00 hours, 15 May 1948, a Haganah Intelligence Service radio intercept, IDFA 661\69\\36.

[442] Segev (ed.), *Through Enemy Eyes*, 151-52. Bar-Joseph, *Enemies*, 75-78, argues that the 4th Battalion moved into Bab al Wad and Latrun as a result of an initiative by the Arab junior officers and contrary to the plans and wishes of the senior British commanders, who were wary of a clash with the Jews. But Ghussan, on whom Bar-Joseph bases himself, does not actually say this: Ghussan states that during 15-16 May there was pressure on the Legion officers, from villagers around Latrun (Imwas, Beit Nuba, Yalu, etc.) to push into the area and protect them from the Jews, and that on 17 May the senior Legion commanders, bowing to this pressure and believing that the Haganah was, indeed, about to attack, ordered the 4th Battalion in (*Through Enemy Eyes*, 151).

[443] Kirkbride to Bevin, 13 February 1948, PRO FO 816\116.

[444] 'Haganah Intelligence Service Information, Daily Brief', Haganah Intelligence Service, 20 April 1948, IDFA 900\52\\58.

[445] Kirkbride to Bevin (No. 244), 23 April 1948, enclosing Abdullah to Cunningham, and Kirkbride to Bevin (No. 243), 23 April 1948, both in PRO FO 816\117. Abdullah clearly was moved by the Jewish onslaughts on Deir Yassin and the Arab neighbourhoods of Tiberias and Haifa.

[446] Kirkbride to Bevin (No. 270), 1 May 1948, PRO FO 816\118.

[447] Kirkbride to Bevin (No. 273), 1 May 1948, PRO FO 816\118.

[448] Kirkbride to Bevin (No. 275), 1 May 1948, PRO FO 816\118. Kirkbride responded that Britain couldn't propose this at the UN as there would be a suspicion that Britain wanted to get back into Palestine through the back door, by a 'trick.' He suggested to Abul Huda that the Arab states raise the idea, if they wanted, at the UN. He said that the Arabs should intensify their efforts to secure a truce in Jerusalem and Bevin concurred (see Bevin to Kirkbride, 5 May 1948, PRO FO 816\119).

[449] Kirkbride to FO (No. 282), 3 May 1948, PRO FO 816\118.

[450] Kirkbride to FO (No. 282), 3 May 1948, PRO FO 816\118.

[451] Bevin to Kirkbride, 5 May 1948, PRO FO 816\119.

[452] Cabinet protocol for 16 May 1948, 5, ISA.

[453] Steiger, 'Arab Legion', 74.
[454] 'Arab [Affairs] Information Bulletin from 18.5.48', Haganah Intelligence Service, 19 May 1948, IDFA 500\48\\55.
[455] 'Protocol of the Meeting of the Arab Division on Thursday 22.4.48,' CZA S-25/9664.
[456] Yadin to Etzioni, 11 May 1948, 22:15 hours, IDFA 500\48\\54.
[457] Reproduced in Oded Messer, *The Haganah's Operational Plans, 1937-1948*, 168-75
[458] 'Arab [Affairs] Information Bulletin from 18.5.48', Haganah Intelligence Service, 19 May 1948, IDFA 500\48\\55.
[459] Glubb, *Soldier*, 108-9; and Kirkbride, *Wings*, 31.
[460] Kirkbride to Bevin (No. 331), 15 May 1948, PRO FO 816\120.
[461] Abdullah to Kirkbride, 16 May 1948, PRO FO 816\120. See also Shlaim, *Collusion*, 241.
[462] Kirkbride to Bevin, 15 May 1948, PRO FO 816\120.
[463] No doubt a great deal of misinformation reached Amman from its allies during those days. For example, the Iraqis apparently informed Jordan that they had conquered Kibbutz Gesher - which, of course, they had not (see Kirkbride to Bevin, 15 May 1948 (13:30 hrs.), PRO FO 816\120).
[464] Text of letter, apparently published in *Al Nisr*, 17 May 1948, in PRO FO 816\120.
[465] Nevo, *Abdallah*, 137. The source of this quotation is unclear.
[466] 'Tene Information, Daily Summary', Haganah Intelligence Service, 27 May 1948, IDFA 900\52\\58.
[467] 'Palestinian Arab Information, (according to Arab broadcasts, 14-15 May)', undated, unsigned but produced by Haganah Intelligence Service, HA 105\88, and Arab Department, Haganah Intelligence Service, 'Monitoring Report of Arab Radio Stations for 14.5.1948', HA 105\90.
[468] Kirkbride to Bevin, 17 May 1948 (17.41 hrs.), PRO FO 816\120; and Kirkbride to Abdullah, 22 May 1948, PRO FO 816\120.
[469] Kirkbride to Bevin, 18 May 1948, PRO FO 816\120.
[470] Glubb, *Soldier*, 118, reproduces the full text. Sela, 'Transjordan', 651, dates the cable 16 May.
[471] Glubb, *Soldier*, 110.
[472] Kirkbride to FO, 19 May 1948, PRO FO 371-68829 E6577\G. According to Sela, 'Transjordan', 651, the King, at a Cabinet meeting in Amman on the morning of 17 May, attended by the Legion's senior officers, including Glubb, ordered the chief of staff and his second-in-command to advance on Jerusalem - but this seems to contradict Kirkbride's more reliable, cited testimony that Glubb had deliberately avoided direct contact with the King and Abdullah's orders of 17 May, which implied that Glubb had not attended the meeting and had been away in the West Bank that morning. Sela's competent essay suffers from an over-reliance, at certain junctures, on the 'evidence' proffered by undocumented Arab memoirs and secondary works produced long after the events described.
[473] Kirkbride, *Wings*, 32.
[474] Bevin to Kirkbride, 19 May 1948, PRO FO 816\120.
[475] Sela, 'Transjordan', 647.
[476] Glubb, *Soldier*, 111 and 113. The presence of his father's tomb in Jerusalem no doubt contributed to Abdullah's decision to send the Legion in. The first thing King Abdullah did when arriving in Jerusalem's Old City, on 27 May -

even before its Jewish Quarter had fallen to the Legion - was to visit the tomb (see Commander-in-Chief, Middle East Land Forces, to War Office, 29 May 1948, PRO CO 537-3868).

[477] Leo Kohn to the chairman, Palestine Truce Commission, Jerusalem, 19 May 1948, IDFA 5254\49\\146.

[478] 'Report by C.V. Herzog', 21 May 1948, in Freundlich (ed.), *Documents on the Foreign Policy of Israel, May-September 1948*, I, 50.

[479] Kirkbride to Foreign Office, 19 May 1948, PRO FO 371-68829 E6577\G.

[480] Minute, possibly by Beith, 20 May 1948, PRO FO 371-68829 E6577\G. L.F.L. Pyman, another Foreign Office official, agreed: 'The action of the Arab Legion at Jerusalem may make [political] difficulties for us, though less than a crossing of the Jewish frontier would have done. But the fundamental fact about Jerusalem is that it is in the middle of an Arab area ...' (Minute by L.F.L. Pyman, 20 May 1948, PRO FO 371-68829 E6577\G).

[481] Glubb, *Soldier*, 121.

[482] Glubb, *Soldier*, 114-17.

[483] Sela, 'Transjordan', 654, incorrectly states that this link-up occurred on the 24th.

[484] Kirkbride to Bevin, 21 May 1948, PRO FO 816\120. Shlaim, *Collusion*, 253-54, says that Glubb already asked the Iraqis to move 'some units' from Jisr Majami to Nablus at a meeting in Amman on 20 May with Abdullah, 'Azzam and 'Abd al Illah, the Iraqi Regent, and senior military commanders. The Iraqis preferred not to split their forces and decided to move the whole expeditionary force to Samaria. This re-deployment occurred on 22-24 May, not as Sela, 'Transjordan', 658, says, on '28' May.

[485] Kirkbride to FO (no. 372), 22 May 1948, PRO CO 537-3902.

[486] Glubb, *Soldier*, 123-26.

[487] Glubb, *Soldier*, 130.

[488] For example, Nevo, *Abdallah*, 136-37: 'The Legion had given up efforts to invade the Jewish sector (west Jerusalem) after earlier attempts ... via the Notre Dame monastery and Sheikh Jarah quarter proved unsuccessful.'

[489] Ben-Gurion's statement, protocols of the Cabinet Meeting of 23 May 1948, ISA. Similarly, Israel's interior minister, Yitzhak Grunbaum, commented a month later: 'Till today we do not understand, why the Arab Legion, when it took Sheikh Jarah, did not advance further. Had it advanced - perhaps it would have conquered all of Jewish Jerusalem or a large part of it. But we had a miracle and we were saved from this catastrophe' (protocols of the Israeli Cabinet meeting of 20 June 1948, ISA). It would appear, then, that in mid-May Ben-Gurion and others in the Israeli hierarchy were far from convinced that Abdullah intended to abide by the November 1947 understanding and occupy only the Arab areas of Palestine.

[490] Ben-Gurion's statement, protocols of the Cabinet Meeting of 30 May 1948, ISA.

[491] Freundlich (ed.), *Documents*, I, Shertok to Weizmann (New York), 23 May 1948, 66. Needless to say, the Legion played no part in the battle for Degania.

[492] Glubb, *Soldier*, 146.

[493] Kirkbride to Bevin, 21 May 1948, PRO FO 816\120.

[494] Steiger, 'Arab Legion', 40.

[495] Steiger, 'Arab Legion', 73, 75. Steiger wrote his study after the publication of Glubb's memoir of the war and no doubt was influenced by it. Sela,

'Transjordan', 654, who apparently never saw Steiger's study, endorses his interpretation: 'What appeared to be the Legion's only attempt during the war to breach the Jewish line of defence [at Notre Dame and, possibly, the Mandelbaum Gate] and storm the New City [i.e., Jewish Jerusalem] was in fact no more than an attempt to broaden the land corridor along the Ramallah-Damascus Gate axis ... Given the Legion's order of battle and missions in this period, the capture of the New City, let alone the holding of it, was totally out of the question.'

[496] Kirkbride to FO, 22 May 1948 (No. 370), PRO CO 537-3902.

[497] Glubb, *Soldier*, 110. See also Royle, *Glubb*, 363; Itzchaki, *Latrun*, I, 153-55; and Shlaim, *Collusion*, 244.

[498] Steiger, 'Arab Legion', 109.

[499] Kirkbride to Bevin, 26 May 1948, PRO FO 816\121. In his memoirs (*Soldier*, 132), Glubb wrote that 'the [defending] 4th Regiment [Battalion] counted six hundred dead Jews in front of our positions' - which reflects poorly on the beduins' arithmetical abilities.

[500] Glubb, *Soldier*, 132.

[501] Glubb, *Soldier*, 132. The IDF was extremely impressed by the Legion's performance at Latrun. On 4 June, the intelligence officer of the 7th Brigade wrote: '...The enemy [i.e., the Legion] used his 3" mortars extremely efficiently ... The enemy's speed and accuracy ... stood out during the past fortnight's operations ...' More generally, the Israeli officer concluded: 'The Legion's strength lies in his quick mobility and flexibility. Units are moved from one place to the next in relation to defensive or offensive needs of the brigade ... (7th Brigade Intelligence Officer, 'Intelligence Survey - as of the Situation on 3 June 24:00 hours', 4 June 1948, IDFA 922\75\\1018). Ben-Gurion himself was filled with admiration. He told his Cabinet colleagues: 'I must say a word in praise of the enemy ... This is a trained, disciplined and brave enemy. The Arab Legion sparked respect among all our boys. It knows how to fight, does not run away, [and] it also knows how to assault, if needs be. It has good command and weapons ...' (Protocol of Israeli cabinet meeting, 14 June 1948, ISA).

[502] Interestingly, in Israel's collective memory 'Latrun' is remembered as a major defeat in which Israel had suffered many hundreds of dead (see Anita Shapira, 'Historiography and Memory: The Case of Latrun', *Alpayim* 10 (1994)).

[503] Sela, 'Transjordan ...', 658-59.

[504] Foreign Office Research Department and Glubb, 'The Part Played by the AL in the Arab-Jewish Hostilities in Palestine 1948-49', August\October 1950, PRO FO 816\89.

[505] Kirkbride to Bevin (No. 660), 17 August 1948, PRO FO 816\127. For the Israeli perspective on the Sasson-Haidar meetings in August, see Sasson to Y. Shimoni, 3 August 1948, and Shertok to Sasson, 5 August 1948, in Freundlich (ed.), *Documents*, I, 453 and 490. Kirkbride was certainly misinformed about Israel's position in the Sasson-Haidar talks. Far from agreeing to a return to the 29 November 1947 UN partition boundaries, Israel insisted on major territorial changes in its favour, including the inclusion in the Jewish state of West Jerusalem and the corridor to it from the coastal plain.

[506] Bevin to Kirkbride, 24 May 1948, PRO FO 816\120.

[507] Kirkbride to Bevin, 25 May 1948, PRO FO 816\121. Indeed, Kirkbride already on 23-24 May was reporting that the Egyptian advance had ground to a

halt. On 23 May he wrote: 'The Egyptian Army is now halted on the line Hebron-Majdal and if the local Egyptian Liaison Officer [in Amman] is to be credited, intends to stay there' (Kirkbride to Bevin, 23 May 1848, PRO FO 816\121); and on 24 May he added: 'The Egyptians seem to have decided no doubt wisely to advance no further and yesterday declined to make a small movement forward which was suggested by Glubb ...' (Kirkbride to Bevin, 24 May 1948, PRO FO 816\121). These reports, incidentally, run completely contrary to the thrust of Israeli military historiography regarding the Egyptian push into Palestine, which holds that the Egyptians only came to a halt as a result of a surprise Israel Air Force strafing attack on 29 May or, alternatively, as a result of the Givati and Negev brigades' offensive against the northernmost Egyptian units, at Isdud, on 2-3 June. If the Egyptians indeed came to a halt on their own volition somewhat earlier (probably on 28 May, having advanced a few more kilometres after 24 May), as appears likely, then it was either because of logistical or operational difficulties or because the Egyptian Government had decided to order the force to halt at the northernmost boundary of the southern ('Auja-Gaza-Isdud') chunk of territory earmarked by the UN Partition Resolution for Arab sovereignty, or out of a combination of these reasons. Incidentally, on 26 May (Kirkbride to Bevin (No. 396), PRO FO 816\121) Kirkbride noted that news of the Legion's victory the day before at Latrun made the Arab states more reluctant to consider a ceasefire.

508 On 27 May Kirkbride cabled Bevin (quite accurately, probably on the basis of briefings by Glubb): 'My forecast of future events is that the military situation will become less favourable to the Arabs as time goes on and that in about a fortnight from now they will be in serious difficulties about supplies' (in PRO FO 816\121).

509 Nevo, *Abdallah*, 138.

510 Kirkbride to Bevin (No. 461), 6 June 1948, PRO FO 816\122.

511 Kirkbride, *Wings*, 63.

512 Bevin to Kirkbride, 25 May 1948, PRO FO 816\120; and Kirkbride to Bevin, 25 May 1948, PRO FO 816\120.

513 Bevin to Kirkbride, 27 May 1948, PRO FO 816\121.

514 Kirkbride, *Wings*, 35.

515 Kirkbride, *Wings*, 34.

516 Glubb, *Soldier*, 142; and Pirie-Gordon (Amman) to B.A.B. Burrows, 25 July 1948, PRO FO 371-68822 E10325.

517 Glubb, *Soldier*, 143. Nevo, *Abdallah*, 150, suggests that the decision was taken partly on political grounds; Ramle and Lydda were regarded as Husseini strongholds.

518 Kadish, Sela, Golan, *Lydda*, 24.

519 'Alexandroni Brigade Bulletin', 24 May 1948, IDFA 2323\49\\6.

520 Glubb, *Soldier*, 145.

521 Arab Legion 4th Brigade to Legion HQ, 13 June 1948 22:02 hours, quoted in IDF\General Staff\Intelligence, 'Monitoring', 14 June 1948, HA 105\92. The monitored signal reported that Abdullah said these things to a United Press correspondent.

522 Kirkbride to Bevin (No. 538), 7 July 1948, PRO FO 816\125.

523 Glubb, *Soldier*, 149-50. See also Bilby, *New Star*, 70-1, in which he quotes from 'the gist of a note' by Glubb from 21 June, in which Glubb bewailed the Arabs' lack of 'unified command' and his own lack of 'artillery ammunition.'

[524] Kirkbride to Bevin (No. 546), 9 July 1948, PRO FO 816\125.
[525] Glubb, *Soldier*, 152.
[526] Kirkbride, *Wings*, 41.
[527] Bevin to Kirkbride, 8 July 1948, PRO FO 816\125.
[528] Kirkbride to Bevin (No. 546), 9 July 1948, PRO FO 816\125.
[529] Kirkbride to Bevin (No. 548), 10 July 1948, PRO FO 816\125.
[530] Ben-Gurion and Grunbaum statements, protocol of Israeli cabinet meeting of 6 October 1948, ISA.
[531] Kirkbride to Bevin (No. 547), dated 9 July 1948 but apparently sent on 8 July and received 9 July, PRO FO 816\125.
[532] See, for example, 'Summary of Information on the Enemy before the End of the Truce on the Ramle-Lydda Front and its Environs on 28.6.48', Kiryati Brigade Intelligence, 3 July 1948, IDFA 2323\49\\7, which said that in Ramle there were 500-600 Legionnaires, backed by 400 Transjordanian auxiliaries and 500 local militiamen, and in Lydda, 650 Legionnaires, 300 Transjordanian auxiliaries and about 1,000 local militiamen - all vast exaggerations.
[533] Glubb, *Soldier*, 158.
[534] Glubb, *Soldier*, 158. Steiger, 'Arab Legion,' 192 and 244, argues that Glubb could and should have defended the two towns, given the Legion's superiority in mobility and armour. Steiger, writing in the mid-1950s, may not have been sufficiently aware of Glubb's ammunition problem in July 1948.
[535] Glubb, *Soldier*, 158.
[536] Kirkbride to Bevin (No. 555), 12 July 1948, PRO FO 816\125.
[537] Kirkbride to Bevin (No. 555), 12 July 1948, PRO FO 816\125.
[538] Steiger, 'Legion', 206, quoting from an intercepted OC 4th Regiment signal to Division HQ, 14 July 1948, 18:30 hours. For a full description of the events in Lydda and Ramle on 11-13 July 1948, see B. Morris, 'Operation Dani and the Palestinian Exodus from Lydda and Ramle in 1948', *MEJ* 40\1, winter 1986.
[539] Kirkbride, *Wings*, 46-47.
[540] Shlaim, *Collusion*, 263-65. Glubb in desperation apparently turned to the Iraqis - but Baghdad said it had no shells to spare.
[541] Shlaim, *Collusion*, 269.
[542] Pirie-Gordon to Bevin (No. 570), 14 July 1948, PRO FO 816\126; and HM Ambassador in Cairo to HM Minister in Amman, 16 July 1948, PRO FO 816\126. Kirkbride fell sick on 13 July and then flew to England, returning to Amman in early August. His deputy, Christopher Pirie-Gordon, filled in.
[543] Glubb, *Soldier*, 164: 'I had never foreseen that the operations in Lydda and Ramle would have led to a human catastrophe on this scale. But even if I had known, what else could I have done?'
[544] Kirkbride, *Wings*, 47 and 65.
[545] 'Hiram' to 'Da`at,' 17 July 1948, ISA 2569\13.
[546] Kirkbride, *Wings*, 48.
[547] Pirie-Gordon to Bevin (No. 590), 19 July 1948, PRO FO 816\126.
[548] 'Report from Informants who Returned from a Trip through Nazareth-Irbid-Zerka-Amman-Jericho-Nablus,' by 'Shafik,' 16 September 1948, ISA 2569\13.
[549] Glubb, *Soldier*, 163-64.
[550] Kirkbride, *Wings,* 65.
[551] Glubb, *Soldier*, 163-64.
[552] Political Department to Y. Shimoni, etc., 2 August 1948, ISA 2569\13.

[553] Comment by Minorities Minister Bechor Shitrit, Protocol of Israeli cabinet meeting, 16 July 1948, ISA.
[554] Glubb, *Soldier*, 165-66.
[555] Pirie-Gordon, Amman, to B.A.B. Burrows, 25 July 1948, PRO FO 371-68822 E10325; and Glubb, *Soldier*, 165-66.
[556] Pirie-Gordon to Bevin (No. 570), 14 July 1948, PRO FO 816\126.
[557] Pirie-Gordon, 'Major General Glubb's Relations with the Trans-Jordan Government', 15 July 1948, quoted in Norton, 'Pasha', 358.
[558] Glubb, *Soldier*, 164-65; and 'Palcor' (London) to Tel Aviv, 24 July 1948, ISA 2569\13.
[559] Nevo, *Abdallah*, 152.
[560] Kirkbride to Bevin, 25 September 1948, PRO FO 371-68832 E12875.
[561] Pirie-Gordon to Bevin (No. 586), 18 July 1948, PRO FO 816\126.
[562] Kirkbride to FO, 5 August 1948, PRO FO 371-6883 E10502.
[563] Kirkbride to Bevin, 11 August 1948, PRO FO 371-68830 E10986.
[564] Kirkbride to FO, 6 August 1948, PRO FO 371-68830 E10512.
[565] Middle East Affairs Department, Israel Foreign Ministry, 'Information from the Middle East countries', No. 16, 3-4 and 14 October 1948, HA 105\88.
[566] Pirie-Gordon to Burrows, 25 July 1948, PRO FO 916\127. Pirie-Gordon pointed out that during the 'Ten Days,' the Legion had expended some 500 shells daily.
[567] Pirie-Gordon to Bevin (No. 585), 18 July 1948, PRO FO 816\126.
[568] 'Initial Summary of Activities During 9.7-18.7.48', IDF Intelligence Department\Operations\General Staff, 21 July 1948, IDFA 7011\49\\5.
[569] Pirie-Gordon to FO, 27 July 1948, PRO FO 816\127.
[570] Pirie-Gordon to FO (No. 614), 27 July 1948, PRO FO 816\127.
[571] Nevo, *Abdallah*, 152, interprets Glubb's leave as a sign of Abdullah's displeasure with him, but there is no evidence for this. The evidence points in the opposite direction - that Abdullah, taking advantage of the truce, decided to send Glubb to London to plead for ammunition and political support.
[572] Abdullah to Bevin, 12 August 1948, and Bevin to Abdullah, 23 August 1948, both in PRO FO 371-68822 E11049G. Bevin's response was bland and unforthcoming.
[573] The two memoranda are in PRO FO 371-68822 E11049G.
[574] Elias Sasson, the director of the Israel Foreign Ministry's Middle East Affairs Department, aware of Glubb's efforts, wrote to Abdul Majid Haidar, Jordan's minister in London, asking him to persuade Glubb of 'the advantages of an understanding between Israel and Transjordan,' not 'to hinder' this goal. 'I often wonder whether Glubb Pasha realizes to what extent such an agreement ... would benefit our two countries,' he wrote (Sasson to Haidar, 26 August 1948, ISA 2569\13).
[575] Statement by Abba Eban, Israel's representative to the United Nations, at a meeting of the Israeli cabinet, 5 September 1948, (protocol of the Israeli cabinet meeting of 5 September 1948, ISA). Apparently Israeli intelligence had obtained a (secret) FO report on the Bevin-Glubb meeting.
[576] Bevin to Kirkbride, 21 August 1948, PRO FO 371-68831 E11168\18\80G. As instructed, Kirkbride subsequently told Abdullah and Abul Huda that HMG had 'never urged Transjordan to intervene in Palestine ... The former made no direct comment and the latter asked me to say that he realised fully that the suggestion in the King's letter to you that there had been prior agree-

ment about the Arab Legion entering Palestine was not correct' (Kirkbride to FO, 28 August 1948, PRO FO 371-68831 E11350\28\80G).

[577] Extract from Chiefs of Staff 112th Meeting, 11 August 1948, PRO FO 371-68822 E11049G.

[578] Burrows Minute, 25 August 1948, PRO FO 371-68822 E11403\G.

[579] Burrows to Glubb, 15 September 1948, PRO FO 371-68831 E11497\28\80G.

[580] BMEO (Cairo) to Eastern Department, FO, 4 September 1948, PRO FO 371-68831 E11710. Zionist sources had it that already in July the Legion had been 'promised further supplies [of ammunition] - albeit in an indirect manner' (see 'Meeting: I.J. Linton-H. Beeley (London, 1 July 1948)', I.J. Linton, 5 July 1948, Freundlich (ed.), *Documents*, I, 272). But this report was probably untrue.

[581] Glubb, *Soldier*, 258.

[582] Kirkbride to Foreign Office, 5 August 1948, PRO FO 371-68830 E10466\G. In his memoirs, Glubb related that 'Azzam had promised him £3 million and actually gave him £250,000 in cash, which he had gone on to 'over-spend' (he does not say by how much). 'Azzam declined to pay up the residue. So Glubb went to Prime Minister Abul Huda, who said: 'Don't you know Finance Regulations? Where am I to get the money from?' Glubb responded, 'sarcastically': 'I suggest you deduct it from my pay.' A furious Abul Huda sped off to complain to the King, who suggested that Glubb take a month's leave (Glubb, *Soldier*, 178-9).

[583] Kirkbride to Bevin, 9 August 1948, PRO FO 371-68830 E10894.

[584] Glubb, *Soldier*, 258.

[585] Kirkbride to Bevin, 25 September 1948, PRO FO 371-68832 E12875.

[586] Foreign Ministry Research Division to Y. Shimoni, 19 July 1948, ISA 2569\13. The IDF at the end of 'the Ten Days' noted the Legion's supply problems (based on signals intercepts): Legion officers were buying the odd rifle and machinegun from West Bankers, paying 'in cash.' Moreover, the Legion was short of fuel, vehicles, and food stocks; was suffering from a rash of desertions; and was burdened by the refugee concentrations, who undermined local morale and required various types of supplies. However, it is by no means clear that the IDF command or the political echelon fully absorbed the import of these intercepts.

[587] Kirkbride to FO, 3 November 1948 (No. 854), PRO FO 371-68822 E14189\14\80G.

[588] Glubb to Burrows, 22 September 1948, quoted in Shlaim, *Collusion*, 297.

[589] For the Legion's suppression of the Palestinian bands, see Mordechai Abir, 'The Local Arab Element in the War of Independence (the Jerusalem Area)', 1957/58, 14, IDFA 1046/70//185, and Gelber, *Palestine 1948,* 174-82. For the Jordanian-Egyptian rivalry, see Doran, *Pan-Arabism before Nasser,* 165; and Shlaim, *Collusion*, 328-330.

[590] See 'Tene (Ayin) Information', date unclear, probably 6 June 1948, and 'Summary of Information', 'Tene,' date unclear but probably 7 July 1948, both in IDFA 922\1975\\1205.

[591] Arab Department, Haganah Intelligence Service, 'Information Circular', 1 July 1948, HA 105\147.

[592] Translation into Hebrew of an intercepted cable from a Mufti supporter in Jerusalem to Haj Amin al Husseini ('SVG' to 'SVT'), 1 August 1948; and unsigned, but by IDF intelligence, 'Information Summary 4.8.1948', both in

HA 105\104. And Abir, 'The Local Arab Element in the War of Independence (the Jerusalem Area)', 20-21, IDFA 1046\70\\185.

[593] Unsigned but by IDF intelligence, 'Information Circular on Arab Matters (from 7.8.1948)', 8 August 1948, IDFA 500\48\\60.

[594] Arab Department, IDF Intelligence Service, 'Information Circular', 1 August 1948, HA 105\147.

[595] See, for example, Glubb, *Soldier*, 164.

[596] See the protocols of the Israeli Cabinet meetings of 1, 16 and 20 June, 2, 4, 14 and 28 July, 11 and 25 August, and 12 September 1948, ISA. At the meeting of 16 June a majority, if not a consensus, formed around the policy of not allowing a refugee return before the end of hostilities. Formalizing this policy, on 28 July the Cabinet decided, by 9 votes to 2, 'that so long as the war continues there is no agreement to a return of the refugees.' A second vote on the matter, amplifying the original decision, took place on 12 September, when it was decided, by 7 votes to 3, 'not to discuss the return of the refugees before a peace settlement.'

[597] Glubb to Burrows, 7 September 1948, PRO FO 371-68859 E12069. See also Glubb, 'Note by Glubb Pasha', 19 August 1948, PRO FO 371-68822, and Glubb to G. Lewis Jones, US Embassy, London, 15 September 1948, PRO FO 371-68859 E12069.

[598] Glubb to Pirie-Gordon, 19 June 1949, PRO FO 816\147.

[599] For example, see Glubb to Furlonge, 1 June 1952, PRO FO 816\179.

[600] Kirkbride, *Wings*, 68.

[601] Shlaim, *Collusion*, 299-301; and Doran, *Pan-Arabism*, 178.

[602] Glubb, undated but early 1949, SAMECA, Glubb Papers, Transjordan (5).

[603] Glubb, 'A Note on the Need for a Longer Term Plan for the Arab Legion', undated but received in UK on 23 May 1950, PRO FO 371-82752 ET1202\28.

[604] Glubb, 'Suggested Partition Frontiers in Palestine', early 1949, SAMECA, Glubb Papers, Transjordan (5). For the process of the destruction of the Arab villages and settlement of emptied Arab villages and neighbourhoods by new Jewish immigrants, see Morris, *Birth*, 155-196

[605] Glubb to Goldie, 16 October 1948, quoted in Shlaim, *Collusion*, 329.

[606] Glubb to Goldie, 21 October 1948, quoted in Shlaim, *Collusion*, 332-333, and Shlaim's own analysis of the move. A week later, Kirkbride explained that the Legion push to Hebron was at least in part designed 'to prevent a panic amongst the local population which would have resulted in a new wave of refugees which Transjordan simply would not have been in a position to cope with' (Kirkbride to Bevin (No. 836), 30 October 1948, PRO FO 816\132).

[607] Marshud to Glubb, 9 December 1948, IDFA 922\1975\\693.

[608] Kirkbride to FO, 3 November 1948 (No. 853), PRO FO 371-68822 E14188\14\80G.

[609] Kirkbride to FO, 3 November 1948 (No. 853), PRO FO 371-68822 E14188\14\80G; and FO to Kirkbride, 6 November 1948, PRO FO 371-68822 E14189\14\80G.

[610] Kirkbride to Bevin (No. 775), 4 October 1948, PRO FO 816\130.

[611] Glubb to Burrows, 22 September 1948, PRO FO 371-68861 E12651\G. The transfer to Jordanian sovereignty of a strip of coastline around Gaza, possibly as far north as Majdal\Ashkelon, and a sovereign passage to it from the Hebron Hills, was to be a constant demand in Jordanian negotiations with Israel

during the following months (see 'A Meeting between Representatives of the State of Israel, R. Shiloah and Lt. Col. Moshe Dayan, and the Representative of King Abdullah, Col. Abdullah Tall, 30.12.48', 31 December 1948, unsigned, ISA FM 3738\8; and E. Sasson to M. Shertok, 1 February 1949, ISA FM 3738\9).

612 Kirkbride to Bevin (No. 769), 30 September 1948, PRO FO 816\129; and Glubb, 'Trans-Jordan and Palestine', 5 October 1948, PRO FO 816\130.

613 Kirkbride to Burrows, 6 October 1948, PRO FO 816\130.

614 Glubb to Kirkbride, 21 November 1948, untitled draft plan, Arab Legion Headquarters, 21 November 1948; and Kirkbride to Bevin (No. 910), 26 November 1948 - both in PRO FO 816\134.

615 Kirkbride to Bevin (No. 854), 3 November 1948, PRO FO 816\132. Kirkbride presented all the foregoing as his view - but ended the cable with: 'Glubb agrees with these views.'

616 Kirkbride to Bevin (No. 844), 2 November 1948, PRO FO 816\132.

617 Glubb, *Soldier*, 217.

618 Glubb, *Soldier*, 213.

619 Kirkbride to FO, 31 August 1948, PRO FO 371-68822.

620 Kirkbride to FO, 3 November 1948 (No. 854), PRO FO 371-68811 E14189\14\80G.

621 Kirkbride to Foreign Office, 6 December 1948, PRO FO 371-68822\E15533.

622 It is not altogether clear when the Legion 'occupied' the southern Negev wedge. There is evidence that it occurred in May-June 1948, during the pan-Arab invasion of Palestine; and there is also testimony that it occurred in late October-November 1948, after the Egyptian defeat in Operation Yoav. In either case, it was a violation of General Assembly Resolution 181. And in either case, Glubb, strictly speaking, lied when he maintained, as he frequently did during and after 1948, that the Legion had never tried to invade, or had never invaded, areas allotted to the Jewish state in the partition resolution (though he could well have claimed that the Legion penetration of the southern Negev was more in the nature of 'patrolling' than conquest and occupation). It is possible that Legion units penetrated the area twice - once in May-June and then again in late October-November. Indeed, I have seen no evidence of a Legion presence in the southern Negev during July-mid-October 1948.

In *Soldier*, 229, Glubb wrote that the area was occupied by the Legion after the Egyptian collapse of 15-22 October. But Kenneth Bilby, *New Star*, 102-5, quotes a long document which he said Glubb wrote in his presence in March 1949 which stated that the Legion had occupied 'Hisb and Kurneb ... on 12 June 1948' and remained there until November. On 6 November, the Legion withdrew from 'Hisb' - presumably present-day Hatzeva, in the northern 'Arava, just south of the Dead Sea - which was occupied by the IDF two days later. The Legion re-established itself in 'Ain al Weibe (present-day Yahav), to the south. On 1 December, Legion and IDF forces clashed at 'Ain el Weibe and the Legion 'took up a position at [Bir] Meliha,' still further south, and the Jews at 'El Ghamr. Later, the Jews withdrew and the Legion reoccupied 'Ain al Weibe'. The Legion, sensitive to possible danger to 'Aqaba, Jordan's only sea port, at this time established the 'Southern Column,' a mobile unit responsible for the Ma`an-'Aqaba road and the 'Arava area, and appointed the commander of the 9th Regiment (battalion) military governor of 'Aqaba. According to IDF intelligence, the Legion's focus had steadily 'moved southward' during the second half of 1948 (Military Intelligence 1, 'Weekly Intelligence Report', 9 December 1938 [sic, should be 1948], IDFA 1041\49\\13.) Between 24 and 28 February 1949, according to Glubb, an IDF reconnaissance group drove through the southern Negev to Ras al Naqb and back, and on '7 March' 1949 the IDF began its decisive push southwards down the 'Arava and central Negev to Um Rashrash.

[623] Glubb, 'Suggested Partition Frontiers in Palestine', undated but from early 1949, SAMECA, Glubb Papers, Transjordan (5).

[624] For example, see Yaakov Shimoni to prime minister and foreign minister, 'Meeting with Representatives of King Abdullah', undated but from early 1949, ISA FM 2408\13. At the meeting, the Jordanians read out a letter from Abdullah, which, among other things, stated: 'The most important thing is that we [the Jordanians] reach Lydda and Ramle and return their inhabitants to them ... If this is implemented then all the [other] problems and obstacles will be removed from the path of both sides.'

[625] Glubb, 'Suggested Partition Frontiers in Palestine', early 1949, SAMECA, Glubb Papers, Transjordan (5).

[626] Bilby, *New Star*, 105-6, quotes an interview with IDF General Moshe Dayan in late 1949, with Dayan saying, about the IDF takeover of the central and southern Negev on 5-10 March 1949: 'Assuredly ... we violated the truce when we made our move. It was one of those calculated violations which we had to carefully weigh against political risks.'

[627] Glubb, 'The Palestine Situation', 15 March 1949, PRO FO 816\144.

[628] Bilby, *New Star*, 22.

[629] Glubb, text of speech delivered at a dinner in London of the Anglo-Arab Association, 6 May 1949, PRO FO 371-75295 E6180. Kirkbride, *Wings*, 65, incorrectly recalled that there were 'no Arab troops' stationed at the time south of the Dead Sea.

[630] Glubb, *Soldier*, 231-33. IDF documentation states that by March 1949 this Jordanian force, with headquarters in Gharandal, consisted of some two companies of regular troops and mounted police (see 'Intelligence Annex to Operation Uvda Operational Order', 12th (Hanegev) Brigade Intelligence, 3 March 1948, IDFA 6308\49\\146).

[631] Some shots were traded between the advancing Israelis and the Jordanians, and one Jordanian armoured car was lost - but there appear to have been no fatalities on either side (Glubb, *Soldier*, 232).

[632] Kirkbride to B.A.B. Burrows, 9 March 1949, PRO FO 371-75300 E3381\G31.

[633] Glubb, *Soldier*, 233; and Morris, *Border Wars*, 150-152.

[634] Bilby, *New Star*, 106-8.

[635] Glubb, *Soldier*, 234.

[636] Glubb, *Soldier*, 235-37.

[637] Glubb to Pirie-Gordon, 14 March 1949, PRO FO 816\144; and Glubb to Pirie-Gordon, 15 March 1949, PRO FO 816\144.

[638] Glubb to Pirie-Gordon, 23 March 1949, PRO FO 816\144.

[639] Shlaim, *Collusion*, 414-15.

[640] Glubb to Pirie-Gordon, 23 March 1949, PRO FO 816\144.

[641] Shlaim, *Collusion*, 418.

[642] Glubb, *Soldier*, 237.

[643] Glubb speech at dinner in London of Anglo-Arab Association, 6 May 1949, PRO FO 371-75295 E6180.

[644] Bar-Joseph, *Best of Enemies,* 163-64, seems to me to exaggerate when he writes that 'Glubb ... played virtually no role in the political negotiations throughout this period [i.e., the reference apparently is to 1949-51].'
[645] Glubb to Pirie-Gordon, 11 June 1949, PRO FO 816\146.
[646] Glubb, *Soldier*, 241-43.
[647] Capt. Karl Kosman in the name of the director of IDF Intelligence Department, to Foreign Ministry Research Department, 'Public Opinion in the Triangle', 5 June 1949, IDFA 880\49\\202.
[648] Untitled, undated, unsigned memorandum from June 1949, PRO FO 816\147.
[649] Glubb, *Soldier*, 243-44. Glubb writes that an 'anonymous defender' of the Legion had produced the poster - but it was clearly he himself.
[650] Glubb to Kirkbride, 7 June 1949, SAMECA, Glubb Papers, Transjordan\Iraq (8).
[651] Glubb, *Soldier*, 257. Ben-Gurion, similarly, understood that Abdullah sincerely wanted peace. In 1949 he told Bilby: 'I think he really wants peace' (quoted in Shlaim, *Collusion*, 353).
[652] Glubb, *Soldier*, 258.
[653] Kirkbride to Bevin (No. 931), 6 December 1948, PRO FO 816\134.
[654] Glubb, 'A Note on the Palestine Situation 28\5\49', PRO FO 816\146. See also, for example, OC Samaria District, Arab Legion, to Glubb, 27 May 1949, PRO FO 816\146.
[655] Glubb, 'The Situation in Palestine 24th July, 1949', PRO FO 816\147.
[656] Glubb, 'The Situation in Jordania', 15 October 1949, PRO FO 816\148.
[657] Wilson, *King Abdullah,* 197-198.
[658] Glubb, 'The State of Jordan 25th April 1950', PRO FO 816\162.
[659] Glubb, 'The State of Jordan 25th April 1950', PRO FO 816\162.
[660] British Legation, Amman, to FO, 17 September 1951, PRO FO 816\172.
[661] Gelber, *Jewish-Transjordanian*, 289, argues that it was Palestinian resentment against Abdullah's annexation of the West Bank and rule over them rather than rumours or information about the clandestine Israeli-Hashemite peace contacts that triggered the assassination. Shlaim, *Collusion*, 606, ascribes the assassination to 'the long-standing rivalry between Abdullah and the Husseinis,' though suggests that the 'contacts with the Israelis and ... his ... desire to make peace' also played a part.
[662] Glubb, *Soldier*, 276 and 279-280.
[663] Sasson to Foreign Ministry Director General Walter Eytan, 21 July 1951, ISA FM 2408\11 aleph. Sasson criticized Israel Radio's Arabic service for failing, when reporting the assassination, to say 'may God's mercy be upon him,' which could be seen as a sign that Israel 'does not keep faith with our loyal friends when they pass on.'
[664] Glubb, *Soldier*, 278.
[665] British Legation, Amman, to FO, 27 July 1951, PRO FO 816\172.
[666] Kirkbride to Furlonge, FO, 27 July 1951, PRO FO 816\172.
[667] Glubb to Kirkbride, 12 August 1951; and OC Nablus District to Glubb, 15 July 1951, both in PRO FO 816\174.
[668] Gazit to Ambassador, 23 June 1954, ISA FM 3745\3.
[669] Gershon Avner to Gideon Rafael, 5 August 1954, ISA FM 3745\3.
[670] Lt. General Sir Harold Redman, CIGS, to Sir James Marshall-Cornwall, 17 July 1953; Marshall-Cornwall to Redman, 24 August 1953; and Marshall-Cornwall to Glubb, 24 August 1953 - all in ISA FM 3745\3.

[671] Chiefs of Staff Committee, 'Size and Shape of the Arab Legion for 1949\50,' 31 December 1948.
[672] Glubb, 'A Note on the Attitude of Israel in Event of a Major War', 11 January 1951, PRO FO 816\175.
[673] Glubb to Kirkbride, 13 January 1951, PRO FO 816\175.
[674] Glubb, 'A Note on the Future of Jerusalem', 18 July 1949, PRO FO 816\147.
[675] See Morris, *Border Wars* (1997 ed.), 10-13.
[676] Eban to prime minister and foreign minister, 26 December 1952, ISA FM 2408\13.
[677] Shiloah to Sharett, 27 January 1953, ISA FM 2408\13
[678] David Ben-Gurion Diary, entries for 7 and 13 February, 1951, Ben-Gurion Archive; and Bar-On, *Challenge*, 249, 253.
[679] Glubb to MacKnight, 'Reflections on Border Problems,' 7 December 1953, PRO FO 371-655954.
[680] Glubb to Furlonge, 1 June 1952, PRO FO 816\179.
[681] Glubb, 'A Note on the Need for a Longer Term Plan for the Arab Legion', undated but received in the Foreign Office on 23 May 1950, and attached Minute by Furlonge, 23 May 1950, PRO FO 371-82752 ET1208.
[682] Glubb to Col. R.K. Melville, 9 April 1955, PRO FO 371-115899.
[683] Glubb, 'An (Extremely Conjectural) Memo on Egyptian Policy', 22 October 1955, PRO FO 371-115907.
[684] For example, see Glubb, 'A Note on Refugee Vagrancy', February, 1953 (misdated 'end March, 1953'), PRO FO 371-104778.
[685] Glubb, 'A Note on Refugee Vagrancy', February, 1953, PRO FO 371-104778.
[686] Glubb to Kirkbride, 18 March 1951, PRO FO 816\173; and Glubb, 'A Note on Refugee Vagrancy', February, 1953, PRO FO 371-104778.
[687] Glubb, 'A Note on Refugee Vagrancy', February 1953, PRO FO 371-104778.
[688] Evans to A.D.M. Ross (London), 28 February 1953, PRO FO 371-104779 ER1091\69.
[689] Glubb to Kirkbride, 18 March 1951, PRO FO 816\173
[690] Glubb, *Soldier*, 245.
[691] Glubb, 'After Qibya', 14 January 1954, PRO FO 371-111069 VR1072\10
[692] Glubb to Melville, 15 June 1953, PRO FO 371-104784.
[693] Glubb to Melville, 12 June 1953, PRO FO 371-104784. See also Furlonge to FO, 3 June 1953, PRO FO 371-104783 E21091\200.
[694] Moore (Tel Aviv) to FO, 19 June 1953, PRO FO 371-104784 ER 1091\239; and Glubb, *Soldier*, 305-6.
[695] Glubb, 'A Note on Refugee Vagrancy', February 1953, PRO FO 371-104778.
[696] Glubb, 'A Note on the Situation in Jordan', 1 July 1952, PRO FO 371-98861.
[697] Glubb to Riley, 8 February 1951, PRO FO 371-91385 E1091\23.
[698] Knox Helm to Kirkbride, 2 April 1951, PRO FO 816\173.
[699] Glubb, 'A Note on Refugee Vagrancy', February 1953, PRO FO 371104778.
[700] Glubb, 'A Note on Refugee Vagrancy', February 1953, PRO FO 371-104778:
[701] Glubb, *Soldier*, 323
[702] Glubb, 'A Note on Refugee Vagrancy', February 1953, PRO FO 371-104778.

[703] Glubb, 'A Note on the Situation in Jordan', 1 July 1952, PRO FO 371-98861. See also Glubb, 'A Note on Refugee Vagrancy,' February 1953, PRP FO 371-104778.
[704] Glubb, 'A Note on Refugee Vagrancy', February 1953, PRO FO 371-104778.
[705] Glubb to Furlonge, 4 April 1953, PRO FO 816\189.
[706] Glubb, *Soldier*, 247-9; and Morris, *Border Wars*, 170-78.
[707] Glubb to Kirkbride, 28 June 1950, PRO FO 371-82205. As to the support by leaders like Ben-Gurion and Sharett of Arab emigration from Israel in those early years of the state, see Benziman and Mansour, *Sub-Tenants*, 54-60; and Masalha, *A land Without a People*, 14-21. But Glubb's charge, that the Israeli leadership and IDF command authorised or condoned the beatings and torture, appears to be unfounded. A number of soldiers were reportedly tried in connection with the 'Arava incident and the Mapai Party leaders discussed the incident at length and critically (see Morris, *Border Wars*, 174-78).
[708] Glubb to Kirkbride, 28 June 1950, PRO FO 371-82205.
[709] Glubb, 'After Qibya', 14 January 1954, PRO FO 371-111069 VR1072\10.
[710] Glubb, 'After Qibya', 14 January 1954, PRO FO 371-111069 VR1072\10.
[711] Glubb, 'A Note on the Situation in Jordan', 1 July 1952, PRO FO 371-98861.
[712] Glubb, 'After Qibya', 14 January 1954, PRO FO 371-111069 VR1072\10.
[713] Glubb, 'A Note on Refugee Vagrancy', February 1953, PRO FO 371-104778.
[714] Glubb, *Soldier*, 342.
[715] Glubb, *Soldier*, 340.
[716] Glubb to Riley, 8 February 1951, PRO FO 371\91385 E1091\23.
[717] Glubb to General E.L.M. Burns, chief of staff, UNTSO, 18 October 1954, PRO FO 371-11106.
[718] Glubb to Riley, UNTSO, 8 February 1951, PRO FO 371-91385 E1091\23.
[719] Glubb, 'A note on the Situation in Jordan', 1 July 1952, PRO FO 371-98861. See also Moore (Tel Aviv) to Foreign Office, 19 June 1953, PRO FO 371-104784 ER 1091\239.
[720] See Morris, *Border Wars*, 257-76; and Glubb, *Soldier*, 308-13.
[721] Glubb, *Soldier*, 382, relates how he twice indirectly tried to persuade Nasser to desist from such operations, which were usually organized by the Egyptian Embassy in Amman, to kill soldiers and civilians and blow up military and civilian installations.
[722] Golani, *There Will be War Next Summer*, 27-44, argues that the Israeli policy to provoke war with Egypt was initiated by Ben-Gurion and Dayan in March 1955. Bar-On, *The Gates of Gaza*, 13-16, dates the initiation of the policy from September-October 1955, when Nasser first announced to the world the massive Egyptian-Soviet (the 'Czech') arms deal.
[723] Glubb to Melville, 9 April 1955, PRO FO 371-115899; and Glubb to Melville, 8 April 1955, PRO FO 371-115899.
[724] Glubb, 'An (Extremely Conjectural) Memo on Egyptian Policy', 22 October 1955, PRO FO 371-115907.
[725] Glubb, 'A Note on Refugee Vagrancy', February 1953, PRO FO 371-104778.
[726] M.T. Walker (Amman) to G.W. Furlonge, Foreign Office, 15 June 1951, PRO FO 371-91387 EE1091\56.
[727] *Palestine Post*, 6 July 1949.

[728] Knox Helm to FO, 17 July 1949, PRO FO 371-75295 E8695.
[729] Pirie-Gordon to FO, 22 July 1949, PRO FO 371-75295 E8954.
[730] Judd (Jerusalem) to FO, 23 July 1949, PRO FO 371-75295 E8955.
[731] 'H.Mc.' minute, 6 August 1949, PRO FO 371-75295.
[732] *NYT*, 18 June 1953, p. 26, 'Glubb Says Israel Seeks Territory'.
[733] FO memorandum on conversation, illegible signature, 22 June 1953, PRO FO 371-104784 ER1091\232A.
[734] Moore to FO, 23 June 1953, PRO FO 371-104785 ER1091\265.
[735] Glubb to Furlonge, 1 Feb. 1953, PRO FO 816\189.
[736] Glubb, *Soldier*, 392-401. See also Vatikiotis, *Arab Legion*, 121-24.
[737] Glubb, *Soldier*, 411.
[738] Glubb to Kirkbride, 27 May 1950, PRO FO 816\165.
[739] General Brian Robertson, OC MELF, 24 October 1952; and Glubb to Robertson, 5 November 1952 - both in PRO FO 816\182.
[740] Kirkbride to G.W. Furlonge, Eastern Department, FO, 5 December 1950, PRO FO 186\167.
[741] See, for example, 'J.C.B.' minute, 30 March 1954, PRO FO 816\190.
[742] For example, see C.B. Duke minute on meeting with Jordan's foreign minister, 7 Aug. 1954, PRO FO 816\191.
[743] 'Jordan' 2 March 1956, an unsigned Israeli intelligence memorandum on Glubb's dismissal, ISA FM 2408\11 bet. See also Vatikiotis, *Arab Legion*, 117-18 and 124.
[744] Dann, *Hussein*, 32-3; and Glubb, *Soldier*, 423-26.
[745] Glubb, *Soldier*, 423-26.
[746] Cabinet meeting minute, 5 March 1956, PRO CAB 128-30.
[747] Cabinet meeting minute, 9 March 1956, PRO CAB 128-30.
[748] Uriel Dann, *Hussein,* especially chapter 4; and Vatikiotis, *Politics*, 127-34.
[749] Dann, *Hussein*, 34.
[750] Wolfgang Saxon, Glubb Pasha obituary, *NYT*, 18 March 1986.
[751] Hodder and Stoughton, London, 1967, revised ed. 1969.
[752] Glubb quoted in 'The Times Diary,' *The Times* (London), 26 August 1967.
[753] Glubb, 'Middle East Crisis,' 1969 ed., 7.
[754] Glubb, 'Middle East Crisis,' 1969 ed., 11-23; Glubb quoted in 'The Times Diary', *The Times* (London), 28 June 1967; and Glubb, *Peace*, 331-33.
[755] Glubb, 'Middle East Crisis', 1969 ed., 14-18. On p. 17 he actually refers to 'poor little Jordan.'
[756] Glubb, *Peace*, 337.
[757] Glubb, *Peace*, 339.
[758] Glubb, *Soldier*, 211-212, and 251.
[759] Glubb, *Peace*, 299.
[760] Glubb letter to the editor, *The Times* (London), 21 February 1968.
[761] Glubb letter to *The Times*, 8 January 1969.
[762] Glubb letter to *The Times* (London), 28 November 1969.
[763] Glubb to the editor, *The Times* (London), 25 March 1978. Whatever had happened in Palestine in 1948, there was no truth to the charge about destroying Lebanese towns and villages in 1978. See also Glubb to the editor, *The Times* (London), 6 December 1979.
[764] See Glubb 'Middle East Crisis,' 1969 ed., 59-60: 'It is not difficult to understand the Jewish desire for a state … Israel has now achieved a Jewish State ... It is unwise ... to demand an empire ...'
[765] Glubb letter to *The Times* (London), 14 June 1972.

[766] Quoted in Royle, *Glubb*, 498.
[767] Shlaim, *Collusion*, 224. This view also underlies Norton's 'Pasha'.
[768] See, for example, al-Nashashibi, *What Happened in the Middle East*, 171-72.
[769] Glubb, *Soldier*, 445.
[770] Glubb, *Soldier*, 446. At the time, Jordan also included the West Bank, with Bethlehem and East Jerusalem.
[771] Glubb, *Soldier*, 299.
[772] Al-Nashashibi, *What Happened in the Middle East*, 156.
[773] Protocol of Israel Cabinet Meeting, 14 July 1948, ISA.
[774] Glubb to Furlonge, 31 October 1953, PRO FO 816\189.
[775] Norton, 'Pasha', 225.

INDEX

'A Further Note on Peace Terms in the Middle East', 67

'A Further Note on the Palestine Question', 79

'A Note on the Exact Siting of the Frontier in the event of the adoption of Partition', 87

'A Note on the Report of [the] Anglo-American Commission', 75

A Soldier with the Arabs, 9, 114

'Abd al-Ilah, 131

Abdullah (Emir, later King, of Jordan), 3, 33, 34, 36, 37, 38, 39, 41, 42, 44, 51, 57, 74, 78, 80, 82, 85, 89, 91, 92, 93, 94, 95, 96, 97, 98, 99, 100, 101, 102, 103, 104, 106, 107, 108, 109, 110, 111, 112, 113, 115, 116, 117, 118, 119, 120, 121, 122, 124, 125, 126, 127, 128, 129, 130, 131, 132, 133, 134, 135, 136, 137, 138, 140, 142, 143, 144, 147, 148, 149, 150, 151, 152, 153, 154, 155, 156, 157, 158, 159, 160, 161, 162, 163, 165, 167, 168, 170, 171, 172, 173, 174, 176, 178, 179, 180, 182, 183, 185, 186, 187, 189, 192, 193, 196, 201, 202, 203, 204, 205, 206, 207, 238, 240, 241

Abu Durra, Yusuf, 54, 55

Abu Ibrahim the Elder, 53

Abu Nawar, 'Ali, 231, 232

Abu Tor, 155

Abul Huda, Tewfiq, 71, 107, 109, 110, 111, 112, 113, 114, 115, 116, 120, 131, 132, 154, 156, 157, 159, 160, 171, 172, 173, 174, 175, 176, 179, 180, 181, 197

Acre (Akko), 82, 87, 124, 140, 174

Al Ahram, 128

Ajlun, 51, 52

al Aksa, 156, 206

al Alami, Musa, 118

Alexandroni Brigade (Haganah/IDF), 173

Allenby Bridge, 119, 149, 152, 156, 178

All-Palestine Government, 189, 192

Amman, 2, 4, 12, 35, 37, 38, 39, 42, 43, 44, 45, 46, 51, 61, 71, 75, 93, 94, 95, 105, 117, 118, 122, 123, 125, 127, 129, 131, 136, 140, 142, 144, 147, 148, 149, 150, 151, 154, 156, 157, 159, 160, 173, 174, 176, 177, 178, 180, 181, 186, 193, 196, 200, 201, 202, 204, 207, 208, 213, 223, 227, 228, 229, 231, 232, 233, 237, 245, 249

Anglo-American Commission of Inquiry, 74, 77, 78, 79, 80, 247

Anglo-Iraqi Treaty of 1930, 179

Anglo-Transjordan Treaty of 1946, 179

Antiochus Epiphanes, 24

A'Aqaba, 46, 49, 113, 121, 171, 184, 195, 198, 199, 212, 234

Arab Higher Committee, 104, 118, 204

Arab League, 76, 96, 106, 108, 112, 116, 126, 127, 129, 145, 148,

150, 165, 171, 173, 174, 175, 181, 184, 196, 197, 204
Arab League Military Committee, 129, 145, 165
Arab League Political Committee, 129, 171, 174
Arab Liberation Army, 116, 118, 124, 132, 151, 152, 241, 247
Arab Revolt, 15, 18, 41
'Arava (Wadi 'Araba), 46, 52, 220, 226
'Arava Expulsion, 226
Ashdod, 191
Attlee, Clement, 78
Augusta Victoria, 155
Austria, 50
Axis, 3, 56, 57, 59, 60
Ayalon Valley, 169
'Azzam Pasha, Abd al Rahman, 129, 131, 132, 148, 151, 184, 186

Bab al Wad, 152
Baghdad Pact, 224, 228, 229
Balfour Declaration, 34, 48, 158
Bani Sakhr, 36, 38, 42, 46
Bar-Joseph, Uri, 6, 243
Bar-Kochba Revolt, 25
Basra, 60
Beduin, 10, 11, 17, 18, 38
Beeley, Harold, 89, 98
Beersheba, 46, 47, 48, 82, 89, 109, 117, 118, 128, 136, 190, 191, 192, 193, 194, 195, 198, 199, 212, 243
Begin, Menachem, 210, 216
Beirut, 44, 60, 94, 236, 245
Beisan, 124
Beit Jala, 193
Beit Jibrin, 130, 186, 191, 192, 193
Beit Liqya, 222
Beith, John, 4, 162, 249
Ben-Gurion, David, 5, 70, 91, 105, 142, 155, 165, 175, 176, 210, 218, 223, 236, 241, 243, 244, 247
Berlin, Isaiah, 29
Bernadotte, Folke B., 198
Bethany (al Azariya), 203
Bethlehem, 22, 41, 104, 130, 135, 136, 153, 154, 162, 185, 186, 187, 191, 192, 193, 195
Bevin, Ernst, 78, 94, 97, 99, 100, 106, 107, 108, 109, 110, 111, 112, 113, 114, 115, 116, 117, 120, 122, 123, 128, 132, 134, 149, 154, 155, 160, 166, 171, 175, 179, 181, 182, 183, 204, 238, 240
Broadhurst, Ronald, 123, 249
Burma Road, 170
Burrows, B.A.B., 98, 99, 100, 110, 112, 183, 195, 249
Burton, Richard, 13, 16

Cadogan, Alexander, 166
Campbell, R.I., 115
Christians, 25, 26, 28, 40, 47, 76, 153, 158, 240
Churchill, Winston, 43, 71
Coaker, Charles, 140, 141, 142, 201
Coastal Plain, 82, 85, 105, 116, 162
Coghill, Patrick, 231
Colonial Office, 106, 115, 124, 247
Communism, 189, 210
Communists, 190, 204
Cox, C.H.F, 37
Cromwell, Oliver, 28
Crusades, 21, 44. 75, 78, 79
Cunningham, Alan, 78, 116, 129, 130, 134, 153, 243
Czechoslovakia, 124, 173, 198

Daily Mail, 78
Damascus, 44, 45, 52, 53, 60, 77, 145, 147, 165, 216
Damascus (Shechem) Gate, 165
Damiya Bridge, 119
Danin, Ezra, 101, 102, 103, 142, 143
Darwaza, Izzat, 53, 54
Daskal, Avraham, 134
Dawayima, 214
Dayan, Moshe, 5, 60, 167, 210, 218
Dead Sea, 141, 199, 213
Degania A, 166

Deir Aiyub, 169
Deir as Sana, 52
Deir Tarif, 178
Deir Yassin, 127, 128, 129, 130, 138, 143, 156, 165, 173, 214
Desert Camel Corps, 1
Desert Mechanised Regiment, 60
Desert Patrol, 2, 11
Displaced Persons, 74, 75, 76
Dogara, 51
Duke, Charles, 231

East Jerusalem, 3, 22, 149, 150, 151, 153, 154, 155, 156, 158, 160, 162, 163, 167, 169, 184, 197, 206, 238, 240, 241, 242
Eastern Galilee, 116, 124
Eban, Abba, 211
Eden, Anthony, 43, 231
Egypt, 5, 13, 19, 44, 56, 57, 59, 62, 78, 79, 83, 84, 107, 108, 116, 136, 145, 149, 179, 181, 185, 188, 189, 191, 194, 195, 197, 198, 199, 200, 204, 206, 223, 224, 225, 228, 232, 234, 241, 247
Eighth Army (British), 57
'Ein Tzurim, 135, 139
Esdraelon (see Jezreel Valley)
Ethiopia (Abyssinia), 33
Etzion Bloc, 135, 136, 137, 138
Etzioni Brigade (Haganah/IDF), 156
Ezra, 23, 24, 101, 142

Faluja Pocket, 192, 196
Fascism, 40, 50
First Truce, 172, 173, 176
Flanders, 1, 239
Foreign Office (British), 4, 89, 96, 106, 110, 115, 120, 123, 124, 139, 144, 203, 208, 218, 224, 226, 227, 238, 240, 247, 249
France, 30, 60, 62, 72, 76, 79, 165, 224
Furlonge, Geoffrey, 12, 208, 213

Galilee, 82, 159, 188, 190, 195, 199, 212
Galili, Yisrael, 210
Gaza, 4, 22, 82, 83, 97, 113, 117, 118, 128, 129, 130, 186, 188, 189, 191, 192, 194, 195, 196, 198, 214, 219, 223, 224, 235, 236, 243
Gaza Raid, 223
Gazit, Mordechai, 207, 208
Gelber, Yoav, 240, 244
Germany, 30, 33, 49, 50, 54, 55, 56, 57, 58, 59, 82, 220
Gesher, Kibbutz, 134
al Ghilani, Rashid 'Ali, 3, 60
Glubb, Frederic Manley, 1
Glubb, Godfrey, 16
Glubb, Mary, 16, 246
Glubb, Naomi, 16, 246
Golani Brigade (Haganah/IDF), 140, 199, 244
Goldie, Desmond, 123, 140, 141, 142, 192, 193
Great Revolt, 25
Greater Syria, 34, 72, 96, 100, 109
Griswold, Lawrence, 226
Grunbaum, Yitzhak, 175
Gulf of Aqaba (Gulf of Eilat), 108, 198

H3, 60
Habbaniyah, 60
Haganah, 3, 6, 60, 105, 117, 118, 119, 121, 124, 125, 126, 127, 128, 129, 130, 133, 134, 135, 136, 137, 138, 140, 141, 142, 147, 149, 150, 153, 154, 155, 156, 160, 161, 162, 165, 168, 169, 170, 172, 210, 241, 243, 245, 247
Haganah Intelligence Service, 118, 125, 126
Haidar, Abdul Majid, 38, 170
Haifa, 62, 63, 72, 82, 83, 85, 87, 94, 124, 126, 129, 130, 131, 133, 136, 145, 153, 156, 162, 191, 212

Hamid, Hamad, 222
Hashim, Ibrahim Pasha, 37, 91, 93
al Hashimi, Taha, 165
Hebron, 82, 96, 109, 116, 117, 118, 128, 130, 135, 136, 137, 138, 139, 149, 156, 162, 185, 186, 187, 189, 190, 191, 192, 193, 195, 198
Hebron Hills, 186, 187, 191, 193, 198
Heikal, Yusuf, 118, 119
Herut Party (the Revisionists), 5, 210, 212, 247
Herzl, Theodor, 30
Hijaz, 10, 39, 153, 160
Hitler, Adolf, 23, 24, 81, 201, 213
Holocaust, 21, 57, 64, 70, 74, 79, 239
Holy War Army, 189
House of Commons, 78
Hussein (King of Jordan), 3, 9, 22, 208, 234, 235, 237, 238, 244
Hussein (King of the Hijaz, Sharif of Mecca), 78, 153, 160
al Husseini, Abd al Qadir, 45, 189
al Husseini, Muhammad Haj Amin, 33, 34, 37, 39, 40, 41, 44, 51, 56, 58, 60, 85, 105, 118, 133, 138, 157, 186, 189, 195, 204, 205, 206Hyrkanus, John, 24

Ibn Saud, 36, 40, 44, 54, 57, 66, 107, 112, 115, 153
IDF Central Command, 223
IDF History Department, 169
Idna, 199
Infiltration problem, 218, 245
'Innab, Radi, 231
Iran (Persia), 77
Iraq (Mesopotamia), 1, 2, 3, 13, 16, 17, 40, 44, 48, 49, 51, 56, 59, 60, 62, 67, 68, 69, 71, 77, 92, 96, 98, 107, 113, 124, 131, 134, 144, 145, 147, 149, 150, 154, 163, 165, 168, 170, 174, 178, 179, 180, 183, 188, 194, 196, 200, 202, 207, 211, 228, 231, 232, 238, 240, 241
Iraq Petroleum Company pipeline, 48, 52
Irgun Zvai Leumi (IZL, National Military Organisation), 46, 80, 124, 127, 135, 141, 247
Iskanderoun, 60
Islam, 26, 27, 153, 161, 240, 241
Israel Defence Forces, 3, 5, 6, 10, 21, 60, 123, 137, 138, 139, 150, 155, 162, 167, 169, 170, 172, 173, 175, 176, 177, 181, 182, 184, 187, 188, 192, 193, 194, 195, 196, 199, 200, 202, 203, 210, 213, 215, 219, 220, 222, 223, 230, 234, 235, 236, 241, 242, 243, 244, 245, 247
Israel-Jordan General Armistice Agreement, 201
Israel-Jordan Mixed Armistice Commission, 220, 227

al Ja'abri, Muhammad Ali, 118, 186
Jaffa, 82, 83, 87, 88, 97, 105, 117, 118, 128, 129, 135, 141, 149, 154, 156, 172
Jaffa Gate, 156
Japan, 33, 56
Jarvis, C.S., 47, 245, 249
Jenin, 109, 163, 202
Jericho, 119, 149, 151, 152, 155, 159, 162, 193, 203, 215
Jerusalem, 14, 20, 25, 33, 37, 41, 56, 62, 71, 75, 78, 80, 83, 85, 86, 87, 89, 91, 104, 109, 115, 117, 127, 128, 130, 131, 133, 135, 136, 137, 138, 140, 141, 142, 143, 147, 148, 149, 150, 152, 153, 154, 155, 156, 157, 158, 159, 160, 161, 162, 163, 164, 165, 166, 167, 168, 169, 170, 171, 172, 176, 183, 189, 190, 193, 201, 203, 204, 206, 207, 211, 212, 214, 215, 217, 234, 240, 241, 243, 244, 245, 246, 247, 249

Jerusalem National Committee, 155
Jewish Agency, 29, 70, 78, 80, 92, 93, 94, 100, 101, 102, 104, 105, 125, 128, 134, 139, 142, 144
Jewish Agency Political Department, 29, 92, 100, 102, 125
Jewish Quarter (in Jerusalem's Old City), 155, 160, 161, 163, 165
Jezreel Valley (Plain of Esdraelon), 82, 85, 124, 145
John of Gischala (Yohanan of Gush-Halav), 25
Jones, William, 10
Jordan River, 51, 101, 110, 119, 176, 185, 186, 195, 210, 212, 213, 215, 217, 223, 242
Jordan Valley, 42, 51, 52, 54, 85, 92, 119, 145, 149, 151, 162
Josephus Flavius (Yosef ben Matityahu), 82
Journal of the Royal Central Asian Society, 47
Judea, 24, 25, 88, 91, 104, 149, 162, 172, 176, 210
al Jundi, Abd al Qadir, 45

Karameh, 51
Kfar Etzion, 135, 137, 138, 139
Khirbet Beit Awwa, 199
King David, 23, 80
King David Hotel, 80
King Farouk (of Egypt), 205
Kirkbride, Alec, 2, 71, 91, 93, 96, 97, 98, 99, 100, 102, 104, 106, 107, 108, 113, 114, 115, 116, 122, 123, 126, 127, 128, 129, 130, 131, 132, 134, 139, 143, 144, 145, 147, 148, 149, 151, 153, 154, 155, 156, 158, 159, 160, 161, 162, 163, 166, 168, 170, 171, 172, 173, 175, 176, 177, 178, 179, 180, 184, 185, 189, 194, 195, 196, 197, 199, 202, 203, 204, 208, 217, 220, 226, 229, 230, 231, 240, 245, 249
al Kurasha, Haditha, 36
Kuwait, 62

Lash, Norman, 89, 123, 141
Latrun, 135, 151, 152, 162, 163, 168, 169, 170, 172, 175, 176, 177, 178, 184, 241, 245
Lawrence, T.E., 44, 226
Lebanon, 13, 56, 57, 60, 62, 71, 72, 73, 82, 92, 94, 96, 97, 102, 107, 147, 149, 188, 195, 200, 236, 241
Lidice, 70
Litani River, 236
Lohamei Herut Yisrael (LHI, Freedom fighters of Israel), 5, 57, 124, 127, 247
Lydda, 109, 118, 128, 157, 170, 172, 175, 176, 177, 179, 180, 184, 190, 198, 203, 245
Lydda Airport, 157

Maccabbees, 24, 25
MacMichael, Harold, 63, 64, 66, 71
McMillan, Gordon, 135
McNeil, Hector, 78, 226
Majali, Habis, 134, 187, 206
Majdal (Ashkelon), 118, 191, 192, 195
Mandelbaum Gate, 163, 165, 166
Mapai, 142, 222
Mapai Party Centre, 142
Marcus (Stone), Mickey, 123
Marshall, George, 117
Marshud, Arshid, 137
al Masmiya al Kabira, 119
Medina, 26, 27, 153
Meir (Myerson), Golda, 100, 101, 102, 103, 125, 132, 142, 144, 155, 245
Middle East Command, 3
Mithgal ibn Faiz, 36, 38, 39
Montgomery, Bernard, 183
Moore, Tony, 227
Morrison-Grady plan, 92
Mossad, 211
Mount of Olives, 160

Mount Scopus, 203
Mount Zion, 161
Moyne, W.E. Guinness, 62, 71
Muhammad, 3, 26, 27, 33, 118, 186, 240, 244
al Mukdadi, Darwish, 118
al Mulki, Fawzi, 109, 111, 112, 176, 208
Munich Conference, 50
Muslim Brotherhood, 186
Musrara, 163, 165

Nabi Samwil, 160
Nablus, 37, 44, 46, 82, 96, 109, 117, 118, 128, 140, 149, 151, 152, 157, 159, 162, 163, 165, 178, 201, 202
Naharayim, 101, 134, 140, 163, 208
Naharayim (Jisr al Majami), 101, 119, 134, 149, 158, 163, 208
al Naqba (catastrophe), 15
Nashashibi, 'Azmi, 16, 245, 249
Nashashibi, Nasir al-Din, 16, 245
Nasser, Gamal Abdel, 19, 52, 223, 228, 229, 232, 236, 244
National Guard, 221
National Religious Party (Mizrahi), 212
Nazareth, 87, 130, 153, 154
Nazism, 24, 50, 69, 70, 82
Negev Brigade (Haganah/IDF), 199
Negev Desert (Neqeb), 47, 88, 89, 95, 97, 104, 105, 113, 191, 192, 195, 196, 198, 199, 212, 219, 220, 241, 243
Nejd (Saudi Arabia), 16, 36
Newbold, David, 70'
Note by Glubb', 182
Notre Dame de France, 165, 166
Nur a Din, Mahmud, 147, 148

Old City (of Jerusalem), 133, 150, 151, 153, 155, 156, 159, 160, 161, 163, 165, 166, 167, 206, 212, 240
Operation Dani, 172, 175, 176, 181, 245
Operation HaHar, 193
Operation Hiram, 188, 190
Operation Horev, 196
Operation Kilshon, 155
Operation Litani, 236
Operation Yekev, 193
Operation Yoav, 187, 188, 191, 192, 195
Ormsby-Gore, William, 38

Packard, C.D., 109
Palestinian Arabs, 14, 15, 18, 22, 31, 32, 33, 34, 35, 37, 40, 41, 43, 45, 46, 47, 54, 57, 65, 69, 71, 76, 85, 86, 91, 92, 102, 104, 110, 117, 118, 124, 126, 127, 135, 142, 143, 170, 178, 179, 189, 190, 191, 194, 195, 201, 202, 204, 205, 215, 224, 233, 234, 235, 236, 239, 240, 245
Palestinian Refugees, 20, 21, 70, 127, 130, 131, 148, 170, 172, 176, 177, 178, 182, 185, 187, 188, 190, 191, 193, 197, 198, 201, 206, 214, 215, 216, 220, 221, 224, 235, 236, 237
Palmyra, 60, 63, 150
Pappe, Ilan, 6, 246
Pasha, Mustafa Nahas, 71
Peace in the Holy Land, 22, 23, 25, 26, 244
Peake, Frederick, 2, 11, 33, 42, 43, 45, 51, 207, 245
Peel Commission, 40, 41, 42, 43, 76, 83, 85, 95
Perowne, Stuart, 14
Pirie-Gordon, Christopher, 93, 95, 96, 109, 110, 178, 179, 180, 181, 201, 226
Plan D, 156
Poland, 49

Qalqilya, 125, 127, 200, 205
Qatamon, 154, 166, 203
Qatana, 214
al Qawuqji, Fawzi, 118, 124, 128, 129, 152, 156

Qibya, 222

Rabinovich, Itamar, 6, 246
Rafah, 83, 121, 131, 136, 145, 191
Ramallah, 109, 118, 119, 128, 133, 135, 140, 149, 151, 152, 157, 159, 162, 163, 165, 175, 177, 178, 189, 193, 201, 204
Ramle, 88, 118, 170, 172, 173, 175, 176, 178, 179, 180, 184, 190, 198, 203, 245
Ras al-Naqura, 145
Razek, Aref Abdul, 53
Rehovot, 191
Revadim, 135, 140
Rifa`i, Samir, 96, 98, 111, 231
Riley, William, 5, 217, 249
Rose, E.M., 224
Royal Air Force (RAF), 2, 52, 130, 181, 247
Russia, 30, 59, 74, 77, 84, 105, 182, 189, 190, 204, 209, 210, 223, 224, 228, 234
Rutbah, 60, 62

Sadat, Anwar, 57
Sadlier, George, 17
Safad, 82, 87, 124
Safwat, Ismail, 129, 145
Saib, Salih Pasha, 194
Said, Nuri, 71, 72
Saladin, 44, 78
al Sakakini, Khalil, 56, 246
Samakh, 52, 53, 149, 158
Samaria, 16, 25, 116, 119, 145, 149, 152, 162, 172, 174, 195, 200, 201, 210
Sandstrom, Emil, 93
Sasson, Eliahu (Elias), 92, 94, 101, 103, 126, 170, 206
Saudi Arabia, 2, 13, 16, 17, 36, 39, 40, 44, 49, 57, 62, 63, 65, 66, 68, 69, 93, 94, 107, 112, 207, 216, 224, 246
Schmidt, Dana Adams, 227
Sea of Galilee, 44, 51, 149, 213
Second Truce, 177, 181, 186, 191
Shamir, Shlomo, 140, 141, 142
Shapira, Anita, 6
Sharett (Shertok), Moshe, 29, 70, 142, 166, 211, 218, 226, 238
Sharon, Ariel, 169
Sheikh Hafiz Wahba, 115
Sheikh Hussein Bridge, 119
Sheikh Jarah, 155, 156, 163, 203
Shiloah, Reuven, 211
Shimoni, Yaakov, 102, 126, 156
Shlaim, Avi, 6, 237, 240, 246
Shuckburgh, C.E., 224
Shunat Nimrin, 51
Sinai Peninsula, 6, 47, 48, 49, 192, 196, 223, 224, 234, 244
Sion (Steiger), Dov, 10, 12, 167, 169, 240, 249
Six day War, 234, 242
Six Day War, 60, 233, 234, 242
al Solh, Riad, 107, 131
Somerset de Chair, 60
Southern Desert Camel Corps, 2
Soviet Bloc, 223
Spears, Sir Edward, 71
Spiegel (Golan), Nahum, 140
Stabler, Wells, 200
Stalin, Joseph, 24, 213
Stanley, Oliver, 63
Suez Canal, 48, 59, 62, 121, 136, 183, 184, 198
Suez War, 4, 6, 48, 59, 62, 121, 136, 171, 198, 223, 224, 232, 244, 245
'Suggested Partition Frontiers in Palestine', 189
Syria, 2, 3, 13, 38, 40, 44, 45, 49, 51, 52, 53, 55, 56, 57, 60, 62, 67, 68, 69, 71, 72, 73, 77, 78, 82, 92, 93, 94, 95, 97, 102, 107, 116, 124, 131, 145, 147, 149, 158, 165, 168, 170, 186, 188, 196, 197, 200, 204, 207, 224, 232, 235, 241

Tal, Wasfi, 145
Tall, Abdullah, 121, 135, 137, 138, 140, 144, 150, 206, 207, 246

Tel Aviv, 6, 85, 105, 126, 127, 141, 142, 145, 150, 157, 161, 162, 168, 169, 170, 172, 175, 176, 191, 212, 214, 215, 227, 242, 243, 244, 245, 246, 247
Tel Aviv-Jerusalem road, 124, 126, 127, 152, 161, 168, 169, 172, 175, 176
Temple Mount (Haram ash Sharif), 78, 153
Templer, Sir Gerald, 229
Ten Days, 181
Teveth, Shabtai, 6
The Life and Times of Muhammad, 26, 244
'The Middle East Crisis – A Personal Interpretation', 233, 234, 244
The New York Times, 226, 243
The Palestine Post, 226, 243
The Protocols of the Elders of Zion, 23
The Road Not Taken, 6, 246
The Story of the Arab Legion, 233, 244
The Times, 243
'The Trans-Jordan Situation 12th August 1948', 182
The Way of Love, Lessons from a Long Life, 3
Tiberias, 82, 124, 126, 129, 130, 131, 156
Tidrick, Kathryn, 11, 246, 249
Titus, 25, 161, 234, 249
Tobruk, 56, 62
Transjordanian Frontier Force, 45, 51, 53, 55, 130, 247
Treasury (British), 106, 120
Truman, Harry, 76
Tulkarm, 109, 118, 140, 163, 200, 202, 205
Turkey, 63, 77, 92

Um Rashrash (Eilat), 46, 49, 199, 200
United Nations Emergency Force (UNEF), 234, 247
United Nations General Assembly, 91, 94, 96, 99, 100, 102, 103, 104, 122, 124
United Nations General Assembly Partition Resolution (181), 94, 105, 110, 116, 122, 124, 132, 135, 141, 144, 159, 167, 169, 187, 195, 197, 241
United Nations Relief and Works Agency for Palestinian Refugees in the Near East (UNRWA), 190, 216, 218, 247
United Nations Security Council, 108, 122, 171, 172, 184, 223, 238
United Nations Special Committee on Palestine (UNSCOP), 91, 93, 94, 95, 96, 102, 104, 247
United Nations Truce Supervision Organisation (UNTSO), 5, 217, 247, 249
United States, 30, 63, 67, 68, 74, 75, 76, 79, 84, 92, 105, 172, 189, 193, 196, 200, 215, 224, 225, 226, 243, 245

Vespasian, 25
Vichy, 3, 57, 60

Wailing (Western) Wall, 212
War Office (British), 109, 120, 124, 162, 185, 247
Wauchope, Sir Arthur, 37, 38, 39
Weizmann, Chaim, 30, 31, 50, 144, 166
West Bank, 3, 4, 9, 15, 22, 24, 106, 113, 117, 119, 122, 123, 126, 135, 136, 140, 142, 147, 149, 151, 152, 157, 162, 163, 167, 170, 172, 173, 176, 177, 183, 185, 186, 187, 188, 189, 190, 193, 194, 195, 196, 197, 198, 199, 200, 201, 202, 203, 204, 205, 206, 210, 211, 212, 213, 214, 217, 219, 221, 222, 223, 229, 231, 234, 235, 236, 238, 240, 241, 242